# Lecture Notes in Computer Science 3923

Commenced Publication in 1973
Founding and Former Series Editors:
Gerhard Goos, Juris Hartmanis, and Jan van Leeuwen

Alan Mycroft   Andreas Zeller (Eds.)

# Compiler Construction

15th International Conference, CC 2006
Held as Part of the Joint European Conferences
on Theory and Practice of Software, ETAPS 2006
Vienna, Austria, March 30-31, 2006
Proceedings

 Springer

Volume Editors

Alan Mycroft
Cambridge University
Cambridge, UK
E-mail: am@cl.cam.ac.uk

Andreas Zeller
Saarland University
Saarbrücken, Germany
E-mail: zeller@cs.uni-sb.de

Library of Congress Control Number: 2006922081

CR Subject Classification (1998): D.3.4, D.3.1, F.4.2, D.2.6, F.3, I.2.2

LNCS Sublibrary: SL 1 – Theoretical Computer Science and General Issues

ISSN        0302-9743
ISBN-10     3-540-33050-X Springer Berlin Heidelberg New York
ISBN-13     978-3-540-33050-9 Springer Berlin Heidelberg New York

Springer is a part of Springer Science+Business Media

springer.com

© Springer-Verlag Berlin Heidelberg 2006
Printed in Germany

Typesetting: Camera-ready by author, data conversion by Scientific Publishing Services, Chennai, India
Printed on acid-free paper        SPIN: 11688839        06/3142        5 4 3 2 1 0

# Foreword

ETAPS 2006 was the ninth instance of the European Joint Conferences on Theory and Practice of Software. ETAPS is an annual federated conference that was established in 1998 by combining a number of existing and new conferences. This year it comprised five conferences (CC, ESOP, FASE, FOSSACS, TACAS), 18 satellite workshops (ACCAT, AVIS, CMCS, COCV, DCC, EAAI, FESCA, FRCSS, GT-VMT, LDTA, MBT, QAPL, SC, SLAP, SPIN, TERM-GRAPH, WITS and WRLA), two tutorials, and seven invited lectures (not including those that were specific to the satellite events). We received over 550 submissions to the five conferences this year, giving an overall acceptance rate of 23%, with acceptance rates below 30% for each conference. Congratulations to all the authors who made it to the final programme! I hope that most of the other authors still found a way of participating in this exciting event and I hope you will continue submitting.

The events that comprise ETAPS address various aspects of the system development process, including specification, design, implementation, analysis and improvement. The languages, methodologies and tools which support these activities are all well within its scope. Different blends of theory and practice are represented, with an inclination towards theory with a practical motivation on the one hand and soundly based practice on the other. Many of the issues involved in software design apply to systems in general, including hardware systems, and the emphasis on software is not intended to be exclusive.

ETAPS is a loose confederation in which each event retains its own identity, with a separate programme committee and proceedings. Its format is open-ended, allowing it to grow and evolve as time goes by. Contributed talks and system demonstrations are in synchronised parallel sessions, with invited lectures in plenary sessions. Two of the invited lectures are reserved for "unifying" talks on topics of interest to the whole range of ETAPS attendees. The aim of cramming all this activity into a single one-week meeting is to create a strong magnet for academic and industrial researchers working on topics within its scope, giving them the opportunity to learn about research in related areas, and thereby to foster new and existing links between work in areas that were formerly addressed in separate meetings.

ETAPS 2006 was organized by the Vienna University of Technology, in cooperation with

- European Association for Theoretical Computer Science (EATCS);
- European Association for Programming Languages and Systems (EAPLS);
- European Association of Software Science and Technology (EASST);
- Institute for Computer Languages, Vienna;
- Austrian Computing Society;
- The *Bürgermeister der Bundeshauptstadt Wien*;

- Vienna Convention Bureau;
- Intel.

The organizing team comprised:

| | |
|---|---|
| Chair: | Jens Knoop |
| Local Arrangements: | Anton Ertl |
| Publicity: | Joost-Pieter Katoen |
| Satellite Events: | Andreas Krall |
| Industrial Liaison: | Eva Kühn |
| Liaison with City of Vienna: | Ulrich Neumerkel |
| Tutorials Chair, Website: | Franz Puntigam |
| Website: | Fabian Schmied |
| Local Organization, Workshops Proceedings: Markus Schordan | |

Overall planning for ETAPS conferences is the responsibility of its Steering Committee, whose current membership is:

Perdita Stevens (Edinburgh, Chair), Luca Aceto (Aalborg and Reykjavík), Rastislav Bodík (Berkeley), Maura Cerioli (Genova), Matt Dwyer (Nebraska), Hartmut Ehrig (Berlin), José Fiadeiro (Leicester), Marie-Claude Gaudel (Paris), Roberto Gorrieri (Bologna), Reiko Heckel (Leicester), Michael Huth (London), Joost-Pieter Katoen (Aachen), Paul Klint (Amsterdam), Jens Knoop (Vienna), Shriram Krishnamurthi (Brown), Kim Larsen (Aalborg), Tiziana Margaria (Göttingen), Ugo Montanari (Pisa), Rocco de Nicola (Florence), Hanne Riis Nielson (Copenhagen), Jens Palsberg (UCLA), Mooly Sagiv (Tel-Aviv), João Saraiva (Minho), Don Sannella (Edinburgh), Vladimiro Sassone (Southampton), Helmut Seidl (Munich), Peter Sestoft (Copenhagen), Andreas Zeller (Saarbrücken).

I would like to express my sincere gratitude to all of these people and organizations, the programme committee chairs and PC members of the ETAPS conferences, the organizers of the satellite events, the speakers themselves, the many reviewers, and Springer-Verlag for agreeing to publish the ETAPS proceedings. Finally, I would like to thank the organizing chair of ETAPS 2006, Jens Knoop, for arranging for us to have ETAPS in the most beautiful city of Vienna.

Edinburgh, January 2006                                                  Perdita Stevens
ETAPS Steering Committee Chair

# Preface

The Program Committee is pleased to present the proceedings of the 15th International Conference on Compiler Construction (CC 2006) which was held on March 30 and 31 in Vienna, Austria, as part of the Joint European Conference on Theory and Practice of Software (ETAPS 2006).

Traditionally, CC had been a forum for research on compiler construction. Starting last year, CC has expanded its remit to include a broader spectrum of programming tools, from analysis tools to compilers to virtual machines to debuggers. The submissions we received again reflected the new scope of the conference.

The Program Committee received 71 submissions. From these, 17 research papers and 3 tool demonstrations were selected, giving an overall acceptance rate of 28%.

The Program Committee included 16 members representing 9 countries on 3 continents. Each member reviewed roughly 16 papers and each paper received at least three reviews. In all, 45 external reviewers participated in the review process. Committee members were allowed to submit papers; these would be screened by four reviewers. The Program Committee met on December 5 in London for a one-day meeting. All but three of the members attended the meeting.

Many people contributed to the success of this conference. First of all, we would like to thank the authors for all the care they put into their submissions. Our gratitude also goes to the Program Committee members and external reviewers for their substantive and insightful reviews. Intel generously funded parts of the Program Committee meeting. Special thanks go to Jay McCarthy for maintaining the Continue Conference Server.

CC 2006 was made possible by the ETAPS Steering Committee, in particular by the hard work of Jens Knoop in the role of ETAPS 2006 Organizing Committee Chair, and by that of Anton Ertl in taking care of the local arrangements. We would also like to thank Reinhard Wilhelm and Ras Bodik, recent CC chairs, for on-going helpful discussions about CC's future direction. Finally, we are grateful to George Necula for accepting the invitation to give a keynote talk.

January 2006

Alan Mycroft and Andreas Zeller
CC 2006 Program Chairs

# Conference Organization

## Program Chairs

Alan Mycroft      University of Cambridge, UK
Andreas Zeller      Saarland University, Germany

## Program Committee

| | |
|---|---|
| Radhia Cousot | CNRS, France |
| Koen De Bosschere | Ghent University, Belgium |
| Arie van Deursen | CWI, Netherlands |
| Michael Ernst | Massachusetts Institute of Technology, USA |
| Sergei Gorlatch | University of Münster, Germany |
| Chris Hankin | Imperial College, UK |
| Jens Knoop | TU Vienna, Austria |
| Shriram Krishnamurthi | Brown University, Rhode Island, USA |
| K. Rustan M. Leino | Microsoft Research, Washington, USA |
| Oege de Moor | Oxford University, UK |
| Greg Morrisett | Harvard University, Massachusetts, USA |
| Morten Rhiger | Roskilde University, Denmark |
| Barbara Ryder | Rutgers University, New Jersey, USA |
| Frank Tip | IBM Research, New York, USA |
| Des Watson | University of Sussex, UK |
| Kwangkeun Yi | Seoul National University, Korea |

## Additional Reviewers

| | | |
|---|---|---|
| Martin Alt | Erik D'Hollander | Martin Griebl |
| Gerco Ballintijn | Bruno De Bus | Christoph Herrmann |
| Anne Benoit | John Dias | Oleg Kiselyov |
| Jim Benham | Julian Dolby | Taeke Kooiker |
| Kristof Beyls | Jan Dünnweber | Christoph Kessler |
| Magiel Bruntink | Bruno Dufour | Andreas Krall |
| Dries Buytaert | Rob Economopoulos | Jens Krinke |
| Dominique Chanet | Anton Ertl | Yossi Lev |
| Ophelia Chesley | Chen Fu | Jonas Maebe |
| Jamieson M. Cobleigh | Robert Fuhrer | Guillaume Marceau |
| Bas Cornelissen | Andy Georges | Thomas J. Marlowe |

# Table of Contents

## Optimization

## Code Generation

## Register Allocation

# Using Dependent Types to Port Type Systems to Low-Level Languages

George Necula

University of California, Berkeley, USA

A major difficulty when trying to apply high-level type systems to low-level languages is that we must reason about relationships between values. For example, in a low-level implementation of object-oriented dynamic dispatch we must ensure that the "self" argument passed to the method is the same object from whose virtual table we fetched the pointer to the method. Similarly, in low-level code using arrays we must relate the array address with the variables that store the bounds. We show for several examples that the high-level type system must be extended with dependent types in order to reason about low-level code. The novel feature in this use of dependent types is that they can be used in presence of pointers and mutation.

We discuss three case studies. First, we show a variant of bytecode verification that operates on the assembly language output of a native code compiler. Second, we show how to express and check at the assembly level the invariants enforced by CCured, a source-level instrumentation tool that guarantees type safety in legacy C programs. Finally, we show that dependent types are a natural specification mechanism for enforcing common safe programming practices in C programs. We have used this mechanism to efficiently enforce memory safety for several Linux device drivers.

A. Mycroft and A. Zeller (Eds.): CC 2006, LNCS 3923, p. 1, 2006.
© Springer-Verlag Berlin Heidelberg 2006

# Interprocedural Dataflow Analysis in the Presence of Large Libraries

Atanas Rountev[1], Scott Kagan[1], and Thomas Marlowe[2]

[1] Ohio State University, Columbus, OH, USA
[2] Seton Hall University, South Orange, NJ, USA

**Abstract.** Interprocedural dataflow analysis has a large number of uses for software optimization, maintenance, testing, and verification. For software built with reusable components, the traditional approaches for *whole-program analysis* cannot be used directly. This paper considers *component-level analysis* of a main component which is built on top of a pre-existing library component. We propose an approach for computing summary information for the library and for using it to analyze the main component. The approach defines a general theoretical framework for dataflow analysis of programs built with large extensible library components, using pre-computed summary functions for library-local execution paths. Our experimental results indicate that the cost of component-level analysis could be substantially lower than the cost of the corresponding whole-program analysis, without any loss of precision. These results present a promising step towards practical analysis techniques for large-scale software systems built with reusable components.

## 1 Introduction

*Interprocedural dataflow analysis* is a widely-used form of static program analysis. Dataflow analysis techniques play an important role in tools for performance optimization, program understanding and maintenance, software testing, and verification of program properties. Unfortunately, the use of interprocedural dataflow analysis in real-world software tools is hindered by several serious challenges. One of the central problems is the underlying analysis model implicit in most of the work in this area. The key feature of this model is the assumption of a *whole-program analysis for a homogeneous program*. Interprocedural whole-program analysis takes as input an entire program and produces information about the behavior of that program. This classical dataflow analysis model [28] assumes that the source code for the whole program is available for analysis.

Modern software presents serious challenges for this traditional model. For example, systems often contain reusable components. Whole-program analysis assumes that it is appropriate to analyze the source code of the entire program as a single unit. However, for software built with reusable components,

- Some program components may be available only in binary form, without source code, which makes whole-program analysis impossible.

A. Mycroft and A. Zeller (Eds.): CC 2006, LNCS 3923, pp. 2–16, 2006.

- It is necessary to re-analyze a component every time this component is used as part of a new system. For example, a library may be used in many applications, and whole-program analysis requires re-analysis of this library from scratch in the context of each such application.
- Code changes in one component typically require complete re-analysis of the entire application.
- The cost of whole-program analysis is often dominated by the analysis of the underlying large library components (e.g., standard libraries, middleware, frameworks, etc.). To achieve practical cost, analysis designers are often forced to use semantic approximations that reduce the precision and usefulness of the analysis solution.

These issues limit the usefulness of many existing analyses. In some cases the analyses cannot be used at all. Even if they are possible, the analyses have to be relatively approximate in order to scale for large-scale software with hundreds of thousands (or even millions) lines of code. Such approximations lead to under-optimized code in optimizing compilers, spurious dependencies in program understanding tools, false warnings in verification tools, and infeasible coverage requirements in testing tools.

*Component-Level Dataflow Analysis.* In this paper we consider a model of interprocedural dataflow analysis which we refer to as *component-level analysis* (CLA). A component-level analysis processes the source code of a single program component, given some information about the environment of this component. The general CLA model is discussed in [20] (without any formalisms, proofs, or experiments.) Here, we focus on one particular scenario for CLA: analysis of a main component *Main* which is built on top of a library component *Lib*. In this scenario, the source code of *Lib* is pre-analyzed independently of any library clients. This pre-analysis produces *summary information* for *Lib*. This information is used subsequently for component-level analysis of the source code of any main component built on top of *Lib*.

This form of CLA has significant real-world relevance. In particular, there are large standard libraries that are associated with languages such as C++, Java, and C#. A library could be considered as component *Lib*, while a program written on top of it is component *Main*. CLA allows (1) analysis of *Main* without the source code of *Lib*, by using the summary information, (2) reduction in the cost of analyzing *Main*, because the source code of *Lib* has already been analyzed, (3) reuse of the summary information across multiple main components, in order to avoid repeated re-analysis of *Lib*, and (4) reduced work to handle code changes, since changes in *Main* do not require re-analysis of *Lib*.

*Contributions.* The main goal of our work is to define general theoretical machinery for designing component-level analyses of *Main*. We achieve this goal by generalizing the "functional approach" to whole-program analysis due to Sharir and Pnueli [28]. The key technical issue that this generalization needs to address is *the lack of complete call graph information when performing pre-analysis of a library.* An example of this problem is the presence of callbacks from the library to the main component. The contributions of our work are:

- **General theoretical framework:** This paper defines a general approach for component-level analysis in the absence of complete information about calling relationships within *Lib* and from *Lib* to *Main*. The approach is defined for the most general category of monotone dataflow problems. As a result, it becomes possible to define CLA versions for many important and widely-used whole-program analyses.
- **Framework instantiation:** Our long-term goal is to design CLA versions of existing whole-program analyses, based on the framework from above. In this paper, we show how to instantiate the general approach to a particular form of the *interprocedural reaching definitions analysis*, which is a classical dataflow problem. This analysis exemplifies the category of flow- and context-sensitive dataflow analyses, which present the most challenging targets for our theoretical approach.
- **Experimental comparison:** We present an experimental study which compares CLA with its whole-program counterpart. The experiments indicate that the CLA approach can produce significant reduction in analysis cost, while at the same time achieving exactly the same precision.

## 2   Whole-Program Analysis

This section describes, at a high level, the classical formulation of whole-program interprocedural dataflow analysis [28]. The input to the analysis is the source code for a complete program. One of the procedures[1] is designated as the main procedure *main*. In the traditional model presented below, each call site invokes only one procedure. A call that could invoke many procedures (e.g., due to virtual dispatch or function pointers) can be modeled as a case statement where each case corresponds to one unique target procedure. Given a complete program, a whole-program analysis constructs a tuple $\langle G, L, F, M, \eta \rangle$ where

- $G = (N, E)$ is an interprocedural control-flow graph (ICFG).
- $L$ is a meet semi-lattice, with partial order $\leq$, meet operation $\wedge$, and greatest element $\top$. To simplify the discussion, we assume that $L$ has finite height.
- $F \subseteq \{f \mid f : L \to L\}$ is a monotone[2] function space that is closed under functional composition and functional meet.
- $M : E \to F$ is an assignment of dataflow functions to graph edges. Function $f_e = M(e)$ encodes the effects of $e$'s execution.
- $\eta \in L$ is the solution at the start node of *main*.

Graph $G$ contains the control-flow graphs (CFGs) for the individual procedures. Nodes $n \in N$ correspond to statements, and intraprocedural edges $e \in E$ represent flow of control within the same procedure. The CFG for a procedure $p$ has an artificial start node $start_p$ and an artificial exit node $exit_p$. Each single-target call is represented by two nodes: a *call-site* node and a *return-site* node.

---

[1] We will use "procedure" to refer to both procedures and methods.
[2] That is, $x \leq y$ implies $f(x) \leq f(y)$ for any $f \in F$ and $x, y \in L$.

There is an interprocedural edge $e \in E$ from a call-site node to the start node of the invoked procedure $p$; there is also a corresponding edge $e \in E$ from $exit_p$ to the return-site node. Dataflow functions are associated with these edges to represent the effects of parameter passing and return values.

A path in $G$ is a sequence of edges $q = (e_1, \ldots, e_k)$ such that the target of $e_i$ is the same as the source of $e_{i+1}$. The dataflow function associated with $q$ is the composition of the edge functions: $f_q = f_{e_k} \circ \ldots \circ f_{e_1}$. Not all ICFG paths represent possible executions. A *valid* path has interprocedural edges that are properly matched: each (exit,return-site) edge is matched correctly with the last unmatched (call-site,start) edge on the path.

The *meet-over-all-valid-paths solution* $MVP_n$ for an ICFG node $n$ describes the program properties immediately before the execution of $n$. This solution is $MVP_n = \bigwedge_{q \in VP(n)} f_q(\eta)$ where $VP(n)$ is the set of all valid paths $q$ leading from the start node of *main* to $n$ (paths $q$ do not include $n$ itself). An analysis algorithm computes a solution $S_n \in L$ at each node $n$; this solution is *safe* (i.e., correct) if $S_n \leq MVP_n$. There are well-known general algorithms for computing safe solutions for dataflow problems; one such algorithm is outlined in Section 2.2.

## 2.1   Running Example

We will use the example in Figure 1 throughout the rest of the paper; the figure also shows the corresponding ICFG. The example uses a C-style language to illustrate a whole program built with two components: a library component and a main component. We consider the classical *reaching definitions* problem. The definitions k=0, k=2, k=3, k=7, and k=9 will be denoted by $d_0$, $d_2$, $d_3$, $d_7$, and

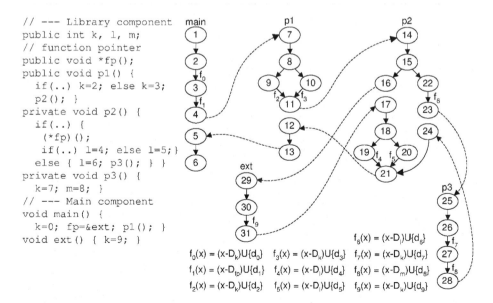

**Fig. 1.** Whole program, ICFG, and dataflow functions

$d_9$ respectively. The set of all definitions of k will be denoted by $D_k$. Similar notation will be used for the remaining variables. The lattice for the problem is the powerset of $D = \{d_0, \ldots, d_9\}$, with partial order $\supseteq$, meet operation $\cup$, top element $\top = \emptyset$, and bottom element $\bot = D$. The non-identity dataflow functions are shown next to the corresponding edges in Figure 1. For example, the function for k=3 is $f_3(x) = (x - D_k) \cup \{d_3\}$, where $x \subseteq D$.

## 2.2   The Functional Approach of Sharir and Pnueli

One of the classical techniques for solving whole-program dataflow problems is the "functional approach" by Sharir and Pnueli [28]. The essence of this approach is the creation and use of *summary functions*. A summary function $\phi_n : L \to L$ for a node $n$ represents the solution at $n$ as a function of the solution at the start node of the procedure containing $n$. For example, in Figure 1, $\phi_{27} = f_7$, $\phi_{28} = f_8 \circ f_7$, and $\phi_{11} = f_2 \wedge f_3$. (As usual, for any $g, h : L \to L$, the functional meet $k = g \wedge h$ is such that $k(x) = g(x) \wedge h(x)$ for any $x$.) In the case when $n$ is the exit node of a procedure $p$, $\phi_n$ can be used as a summary function $f_p$ for the entire procedure.

Phase I of Sharir-Pnueli's analysis computes summary functions for all ICFG nodes. This fixed-point computation uses the summary functions for $p$'s callees to compute the summary function for nodes inside $p$. For example, in Figure 1, $f_{p3} = f_8 \circ f_7$ and $f_{ext} = f_9$. Inside p2, these functions can be used to compute, for example, $\phi_{19} = f_{ext}$ and $\phi_{21} = (f_4 \circ f_{ext}) \wedge (f_5 \circ f_{ext}) \wedge (f_{p3} \circ f_6)$. In the output of the first phase, we have $f_{p3} = \phi_{28} = f_8 \circ f_7$, $f_{ext} = \phi_{31} = f_9$, $f_{p2} = \phi_{21}$, $f_{p1} = \phi_{13} = (f_{p2} \circ f_2) \wedge (f_{p2} \circ f_3)$, and $f_{main} = \phi_6 = f_{p1} \circ f_1 \circ f_0$.

Phase II of the analysis propagates lattice elements using the summary functions. In Figure 1, the value $\eta = \emptyset$ at the start node 1 of main is propagated to call-site node 4, as $\phi_4(\eta) = (f_1 \circ f_0)(\emptyset) = \{d_0, d_1\}$. This value is then propagated to the start node of p1, and from there to call-site node 11 as $\phi_{11}(\phi_4(\eta))$. In turn, the value at 11 is propagated to the start node of p2, and to call-site nodes 16 and 22 as $\phi_{16}(\phi_{11}(\phi_4(\eta)))$ and $\phi_{22}(\phi_{11}(\phi_4(\eta)))$, respectively. In general, the propagation occurs only among start nodes and call-site nodes, and stabilizes when the solutions at start nodes are fully computed. Phase III of the analysis can be performed on demand. Whenever the solution at a node $n$ is needed, it can be computed as $\phi_n(S_{start})$, where $S_{start}$ is the solution computed by phase II for the start node of $n$'s procedure.

## 2.3   Using the Functional Approach for Component-Level Analysis

In Sharir-Pnueli's approach the bulk of the computation is performed during phase I when all ICFG nodes need to be visited, possibly multiple times. Phase II involves only start nodes and call-site nodes. Phase III is performed on demand, and its cost is proportional to the number of distinct queries made by an analysis client. In this paper we focus our efforts on reducing the cost of phase I by using pre-analysis of *Lib*.

In the simplest case, the pre-analysis of *Lib* and the subsequent component-level analysis of *Main* are trivial. Suppose each call site in *Lib* is monomorphic and its target does not depend on the code in the main component. For example, this is true for C programs that do not use function pointers, and for Java programs that do not make virtual calls. Clearly, the phase I computation for all library procedures can be performed independently of any main component. The summary functions $f_p$ for all exported library procedures $p$ can be stored as the library summary. Later, when CLA of some main component is performed, the phase I computation for that *Main* will compute $\phi_n$ for all nodes $n$ in this main component, using the pre-computed summary functions for library procedures. Phase II can be restricted only to the portion of the call graph that is in *Main*, and phase III can answer on-demand questions about the node solutions in *Main*.

Unfortunately, this approach is possible only in the *absence of callbacks* from *Lib* to *Main*. However, callbacks are common in real-world software. For example, in C code, one of the parameters of a library function p could be a function pointer g to a callback function defined in *Main*. A call (*g)(..) inside p invokes the callback function. Clearly, the complete behavior of p is not known at summary-generation time, and it is not possible to create a summary function $f_p$. This is a realistic problem, because callbacks through function pointers occur often in C libraries [17]. Callbacks also occur often in object-oriented software. Consider a library method m(A *a) in C++ or m(A a) in Java, where A is a library class. Suppose some *Main* creates a subclass B of A that overrides some of A's methods. If *Main* calls m with an actual parameter that is a pointer to an instance of B, a virtual call through a inside m may invoke a method defined in B. Of course, this situation is common for extensible object-oriented libraries.

Even in the absence of callbacks, in many cases it is still not possible to create a precise summary function for a library procedure. Consider the following Java example: the library contains a procedure p with a virtual call a.m(), where the static type of a is library class A. Suppose the library contains classes B and C that are subclasses of A, and method A.m is overridden by B.m and C.m. A conservative pre-analysis of the library has to assume that a.m() could invoke any of these three methods, and as a result the summary function for p will depend on all three callees. But if some *Main* instantiates and uses only C, for example, the pre-computed summary function for p will be overly conservative. Since the calling relationships at virtual calls in *Lib* depend on the execution context created by *Main*, any library procedure that contains polymorphic calls presents a problem for the functional approach.

## 3   Summary Computation for Component-Level Analysis

Consider again the program in Figure 1. Suppose the library component *Lib* were built as a reusable component, independent of the particular main component in the figure. Furthermore, for the sake of the example, assume that p1 were made visible to (and callable by) future main components, while the remaining library procedures were hidden from such components using some language mechanism.

Suppose we wanted to compute summary information for *Lib* in order to use it later when performing component-level analysis of any main component *Main* (including the main component from Figure 1). The summary will be main-component-independent, and the only information used for computing this summary will be the source code of *Lib*. Our goal is to construct a library summary with the following property: the subsequent summary-based CLA of *Main* must produce for each ICFG node $n$ in the main component *the same solution* as the solution that would have been computed for $n$ by a whole-program analysis of the source code of $Main \cup Lib$.

One possible summary information contains the ICFG of the library together with some encoding of the dataflow functions at the ICFG edges. However, such a summary contains redundant details that are irrelevant for the CLA of *Main*. As a result, phase I of CLA will have *the same cost* as phase I of a whole-program analysis would have had. Furthermore, due to the redundant information, the summary would be unnecessarily large, making it expensive to store and read.

We propose a general approach that can be used to create a more concise library summary. The approach will be illustrated for the example in Figure 2, but this technique is conceptually applicable to any interprocedural dataflow analysis. (In [22] we show how to handle flow- and context-insensitive analyses.) The basic idea is to compute summary functions that capture the effects of all relevant *library-local ICFG paths*. The functions are then included in the library summary together with information about the program points that could be affected by future main components. Figure 2 shows the summary information computed for *Lib* by our approach. Combining this summary with the ICFG for any main component *Main* allows component-level analysis of *Main*.

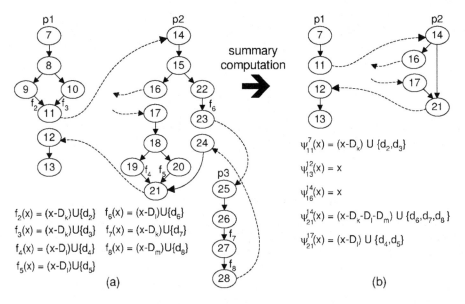

**Fig. 2.** (a) ICFG for *Lib* (b) condensed ICFG and summary functions for *Lib*

### 3.1   Library Pre-analysis for Summary Generation

*Fixed calls.* The pre-analysis of the source code of *Lib* constructs the ICFG for the library and identifies the calls at which the target procedures may depend on the main component. If a call site in *Lib* always invokes the same library procedure, regardless of the code in any main component, we will refer to it as a *fixed call*. In C code, any call that is not through a function pointer is a fixed call. In Java, we can use the following simple criterion for fixed calls: (1) any call that does not correspond to the bytecode instructions `virtualinvoke` or `interfaceinvoke` is a fixed call, and (2) a `virtualinvoke` call is fixed if the static type of the receiver is a final class, or the compile-time target method is a final or private method. Note that it may be possible to employ conservative analyses (e.g., [23, 13]) to identify additional fixed calls that do not satisfy these rather restrictive criteria; such analyses can be performed with worst-case assumptions about the behavior of the unknown main components.

*Fixed procedures.* We will recursively define a library procedure $p$ to be *fixed* if (1) $p$ contains no calls, or (2) $p$ contains only fixed calls and they invoke only fixed procedures. All transitive callees of $p$ are known at library pre-analysis time, and the Sharir-Pnueli approach can be used to compute a summary function $f_p$. The library pre-analysis identifies all fixed procedures $p$ and computes the corresponding summary functions. In Figure 2 the only fixed procedure is p3 and the analysis computes $f_{p3} = f_8 \circ f_7$.

*Non-fixed procedures.* After processing the fixed procedures, the library pre-analysis considers all non-fixed procedures. The analysis computes a set of summary functions $\psi_n^k : L \to L$ for each ICFG node $n$ in each such procedure. Here $k$ is an ICFG node that belongs to the same procedure as $n$, and is one of the following: (1) the start node of the procedure, (2) the return-site node for a non-fixed call, or (3) the return-site node for a fixed call to a non-fixed procedure. Intuitively, $k$ represents a program point which depends on unknown main components. For example, for node 21 in Figure 2, the approach would construct two functions $\psi_{21}^{14}$ and $\psi_{21}^{17}$. During phase I of the subsequent component-level analysis of a main component, these functions allow us to express the summary function at 21 as $\phi_{21} = \psi_{21}^{14} \wedge (\psi_{21}^{17} \circ f_{callback} \circ \psi_{16}^{14})$, where $f_{callback}$ is the summary function for the callback procedure from the main component.

*Computation of summary functions.* Figure 3 defines a worklist-based algorithm for computing the summary functions. The algorithm first initializes functions $\psi_k^k$ to the identity function $\lambda x.x$. For all other $n$, $\psi_k^k$ is initialized to a function that maps every lattice element to $\top$; as usual, $\top$ represents the lack of any information. In our running example, the identity function is associated with nodes 7, 12, 14, and 17. After initialization, functions $\psi_n^k$ are computed incrementally using functional composition and functional meet. A function $\psi_n^k$ captures the semantic effects of certain ICFG paths from $k$ to $n$. For example, there are two paths from node 7 to node 11 in Figure 1. Function $f_2$ is propagated to 11 along

**procedure** *Summary_Computation_For_Nonfixed_Procedures*
**for** each non-fixed procedure $p$ **do**
    initialize $\psi_{start_p}^{start_p} := \lambda x.x$ and put $(start_p, start_p)$ on the worklist
**for** each return-site $r$ for a non-fixed call, or for a fixed call to a non-fixed procedure **do**
    initialize $\psi_r^r := \lambda x.x$ and put $(r, r)$ on the worklist
**for** each other node $n$ and each applicable $k$ **do** initialize $\psi_n^k := \lambda x.\top$
**while** the worklist is not empty **do**
    remove pair $(k, n)$ from the worklist
    **case 1: if** $n$ is not a call-site node or a method exit **do**
        **for** each ICFG successor node $n'$ of $n$ **do** $propagate(k, n', f_{(n,n')} \circ \psi_n^k)$
    **case 2: if** $n$ is a fixed call-site, with return-site $r$, calling fixed procedure $p$ **do**
        $propagate(k, r, f_{(exit_p, r)} \circ f_p \circ f_{(n, start_p)} \circ \psi_n^k)$
    **case 3:** in all other cases, do nothing
**procedure** $propagate(k, n, f)$
    $\psi_n^k := \psi_n^k \wedge f$
    if $\psi_n^k$ has changed, put $(k, n)$ on the worklist

**Fig. 3.** Computation of summary functions for non-fixed library procedures

one path, and function $f_3$ is propagated along the other path. Thus, the summary analysis will compute $\psi_{11}^7 = f_2 \wedge f_3 = \lambda x.(x - D_k) \cup \{d_2, d_3\}$. As another example, at return-site 24 we have $\psi_{24}^{14} = f_{p3} \circ \psi_{23}^{14} = f_8 \circ f_7 \circ f_6$.

The computed summary functions are then used to construct the library summary. First, for every fixed procedure $p$ that is visible to future main components, the summary includes the summary function $f_p$. For every non-fixed $p$, the summary contains the set $\Psi_p$ of all functions $\psi_n^k$ such that $n$ is (1) the exit node of $p$, (2) the call-site node for a non-fixed call in $p$, or (3) the call-site node for a fixed call in $p$ to a non-fixed procedure. For example, for **p1** in Figure 2, $\Psi_{p1} = \{\psi_{11}^7, \psi_{13}^{12}\}$ because 11 is a call-site node for a fixed call to the non-fixed procedure **p2**. Similarly, for **p2**, the summary contains $\Psi_{p2} = \{\psi_{21}^{14}, \psi_{16}^{14}, \psi_{21}^{17}\}$.

The functions in $\Psi_p$ implicitly define a "condensed" CFG for $p$. The nodes in this condensed graph are all $k$ and $n$ such that $\psi_n^k \in \Psi_p$. For every $\psi_n^k \in \Psi_p$ that is different from $\lambda x.\top$, there is an edge from $k$ to $n$ in the condensed CFG, with edge dataflow function $\psi_n^k$. These edges represent sets of paths from the original CFG. Figure 2(b) shows the condensed graphs for non-fixed procedures **p1** and **p2**. The condensed CFG for **p3** (not shown in the figure) has only a start node, an exit node, and a single edge with edge dataflow function $f_{p3}$.

Note that the summary functions are being constructed without any knowledge about the future main components and about the lattice elements that correspond to these main components. For the running example, the summary analysis has no information about the definitions that are generated by main components. For example, in $\psi_{11}^7 = \lambda x.(x - D_k) \cup \{d_2, d_3\}$, the set $D_k$ of definitions of **k** is not known completely. However, complete knowledge of $D_k$ is not necessary to encode this function. It is enough to represent the fact that *all* definitions of **k** are killed—both the known ones from the library and the unknown ones created by future main clients.

## 3.2   Analysis of a Main Component

The summary functions and the condensed CFGs defined by them can be used to perform component-level analysis of any main component that is built on top of *Lib*. Such an analysis is straightforward. First, the condensed CFGs for the library procedures are added to the ICFG for the main component, together with the appropriate interprocedural edges. The resulting condensed ICFG is used as input to phase I of Sharir-Pnueli's whole-program analysis. For any node $n$ in the condensed ICFG, the summary function $\phi'_n$ computed by this phase I is a safe approximation of the summary function $\phi_n$ that would have been computed for $n$ by phase I of the standard whole-program analysis of the "normal" non-condensed ICFG—in other words, we have $\phi'_n(x) \leq \phi_n(x)$ for any $x \in L$. In the case when all dataflow functions are distributive—that is, $f(x \wedge y) = f(x) \wedge f(y)$—there is no loss of precision, and $\phi'_n = \phi_n$.

Phases II and III on the condensed ICFG are similar to phases II and III on the original ICFG. For any node $n$, the solution $S'_n$ computed by phase III of the analysis on the condensed graph is a safe approximation of the solution $S_n$ computed by phase III of the analysis of the original ICFG—that is, $S'_n \leq S_n$. If the dataflow functions are distributive, we have $S'_n = S_n$, and the component-level analysis achieves the same precision as the whole-program analysis.

## 3.3   Analysis Implementation

The approach described above provides the conceptual foundations for designing CLA versions of whole-program analyses. In order to implement an actual analysis, an analysis builder has to address two important issues.

First, the library summary should contain enough information so that the CLA of *Main* can compute a whole-program call graph, in order to construct the *inter*procedural edges in the condensed ICFG. As a simple example, for Figure 2, the summary could record the fact that the call at node 16 is through a function pointer, and that no function addresses are taken in the library. The CLA of *Main* can resolve the call at 16 to any procedure whose address is taken in *Lib* or in *Main*; for the particular main component in Figure 1, the only possible target is ext. As another simple example, for a Java library, the summary can store the static receiver type and static target method for each non-fixed call site. When the code of *Main* becomes available, the whole-program class hierarchy can be constructed and used to determine the potential target methods at non-fixed library calls. Of course, more sophisticated approaches for call graph construction are possible. The adaptation of these techniques to component-level analysis is beyond the scope of this paper; some existing work already solves certain instances of this problem (e.g., [24]).

A second key issue for component-level analysis is the representation, composition, and meet of dataflow functions. The function space should allow compact representation of functions. For a large number of important dataflow problems, such compact representations have already been defined. In particular, interprocedural finite distributive subset (IFDS) problems [18] and interprocedural distributive environment (IDE) problems [27] have compact function representations and efficient functional composition and functional meet [19, 18, 27]. These two categories of problems are significant because they cover a large number of widely used interprocedural analyses [19] such as reaching definitions, available expressions, live variables, truly-live variables, possibly-uninitialized variables, several forms of constant propagation, flow-sensitive side-effects, some forms of may-alias and must-alias analysis, interprocedural slicing, 0-CFA type analysis for Java [9], field-based points-to analysis for Java [15], and object naming analysis [21]. The general theoretical approach described earlier can be instantiated to IFDS/IDE problems by using *graph-based analysis algorithms* similar to the whole-program algorithms from [19, 18, 27]. Using these techniques, it becomes possible to design CLA versions of many important and widely-used analyses.

In the particular case of the reaching definitions analysis, a function $f$ can be represented by a pair $(K, G)$ where $K$ is the set of definitions killed by $f$, and $G$ is the set of definitions generated by $f$. The functional meet of $f_1 = (K_1, G_1)$ and $f_2 = (K_2, G_2)$ is represented by $(K_1 \cap K_2, G_1 \cup G_2)$. The functional composition $f_2 \circ f_1$ corresponds to $(K_1 \cup K_2, (G_1 - K_2) \cup G_2)$.

## 4      Experimental Study

This section presents an experimental study which evaluates the effectiveness of the proposed approach for CLA. The study was performed on the 19 Java programs shown in Table 1. Each program was processed using the Soot frame-

**Table 1.** Analyzed programs

| Program | User Methods | All Methods | User CFG Nodes | All CFG Nodes |
|---------|--------------|-------------|----------------|---------------|
| jb-6.1 | 149 | 7130 | 2888 | 117781 |
| socksproxy | 113 | 7178 | 2449 | 118969 |
| jlex-1.2.6 | 133 | 7113 | 7210 | 122095 |
| RabbIT2 | 184 | 7368 | 3455 | 122755 |
| javacup-0.10j | 332 | 7312 | 9066 | 124000 |
| sablecc-2.18.2 | 1744 | 8755 | 24149 | 139498 |
| db | 96 | 17755 | 2397 | 303193 |
| compress | 100 | 17760 | 2399 | 303201 |
| fractal | 184 | 17919 | 3526 | 305731 |
| raytrace | 219 | 17878 | 5179 | 305973 |
| socksecho | 176 | 17966 | 3562 | 306658 |
| jack | 349 | 18008 | 11541 | 312333 |
| jtar-1.21 | 224 | 18152 | 6145 | 312562 |
| jess | 641 | 18323 | 12365 | 313375 |
| mpegaudio | 307 | 17967 | 14304 | 315094 |
| jflex-1.4.1 | 509 | 18217 | 14826 | 315936 |
| mindterm-1.1.5 | 598 | 18385 | 17792 | 321948 |
| muffin-0.9.3a | 933 | 18820 | 18383 | 323560 |
| javac | 1185 | 18868 | 25496 | 326524 |

work [30] version 2.2.2, on top of the J2SE 1.4.2 libraries. The experiments were performed on a 2.8GHz Pentium4 PC with 2GB of RAM running Sun's HotSpot Client VM version 1.4.2 using a maximum heap size of 1.5GB (JVM option Xmx).

For each of the data programs, we utilized Soot's call graph construction algorithm based on class hierarchy analysis. Column *User Methods* shows the number of reachable methods which are declared in the program code (i.e., all reachable non-library methods). The total number of reachable methods is listed in column *All Methods*. As Table 1 shows, the vast majority (80.1% to 99.5%) of reachable methods were contained in the libraries. These measurements clearly indicate that the cost of whole-program analysis will be dominated by the cost to analyze the relevant library code. This observation provides a very strong motivation for using summary-based component-level analysis of *Main*.

For each of the data programs, we constructed the whole-program ICFG. Columns *User CFG Nodes* and *All CFG Nodes* of Table 1 describe the number of ICFG nodes. Again, the large majority of nodes (between 82.7% and 99.2%) were in the Java libraries. Using the techniques described in Section 3.1, we constructed the "condensed" version of the ICFG. The reduction of the number of nodes (shown in Table 2) was substantial, with the condensed ICFGs containing 59.2% to 71.4% fewer nodes than the original ICFGs. Our experiments also showed that the reduction in the number of ICFG edges was equally significant; for brevity, we do not present these results. Since the cost of dataflow analyses typically depends on ICFG size, these results clearly show that a summary-based approach can achieve considerable cost reduction.

To measure the savings achieved by our technique, we implemented Sharir-Pnueli's Phase I for a variation of the reaching definitions problem for Java. Java has three types of memory locations: local variables, instance fields, and static fields. For local variables, the reaching definitions problem is purely intra-procedural. For instance fields, an alias analysis must be used to resolve indirect accesses through object references. Since such resolution is typically done with a *may-alias* analysis, field definitions cannot be killed safely; as a result, the dataflow functions are different from the ones in the classical reaching definitions

**Table 2.** Reduction in the number of ICFG nodes

| Program | Condensed Nodes | Reduction | Program | Condensed Nodes | Reduction |
|---|---|---|---|---|---|
| jb | 35556 | 69.8% | socksecho | 88453 | 71.2% |
| socksproxy | 35604 | 70.1% | jack | 95926 | 69.3% |
| jlex | 39876 | 67.3% | jtar | 91722 | 70.7% |
| RabbIT2 | 37155 | 69.7% | jess | 96817 | 69.1% |
| javacup | 41733 | 66.3% | mpegaudio | 98689 | 68.7% |
| sablecc | 56954 | 59.2% | jflex | 99376 | 68.6% |
| db | 86783 | 71.4% | mindterm | 102769 | 68.1% |
| compress | 86789 | 71.4% | muffin | 103864 | 67.9% |
| fractal | 88195 | 71.2% | javac | 109965 | 66.3% |
| raytrace | 89563 | 70.7% | | | |

**Table 3.** Running time of the analysis (in seconds) and % time reduction

| Program | WPA | CLA | Program | WPA | CLA |
|---------|-----|-----|---------|-----|-----|
| jb | 97.3 | 19.2 (80.2%) | socksecho | 658.5 | 328.6 (50.1%) |
| socksproxy | 96.1 | 20.5 (78.6%) | jack | 665.2 | 322.6 (51.5%) |
| jlex | 101.2 | 17.5 (82.8%) | jtar | 682.3 | 349.6 (48.8%) |
| RabbIT2 | 101.1 | 22.1 (78.2%) | jess | 665.1 | 334.6 (49.7%) |
| javacup | 116.6 | 24.0 (79.4%) | mpegaudio | 585.9 | 240.1 (59.0%) |
| sablecc | 139.3 | 34.5 (75.2%) | jflex | 686.0 | 454.1 (33.8%) |
| db | 656.1 | 392.5 (40.2%) | mindterm | 648.6 | 342.0 (47.3%) |
| compress | 597.5 | 300.4 (49.7%) | muffin | 658.1 | 366.1 (44.4%) |
| fractal | 676.0 | 261.5 (61.3%) | javac | 656.1 | 346.7 (47.2%) |
| raytrace | 651.3 | 417.1 (36.0%) | | | |

problem. Thus, we implemented a reaching definitions analysis for static fields only, where the dataflow functions are of the form described in Section 2.

Table 3 shows the analysis running time (in seconds) using both whole-program analysis (column *WPA*) and component-level analysis (column *CLA*). The reduction in running time ranged from 33.8% to 82.8%, with an average of 57.5%. Even though Table 3 only shows results for one particular dataflow analysis, we believe that due to the ICFG reduction, such dramatic savings will not be limited to the reaching definitions problem. Studying the effects of CLA on other dataflow analyses remains open for future investigations.

## 5   Related Work

Many techniques have been introduced for efficient dataflow analysis, with various representations of the flow of control and data. Examples include the elimination algorithms from [26] and the flow graph summarization of Callahan [1]. Our condensed ICFG is conceptually similar to the program summary graph from [1]. Efficient data flow representation is typically in terms of groups of problems, beginning with the slot-wise problems (e.g., [7]), eventually leading to the formulation of the IFDS and IDE frameworks [18, 27].

Various whole-program dataflow analyses construct summary information about a procedure, and then use this information when analyzing the callers of that procedure. An early example are the jump functions used for interprocedural constant propagation [10]. As another example, several analyses [2, 4, 31, 3, 25] perform a bottom-up traversal of the program call graph and compute a summary function for each visited procedure. This summary function is then used when analyzing the callers of that procedure and when constructing their summary functions. Summary functions can also be created in top-down manner, by introducing all possible contexts at the entry of the analyzed procedure [11]. Some approaches compute summary information for a software component independently of the callers and callees of that component. One particular technique is to compute partial analysis results for each component, to combine the results for all components in the program, and then to perform the rest of the analysis work (e.g., [5, 8, 6, 12, 24]). Sometimes conservative assumptions are used instead of pre-computed summaries (e.g., [29]). Finally, there is related work on incremental and parallel dataflow analysis (e.g., [16, 14]) in which the idea of a representative problem is introduced, and in which intensive local analysis is followed by a quick postpass to recover the actual solutions.

# 6 Conclusions and Future Work

The use of library summaries is essential for interprocedural dataflow analysis of modern software systems that are built with large library components. We propose a general theoretical framework for summary-based analysis, and present initial results that strongly indicate the potential of this technique to reduce analysis cost. In future work, we will (1) instantiate the framework to a range of popular dataflow analyses, starting with IFDS and IDE analyses, and (2) implement and evaluate these analyses, in order to gather experimental evidence of the benefits of the proposed approach. We will also consider systems built with multiple library components (e.g., libraries that use other libraries).

*Acknowledgment.* We would like to thank the CC reviewers for their helpful comments and suggestions.

# References

1. D. Callahan. The program summary graph and flow-sensitive interprocedural data flow analysis. In *Conf. Programming Language Design and Implementation*, pages 47–56, 1988.
2. R. Chatterjee, B. G. Ryder, and W. Landi. Relevant context inference. In *Symp. Principles of Programming Languages*, pages 133–146, 1999.
3. B. Cheng and W. Hwu. Modular interprocedural pointer analysis using access paths. In *Conf. Programming Language Design and Implementation*, 2000.
4. J. Choi, M. Gupta, M. Serrano, V. Sreedhar, and S. Midkiff. Escape analysis for Java. In *Conf. Object-Oriented Programming Systems, Languages, and Applications*, pages 1–19, 1999.
5. M. Codish, S. Debray, and R. Giacobazzi. Compositional analysis of modular logic programs. In *Symp. Principles of Programming Languages*, pages 451–464, 1993.
6. M. Das. Unification-based pointer analysis with directional assignments. In *Conf. Programming Language Design and Implementation*, pages 35–46, 2000.
7. D. Dhamdhere, B. Rosen, and K. Zadeck. How to analyze large programs efficiently and informatively. In *Conf. Programming Language Design and Implementation*, pages 212–223, 1992.
8. C. Flanagan and M. Felleisen. Componential set-based analysis. *ACM Trans. Programming Languages and Systems*, 21(2):370–416, Mar. 1999.
9. D. Grove and C. Chambers. A framework for call graph construction algorithms. *ACM Trans. Programming Languages and Systems*, 23(6):685–746, Nov. 2001.
10. D. Grove and L. Torczon. Interprocedural constant propagation: a study of jump function implementation. In *Conf. Programming Language Design and Implementation*, pages 90–99, 1993.

11. M. J. Harrold and G. Rothermel. Separate computation of alias information for reuse. *IEEE Tran. Software Engineering*, 22(7):442–460, July 1996.
12. N. Heintze and O. Tardieu. Ultra-fast aliasing analysis using CLA. In *Conf. Programming Language Design and Implementation*, pages 254–263, 2001.
13. F. C. Kuck. Class analysis for extensible Java software. Master's thesis, Ohio State University, Sept. 2004.
14. Y.-F. Lee and B. G. Ryder. A comprehensive approach to parallel data flow analysis. In *Int. Conf. Supercomputing*, pages 236–247, 1992.
15. O. Lhoták and L. Hendren. Scaling Java points-to analysis using Spark. In *Int. Conf. Compiler Construction*, LNCS 2622, pages 153–169, 2003.
16. T. J. Marlowe and B. G. Ryder. An efficient hybrid algorithm for incremental data flow analysis. In *Symp. Principles of Programming Languages*, pages 184–196, 1990.
17. A. Milanova, A. Rountev, and B. G. Ryder. Precise call graphs for C programs with function pointers. *Int. J. Automated Software Engineering*, 11(1):7–26, 2004.
18. T. Reps, S. Horwitz, and M. Sagiv. Precise interprocedural dataflow analysis via graph reachability. In *Symp. Principles of Programming Languages*, p. 49–61, 1995.
19. T. Reps, M. Sagiv, and S. Horwitz. Interprocedural dataflow analysis via graph reachability. Technical Report TR 94-14, Datalogisk Institut, University of Copenhagen, Apr. 1994.
20. A. Rountev. Component-level dataflow analysis. In *Int. Symp. Component-Based Software Engineering*, LNCS 3489, pages 82–89, 2005.
21. A. Rountev and B. H. Connell. Object naming analysis for reverse-engineered sequence diagrams. In *Int. Conf. Software Engineering*, pages 254–263, 2005.
22. A. Rountev, S. Kagan, and T. Marlowe. Interprocedural dataflow analysis in the presence of large libraries. Technical Report OSU-CISRC-1/06-TR01, Jan. 2006.
23. A. Rountev, A. Milanova, and B. G. Ryder. Fragment class analysis for testing of polymorphism in Java software. *IEEE Tran. Software Engineering*, 30(6):372–387, June 2004.
24. A. Rountev and B. G. Ryder. Points-to and side-effect analyses for programs built with precompiled libraries. In *Int. Conf. Compiler Construction*, LNCS 2027, pages 20–36, 2001.
25. E. Ruf. Effective synchronization removal for Java. In *Conf. Programming Language Design and Implementation*, pages 208–218, 2000.
26. B. G. Ryder and M. C. Paull. Elimination algorithms for data flow analysis. *ACM Computing Surveys*, 18(3):277–316, 1986.
27. M. Sagiv, T. Reps, and S. Horwitz. Precise interprocedural dataflow analysis with applications to constant propagation. *Theoretical Comp. Sci.*, 167:131–170, 1996.
28. M. Sharir and A. Pnueli. Two approaches to interprocedural data flow analysis. In *Program Flow Analysis: Theory and Applications*, pages 189–234. 1981.
29. F. Tip, P. Sweeney, C. Laffra, A. Eisma, and D. Streeter. Practical extraction techniques for Java. *ACM Trans. Programming Languages and Systems*, 24(6):625–666, 2002.
30. R. Vallée-Rai, E. Gagnon, L. Hendren, P. Lam, P. Pominville, and V. Sundaresan. Optimizing Java bytecode using the Soot framework: Is it feasible? In *Int. Conf. Compiler Construction*, LNCS 1781, pages 18–34, 2000.
31. J. Whaley and M. Rinard. Compositional pointer and escape analysis for Java programs. In *Conf. Object-Oriented Programming Systems, Languages, and Applications*, pages 187–206, 1999.

# Efficient Flow-Sensitive Interprocedural Data-Flow Analysis in the Presence of Pointers

Teck Bok Tok[1], Samuel Z. Guyer[2], and Calvin Lin[1]

[1] Department of Computer Sciences,
The University of Texas at Austin, Austin, TX 78712, USA
[2] Department of Computer Science,
Tufts University, Medford, MA 02155, USA

**Abstract.** This paper presents a new worklist algorithm that significantly speeds up a large class of flow-sensitive data-flow analyses, including typestate error checking and pointer analysis. Our algorithm works particularly well for inter-procedural analyses. By contrast, traditional algorithms work well for individual procedures but do not scale well to interprocedural analysis because they spend too much time unnecessarily re-analyzing large parts of the program. Our algorithm solves this problem by exploiting the sparse nature of many analyses. The key to our approach is the use of interprocedural def-use chains, which allows our algorithm to re-analyze only those parts of the program that are affected by changes in the flow values. Unlike other techniques for sparse analysis, our algorithm does not rely on precomputed def-use chains, since this computation can itself require costly analysis, particularly in the presence of pointers. Instead, we compute def-use chains on the fly during the analysis, along with precise pointer information. When applied to large programs such as nn, our techniques improve analysis time by up to 90%—from 1974s to 190s—over a state of the art algorithm.

## 1 Introduction

Flow-sensitive analysis is important for problems such as program slicing [22] and error checking [6, 7]. While recent work with BDD's has produced efficient algorithms for solving a variety of flow-insensitive analyses [24, 25], these techniques have not translated to flow-sensitive problems. Other techniques, such as demand interprocedural analysis [11], do not apply to pointer analysis. Thus, the most general technique for solving flow-sensitive problems continues to be iterative data-flow analysis. Existing iterative data-flow analysis algorithms work well within a single procedure, but they scale poorly to interprocedural analysis because they spend too much time unnecessarily re-analyzing parts of the program.

At issue is the manner in which worklists are managed, which can greatly affect the amount of work performed during each iteration. The most basic algorithm maintains a worklist of basic blocks for each procedure. Basic blocks are repeatedly removed from the worklist and applied with the flow functions. If any changes to the flow values occur, all reachable blocks are added to the worklist. This basic algorithm becomes extremely inefficient when used for interprocedural analysis: when re-analyzing a block

A. Mycroft and A. Zeller (Eds.): CC 2006, LNCS 3923, pp. 17–31, 2006.

that contains procedure calls, the algorithm may revisit all of the called procedures, even though many of them may not require re-analysis. Extensions to this basic algorithm, such as Hind and Pioli's priority queue approach [10], which considers the structure of the control flow, also suffer from this problem of useless work. For example, when the Hind and Pioli algorithm is applied to the nn program (about 36K lines of C), we find that only 3% of the basic block visits are useful—the others do not update any flow values.

In this paper we present a new algorithm for interprocedural iterative data-flow analysis that is significantly more efficient than previous algorithms. The algorithm exploits data dependences to reduce the number of times that blocks are revisited. The algorithm builds on an insight from previous work on intraprocedural algorithms: def-use chains can be used to directly identify those blocks that are affected by flow value updates [23]. This goal, however, is complicated by the fact that the computation of def-use chains is itself an expensive flow-sensitive computation, particularly in the presence

```
p = &x;
while (cond) {
    y = x;
    *p = 7;
    p = &z;
}
y = z;
```

**Fig. 1.** A loop example

of pointers. The example in Fig.1 shows why: the first time through the loop "*p" refers to x and therefore implies a def-use chain to the statement above it. The second time through the loop, however, "*p" refers to z, which implies a def-use chain to the block following the loop.

Our algorithm solves this problem by computing data dependences on the fly, along with precise pointer information, while solving the client data-flow analysis problem. The key to our approach is that as the pointer analysis computes the uses and defs of variables, it builds a network of use-def and def-use chains: the use-def chains enable fast lookup of flow values, while the def-use chains are used to narrow the scope of re-analysis when flow values change. Initially, the framework visits all basic blocks in a procedure to compute a first approximation of (1) the pointer information, (2) the data dependences, and (3) the client data-flow information. Subsequent changes in the flow values at a particular def only cause the corresponding uses to be re-analyzed. More importantly, our system incorporates new dependences into the analysis as the pointer analysis discovers them: changes in the points-to sets cause reevaluation of pointer expressions, which in turn may introduce new uses and defs and force reevaluation of the appropriate parts of the client analysis problem. Occasionally, we find pairs of basic blocks that are connected by large numbers of def-use chains. For these cases we have explored a technique called *bundling* which groups these def-use chains so that they can be efficiently treated as a single unit.

This paper makes the following contributions. First, we present a metric that allows us to compare the relative efficiency of different worklist algorithms. Second, we present a new worklist management algorithm, which significantly improves efficiency as measured by our metric. Third, we evaluate our algorithm by using it as the data-flow engine for an automated error checking tool [7]. We compare our algorithm against a state-of-the-art algorithm [10] on a large suite of open source programs. We show that improved efficiency translates into significant improvements in analysis time. For our set of 19 open source benchmarks, our algorithm improves efficiency by an average of 500% and improves analysis time by an average of 55.8% when compared with the Hind and Pioli algorithm. The benefits of our algorithm increase with larger and more complex benchmarks. For example, the nn benchmark sees an order of magnitude improvement in efficiency, which translates to a 90% improvement in analysis time.

This paper is organized as follows. We review related work in Section 2. Section 3 briefly describes the analysis framework. Section 4 presents our worklist algorithm, $\mathcal{DU}$ that enables sparse analysis, and a variant, $\mathcal{DU}_{loop}$ that exploits loop structures. Section 5 presents our empirical setup and results. We conclude in Section 6.

## 2  Related Work

There are two families of data-flow algorithms: elimination methods [21] and iterative algorithms. Elimination methods, such as interval analysis, solve systems of equations and do not work well in the presence of pointers. The class of iterative algorithms include worklists, round robin, and node listing algorithms [13, 1]. Both the round-robin and node listing approaches are dense analyses in the sense that blocks are re-analyzed needlessly.

Previous work on comparing worklist algorithms includes Atkinson and Griswold's work [2], which shows that the performance difference between a round-robin algorithm and a worklist algorithm can be huge. They propose a hybrid algorithm that combines the benefits of the two. In separate work, Hind and Pioli [10] exploit loop structure by using a priority queue. We find that Atkinson and Griswold's hybrid algorithm can sometimes be better and sometimes worse than Hind and Pioli's algorithm. To provide a basis for comparison with our new algorithm, we use as our baseline a version of the priority-queue approach that does not use the identity transfer function or *IN/OUT* sets.

Wegman and Zadeck pioneered the notion of sparse analysis in their sparse constant propagation algorithm [23]. We extend their approach to handle pointers, and we address the need to discover def-use chains on the fly as the analysis progresses.

Another possible method of exploiting sparsity is to use a sparse evaluation graph (SEG) or its variants [4, 17], which are refinements of CFGs that eliminate irrelevant statements. Hind and Pioli report improvement with pointer analysis when SEG is used [10], but because their use of *IN/OUT* sets does not fully exploit sparsity. It is unclear how much our sparse analysis can benefit from an SEG, and we leave this study as future work.

For some classes of data-flow analysis problems, there exist techniques for efficient analysis. For example, demand interprocedural data-flow analysis [11] can produce precise results in polynomial time for interprocedural, finite, distributive, subset problems (IFDS). Unfortunately, this class excludes pointer analysis, and a separate pointer analysis phase may be required.

In the context of pointer analysis itself, previous work on flow-sensitive pointer analysis algorithms that makes use of worklists [18, 3] do not attempt to tune the worklist, so our worklist algorithm can be applied to such work to improve their performance. Other pointer analysis algorithms sometimes tradeoff precision for scalability [9]. Our algorithm improves the efficiency of the worklist component that drives the analysis, without affecting the precision of the analysis.

Worklist algorithms have also been studied from other perspectives. For example, Cobleigh et at. [5] study the effects of worklist algorithms in model checking. They identify a few dimensions along which an algorithm can be varied. Their main result is that different algorithms perform best during different phases of analysis. We do not attempt to partition an analysis into phases. Similarly we do not address the issue of partitioning the problem into subproblems [20], nor do we divide a large program into manageable modules [19, 15].

## 3 Analysis Framework

This section provides background about our data-flow analysis framework, including details about how we efficiently compute reaching definitions using dominance information.

We assume an iterative-based whole-program flow-sensitive pointer analysis that uses a worklist for each procedure, where each worklist maintains a list of unique CFG blocks. An alternative is a single worklist of nodes from a supergraph [16], eliminating procedure boundaries, but we believe that such a large worklist would be too expensive.

Our algorithm requires accurate def-use chains. Since definitions are created on the fly during pointer analysis, we need to update chains whenever a new definition is discovered. To perform such updates efficiently, we assume SSA form for all variables, including heap objects. SSA has well-understood properties: every use $u$ has a unique reaching definition $d$, and $d$ must dominate $u$ if $u$ is not a *phi*-use. These properties, together with dominance relations (described below), allow us to quickly determine if a newly-discovered definition invalidates any existing def-use pairs. Finally, to merge flow values at different call sites, the system uses interprocedural $\phi$-functions at procedure entries.

Our system does not use *IN/OUT* sets to propagate flow values [3] because their use would mandate a dense analysis: any update on a node would force all of its successors to be revisited. Our sparse analysis instead uses dominance information to efficiently retrieve flow values across use-def chains. To obtain the nearest reaching definition for a given use, we build from the CFG an expanded dominator tree where each node represents a statement. We assign to each node $n$ a preorder number and a postorder number, denoted $min(n)$ and $max(n)$, respectively, so that given two distinct statements $m$ and $n$, $m$ dominates $n$, denoted by $DOM(m, n)$, if and only if $min(m) < min(n) \wedge max(m) > max(n)$. These numbers are assigned by performing a depth-first traversal and incrementing a counter each time we move either up or down the tree. Fig.2 shows the numbers assigned to an example expanded dominator tree. The number to the left of each node is its $min$ number and the number to the right of each node is its $max$ number.

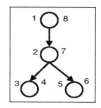

**Fig. 2.** Node numbering on an expanded dominator tree

To use this expanded dominator tree, each definition of a variable is associated with a unique statement, and we store all definitions of a variable in a list that satisfies the following invariant: let $d_i$ be the $i^{th}$ definition in the list, and let $n_i$ be the statement associated with $d_i$, then the $min$ of the statements are stored in decreasing order:

$$\forall i < j : min(n_i) > min(n_j)$$
$$\Rightarrow \quad \forall i < j : \neg DOM(n_i, n_j) \tag{1}$$

To find the nearest reaching definition that strictly dominates a statement $m$, we (1) perform a binary search to obtain the minimum $i$ such that $d_i$ in the list satisfies $min(n_i) < min(m)$; and (2) perform a linear scan from $i$ to the end of the list to find the first $d_i$ such that $max(n_i) > max(m)$. For the resulting $d_i$, $DOM(n_i, m)$. Without the binary search, a linear search alone (starting from $i = 1$) can still find the correct result if the $DOM(n_i, m)$ test is used, because by Invariant (1) the first $n_i$ that dominates $m$ must also be the nearest.

# 4 $\mathcal{DU}$: Worklist Management

Our algorithm is based on a well-known idea: use def-use chains to identify those blocks that may be affected by the most recent updates, thereby exploiting the sparsity of the analysis. To compute def-use chains in the presence of pointers, we present $\mathcal{DU}$, a worklist algorithm that is coupled with pointer analysis. This algorithm can exploit both intra- and inter-procedural def-use chains.

To simplify our presentation, we start off with a naive, inefficient version and gradually add details to build our full version at the end of this section. We will use Fig.3 as a running example.

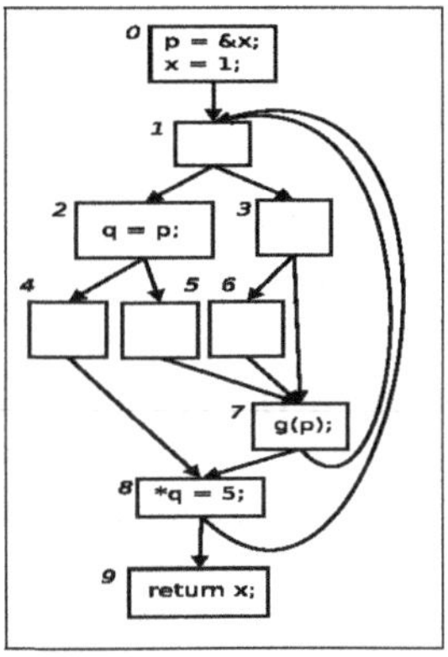

Fig. 3. An example CFG

**Structure of a Worklist Algorithm**
The left box of Fig.4 gives a high-level description of a generic worklist algorithm. It maintains a queue of CFG blocks, initially set to include all blocks in reverse post-order. The pointer analysis retrieves and analyzes one block from the worklist. The pointer analysis then identifies the set of *changes*, which is the set of variables whose flow values have been updated. The algorithm then uses a function $R$ to compute and add to the worklist the blocks that will be revisited. The worklist may then be reordered, as we discuss in Section 4.1. The entire process is repeated until the worklist becomes empty. Different implementations differ in the computation of $R$ and in the worklist reordering.

**Naive Worklist Algorithms**
The behavior of the function $R$ is crucial to the worklist efficiency. If we do not know which blocks are affected by the changes in the last block visit, then we must conservatively return all the reachable blocks of the given block $n$. We refer to this version as $R_{reach}$, shown in the right box of Fig. 4. Considering the example in Fig.3, suppose we

have just revisited the loop header (block 1), where a new $\phi$-function for variable $x$ is created. $R_{reach}$ will return blocks 2–9, a total of 8 blocks.

### Worklist Algorithm Using Intraprocedural Def-Use Chains

$R_{reach}$ is easy and cheap to compute, but it adds too many blocks. We introduce $R_{DU}$, shown in the right of Fig.4. This function iterates over the set of variable changes, retrieves their last definitions in the block, and obtains their use sites in the procedure. The blocks containing these use sites are returned and added to the worklist. For now, assume that only intraprocedural def-use chains are used. In the example of Fig.3, only two blocks (7 and 8) are returned by $R_{DU}$, so $R_{DU}$ is more efficient than $R_{reach}$.

| | |
|---|---|
| **Initially:**<br>$WL$ = reverse_post_order($CFG$)<br><br>**Main loop:**<br>while $WL \neq \emptyset$ do<br>  block $n$ = remove_front($WL$);<br>  $var\_changes$ = visit_block($n$);<br>  if $var\_changes \neq \emptyset$ then<br>    $more$ = $R(n, var\_changes)$;<br>    merge($more, WL$); | $R_{reach}(n, var\_changes)$ {<br>  return reachable_blocks($n$);<br>}<br>$R_{DU}(n, var\_changes)$ {<br>  for $v \in var\_changes$ do<br>   $d$ = last_def_of($v,n$);<br>    for $u \in$ uses($d$) do<br>     add(block_of($u$), $result$);<br>   return $result$;<br>} |

**Fig. 4.** Initial version of algorithm $\mathcal{DU}$. The function $R$ computes what blocks need to be added to the worklist. The first version, $R_{reach}$, simply returns reachable blocks from block $n$. $R_{DU}$ uses def-use chains to compute the blocks affected by the latest variable updates during the last block visit.

### Dynamic Def-Use Computation

Def-use chains are computed on the fly as new pointer information is discovered, so the worklist algorithm needs to be aware that some defs may temporarily have no uses. As we shall see, the solution requires a new form of communication between the pointer analysis and the worklist algorithm.

New definitions are created at indirect assignments, function calls, and $\phi$-functions. There are three cases to consider: (i) a new def leads to a new $\phi$-function; (ii) a new def resides between an existing def-use pair; (iii) a new def temporarily has no reaching definition.

Consider case (i). SSA form requires that whenever a new definition $d$ is created, a $\phi$-function is also created at dominance frontiers. Because pointer information is not yet available, many $\phi$-functions cannot be computed in advance.[1] Therefore after $d$ is created, the algorithm must make sure that the dominance frontiers are eventually revisited, so that the $\phi$-functions can be created.

Cases (ii) and (iii) are similar because any existing use below the new def $d$ may need to update its reaching definition. Such situations often occur in the presence of loops when a use is visited before its reaching definition is created. In the example of Fig.3, if a new $\phi$-function for $p$ is created at the loop header, we need to make sure that block 7 is revisited, even if the new def has no known use yet.

---

[1] Short of exhaustive up-front creation.

There are two possible solutions. The first method identifies those uses that need to be revisited by simply searching through existing def-use chains and through existing uses without defs. (It only needs to inspect those chains whose def is the nearest definition above $d$.) The second solution handles (iii) as follows: whenever a use $u$ without a reaching definition is discovered, statements above $u$ are marked if they are merge points or if they contain indirect assignments or function calls. Later when $d$ is discovered at one of these statements, $u$ is revisited.

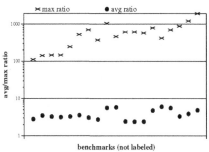

The first method can be quite expensive, while the second method does not handle case (ii). We have found that combining the two is cost effective. We use the second method on case (iii) by marking only loop headers, and we use the first method otherwise. This combination works well in practice, most likely because uses that initially have no reaching definition typically occur in loops, so marking and inspecting loop headers is sufficient. Because in practice there is usually a small, fixed number of loop headers in any procedure, the overhead due to the markings is small.

**Fig. 5.** Maximum and average ratio $r = C/(B + 1)$, in log scale. The set of benchmarks is explained in Section 5. The high ratios indicate potential for high overhead due to def-use chains.

## Bundles

One problem with $R_{DU}$ is that it can be expensive to follow du-chains if there are many du-chains that connect the same two basic blocks. We can measure the extent of this problem as follows. Define $C$ to be the number of variables whose flow values change after analyzing a given basic block. Define $B$ to be the number of unique basic blocks that contain uses of these $C$ variables. If the ratio $r = C/(B + 1)$ is large, then there is a large amount of redundancy in the dependence information represented by the du-chains. (The $+1$ term prevents division by zero.) Fig.5 shows the maximum and average values of this ratio for the benchmarks that we use in our later experiments. We omit the minimums, which are all close to zero. We see that the average ratios hover between two and ten, while the maximums are two orders of magnitude larger. One reason for the large maximums is the large number of global and heap variables defined at merge points near the end of procedures, which leads to large values of $C$ with no further uses in the procedure ($B = 0$).

To handle the cases where the value of $r$ is large, we define a *bundle* $\langle D, U \rangle$ to be the set of all def-use chains whose definitions and uses share the blocks $D$ and $U$, respectively. A bundle is used as follows (see Fig.6). After analyzing a block $n$, all bundles of the form $\langle n, u \rangle$ are retrieved. $R_{bundle}$ then iterates through these bundles: for

```
R_bundle(n, changes) {
    bundles = set of bundles {⟨n, *⟩};
    for b ∈ bundles do
        if b contains var∈ changes then
            let b = ⟨n, u⟩;
            add u to result;
    return result;
}
```

**Fig. 6.** Efficient $R_{bundle}$ that uses bundles

each bundle that contains a variable in the *changes* set, the $u$ stored in the bundle is added to the worklist. When there is no bundle ($B = 0$), no overhead will be incurred even if there is a large number of changes.

Our experimental results with an earlier implementation of our $\mathcal{DU}$ algorithm shows that bundles are quite effective for reducing analysis time. Our results also show that bundles can consume considerable space. Given the space overhead of bundles and the bi-modal distribution of $r$ values, we use a simple heuristic to apply bundles selectively. This heuristic compares $C$ to a threshold that is defined as some factor of the size of the basic block in question (as defined by the number of statements in the block).

Because we have not yet tuned the selective use of bundles for the current implementation of our worklist algorithms, the results shown later in this paper do *not* use bundles. We expect to see improved results once this tuning has been completed.

### Handling Interprocedural Def-Use Chains

Our system allows def-use chains to cross procedure boundaries, which typically occurs when a procedure accesses global variables or accesses variables indirectly through pointers. The framework treats these variables as if they were inputs or outputs to the procedure but not explicitly mentioned in the formal parameters. During interprocedural analysis, these def-use chains can be used to further improve worklist efficiency.

A procedure input is a variable that has a use inside a procedure and a reaching definition inside a caller. When re-analyzing a procedure due to changes to procedure inputs, we revisit only the affected use sites—which are often a subset of the procedure's blocks—because we know which inputs' flow values have changed. To identify these changed flow values, we use interprocedural $\phi$-functions, which merge flow values at procedure entries. As before, these $\phi$-functions are created on the fly.

A procedure output has a definition inside the procedure with some use inside a caller. The output can export a new variable, for example, a heap allocated object, or it can export a side effect on an input. We use information about the procedure output to help manage the worklists of the callers: if there is change in flow value in an output variable, the worklist of each caller marks the sites that need to be revisited. For this idea to work, we require a departure from the usual way worklists are used.

In many existing algorithms, analysis is performed one procedure at a time: analysis of a procedure $P$ is started by placing all of its blocks on its worklist. To exploit interprocedural def-use chains, we no longer initialize the worklist to all blocks, except when the procedure is analyzed for the first time. Instead, a procedure $P$'s blocks are marked to identify callers of $P$ that change $P$'s inputs and to identify callers of $P$ that are affected by $P$'s outputs.

In conjunction with a call graph worklist, this strategy allows us to exploit sparsity at the granularity of the procedure level. Thus, a procedure need not appear in the call graph worklist if its corresponding worklist is empty.

### Full Version of Algorithm $\mathcal{DU}$

Fig.7 presents our full algorithm. It first computes the reverse post-order, $rpo$, of the procedure, which is used as the worklist if the procedure is analyzed for the first time. Otherwise, the inputs are processed, searching for those with new flow values, so that

| **Initially:**<br>```if analyze proc for 1st time then```<br>    $rpo$ = ```reverse_post_order(```$CFG$```)```;<br>    $WL$ = $rpo$;<br>    $marked$ = $\emptyset$;<br>```else```<br>    $WL$ = ```process_proc_inputs()```;<br>    ```merge(```$marked$, $WL$```)```;<br>    ```sort``` $WL$ ```according to``` $rpo$;<br><br>**Main loop:**<br>```while``` $WL \neq \emptyset$ ```do```<br>    $n$ = ```remove_front(```$WL$```)```;<br>    $changes$ = ```visit_block(```$n$```)```;<br>    ```if``` $changes \neq \emptyset$ ```then```<br>        $more$ = $R_{bundle}(n, changes)$;<br>    ```merge(```$more$, $WL$```)```; | **Finally:**<br>```// worklist done; export variables.```<br>$outputs$ = ```vars to export```;<br>```if``` $outputs \neq \emptyset$ ```then```<br>    ```add(```$exit\_block()$, $outputs$```)```;<br><br>**Addition interface:**<br>```add(```$e$, $changes$```) {```<br>    $bundles$ = ```set of``` $\{\langle e, * \rangle\}$;<br>    ```for``` $b \in bundles$ ```do```<br>        ```if``` $b$ ```contains var```$\in$<br>        $changes$ ```then```<br>            ```let``` $b = \langle e, u \rangle$;<br>            $p$=```proc_of(```$u$```)```;<br>            $p\_marked$=```marked_set(```$p$```)```;<br>            ```add``` $u$ ```to``` $p\_marked$;<br>```}``` |

**Fig. 7.** Full version of algorithm $\mathcal{DU}$, when it considers both intra- and interprocedural def-use chains. Note that we also use bundles to export variables.

their use sites are put in the worklist. Those blocks marked for re-analysis are placed on the worklist, which is then sorted according to $rpo$.

The main loop is the same as that of Fig.4. After the loop, all outputs with changed flow values are gathered, and the callers' callsites are processed. During this final stage, bundles can again be used in the add routine to avoid looping through all the variables in $changes$. We assume that there is a definition for each output variable at the callee's exit block $e$. Each bundle of the form $\langle e, u \rangle$ therefore has a use site in a caller. We can then mark this use site in the caller's $marked$ set, enabling the caller to re-analyze it later.

### 4.1 Exploiting Loop Structure

By always adding blocks to the rear of the worklist, our $\mathcal{DU}$ algorithm ignores loop structure, which would seem to be a mistake because CFG structure seems to be closely related to convergence. For example, Kam and Ullman [14] show that for certain types of data-flow analyses, convergence requires at most $d + 3$ iterations, where $d$ is the largest number of back edges found in any cycle-free path of the CFG. Thus, it seems desirable to exploit knowledge of CFG structure when ordering the worklist, which is precisely what Hind and Pioli's algorithm does [10], although their algorithm does not distinguish different types of loops.

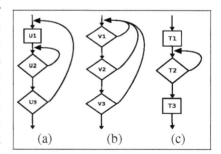

**Fig. 8.** Three loop examples: s simple loop, a nested loop, and a loop with multiple back-edges

To understand the complexities that arise from handling different types of loops, consider two types of loops. First, in a nested loop

(Fig.8(a)), which loop should we converge first? Second, in a loop with multiple back-edges (Fig.8(b)), which back edge should get priority, ie, after visiting V2 in the figure, should V1 be revisited before or after V3? After exploring many different heuristics, we evaluate a minor variant of our $\mathcal{DU}$ algorithm that ignores inner loops and uses a round-robin schedule for each loop. This algorithm, $\mathcal{DU}_{loop}$ does not try to converge an inner loop because the loop will be revisited when trying to converge the outer loop. The round-robin schedule ensures that all blocks in a loop are visited before any block is revisited.

In general, we believe that exploiting loop structure alone is not enough to yield significant improvement—we need to also account for data dependences in loops. Unfortunately, these dependences can be indirect. For example, in Fig.8(c) we have implicitly assumed that there is only a forward dependence from block T2 to T3. However, a backward, indirect dependence from block T3 to T2 can exist via a sequence of interprocedural def-use chains, so that a change in T3 could force T2 to be revisited. This phenomenon reduces the effectiveness of any techniques that try to exploit loop structures.

## 5   Experiments

### 5.1   Benchmarks and Metrics

Our experiments use 19 open source C programs (see Table 1), which—except for sendmail—were used in previous work [7]. In addition to measuring analysis time, we define metrics to evaluate the efficiency of worklist algorithms.

**Table 1.** Properties of the benchmarks. Lines of code (LOC) are given before preprocessing.

| Program | Description | LOC | Procs | Stmts | CFG nodes | Call sites |
|---|---|---|---|---|---|---|
| stunnel 3.8 | Secure TCP wrapper | 2K | 42 | 2,067 | 511 | 417 |
| pfingerd 0.7.8 | Finger daemon | 5K | 47 | 3,593 | 899 | 545 |
| muh 2.05c | IRC proxy | 5K | 84 | 4,711 | 1,173 | 666 |
| muh 2.05d | IRC proxy | 5K | 84 | 4,921 | 1,245 | 669 |
| pure-ftpd 1.0.15 | FTP server | 13K | 116 | 10,772 | 2,537 | 1,180 |
| crond (fcron-2.9.3) | cron daemon | 9K | 100 | 11,252 | 2,426 | 1,249 |
| apache 1.3.12 (core only) | Web server | 30K | 313 | 16,717 | 3,933 | 1,727 |
| make 3.75 | make | 21K | 167 | 18,787 | 4,629 | 1,855 |
| BlackHole 1.0.9 | E-mail filter | 12K | 71 | 20,227 | 4,910 | 2,850 |
| openssh client 3.5p1 | Secure shell client | 38K | 441 | 21,601 | 5,084 | 4,504 |
| wu-ftpd 2.6.0 | FTP server | 21K | 183 | 22,185 | 5,377 | 2,869 |
| wu-ftpd 2.6.2 | FTP server | 22K | 205 | 23,130 | 5,629 | 2,946 |
| named (BIND 4.9.4) | DNS server | 26K | 210 | 23,405 | 5,741 | 2,194 |
| privoxy 3.0.0 | Web server proxy | 27K | 223 | 23,615 | 5,765 | 3,364 |
| openssh daemon 3.5p1 | Secure shell server | 50K | 601 | 28,877 | 6,993 | 5,415 |
| cfengine 1.5.4 | System admin tool | 34K | 421 | 38,232 | 10,201 | 6,235 |
| sqlite 2.7.6 | SQL database | 36K | 386 | 43,489 | 10,529 | 3,787 |
| nn 6.5.6 | News reader | 36K | 493 | 47,058 | 11,739 | 4,104 |
| sendmail 8.11.6 | Mail server | 69K | 416 | 67,773 | 15,153 | 7,573 |

1. *Basic block visitation*, or *BB-visit*, is the number of times blocks are retrieved from the worklists and analyzed.
2. *Basic block changes*, or *BB-change*, is the number of basic block visitations that update some data-flow information. *BB-change* is a measure of useful work.
3. *Efficiency*, $\mathcal{E}$, is the percentage of basic block visitations that are useful, i.e. the ratio *BB-change/BB-visit*.

## 5.2  Setup

We implement our worklist algorithms using the Broadway compiler system [8], which employs an interprocedural pointer analysis that computes points-to sets for all variables. The system supports flexible precision policies, such as fixed-modes context sensitive (CS) and insensitive modes (CI), and Client Driven (CD) mode [7]. CD allows a subset of procedures to be analyzed context sensitively, according to the needs of the client analysis. To handle context sensitivity correctly, the $\mathcal{DU}$ algorithm is modified to mark a block for re-analysis under specific contexts. Broadway also supports flexible heap models; in this paper we use one abstract heap object per allocation site in CI mode, and one object per allocation context in CS mode.

To evaluate our worklist algorithm, we need to choose a pointer analysis algorithm. Because the characteristics of the pointer analysis will affect the performance of our worklist algorithm, we present results for pointer analysis algorithms that represent two extreme points, CI and CS.

All experiments are performed on a 1.7GHz Pentium 4 with 2GB of main memory, running Linux 2.4.29. We compare our algorithms against a priority-queue worklist. This algorithm assigns a unique priority to each block in a CFG, and uses $R_{reach}$. Procedure exits always have lowest priority, so loops are always converged first. This algorithm is similar to that used by Hind and Pioli [10], except we don't use *IN/OUT* sets. When we tried using *IN/OUT* sets, the compiler ran out of memory for many of the larger benchmarks.

## 5.3  Empirical Lower Bound Analysis

To see how much room there is for further improvement, we empirically estimate a lower bound as follows. First, we execute $\mathcal{DU}$ to produce a trace of block visitations where data-flow information is updated, so the length of the trace is *BB-change*. We then re-execute the analysis, visiting blocks using the trace. In theory, this second execution should yield 100% efficiency. In practice we do not get 100% efficiency because, due to implementation details, the compiler has to visit additional blocks to ensure state consistency between useful visits. We measure this second execution to approximate a lower bound,[2] which on subsequent graphs is labeled as 'bound'.

## 5.4  Results

We first consider the behavior of our worklist algorithms in conjunction with CI pointer analysis. Each graph in Fig.9 shows the performance of $\mathcal{DU}$, $\mathcal{DU}_{loop}$ and our

---

[2] Note that a better ordering of the visits in the first execution may lead to an even lower bound.

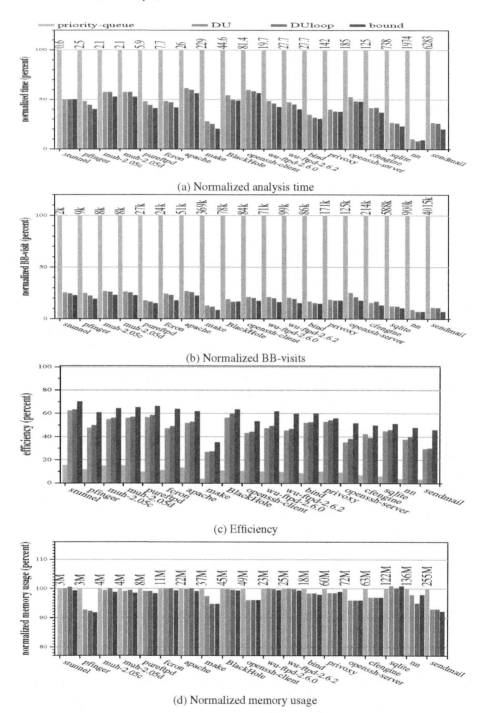

(a) Normalized analysis time

(b) Normalized BB-visits

(c) Efficiency

(d) Normalized memory usage

**Fig. 9.** Performance results of $\mathcal{DU}$ and its variant, on CI pointer analysis

empirical lower bound normalized against our baseline, which uses Hind and Pioli's priority queue. The benchmarks are listed in order of increasing size, so we see that $\mathcal{DU}$ significantly reduces analysis time, with an average reduction of 56%, and that larger benchmarks tend to benefit the most. For example, $\mathcal{DU}$ analyzes sendmail 74% faster than the baseline. We also see that $\mathcal{DU}_{loop}$ only improves upon $\mathcal{DU}$ by a few percentage points and that the main source of improvement is the increased efficiency. For example, for the large benchmarks, the efficiency of the baseline is just a few percent, but for $\mathcal{DU}$ it is in the 30-60% range. The cost of this reduced analysis time is a modest increase in memory usage. Finally, we see that there theoretically is still room for increased efficiency.

Fig.10 shows similar results for context sensitive pointer analysis. Results are only shown for benchmarks that complete under the baseline. The benefit of $\mathcal{DU}$ is larger for CS mode than CI mode because the number of large number of contexts exacerbates any inefficiencies in the worklist. For example, $\mathcal{DU}$ improves the analysis time of wu-ftpd-2.6.2 by about 80%, while in CI mode its improvement is only about 53%. These results are encouraging, and currently we are extending our algorithm to Client Driven mode. We also see that the memory overhead of our algorithms increases under CS mode.

We have repeated our experiments with five different error-checking clients [7]. These are interprocedural analyses that generally yield better precision with

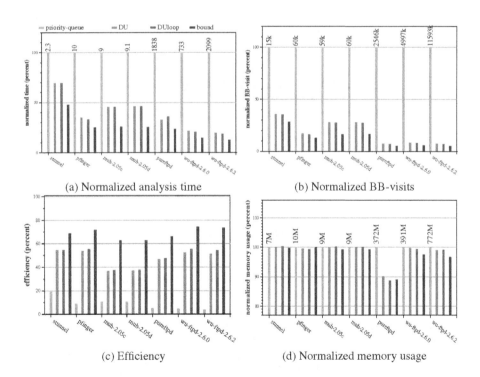

(a) Normalized analysis time

(b) Normalized BB-visits

(c) Efficiency

(d) Normalized memory usage

**Fig. 10.** Performance results of $\mathcal{DU}$ and its variant, on CS pointer analysis

flow-sensitivity. We run each client concurrently with the pointer analysis, and the results generally follow the same pattern as those in Figures 10 and 9, so we omit these to conserve space.

## 6  Conclusion

The ability to accurately analyze large programs is becoming increasingly important, particularly for software engineering problems such as error checking and program understanding, which often require high precision interprocedural analysis. This paper shows that by tuning the worklist, data-flow analysis can be made much more efficient without sacrificing precision.

We have implemented and evaluated a worklist algorithm that utilizes def-use chains. When compared with previous work, our $\mathcal{DU}$ algorithm shows substantial improvement, reducing analysis time for large programs by up to 90% for a context-insensitive analysis and by up to 80% for a context-sensitive analysis. The $\mathcal{DU}$ algorithm works well because it avoids a huge amount of unnecessary work, eliminating 65% to 90% of basic block visitations. We have also explored methods of exploiting CFG structure, and we have found that exploiting loop structure provides a small benefit for most of our benchmarks.

An empirical lower bound analysis reveals that there is room for further improvement. More study is required to determine whether some technique that considers both CFG structure and its interaction with data dependences can lead to further improvement.

*Acknowledgments.* We thank Ben Hardekopf and Kathryn McKinley for their valuable comments on early drafts of this paper. This work is supported by NSF grant ACI-0313263, DARPA Contract #F30602-97-1-0150, and an IBM Faculty Partnership Award.

## References

1. A. V. Aho and J. D. Ullman. Node listings for reducible flow graphs. In *Proc. 7th Annual ACM Symp. on Theory of Computing*, pages 177–185, 1975.
2. Darren C. Atkinson and William G. Griswold. Implementation techniques for efficient data-flow analysis of large programs. In *Proc. IEEE Int'l Conf. on Software Maintenance (ICSM'01)*, pages 52–61, November 2001.
3. J. Choi, M. Burke, and P. Carini. Efficient flow-sensitive interprocedural computation of pointer-induced aliases and side effects. In *POPL*, pages 232–245, 1993.
4. J. Choi, R. Cytron, and J. Ferrante. Automatic construction of sparse data flow evaluation graphs. In *POPL*, pages 55–66, 1991.
5. Jamieson M. Cobleigh, Lori A. Clarke, and Leon J. Osterweil. The right algorithm at the right time: comparing data flow analysis algorithms for finite state verification. In *Int'l Conf. on Software Engineering*, pages 37–46, May 2001.
6. Jeffrey S. Foster, Tachio Terauchi, and Alex Aiken. Flow-sensitive type qualifiers. In *ACM SIGPLAN'02 Proc. 2002 PLDI*, pages 1–12, June 2002.

7. Samuel Z. Guyer and Calvin Lin. Client driven pointer analysis. In Radhia Cousot, editor, *10th Annual Int'l Static Analysis Symp. (SAS'03), volume 2694 of Lecture Notes on Computer Science*, pages 214–236, June 2003.

8. Samuel Z. Guyer and Calvin Lin. An annotation language for optimizing software libraries. In *2nd Conf. on Domain Specific Languages*, pages 39–53, October 1999.

9. Michael Hind and Anthony Pioli. Which pointer analysis should I use? In *ACM SIGSOFT Int'l Symp. on Software Testing and Analysis (ISSTA 2000)*, pages 113–123, August 2000.

10. Michael Hind and Anthony Pioli. Assessing the effects of flow-sensitivity on pointer alias analysis. In *5th Annual Int'l Static Analysis Symp. (SAS'98), volume 1503 of Lecture Notes on Computer Science*, pages 57–81, September 1998.

11. Susan Horwitz, Thomas Reps, and Mooly Sagiv. Demand interprocedural dataflow analysis. In *ACM 3rd Symp. on the Foundations of Software Engineering*, pages 104–115, 1995.

12. Matthew S. Hecht and Jeffrey D. Ullman. Analysis of a simple algorithm for global data flow problems. In *POPL*, pages 207–217, 1973.

13. K. W. Kennedy. Node listings applied to data flow analysis. In *Proc. 2th ACM Symp. on Principles of Programming Languages*, pages 10–21, 1975.

14. John B. Kam and Jeffrey D. Ullman. Global Data Flow Analysis and Iterative Algorithms. *Journal of ACM*, 23(1):158–171, 1976.

15. Sungdo Moon et al. SYZYGY — a framework for scalable cross-module IPO. In *2004 Int'l Symp. on Code Generation and Optimization with Special Emphasis on Feedback-Directed and Runtime Optimization*, pages 65–74, March 2004.

16. Eugene M. Myers. A precise inter-procedural data flow algorithm. In *Proc. 8th ACM Symp. on Principles of Programming Languages*, pages 219–230, January 1981.

17. G. Ramalingam. On sparse evaluation representations. Research Report RC 21245(94831), IBM Research, July 1998.

18. Barbara G. Ryder, William A. Landi, Philip A. Stocks, Sean Zhang, and Rita Altucher. A schema for interprocedural modification side-effect analysis with pointer aliasing", In *ACM Transactions on Programming Languages and Systems*, 23(1):105–186, March 2001.

19. Atanas Rountev, Barbara G. Ryder, and William A. Landi. Data-flow Analysis of Program Fragments. In *Proc. 7th Symposium on the Foundations of Software Engineering*, pages 235–253, September 1999.

20. Erik Ruf. Partitioning dataflow analyses using types. In *Proc. 24th ACM SIGPLAN-SIGACT Symp. on Principles of Programming Languages*, pages 15–26, January 1997.

21. Barbara G. Ryder and Marvin C. Paull. Elimination algorithms for data flow analysis. *ACM Computing Surveys (CSUR)*, 18(3):277–316, September 1986.

22. Frank Tip. A survey of program slicing techniques. *Journal of Programming Languages*, 3, 1995.

23. Mark N. Wegman and F. Kenneth Zadeck. Constant propagation with conditional branches. *ACM Transactions on Programming Languages and Systems*, 13(2):181–210, April 1991.

24. John Whaley and Monica S. Lam. Cloning-Based Context-Sensitive Pointer Alias Analyses Using Binary Decision Diagrams. In *ACM SIGPLAN'04 Proc. 2004 PLDI*, pages 131–144, June 2004.

25. Jianwen Zhu and Silvian Calman. Symbolic Pointer Analysis Revisited. In *ACM SIG-PLAN'04 Proc. 2004 PLDI*, pages 145–157, June 2004.

# Path-Based Reuse Distance Analysis*

Changpeng Fang[1], Steve Carr[2], Soner Önder[2], and Zhenlin Wang[2]

[1] PathScale, Inc., 2071 Stierlin Court Ste. 200, Mountain View, CA 94043, USA
cfang@pathscale.com
[2] Department of Computer Science, Michigan Technological University,
Houghton, MI 49931, USA
{carr, soner, zlwang}@mtu.edu

**Abstract.** Profiling can effectively analyze program behavior and provide critical information for feedback-directed or dynamic optimizations. Based on memory profiling, reuse distance analysis has shown much promise in predicting data locality for a program using inputs other than the profiled ones. Both whole-program and instruction-based locality can be accurately predicted by reuse distance analysis.

Reuse distance analysis abstracts a cluster of memory references for a particular instruction having similar reuse distance values into a locality pattern. Prior work has shown that a significant number of memory instructions have multiple locality patterns, a property not desirable for many instruction-based memory optimizations. This paper investigates the relationship between locality patterns and execution paths by analyzing reuse distance distribution along each dynamic path to an instruction. Here a path is defined as the program execution trace from the previous access of a memory location to the current access. By differentiating locality patterns with the context of execution paths, the proposed analysis can expose optimization opportunities tailored only to a specific subset of paths leading to an instruction.

In this paper, we present an effective method for path-based reuse distance profiling and analysis. We have observed that a significant percentage of the multiple locality patterns for an instruction can be uniquely related to a particular execution path in the program. In addition, we have also investigated the influence of inputs on reuse distance distribution for each path/instruction pair. The experimental results show that the path-based reuse distance is highly predictable, as a function of the data size, for a set of SPEC CPU2000 programs.

## 1 Introduction

The ever-increasing disparity between memory and CPU speed has made effective operation of the memory hierarchy the single most critical element in the performance of many applications. To address this issue, compilers attempt to manipulate the spatial and temporal reuse in programs to make effective use of the cache. While static compiler analysis has achieved some success in improving memory performance, limited compile-time knowledge of run-time behavior decreases the effectiveness of static analysis. Profile analysis of a single run can yield more accurate information, however,

---

* This work was partially supported by U.S. NSF grant CCR-0312892.

A. Mycroft and A. Zeller (Eds.): CC 2006, LNCS 3923, pp. 32–46, 2006.

the use of a single run does not catch memory issues that are sensitive to program input size.

To address the lack of sensitivity to data size in profile analysis, Ding et al. [1, 2] have developed techniques to predict *reuse distance* – the number of unique memory locations accessed between two references to the same memory location. Given the reuse distances of memory locations for two training runs, they apply curve fitting to determine the reuse distance for a third input using the data size of the third input. Ding et al. show that reuse distance is highly predictable given the data size of an input set.

Our previous work [3, 4] maps the reuse distance of memory locations to the instructions that reference those locations and shows that the reuse distance of memory instructions is also highly predictable. Our analysis abstracts a cluster of memory references for a particular instruction having similar reuse distance values into a locality pattern. The results of the analysis show that many memory operations exhibit more than one locality pattern, often with widely disparate reuse distances. Unfortunately, optimization based upon reuse distance often favors reuse distances to be consistently either large or small, but not both, in order to improve memory-hierarchy performance effectively.

In this paper, we extend our previous work to use execution-path history to disambiguate the reuse distances of memory instructions. Specifically, we relate branch history to particular locality patterns in order to determine exactly when a particular reuse distance will be exhibited by a memory operation. Our experiments show that given sufficient branch history, multiple locality patterns for a single instruction can be disambiguated via branch history for most instructions that exhibit such locality patterns.

Being able to determine when a particular locality pattern will occur for a memory instruction allows the compiler and architecture to cooperate in targeting when to apply memory optimizations. For example, the compiler could insert prefetches only for certain paths to a memory instruction where reuse distances are predicted to be large. In this case, the compiler would avoid issuing useless prefetches for short reuse distance paths.

We begin the rest of this paper with a review of work related to reuse-distance analysis and path profiling. Next, we describe our analysis techniques and algorithms for measuring instruction-based reuse distance with path information. Then, we present our experiments examining the effectiveness of path-based reuse-distance analysis and finish with our conclusions and a discussion of future work.

## 2   Related Work

Currently, compilers use either static analysis or simple profiling to detect data locality. Both approaches have limitations. Dependence analysis can help to detect data reuse [5, 6]. McKinley et al. design a model to group reuses and estimate cache miss costs for loop transformations based upon dependence analysis [7]. Wolf and Lam use an approach based upon uniformly generated sets to analyze locality. Their technique produces similar results to that of McKinley, but does not require the storage of input dependences [8]. These analytical models can capture high-level reuse patterns but may miss reuse opportunities due to a lack of run-time information and limited scope. Beyls and D'Hollander advance the static technique to encode conditions to accommodate dynamic reuse distances for the class of programs that fit the *polyhedral model* [9]. Unfortunately, the model currently cannot handle spatial reuse and only works for a subset of numerical programs.

To address the limits of static analysis, much work has been done in developing feedback-directed schemes to analyze the memory behavior of programs using reuse distance. Mattson et al. [10] introduce reuse distance (or LRU stack distance) for stack processing algorithms for virtual memory management. Others have developed efficient reuse distance analysis tools to estimate cache misses [11, 12, 13, 14] and to evaluate the effect of program transformations [11, 15, 16]. Ding et al. [1] have developed a set of tools to predict reuse distance across all program inputs accurately, making reuse distance analysis a promising approach for locality based program analysis and optimizations. They apply reuse distance prediction to estimate whole program miss rates [2], to perform data transformations [17] and to predict the locality phases of a program [18]. Beyls and D'Hollander collect reuse distance distribution for memory instructions through one profiling run to generate cache replacement hints for an Itanium processor [19]. Beyls, D'Hollander and Vandeputte present a reuse distance visualization tool called RDVIS that suggests memory-hierarchy optimization [20]. Marin and Mellor-Crummey [21] incorporate reuse distance analysis in their performance models to calculate cache misses.

In our previous work, we propose a framework for instruction-based reuse distance analysis [3, 4]. We use *locality patterns* to represent the reuse distance distribution of an instruction, where a locality pattern is defined as a set of nearby related reuse distances of an instruction. Our work first builds the relationship between instruction-based locality patterns and the data size of program inputs, and extends the analysis to predict cache misses for each instruction, and identify *critical instructions*, those which produce most of the L2 cache misses. We find that a significant number of instructions, especially critical instructions, have multiple locality patterns. In this paper, we investigate the relationship between branch history and the occurrence of multiple locality patterns. To this end, we extend our reuse-distance analysis framework to path/instruction pairs to predict the path-based reuse distances across program inputs.

Previous research in path profiling usually aims at collecting accurate dynamic paths and execution frequencies for helping optimizing frequent paths [22, 23, 24]. Ammons and Larus use path profiles to identify *hot* paths and improve data flow analysis [22]. Ball and Larus present a fast path profiling algorithm that identifies each path with a unique number. Larus represents a stream of whole program paths as a context-free grammar which describes a program's entire control flow including loop iteration and interprocedural paths [24]. All of the aforementioned work takes basic block paths. We instead track only branch history since many modern superscalar processors already record branch history for branch prediction, allowing us to use the reuse-distance analysis in a dynamic optimization framework in the future.

With the intention of applying latency tolerating techniques to the specific set of dynamic load instructions that suffer cache misses, Mowry and Luk [25] propose a profiling approach to correlate cache misses to paths. While correlation profiling motivates our work, we focus on path-based reuse distance analysis. Reuse distance analysis exposes not only the results of hits or misses of cache accessing, but also the relevant reasons. Further, our analysis can predict locality change on paths across program inputs, which is not mentioned in Mowry and Luk's paper [25].

## 3    Analysis

In this section we first describe previous work on whole-program and instruction-based reuse distance analysis. We then relate branch history to locality patterns at the instruction level. We further discuss locality pattern prediction with respect to the branch history of each instruction.

### 3.1    Reuse Distance Analysis

*Reuse distance* is defined as the number of distinct memory references between two accesses to the same memory location. In terms of memory locations, reuse distance has different levels of granularity, e.g. per memory address or per cache line. With the intention of analyzing data locality, this work focuses on cache-line based reuse distance. According to the access order of a reuse pair, reuse distance has two forms: *backward* reuse distance and *forward* reuse distance. Backward reuse distance is the reuse distance from the current access to the previous one addressing the same memory location. Similarly, forward reuse distance measures the distance from the current to the next access of the same memory location. In this paper, we report only backward reuse distances. The results for forward reuse distance are similar.

Ding et al. [1] show that the reuse distance distribution of each memory location accessed in a whole program is predictable with respect to the program input size. They define the *data size* of an input as the largest reuse distance and use a histogram describing reuse distance distribution. Each bar in the histogram consists of the portion of memory references whose reuse distance falls into the same range. Given two histograms with different data sizes, they predict the histogram of a third data size and find that those histograms are predictable in a selected set of benchmarks. Typically, one can use this method to predict reuse distance for a large data input of a program based on training runs of a pair of small inputs.

Previously, we have extended Ding et al.'s work to predict reuse distance for each instruction rather than memory location. We map the reuse distances for a memory location to the instructions that cause the accesses and show that the reuse distances of each memory instruction are also predictable across program inputs for both floating-point and integer programs [3, 4]. In our approach, the reuse distances for each instruction are collected and distributed in logarithmic scaled bins for distances less than 1K and in 1K-sized bins for distances greater than 1K. The minimum, maximum, and mean reuse distances together with the access frequency are recorded for each bin. We scan the original bins from the smallest distance to the largest distance and iteratively merge any pair of adjacent bins $i$ and $i+1$ if

$$min_{i+1} - max_i \leq max_i - min_i.$$

This inequality is true if the difference between the minimum distance in bin $i+1$ and the maximum distance in bin $i$ is no greater than the length of bin $i$. The merging process stops when it reaches a minimum frequency and starts a new pattern for the next bin. We call the merged bins *locality patterns*, which accurately and efficiently represent the reuse distance distribution on a per instruction basis. Furthermore, we have shown that locality patterns can be predicted accurately for a third input using two small training inputs and curve fitting, and can be used to predict cache misses for fully and set associative caches. These results show that locality patterns are an effective abstraction for data locality analysis.

### 3.2   Using Paths to Disambiguate Reuse Patterns

Although previous results show that over half of the instructions in SPEC CPU2000 contain only one pattern, a significant number of instructions exhibit two or more locality patterns. For the purposes of memory-hierarchy optimization, the compiler may need to know when each locality pattern occurs in order to tailor optimization to the pattern exhibiting little cache reuse.

Typically two backward reuse distance locality patterns of a load come either from different sources which meet at the current load through different paths (otherwise, one access will override the other) as shown in Figure 1(a), or a single source that reaches the current load through distinct paths as shown in Figure 1(b). This suggests that a dynamic basic block history plus the source block can uniquely identify each reuse. However, it is expensive to track a basic block trace at run time and apply it to memory optimizations. Branch history is a close approximation to basic block history and available on most modern superscalar architectures.

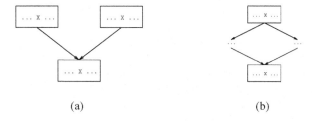

(a)                                    (b)

**Fig. 1.** Path-related reuses, (a) from two separate sources, (b) from a single source

In this work, we use a stack to keep track of the branch history during profiling and collect reuse distances for each distinct branch history of an instruction. During a load, our reuse distance collection tool calculates reuse distance and records the distance with respect to the current branch history. If an instruction has multiple locality patterns and the reuse distances for each branch history form at most one pattern, the branch history can differentiate the multiple patterns and make it possible to determine when each pattern will occur.

Due to the existence of loops in a program, the history stack tends to be quickly saturated, making it difficult to track the reuses from outside the loops. To solve this problem, we detect loop back-edges during profiling and keep the branch history for up to $l$ iterations of a loop, where $l$ is the number of data elements that fit in one cache-line. Note that we choose $l$ based on the cache-line size to differentiate between spatial (references within the same cache line) and temporal reuse patterns (references to the same memory location). After $l$ iterations or at the exit of a loop, the branch history in the loop is squashed with all corresponding history bits cleared from the stack. In this way, we efficiently use a small number of history bits to represent long paths. Furthermore, by squashing loops, the branch histories to an instruction tend to be consistent across program inputs, making it feasible to predict reuse distances along execution paths.

```
if (...)
  for (i = 0; i < n; i++)   // loop 1
    ...A[i]...
else
  for(i = 0; i < n; i++)    // loop 2
    ...A[i]...

for(i = 0; i < n; i++)      // loop 3
  ...A[i]...
```

**Fig. 2.** Multiple reuses

As an example, consider the program shown in Figure 2. A[i] in the third loop has spatial reuse from within the loop $l - 1$ out of every $l$ iterations. Additionally, A[i] has temporal reuse once every $l$ iterations from either loop 1 or loop 2, depending on the condition of the if-statement. For this case, a history of $l + 1$ bits are enough to differentiate all reuse patterns – $l$ bits for reuse from within the loop and one bit for reuse from outside the loop.

After the reuse distances for all paths of each instruction are collected, the patterns are formulated following the merging process discussed in Section 3.1. We then examine whether the path history can help to uniquely identify a pattern and whether the path-based patterns can be predicted for a third input.

### 3.3 Path-Based Reuse Distance Prediction

Previous work has shown that reuse distances are likely to change across program inputs. To make the above analysis useful for optimizations, it is essential to predict reuse distances along execution paths. Our path-based reuse distance prediction is very similar to that for whole programs [1] and instructions [3, 4], except that we form patterns for each path in the two training runs and predict the patterns for the path in the validation run.

In the two training runs, the reuse patterns of each instruction are created for each profiled path. If a path does not occur in both of the two training runs, the reuse patterns for that path are not predictable. Our prediction also assumes a path has an equal number of patterns in the two training runs. We define the *coverage* of the prediction as the percentage of dynamic paths whose reuse distances are predictable based upon the above assumptions.

Given the reuse patterns of the same path in two runs, the predicted patterns for the path in the validation run can be predicted using curve fitting as proposed by Ding et al. [1]. The prediction *accuracy* is computed by comparing the predicted patterns with the observed ones in the validation run. Here accuracy is defined as the percentage of the covered paths whose reuse distances are correctly predicted. A path's reuse distance distribution is said to be correctly predicted if and only if all of its patterns are correctly predicted. The prediction of a reuse pattern is said to be *correct* if the predicted pattern and the observed pattern fall into the same set of bins, or they overlap by at least 90%. Given two patterns $A$ and $B$ such that $B.min < A.max \leq B.max$, we say that $A$ and $B$ overlap by at least 90% if

$$\frac{A.max - \max(A.min, B.min)}{\max(B.max - B.min, A.max - A.min)} \geq 0.9.$$

## 4    Experiment

In this section, we report the results of our experimental evaluation of the relationship between locality patterns and execution paths. We begin with a discussion of our experimental methodology and then, we discuss the effectiveness of using path information in differentiating multiple locality patterns of an instruction. Finally, we report the predictability of the reuse distance distribution along execution paths.

### 4.1    Methodology

In this work, we execute our benchmark suite on the SimpleScalar Alpha simulator [26]. We modify *sim-cache* to generate the branch history and collect the data addresses and reuse distances of all memory instructions. Ding and Zhong's reuse-distance collection tool [1, 2] is used to calculate the reuse distance for each memory access. During profiling, our analysis records a 32-byte cache-line-based backward reuse distance for each individual memory instruction with the current branch history of varying lengths. Given the 32-byte cache-line size, we squash the branch history for loops every 4 iterations to help differentiate spatial and temporal reuse.

Our benchmark suite consists of 10 of the 14 floating-point programs and 11 of the 12 integer programs from SPEC CPU2000, as shown in Figure 3. The remaining five benchmarks (178.galgel, 187.facerec, 191.fma3d, 200.sixtrack and 252.eon) in SPEC CPU2000 are not included because we could not get them to compile correctly with version 5.5 of the Alpha compiler using optimization level -O3. For all benchmarks we use the test and train input sets for the training runs. For floating-point programs, we use the reference input sets for verification. However, for integer programs, we use the MinneSpec workload [27] in order to save profiling time due to the large memory requirements of the reference input set. We collect the reuse distance distribution by running all programs to completion.

### 4.2    Differentiating Multiple Locality Patterns

In this section, we experimentally analyze the ability of using branch history to differentiate between multiple locality patterns for a single instruction on our benchmark suite. We examine branch histories of length 1, 2, 4, 8, 16 and 32 bits using the history collection described in Section 3.2.

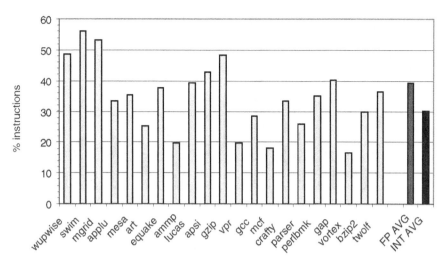

**Fig. 3.** % instructions having multiple reuse patterns

Figure 3 presents the percentage of instructions that have multiple locality patterns in a program. On average, 39.1% of the instructions in floating-point programs and 30.2% of the instructions in integer programs have more than one locality pattern. Floating-point programs, especially 168.wupwise, 171.swim, 172.mgrid and 301.apsi, tend to have diverse locality patterns. Many instructions in these programs have both temporal reuse from outside the loop that corresponds to large reuse distances, and spatial reuse from within the loop that normally has short reuse distances. In integer programs, a high number of conditional branches tends to cause multiple locality patterns. This phenomenon occurs often in 164.gzip, 186.crafty, 254.gap and 300.twolf.

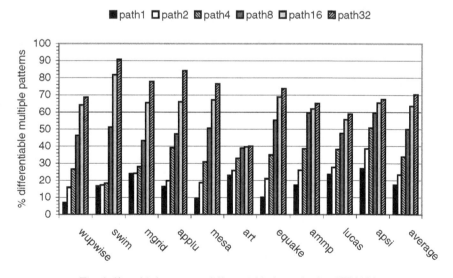

**Fig. 4.** % multiple patterns differentiable by paths for CFP2000

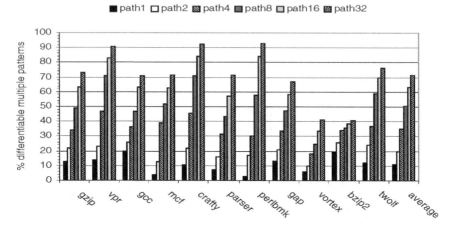

**Fig. 5.** % multiple patterns differentiable by paths for CINT2000

Figures 4 and 5 show the percentage of multiple locality patterns that can be differentiated using branch histories with various lengths. The bars labeled "path*n*" show the differentiation results for a path with *n* bits of history. We see from these two figures that, for both floating-point and integer programs, using execution path context can differentiate a significant percentage of multiple patterns for an instruction. This percentage increases with the increase in the number of history bits used. On average, paths with an 8-bit history can disambiguate over 50% of the multiple patterns. Whereas paths with 32 bits of history can disambiguate over 70% of the multiple patterns.

There are still some multiple patterns that cannot be differentiated by our approach even though a 32-bit history is used. Several factors have been observed to be responsible for this non-differentiability. The first is branch history *aliasing*, where different execution paths have the same branch history. Branch history aliasing occurs when executions from different block traces share the last several bits of the branch history, as shown in Figure 6. In this case, when using a 2-bit history both paths have the history of 01. However, a 3-bit history will solve the problem.

To examine the effect of branch history aliasing on our scheme, we report the percentage of multiple patterns that cannot be differentiated because of history aliasing, as

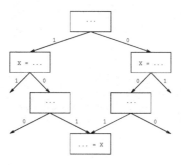

**Fig. 6.** Branch history aliasing

**Table 1.** % multiple patterns that are non-differentiable because of history aliasing for CFP2000

| Benchmark | path1 | path2 | path4 | path8 | path16 |
|-----------|-------|-------|-------|-------|--------|
| 168.wupwise | 62.6 | 53.7 | 42.9 | 23.4 | 5.4 |
| 171.swim | 70.3 | 69.8 | 68.7 | 36.0 | 5.4 |
| 172.mgrid | 51.1 | 50.9 | 46.9 | 31.7 | 9.6 |
| 173.applu | 52.3 | 48.7 | 29.5 | 21.4 | 2.4 |
| 177.mesa | 76.4 | 67.1 | 54.9 | 35.3 | 18.6 |
| 179.art | 40.8 | 38.0 | 30.9 | 24.9 | 24.1 |
| 183.equake | 74.9 | 64.0 | 50.1 | 29.8 | 16.2 |
| 188.ammp | 51.4 | 42.7 | 30.1 | 9.2 | 6.7 |
| 189.lucas | 51.9 | 47.8 | 37.4 | 28.0 | 20.1 |
| 301.apsi | 60.0 | 48.3 | 36.2 | 27.5 | 21.4 |
| average | 59.2 | 53.1 | 42.7 | 26.7 | 13.0 |

**Table 2.** % multiple patterns that are non-differentiable because of history aliasing for CINT2000

| Benchmark | path1 | path2 | path4 | path8 | path16 |
|-----------|-------|-------|-------|-------|--------|
| 164.gzip | 74.0 | 64.6 | 52.6 | 37.7 | 23.4 |
| 175.vpr | 81.3 | 71.8 | 48.2 | 24.0 | 12.0 |
| 176.gcc | 65.0 | 58.7 | 48.5 | 37.9 | 21.7 |
| 181.mcf | 91.8 | 83.0 | 56.5 | 44.3 | 33.3 |
| 186.crafty | 87.6 | 75.9 | 52.7 | 27.3 | 13.9 |
| 197.parser | 82.8 | 74.0 | 59.0 | 46.7 | 32.8 |
| 253.perlbmk | 89.1 | 74.8 | 61.6 | 34.4 | 8.0 |
| 254.gap | 73.6 | 66.2 | 53.5 | 40.1 | 28.6 |
| 255.vortex | 70.1 | 66.5 | 58.1 | 51.4 | 42.4 |
| 256.bzip2 | 59.6 | 52.9 | 44.5 | 43.2 | 40.2 |
| 300.twolf | 74.9 | 63.0 | 50.3 | 28.2 | 17.4 |
| average | 77.3 | 68.3 | 53.2 | 37.7 | 24.9 |

listed in Tables 1 and 2. We identify whether or not a particular history is an aliased one by tracking the block trace associated with this history. We experimentally collect the data for *path*16. For *pathn* where $n < 16$, the non-differentiable multiple patterns due to aliasing are those for *path*16 plus all patterns that can be differentiated by a 16-bit history but not the $n$-bit history. We see from Tables 1 and 2 that the branch history aliasing problem is more severe in integer programs than in floating-point programs, and increasing the number of history bits can greatly reduce the number of non-differentiable patterns.

We have observed that, branch history aliasing most commonly occurs when all locality patterns represent short reuse distances. This is not a severe problem for determining cache misses. There are two ways to reduce the influence of the branch history aliasing problem. We can use more history bits and focus only on those critical instructions which produce most of the cache misses. Or, for those applications considering only short reuse distances, a block trace can be used instead of branch history for path representation. If only short reuse distances are involved, the memory requirement needed for basic block traces will not be excessive.

In addition to branch history aliasing, cache-line alignment causes some multiple patterns to be not differentiable using our scheme. The following code occurs in the function fullGtu(Int32 i1, Int32 i2) in program 256.bzip2.

```
1. c1=block[i1];
2. c2=block[i2];
3. if(c1!=c2) return(c1>c2);
4. i1++;i2++;

5. c1=block[i1];
6. c2=block[i2];
7. if(c1!=c2) return(c1>c2);
8. i1++;i2++;
```

Depending on the value of i1, block[i1] at line 5 may reuse the data touched at line 1 having a short reuse distance, or data from beyond the function having a long reuse distance. The change in the value of i1 may cause the load at line 5 to be in a different cache line from the load at line 1. In this case, our scheme cannot differentiate between the two patterns. Notice that this piece of code is similar to an unrolled loop, which suggests that compile-time loop unrolling may also influence our scheme. Indeed, we have found cases of loop unrolling that cause some multiple patterns to be not differentiable by paths in floating-point programs such as 168.wupwise and 173.applu.

For cache-related optimization, it is important to differentiate multiple patterns of an instruction having both short and long reuse distances. This would allow the compiler to optimize the long reuse distance that is likely a cache miss and ignore the path where the reuse distance is short and a cache hit is likely. Table 3 lists the percentage of multiple patterns that cannot be differentiated and have both short and long patterns. Here we use a threshold of 1K, which corresponds to the size of a 32K-byte L1 cache, to classify reuse distances as short or long. We can see that non-differentiable multiple patterns

**Table 3.** % multiple patterns that cannot be differentiated and have both short and long distances

| CFP2000 | path4 | path8 | path16 | CINT2000 | path4 | path8 | path16 |
|---|---|---|---|---|---|---|---|
| 168.wupwise | 28.5 | 24.3 | 17.5 | 164.gzip | 36.5 | 28.7 | 21.9 |
| 171.swim | 37.1 | 21.5 | 7.2 | 175.vpr | 0.3 | 0.2 | 0.2 |
| 172.mgrid | 10.4 | 8.2 | 6.1 | 176.gcc | 0.3 | 0.3 | 0.2 |
| 173.applu | 11.5 | 10.8 | 6.6 | 181.mcf | 16.8 | 16.7 | 13.9 |
| 177.mesa | 4.8 | 4.6 | 4.6 | 186.crafty | 0.0 | 0.0 | 0.0 |
| 179.art | 18.3 | 12.1 | 11.5 | 197.parser | 0.1 | 0.1 | 0.0 |
| 183.equake | 4.6 | 4.2 | 4.1 | 253.perlbmk | 1.4 | 0.0 | 0.8 |
| 188.ammp | 0.4 | 0.3 | 0.2 | 254.gap | 1.5 | 1.2 | 1.1 |
| 189.lucas | 42.6 | 37.1 | 30.2 | 255.vortex | 0.4 | 0.3 | 0.3 |
| 301.apsi | 5.2 | 4.6 | 3.8 | 256.bzip2 | 14.0 | 14.0 | 11.2 |
| | | | | 300.twolf | 6.8 | 5.0 | 4.2 |
| average | 16.3 | 12.8 | 9.2 | average | 7.0 | 6.1 | 4.9 |

with both short and long reuse distances only account for a small portion of the total number of the multiple patterns in a program, and on average, integer programs have a lower percentage than floating-point programs.

### 4.3  Path Based Reuse Distance Prediction

Tables 4 and 5 list the path-based reuse distance prediction coverage and accuracy for floating-point and integer programs, respectively. For comparison, we also list the instruction-based reuse distance prediction results in the columns labeled "inst". Due to the excessive memory requirements of simulation via SimpleScalar and profile collection, we cannot generate the prediction results for the path32 for integer programs.

**Table 4.** CFP2000 path-based reuse-distance prediction

| Benchmark | inst | coverage (%) | | | | | | inst | accuracy(%) | | | | | |
|---|---|---|---|---|---|---|---|---|---|---|---|---|---|---|
| | | path | | | | | | | path | | | | | |
| | | 1 | 2 | 4 | 8 | 16 | 32 | | 1 | 2 | 4 | 8 | 16 | 32 |
| 168.wupwise | 92.9 | 94.2 | 93.7 | 94.9 | 96.6 | 97.5 | 98.5 | 98.1 | 99.0 | 99.1 | 99.4 | 99.4 | 99.5 | 99.7 |
| 171.swim | 95.5 | 98.6 | 98.7 | 98.9 | 99.2 | 99.7 | 99.8 | 89.0 | 93.6 | 93.5 | 93.6 | 95.9 | 95.7 | 95.7 |
| 172.mgrid | 96.6 | 97.9 | 97.3 | 97.7 | 96.6 | 97.1 | 94.1 | 91.9 | 94.8 | 95.0 | 95.8 | 96.4 | 96.5 | 96.2 |
| 173.applu | 96.4 | 94.0 | 92.2 | 92.3 | 91.9 | 87.8 | 77.0 | 96.0 | 97.0 | 96.2 | 96.2 | 96.1 | 96.3 | 97.1 |
| 177.mesa | 96.9 | 97.0 | 97.1 | 99.2 | 99.2 | 99.9 | 99.8 | 98.6 | 98.6 | 99.3 | 99.3 | 99.3 | 98.9 | 98.9 |
| 179.art | 94.6 | 96.2 | 96.2 | 97.3 | 99.5 | 99.5 | 99.5 | 96.5 | 95.6 | 95.6 | 95.7 | 94.6 | 94.6 | 94.7 |
| 183.equake | 99.2 | 99.6 | 99.6 | 99.6 | 99.2 | 98.9 | 98.0 | 98.3 | 98.6 | 98.6 | 98.8 | 98.6 | 99.0 | 98.9 |
| 188.ammp | 99.9 | 99.9 | 99.9 | 99.9 | 99.9 | 99.8 | 99.4 | 89.6 | 92.8 | 92.8 | 93.9 | 94.0 | 94.1 | 94.3 |
| 189.lucas | 71.7 | 66.5 | 65.3 | 63.3 | 62.4 | 60.1 | 59.3 | 94.1 | 97.5 | 98.6 | 98.6 | 98.3 | 98.8 | 98.8 |
| 301.apsi | 96.6 | 96.6 | 96.8 | 97.1 | 96.1 | 91.4 | 85.9 | 93.0 | 96.5 | 97.0 | 97.2 | 96.9 | 97.2 | 97.7 |
| average | 94.0 | 94.1 | 93.7 | 94.0 | 94.1 | 93.17 | 91.1 | 94.5 | 96.4 | 96.6 | 96.9 | 97.0 | 97.1 | 97.2 |

**Table 5.** CINT2000 path-based reuse-distance prediction

| Benchmark | inst | coverage (%) | | | | | inst | accuracy(%) | | | | |
|---|---|---|---|---|---|---|---|---|---|---|---|---|
| | | path | | | | | | path | | | | |
| | | 1 | 2 | 4 | 8 | 16 | | 1 | 2 | 4 | 8 | 16 |
| 164.gzip | 99.2 | 99.2 | 99.2 | 99.0 | 99.2 | 98.8 | 95.1 | 95.5 | 95.8 | 97.2 | 97.0 | 97.5 |
| 175.vpr | 97.7 | 99.2 | 98.9 | 98.3 | 95.8 | 90.0 | 93.9 | 93.7 | 93.9 | 93.4 | 94.2 | 95.6 |
| 176.gcc | 95.6 | 96.7 | 96.8 | 96.4 | 93.6 | 90.2 | 93.3 | 95.2 | 95.2 | 94.9 | 95.3 | 94.8 |
| 181.mcf | 94.5 | 95.0 | 95.0 | 95.0 | 94.6 | 92.7 | 88.9 | 89.9 | 90.6 | 89.3 | 90.0 | 90.6 |
| 186.crafty | 97.7 | 98.5 | 99.0 | 99.2 | 99.1 | 97.9 | 93.2 | 93.3 | 94.4 | 93.8 | 94.4 | 94.6 |
| 197.parser | 83.3 | 85.5 | 87.1 | 84.8 | 79.1 | 66.4 | 84.9 | 84.4 | 85.2 | 88.5 | 91.6 | 97.0 |
| 253.perlbmk | 99.8 | 99.8 | 99.8 | 99.8 | 99.8 | 99.2 | 97.2 | 97.2 | 97.2 | 97.2 | 98.0 | 97.9 |
| 254.gap | 86.8 | 86.6 | 86.9 | 85.2 | 82.1 | 77.5 | 91.5 | 92.6 | 92.7 | 94.7 | 97.0 | 99.6 |
| 255.vortex | 99.7 | 99.7 | 99.8 | 99.8 | 99.8 | 99.7 | 97.3 | 97.3 | 97.3 | 97.4 | 97.2 | 96.4 |
| 256.bzip2 | 99.9 | 99.9 | 99.9 | 99.9 | 99.9 | 99.9 | 98.0 | 97.8 | 97.8 | 97.8 | 98.1 | 97.9 |
| 300.twolf | 95.6 | 96.2 | 96.1 | 95.4 | 94.1 | 90.1 | 93.3 | 93.3 | 93.4 | 94.0 | 94.0 | 95.0 |
| average | 95.4 | 96.0 | 96.2 | 95.7 | 94.3 | 91.1 | 93.3 | 93.7 | 94.0 | 94.4 | 95.2 | 96.1 |

For floating-point programs, on average, our mechanism can predict reuse distances for over 91% of the paths with accuracies all above 96%, with the number of history bits ranging from 1 up to 32. With less than or equal to 8 bits of branch history, the path-based prediction coverage compares well with using no branch history. When more than 8 bits are used, the prediction coverage decreases slightly. The rightmost part of Table 4 shows that using branch history improves the accuracy of reuse-distance prediction.

Integer programs exhibit similar coverage and accuracy results, as listed in Table 5. On average, we can predict reuse distances for over 91% of the paths with accuracies above 93.5%. While the coverage decreases with the increase in the number of bits used, the path-based reuse distance prediction coverage is higher than the instruction-based one when less than 8 bits are used. With a single-bit history, the average prediction accuracy is 93.7%, while the accuracy for a 16-bit history improves to 96.1% of the covered paths.

We have observed two major factors that influence the prediction coverage. First, our prediction assumes all paths appear in both training runs. However, some paths may only occur when using the reference input set (we call these paths *missing paths*). For example, a conditional branch may be taken when the reference input is used but not when the test input is used. Long execution paths will experience this phenomenon more often than short paths. Another factor determining the predictability is *pattern matching*. For a path or instruction, if the number of locality patterns is not equal in the two training runs, we cannot accurately match the corresponding patterns and thus cannot predict the reuse distances. For this case, relating reuse distances to paths has an advantage because most paths tend to have a single locality pattern.

For 168.wupwise, 171.swim and 179.art, the pattern matching problem dominates the cases where we do not predict reuse correctly. Thus, the coverage monotonically increases with the increase in the number of history bits used. When missing paths are the major factor, the prediction coverage decreases with the path length, as is the case for 173.applu and 189.lucas. For 173.applu, 22.8% of the paths are missing in the training runs for the 32-bit history, leading to a low coverage. For 189.lucas, 197.parser and 254.gap, there is a significant number of instructions that do not appear in the two training runs. Thus, the corresponding paths do not occur in both training runs, resulting in a low coverage for all evaluation cases.

## 5   Conclusions and Future Work

In this paper, we have proposed a novel approach for path-based reuse-distance analysis. We use execution-path history to disambiguate the reuse distances of memory instructions. Specifically, we relate branch history to particular locality patterns in order to determine exactly when a particular reuse distance will be exhibited by a memory operation.

Our experiments show that given sufficient branch history, multiple locality patterns for a single instruction can be disambiguated via branch history for most instructions that exhibit such locality patterns. On average, over 70% of the multiple patterns for static instructions can be differentiated by execution paths with a 32-bit branch history, for both floating-point and integer programs. In addition, we also show that the path based reuse distances can be more accurately predicted than the instruction based reuse distances across program inputs, without a significant decrease in prediction coverage.

Being able to determine when a particular locality pattern will occur for a memory instruction allows the compiler and architecture to cooperate in targeting when to apply memory optimizations. Our next step is to apply the analysis for optimizations like prefetching. Specifically, we are developing software/hardware cooperative approaches to invoke prefetches only when certain paths with large reuse distances are executed. These approaches aim to avoid useless prefetches while achieving high performance.

# References

1. Ding, C., Zhong, Y.: Predicting whole-program locality through reuse distance analysis. In: Proceedings of the 2003 ACM SIGPLAN Conference on Programming Language Design and Implementation, San Diego, California (2003) 245–257
2. Zhong, Y., Dropsho, S., Ding, C.: Miss rate prediction across all program inputs. In: Proceedings of the $12^{th}$ International Conference on Parallel Architectures and Compilation Techniques, New Orleans, LA (2003) 91–101
3. Fang, C., Carr, S., Önder, S., Wang, Z.: Reuse-distance-based miss-rate prediction on a per instruction basis. In: Proceedings of the Second ACM Workshop on Memory System Performance, Washington, D.C. (2004) 60–68
4. Fang, C., Carr, S., Önder, S., Wang, Z.: Instruction based memory distance analysis and its application to optimization. In: Proceedings of the $14^{th}$ International Conference on Parallel Architectures and Compilation Techniques, St. Louis, MO (2005)
5. Goff, G., Kennedy, K., Tseng, C.: Practical dependence testing. In: Proceedings of the SIGPLAN '91 Conference on Programming Language Design and Implementation, Toronto, Canada (1991) 15–29
6. Pugh, W.: A practical algorithm for exact array dependence analysis. Communications of the ACM **35**(8) (1992) 102–114
7. McKinley, K.S., Carr, S., Tseng, C.: Improving data locality with loop transformations. ACM Transactions on Programming Languages and Systems **18**(4) (1996) 424–453
8. Wolf, M.E., Lam, M.: A data locality optimizing algorithm. In: Proceedings of the SIGPLAN '91 Conference on Programming Language Design and Implementation, Toronto, Canada (1991) 30–44
9. Beyls, K., D'Hollander, E.: Generating cache hints for improved program efficiency. Journal of Systems Architecture **51**(4) (2005)
10. Mattson, R.L., Gecsei, J., Slutz, D., Traiger, I.L.: Evaluation techniques for storage hierarchies. IBM Systems Journal **9**(2) (1970) 78–117
11. Almasi, G., Cascaval, C., Padua, D.: Calculating stack distance efficiently. In: Proceedings of the first ACM Workshop on Memory System Performance, Berlin, Germany (2002)
12. Cascaval, C., Padua, D.: Estimating cache misses and locality using stack distance. In: Proceedings of the 17th International Conference on Supercomputing, San Francisco, CA (2003) 150–159
13. Sugumar, R.A., Abraham, S.G.: Efficient simulation of caches under optimal replacement with applications to miss characterization. In: Proceedings of the ACM SIGMETRICS Conference on Measurement & Modeling Computer Systems, Santa Clara, CA (1993) 24–35
14. Zhong, Y., Ding, C., Kennedy, K.: Reuse distance analysis for scientific programs. In: Proceedings of Workshop on Language, Compilers, and Runtime Systems for Scalable Compilers, Washington, DC (2002)

15. Beyls, K., D'Hollander, E.: Reuse distance as a metric for cache behavior. In: Proceedings of the IASTED Conference on Parallel and Distributed Computing and Systems. (2001)
16. Ding, C.: Improving effective bandwidth through compiler enhancement of global and dynamic reuse. PhD thesis, Rice University (2000)
17. Zhong, Y., Orlovich, M., Shen, X., Ding, C.: Array regrouping and structure splitting using whole-program reference affinity. In: Proceedings of the 2004 ACM SIGPLAN Conference on Programming Language Design and Implementation, Washington, D.C. (2004)
18. Shen, X., Zhong, Y., Ding, C.: Locality phase prediction. In: Proceedings of the Eleventh International Conference on Architectural Support for Programming Languages and Operating Systems (ASPLOS-XI), Boston, MA (2004)
19. Beyls, K., D'Hollander, E.: Reuse distance-based cache hint selection. In: Proccedings of the 8th International Euro-Par Conference. (2002)
20. Beyls, K., D'Hollander, E., Vandeputte, F.: RDVIS: A tool that visualizes the causes of low locality and hints program optimizations. In Sunderam, V.e.a., ed.: Computational Science – ICCS 2005, 5th International Conference. Volume 3515., Atlanta, Springer (2005) 166–173
21. Marin, G., Mellor-Crummey, J.: Cross architecture performance predictions for scientific applications using parameterized models. In: Proceedings of the Joint International Conference on Measurement and Modeling of Computer Systems, New York, NY (2004)
22. Ammons, G., Larus, J.R.: Improving data-flow analysis with path profiles. In: Proceedings of the SIGPLAN '98 Conference on Programming Language Design and Implementation, Montreal, Canada (1998) 72–84
23. Ball, T., Larus, J.R.: Efficient path profiling. In: Proceedings of the 29th International Symposium on Microarchitecture, Paris, France (1996) 46–57
24. Larus, J.R.: Whole program paths. In: Proceedings of the SIGPLAN '99 Conference on Programming Language Design and Implementation, Atlanta, GA (1999) 259–269
25. Mowry, T., Luk, C.K.: Predicting data cache misses in non-numberic applications through correlation profiling. In: Proceedings of the 30th International Symposium on Microarchitecture, North Carolina, United States (1997) 314–320
26. Burger, D.C., Austin, T.M.: The SimpleScalar tool set, version 2.0. Computer Architecture News **25**(3) (1997) 13–25
27. KleinOsowski, A., Lilja, D.: Minnespec: A new spec benchmark workload for simulation-based computer architecture research. Computer Architecture Letters **1** (2002)

# Context-Sensitive Points-to Analysis: Is It Worth It?[*]

Ondřej Lhoták[1,2] and Laurie Hendren[2]

[1] School of Computer Science, University of Waterloo, Waterloo, ON, Canada
[2] School of Computer Science, McGill University, Montreal, QC, Canada
olhotak@uwaterloo.ca, hendren@sable.mcgill.ca

**Abstract.** We present the results of an empirical study evaluating the precision of subset-based points-to analysis with several variations of context sensitivity on Java benchmarks of significant size. We compare the use of call site strings as the context abstraction, object sensitivity, and the BDD-based context-sensitive algorithm proposed by Zhu and Calman, and by Whaley and Lam. Our study includes analyses that context-sensitively specialize only pointer variables, as well as ones that also specialize the heap abstraction. We measure both characteristics of the points-to sets themselves, as well as effects on the precision of client analyses. To guide development of efficient analysis implementations, we measure the number of contexts, the number of distinct contexts, and the number of distinct points-to sets that arise with each context sensitivity variation. To evaluate precision, we measure the size of the call graph in terms of methods and edges, the number of devirtualizable call sites, and the number of casts statically provable to be safe.

The results of our study indicate that object-sensitive analysis implementations are likely to scale better and more predictably than the other approaches; that object-sensitive analyses are more precise than comparable variations of the other approaches; that specializing the heap abstraction improves precision more than extending the length of context strings; and that the profusion of cycles in Java call graphs severely reduces precision of analyses that forsake context sensitivity in cyclic regions.

## 1 Introduction

Does context sensitivity significantly improve precision of interprocedural analysis of object-oriented programs? It is often suggested that it could, but lack of scalable implementations has hindered thorough empirical verification of this intuition.

Of the many context sensitive points-to analyses that have been proposed (e.g. [1, 4, 8, 11, 17–19, 25, 28–31]), which improve precision the most? Which are most effective for specific client analyses, and for specific code patterns? For which variations are we likely to find scalable implementations? Before devoting resources to finding efficient implementations of specific analyses, we should have empirical answers to these questions.

This study aims to provide these answers. Recent advances in the use of Binary Decision Diagrams (BDDs) in program analysis [3, 12, 29, 31] have made context sensitive analysis efficient enough to perform an empirical study on benchmarks of significant

---

[*] This work was supported, in part, by NSERC and an IBM Ph.D. Fellowship.

A. Mycroft and A. Zeller (Eds.): CC 2006, LNCS 3923, pp. 47–64, 2006.

size. Using the JEDD system [14], we have implemented three different families of context-sensitive points-to analysis, and we have measured their precision in terms of several client analyses. Specifically, we compared the use of call-site strings as the context abstraction, object sensitivity [17, 18], and the algorithm proposed by Zhu and Calman [31] and Whaley and Lam [29] (hereafter abbreviated ZCWL). Within each family, we evaluated the effect of different lengths of context strings, and of context-sensitively specializing the heap abstraction. In our study, we compared the relative precision of analyses both quantitatively, by computing summary statistics about the analysis results, and qualitatively, by examining specific code patterns for which a given analysis variation produces better results than other variations.

Context-sensitive analyses have been associated with very large numbers of contexts. We wanted to also determine how many contexts each variation of context sensitivity actually generates, how the number of contexts relates to the precision of the analysis results, and how likely it is that scalable context-sensitive representations are feasible. These measurements can be done directly on the BDD representation.

Our results show that although the effect on precision depends on the client analysis, the benefits of context sensitivity are very significant for some analyses, particularly cast safety analysis. We also show that object-sensitivity consistently improves precision most compared to the other variations studied, and that modelling heap objects with context does significantly improve precision.

The remainder of this paper is organized as follows. In Section 2, we provide background about the variations of context sensitivity that we have studied. In Section 3, we list the benchmarks included in our study. We discuss the number of contexts and its implications on precision and scalability in Section 4. In Section 5, we examine the effects of context sensitivity on the precision of the call graph. We evaluate opportunities for static resolution of virtual calls in Section 6. In Section 7, we measure the effect of context sensitivity on cast safety analysis. We briefly survey related work in Section 8. Finally, we draw conclusions from our experimental results in Section 9.

## 2   Background

Like any static analysis, a points-to analysis models the possible run-time features of the program using some chosen static abstraction. A context-sensitive points-to analysis requires an abstraction of pointer targets, pointers, and method invocations. We will denote these three abstractions $\mathcal{O}$, $\mathcal{P}$, and $\mathcal{I}$, respectively. Whenever it is possible for a run-time pointer $p$ to point to the run-time target $o$, the may-point-to relation computed by the analysis must contain the fact $\mathcal{O}(o) \in pt(\mathcal{P}(p))$. The specific choice of static abstraction is a key determining factor of the precision of the analysis, and this paper compares several different abstractions.

**Pointer Target Abstraction:** In Java, the target of a pointer is always a dynamically allocated object. A popular abstraction for a pointer target is the program statement at which the object was allocated. We will write this abstraction as $\mathcal{O}^{as}$.

**Pointer Abstraction:** Each run-time pointer corresponds to either some local variable or some object field in the program. Pointers corresponding to local variables are often statically abstracted by the local variable; we will write this abstraction as $\mathcal{P}^{var}$. For pointers corresponding to fields, we will consider only the field-sensitive abstraction in this paper, because it is more precise than other alternatives (described, for example, in [13, 23]). The field-sensitive abstraction $\mathcal{P}^{fs}(o.f)$ of the field $f$ of run-time object $o$ is the pair $[\mathcal{O}(o), f]$, where $\mathcal{O}(o)$ is our chosen static abstraction of the run-time object $o$.

**Method Invocation (Context) Abstraction:** Because different invocations of a method may have different behaviours, it may be useful to distinguish some of them. A context is a static abstraction of a method invocation; an analysis distinguishes invocations if their abstract contexts are different. In this paper, we compare two families of invocation abstraction (also called context abstraction), call sites [24, 25] and receiver objects [17, 18]. In call-site context sensitivity, the context $\mathcal{I}^{cs}(i)$ of an invocation $i$ is the program statement (call site) from which the method was invoked. In receiver-object context sensitivity, the context of an invocation $i$ is the static abstraction of the object on which the method is invoked. That is, $\mathcal{I}^{ro}(i) = \mathcal{O}(o)$, where $o$ is the run-time object on which the method was invoked.

In either case, the context abstraction can be made even finer by using a string of contexts corresponding to the invocation frames on the run-time invocation stack [18, 24]. That is, having chosen a base abstraction $\mathcal{I}^{base}$, we can define $\mathcal{I}^{string}(i)$ to be $[\mathcal{I}^{base}(i),$ $\mathcal{I}^{base}(i_2), \mathcal{I}^{base}(i_3), \ldots]$, where $i_j$ is the $j$'th top-most invocation on the stack during the invocation $i$ (so $i = i_1$). Since the maximum height of the stack is unbounded, the analysis must somehow ensure that the static abstraction is finite. A simple, popular technique is to limit the length of each context string to at most a fixed number $k$. A different technique is used by the ZCWL algorithm. It does not limit the length of a context string, but it excludes from the context string all contexts corresponding to call edges that are part of a cycle in the context-insensitive call graph. Thus, the number of contexts is bounded by the number of acyclic paths in the call graph, which is finite.

Orthogonal to the choice of context abstraction is the choice of which pointers and objects to model context-sensitively. That is, having chosen a basic context-insensitive pointer abstraction $\mathcal{P}^{ci}$ and a context abstraction $\mathcal{I}$, we can model a run-time pointer $p$ context-sensitively by defining $\mathcal{P}(p)$ to be $[\mathcal{I}(i_p), \mathcal{P}^{ci}(p)]$, where $i_p$ is the method invocation in which $p$ occurs, or context-insensitively by defining $\mathcal{P}(p)$ to be $\mathcal{P}^{ci}(p)$. Similarly, if we have chosen the allocation site abstraction $\mathcal{O}^{as}$ as the basic abstraction for objects, we can model each object $o$ context-sensitively by defining $\mathcal{O}(o)$ to be $[\mathcal{I}(i_o), \mathcal{O}^{as}(o)]$, where $i_o$ is the method invocation during which $o$ was allocated, or context-insensitively by defining $\mathcal{O}(o)$ to be $\mathcal{O}^{as}(o)$.

In the tables in the rest of this paper, we report results for the following variations of points-to analyses. In tables reporting call graph information, the "CHA" column reports baseline numbers obtained using Class Hierarchy Analysis [6]. The "insens." column of each table is a context-insensitive points-to analysis that does not distinguish different invocations of any method. The "object-sensitive" columns are analyses using receiver objects as the context abstraction, while the "call site" columns are analyses using call sites as the context abstraction. Within each of these two sections, in the 1, 2, and 3 columns, pointers are modelled with context strings of maximum length 1, 2, and 3, but pointer targets are modelled context-insensitively. In the 1H columns, both pointers and pointer targets are modelled with context strings of receiver objects or call sites of maximum length 1. The "ZCWL" column is the ZCWL algorithm, which uses call sites as the context abstraction, and allows context strings of arbitrary length. The ZCWL algorithm models pointers with context but pointer targets without context.

In an analysis of an object-oriented language such as Java, there is a cyclic dependency between call graph construction and points-to analysis. In all variations except the ZCWL algorithm, we constructed the call graph on-the-fly during the points-to analysis, since this maintains maximum precision. The ZCWL algorithm requires a context-insensitive call graph to be constructed before it starts, which it then makes context-sensitive, and uses to perform the points-to analysis. For this purpose, we used the call graph constructed by the context-insensitive analysis in the "insens." column.

Interested readers can find additional information about the analysis variations, as well as a detailed presentation of the analysis implementation, in [12, Chapter 4].

## 3   Benchmarks

We performed our study on programs from the SpecJVM 98 benchmark suite [26], the DaCapo benchmark suite, version beta050224 [5], and the Ashes benchmark suite [27], as well as on the Polyglot extensible Java front-end [20], as listed in Table 1. Most of these benchmarks have been used in earlier evaluations of interprocedural analyses for Java. The middle section of the table shows the total number of classes and methods comprising each benchmark. These numbers exclude the Java standard library (which is required to run the benchmark), but include all other libraries that must accompany the benchmark for it to run successfully. All of the measurements in this paper were

**Table 1.** Benchmarks

| Benchmark | Total number of | | Executed methods | |
|---|---|---|---|---|
| | classes | methods | app. | +lib. |
| compress | 41 | 476 | 56 | 463 |
| db | 32 | 440 | 51 | 483 |
| jack | 86 | 812 | 291 | 739 |
| javac | 209 | 2499 | 778 | 1283 |
| jess | 180 | 1482 | 395 | 846 |
| mpegaudio | 88 | 872 | 222 | 637 |
| mtrt | 55 | 574 | 182 | 616 |
| soot-c | 731 | 3962 | 1055 | 1549 |
| sablecc-j | 342 | 2309 | 1034 | 1856 |
| polyglot | 502 | 5785 | 2037 | 3093 |
| antlr | 203 | 3154 | 1099 | 1783 |
| bloat | 434 | 6125 | 138 | 1010 |
| chart | 1077 | 14966 | 854 | 2790 |
| jython | 270 | 4915 | 1004 | 1858 |
| pmd | 1546 | 14086 | 1817 | 2581 |
| ps | 202 | 1147 | 285 | 945 |

done with version 1.3.1_01 of the Sun standard library.[1] The right-most section of the table shows the number of distinct methods that are executed in a run of the benchmark (measured using the *J tool [7]), both excluding and including methods of the Java standard library, in the columns labelled "app." and "+lib.", respectively. About 400 methods of the standard library are executed even for the smallest benchmarks for purposes such as class loading; some of the larger benchmarks make heavier use of the library.

# 4   Number of Contexts

Context-sensitive analysis is often considered intractable mainly because, if contexts are propagated from every call site to every called method, the number of resulting context strings grows exponentially in the length of the call chains. The purpose of this section is to shed some light on two issues. First, of the large numbers of contexts, how many are actually useful in improving analysis results? Second, why can BDDs represent such seemingly large numbers of contexts, and how much hope is there that they can be represented with more traditional techniques?

## 4.1   Total Number of Contexts

We begin by comparing the number of contexts that appear in the context-sensitive points-to relation when the analysis is performed with the different context abstractions. For this measurement, we treat the method invoked as part of the context. For example, suppose we are using abstract receiver objects as the context abstraction; if two different methods are called on the same receiver, we count them as two separate contexts, since they correspond to two necessarily distinct invocations. In other words, we are counting method-context pairs, rather than just contexts.

The measurements of the total numbers of contexts are shown in Table 2. Each column lists the number of contexts produced by one of the variations of context-sensitive analysis described in Section 2. The column labelled "insens." shows the absolute number of contexts (which is also the number of methods, since in a context-insensitive analysis, every method has exactly one context). All the other columns, rather than showing the absolute number of contexts, which would be very large, instead show the number of contexts as a multiple of the "insens." column (*i.e.* they show the average number of contexts per method). For example, for the **compress** benchmark, the total number of 1-object-sensitive contexts is $2596 \times 13.7 = 3.56 \times 10^4$. The empty spots in the table (and other tables throughout this paper) indicate configurations in which the analysis did not complete in the available memory, despite being implemented using BDDs. We allowed the BDD library to allocate a maximum of 41 million BDD nodes (820 million bytes).

The large numbers of contexts explain why an analysis that represents each context explicitly cannot scale to the programs that we analyze here. While a

---

[1] Studying other standard library versions requires models of their native methods. We aim to write such models for a more recent version as future work.

**Table 2.** Total number of abstract contexts

| Benchmark | insens. | object-sensitive | | | | call site | | | ZCWL | (max. $k$) |
|---|---|---|---|---|---|---|---|---|---|---|
| | | 1 | 2 | 3 | 1H | 1 | 2 | 1H | | |
| compress | 2596 | 13.7 | 113 | 1517 | 13.4 | 6.5 | 237 | 6.5 | $2.9 \times 10^4$ | (21) |
| db | 2613 | 13.7 | 115 | 1555 | 13.4 | 6.5 | 236 | 6.5 | $7.9 \times 10^4$ | (22) |
| jack | 2869 | 13.8 | 156 | 1872 | 13.2 | 6.8 | 220 | 6.8 | $2.7 \times 10^7$ | (45) |
| javac | 3780 | 15.8 | 297 | 13289 | 15.6 | 8.4 | 244 | 8.4 | | (41) |
| jess | 3216 | 19.0 | 305 | 5394 | 18.6 | 6.7 | 207 | 6.7 | $6.1 \times 10^6$ | (24) |
| mpegaudio | 2793 | 13.0 | 107 | 1419 | 12.7 | 6.3 | 221 | 6.3 | $4.4 \times 10^5$ | (31) |
| mtrt | 2738 | 13.3 | 108 | 1447 | 13.1 | 6.6 | 226 | 6.6 | $1.2 \times 10^5$ | (26) |
| soot-c | 4837 | 11.1 | 168 | 4010 | 10.9 | 8.2 | 198 | 8.2 | | (39) |
| sablecc-j | 5608 | 10.8 | 116 | 1792 | 10.5 | 5.5 | 126 | 5.5 | | (55) |
| polyglot | 5616 | 11.7 | 149 | 2011 | 11.2 | 7.1 | 144 | 7.1 | 10130 | (22) |
| antlr | 3897 | 15.0 | 309 | 8110 | 14.7 | 9.6 | 191 | 9.6 | $4.8 \times 10^9$ | (39) |
| bloat | 5237 | 14.3 | 291 | | 14.0 | 8.9 | 159 | 8.9 | $3.0 \times 10^8$ | (26) |
| chart | 7069 | 22.3 | 500 | | 21.9 | 7.0 | 335 | | | (69) |
| jython | 4401 | 18.8 | 384 | | 18.3 | 6.7 | 162 | 6.7 | $2.1 \times 10^{15}$ | (72) |
| pmd | 7219 | 13.4 | 283 | 5607 | 12.9 | 6.6 | 239 | 6.6 | | (55) |
| ps | 3874 | 13.3 | 271 | 24967 | 13.1 | 9.0 | 224 | 9.0 | $2.0 \times 10^8$ | (29) |

Note: columns after the second column show multiples of the context-insensitive number.

1-call-site-sensitive analysis must store and process 6 to 9 times more data than a context-insensitive analysis, the ratio grows to 1500 or more times for a 3-object-sensitive analysis.

The ZCWL algorithm essentially performs a $k$-CFA analysis in which $k$ is the maximum call depth in the original call graph after merging strongly connected components (shown in parentheses in the ZCWL column). Because $k$ is different for each benchmark, the number of contexts is much more variable than in the other variations of context sensitivity. On the javac, soot-c, sablecc-j, chart, and pmd benchmarks, the algorithm failed to complete in the available memory.

## 4.2   Equivalent Contexts

Next, we consider that many of the large numbers of abstract contexts are equivalent in the sense that the points-to relations computed in many of the abstract contexts are the same. More precisely, we define two method-context pairs, $(m_1, c_1)$ and $(m_2, c_2)$ to be **equivalent** if $m_1 = m_2$, and for every local pointer variable $p$ in the method, the points-to set of $p$ is the same in both contexts $c_1$ and $c_2$.

When two contexts are equivalent, there is no point in distinguishing them, because the resulting points-to relation is independent of the context. In this sense, the number of equivalence classes of method-context pairs reflects how worthwhile context sensitivity is in improving the precision of points-to sets.

The measurements of the number of equivalence classes of contexts are shown in Table 3. Again, the "insens." column shows the actual number of equivalence classes of contexts, while the other columns give a multiple of the "insens." number (*i.e.* the average number of equivalence classes per method).

**Table 3.** Number of equivalence classes of abstract contexts

| Benchmark | insens. | object-sensitive | | | | call site | | | ZCWL |
|---|---|---|---|---|---|---|---|---|---|
| | | 1 | 2 | 3 | 1H | 1 | 2 | 1H | |
| compress | 2597 | 8.4 | 9.9 | 11.3 | 12.1 | 2.4 | 3.9 | 4.9 | 3.3 |
| db | 2614 | 8.5 | 9.9 | 11.4 | 12.1 | 2.4 | 3.9 | 5.0 | 3.3 |
| jack | 2870 | 8.6 | 10.2 | 11.6 | 11.9 | 2.4 | 3.9 | 5.0 | 3.4 |
| javac | 3781 | 10.4 | 17.7 | 33.8 | 14.3 | 2.7 | 5.3 | 5.4 | |
| jess | 3217 | 8.9 | 10.6 | 12.0 | 13.9 | 2.6 | 4.2 | 5.0 | 3.9 |
| mpegaudio | 2794 | 8.1 | 9.4 | 10.8 | 11.5 | 2.4 | 3.8 | 4.8 | 3.3 |
| mtrt | 2739 | 8.3 | 9.7 | 11.1 | 11.8 | 2.5 | 4.0 | 4.9 | 3.4 |
| soot-c | 4838 | 7.1 | 13.7 | 18.4 | 9.8 | 2.6 | 4.2 | 4.8 | |
| sablecc-j | 5609 | 6.9 | 8.4 | 9.6 | 9.5 | 2.3 | 3.6 | 3.9 | |
| polyglot | 5617 | 7.9 | 9.4 | 10.8 | 10.2 | 2.4 | 3.7 | 4.7 | 3.3 |
| antlr | 3898 | 9.4 | 12.1 | 13.8 | 13.2 | 2.5 | 4.1 | 5.2 | 4.3 |
| bloat | 5238 | 10.2 | 44.6 | | 12.9 | 2.8 | 4.9 | 5.2 | 6.7 |
| chart | 7070 | 10.0 | 17.4 | | 18.2 | 2.7 | 4.8 | | |
| jython | 4402 | 9.9 | 55.9 | | 15.6 | 2.5 | 4.3 | 4.6 | 4.0 |
| pmd | 7220 | 7.6 | 14.6 | 17.0 | 11.0 | 2.4 | 4.2 | 4.2 | |
| ps | 3875 | 8.7 | 9.9 | 11.0 | 12.0 | 2.6 | 4.0 | 5.2 | 4.4 |

Note: columns after the second column show multiples of the context-insensitive number.

The relatively small size of these numbers compared to the total numbers of contexts in Table 2 explains why a BDD can effectively represent the analysis information, since it automatically merges the representation of equal points-to relations, so each distinct relation is only represented once. If we had some idea before designing an analysis which abstract contexts are likely to be equivalent, we could define a new context abstraction in which these equivalent contexts are merged. Each equivalence class of old abstract contexts would be represented by a single new abstract context. With such a context abstraction, the context-sensitive analysis could be implemented without requiring BDDs.

It is interesting that in the 1-, 2-, and 1H-object-sensitive analysis, the number of equivalence classes of contexts is generally about 3 times as high as in the corresponding 1-, 2-, and 1H-call-site-string analysis. This indicates that receiver objects better partition the space of concrete calling contexts that give rise to distinct points-to relations. That is, if at run time, the run-time points-to relation is different in two concrete calls to a method, it is more likely that the two calls will correspond to distinct abstract contexts if receiver objects rather than call sites are used as the context abstraction. This observation leads us to hypothesize that object-sensitive analysis should be more precise than call-site-string analysis; we will see more direct measurements of precision in upcoming sections.

In both object-sensitive and call-site-string analyses, making the context string longer increases the number of equivalence classes of contexts by only a small amount, while it increases the absolute number of contexts much more significantly. Therefore, increasing the length of the context string is unlikely to result in a large improvement in precision, but will significantly increase analysis cost.

It was initially rather surprising that in the analysis using the ZCWL algorithm, the number of equivalence classes of abstract contexts is so small, often even smaller than in the 2-call-site-sensitive analysis. The algorithm essentially performs a $k$-CFA analysis, where $k$ is the maximum call depth in the original call graph; $k$ is always much higher than 2. The number of equivalence classes of contexts when using the ZCWL algorithm is small because the algorithm merges strongly connected components (SCCs) in the call graph, and models all call edges in each such component in a context-insensitive way. In contrast, the 2-call-site-sensitive analysis models all call edges context-sensitively, including those in SCCs. Indeed, a very large number of methods are part of some SCC. The initial call graph for each of our benchmarks contains a large SCC of 1386 to 2926 methods, representing 36% to 53% of all methods in the call graph. In particular, this SCC always includes many methods for which context-sensitive analysis would be particularly useful, such as the methods of the String class and the standard collections classes. These methods are used extensively within the Java standard library, and contain many calls to each other. We examined this large SCC and found many distinct cycles; there was no single method that, if removed, would break the component. In summary, the reason for the surprisingly small number of equivalence classes of abstract contexts when using the ZCWL algorithm is that it models a large part of the call graph context-insensitively.

### 4.3   Distinct Points-to Sets

Finally, we measure the number of distinct points-to sets that appear in the points-to analysis result. This number is an indication of how difficult it would be to efficiently represent the context-sensitive points-to sets in a non-BDD-based analysis implementation, assuming there was already a way to represent the contexts themselves. An increase in the number of distinct points-to sets also suggests an increase in precision, but the connection is very indirect [10, Section 3.2]. We therefore present the number of distinct points-to sets primarily as a measure of analysis cost, and provide more direct measurements of the precision of clients of the analysis later in this paper. In traditional, context-insensitive, subset-based points-to analyses, the representation of the points-to sets often makes up most of the memory requirements of the analysis. If the traditional analysis stores points-to sets using shared bit-vectors as suggested by Heintze [9], each distinct points-to set need only be stored once. Therefore, the number of distinct points-to sets approximates the space requirements of such a traditional representation.

The measurements of the number of distinct points-to sets arising with each context abstraction are shown in Table 4. In this table, all numbers are the absolute count of distinct points-to sets, not multiples of the "insens." column.

The numbers of distinct points-to sets are fairly constant in most of the analysis variations, including object-sensitive analyses, call-site-string analyses, and the analysis using the ZCWL algorithm. Therefore, in a traditional points-to analysis implemented using shared bit-vectors, representing the individual points-to sets should not be a source of major difficulty even in a context-sensitive analysis. Future research in traditional implementations of context-sensitive analyses should therefore be directed more at the problem of efficiently representing the contexts, rather than representing the points-to sets.

**Table 4.** Total number of distinct points-to sets in points-to analysis results

| Benchmark | insens. | object-sensitive | | | | call site | | | ZCWL |
|---|---|---|---|---|---|---|---|---|---|
| | | 1 | 2 | 3 | 1H | 1 | 2 | 1H | |
| compress | 3178 | 3150 | 3240 | 3261 | 34355 | 3227 | 3125 | 38242 | 3139 |
| db | 3197 | 3170 | 3261 | 3283 | 34637 | 3239 | 3133 | 38375 | 3173 |
| jack | 3441 | 3411 | 3507 | 3527 | 37432 | 3497 | 3377 | 40955 | 3541 |
| javac | 4346 | 4367 | 4579 | 4712 | 55196 | 4424 | 4303 | 54866 | |
| jess | 3834 | 4433 | 4498 | 4514 | 51452 | 4589 | 4426 | 42614 | 4644 |
| mpegaudio | 4228 | 4179 | 4272 | 4293 | 36563 | 4264 | 4157 | 67565 | 4175 |
| mtrt | 3349 | 3287 | 3377 | 3396 | 35154 | 3387 | 3263 | 38758 | 3282 |
| soot-c | 4683 | 4565 | 4670 | 4657 | 45974 | 4722 | 4550 | 52937 | |
| sablecc-j | 5753 | 5777 | 5895 | 5907 | 52993 | 5875 | 5694 | 59748 | |
| polyglot | 5591 | 5556 | 5829 | 5925 | 50587 | 5682 | 5516 | 59837 | 5575 |
| antlr | 4520 | 5259 | 5388 | 5448 | 54942 | 4624 | 4535 | 54176 | 4901 |
| bloat | 5337 | 5480 | 5815 | | 55309 | 5452 | 5342 | 49230 | 6658 |
| chart | 9608 | 9914 | 10168 | | 233723 | 9755 | 9520 | | |
| jython | 4669 | 5111 | 5720 | | 74297 | 4968 | 4857 | 46280 | 8587 |
| pmd | 7368 | 7679 | 7832 | 7930 | 94403 | 7671 | 7502 | 103990 | |
| ps | 4610 | 4504 | 4639 | 4672 | 47244 | 4656 | 4521 | 58513 | 4802 |

However, when abstract heap objects are modelled context-sensitively, the elements of each points-to set are pairs of abstract object and context, rather than simply abstract objects, and the number of distinct points-to sets increases about 11-fold. In addition, it is likely that the points-to sets themselves are significantly larger. Therefore, in order to implement such an analysis without using BDDs, it would be worthwhile to look for an efficient way to represent points-to sets of abstract objects with context.

## 5   Call Graph

We now turn our attention to the effect of context sensitivity on call graph construction. For the purposes of comparison, we have constructed context-sensitive call graphs, projected away their contexts, and measured differences in their context-insensitive projections. We adopted this methodology because context-sensitive call graphs using different context abstractions are not directly comparable. Each node in the graph represents a pair of method and abstract context, but the set of possible abstract contexts is different in each context variation. In the context-insensitive projection, each node is simply a method, so the projections are directly comparable. The context-insensitive projection preserves the set of methods reachable from the program entry points, as well as the set of possible targets of each call site in the program; it is these sets that we measure. The set of reachable methods is particularly important because any conservative interprocedural analysis must analyze all of these methods, so a small set of reachable methods reduces the cost of other interprocedural analyses.

We have not included the ZCWL algorithm in our study of call graph construction, because the context-insensitive projection of the context-sensitive call graph that it produces is the same as the context-insensitive call graph that we originally give it as input.

## 5.1 Reachable Methods

Table 5 shows the number of methods reachable from the program entry points when constructing the call graph using different variations of context sensitivity, excluding methods from the standard Java library. In Table 5 and all subsequent tables in this paper, the most precise entry for each benchmark has been highlighted in bold. In the case of a tie, the most precise entry that is least expensive to compute has been highlighted.

**Table 5.** Number of reachable benchmark (non-library) methods in call graph

| Benchmark | CHA | insens. | object-sensitive | | | | call site | | | actually |
| | | | 1 | 2 | 3 | 1H | 1 | 2 | 1H | executed |
|---|---|---|---|---|---|---|---|---|---|---|
| compress | 90 | **59** | 59 | 59 | 59 | 59 | 59 | 59 | 59 | 56 |
| db | 95 | 65 | **64** | 64 | 64 | 64 | 65 | 64 | 65 | 51 |
| jack | 348 | 317 | **313** | 313 | 313 | 313 | 316 | 313 | 316 | 291 |
| javac | 1185 | 1154 | **1147** | 1147 | 1147 | 1147 | 1147 | 1147 | 1147 | 778 |
| jess | 683 | 630 | 629 | 629 | 629 | **623** | 629 | 629 | 629 | 395 |
| mpegaudio | 306 | 255 | **251** | 251 | 251 | 251 | 251 | 251 | 251 | 222 |
| mtrt | 217 | 189 | **186** | 186 | 186 | 186 | 187 | 187 | 187 | 182 |
| soot-c | 2395 | 2273 | **2264** | 2264 | 2264 | 2264 | 2266 | 2264 | 2266 | 1055 |
| sablecc-j | 1904 | 1744 | 1744 | 1744 | 1744 | **1731** | 1744 | 1744 | 1744 | 1034 |
| polyglot | 2540 | 2421 | 2419 | 2419 | 2419 | **2416** | 2419 | 2419 | 2419 | 2037 |
| antlr | 1374 | **1323** | 1323 | 1323 | 1323 | 1323 | 1323 | 1323 | 1323 | 1099 |
| bloat | 2879 | 2464 | **2451** | 2451 | | 2451 | 2451 | 2451 | 2451 | 138 |
| chart | 3227 | 2081 | 2080 | 2080 | | **2031** | 2080 | 2080 | | 854 |
| jython | 2007 | 1695 | 1693 | 1693 | | **1683** | 1694 | 1693 | 1694 | 1004 |
| pmd | 4997 | 4528 | 4521 | 4521 | 4521 | **4509** | 4521 | 4521 | 4521 | 1817 |
| ps | 840 | 835 | 835 | 835 | 835 | **834** | 835 | 835 | 835 | 285 |

For the simple benchmarks like compress and db, the context-insensitive call graph is already quite precise (compared to the dynamic behaviour), and any further improvements due to context sensitivity are relatively small. For the more significant benchmarks, call graph construction benefits slightly from 1-object sensitivity. The largest difference is 13 methods, in the bloat benchmark. All of these methods are visit methods in an implementation of the visitor design pattern, in the class AscendVisitor. This class traverses a parse tree from a starting node upwards toward the root of the tree, visiting each node along the way. Some kinds of nodes have no descendants that are ever the starting node of a traversal, so the visit methods of these nodes can never be called. However, in order to prove this, an analysis must analyze the visitor dispatch method context-sensitively in order to keep track of the kind of node from which it was called. Therefore, a context-insensitive analysis fails to show that these visit methods are unreachable.

In jess, sablecc-j, polyglot, chart, jython, pmd, and ps, modelling abstract heap objects object-sensitively further improves the precision of the call graph. In the sablecc-j benchmark, 13 additional methods are proved unreachable. The benchmark includes an implementation of maps similar to those in the standard library. The maps are instantiated in a number of places, and different kinds of objects are placed in the different maps. Methods such as toString() and equals() are called on some maps but not others. Calling one of the methods on a map causes it to be called on all elements of the map. Therefore, these methods are called on some kinds of map elements, but not others. However, the map elements are kept in generic map entry objects, which are allocated at a single point in the map code. When abstract heap objects are modelled without context, all map entries are modelled by a single abstract object, and the contents of all maps are conflated. When abstract heap objects are modelled with context, the map entries are treated as separate objects depending on which map they were created for. Note that distinguishing the map entries requires receiver objects to be used as context, rather than call-site strings. The code that allocates a new entry is in a method that is always called from the same call site, in another method of the map class. In general, although modelling abstract heap objects with context improved the call graph for some benchmarks in an object-sensitive analysis, it never made any difference in analyses using call-site strings as the context abstraction (*i.e.* the 1-call-site and 1H-call-site columns are the same).

Overall, object-sensitive analysis results in slightly smaller call graphs than call-site-string analysis. The 1-object-sensitive call graph is never larger than the 1-call-site-sensitive call graph, and it is smaller on db, jack, mtrt, soot-c, and jython. On the db, jack, and jython benchmarks, the call-site-sensitive call graph can be made as small as the 1-object-sensitive call graph, but it requires 2-call-site rather than 1-call-site analysis.

Even the most precise context-sensitive analyses produce a much bigger call graph than the dynamic one, shown in the rightmost column of the table. This difference is largely due to unused but complicated features of the Java Runtime Environment (such as network class loading and Jar File signing) which are controlled by external configuration parameters unknown to the analysis.

## 5.2   Call Edges

Table 6 shows the size of the call graph in terms of call edges rather than reachable methods. Only call edges originating from a benchmark (non-library) method are counted.

In general, context sensitivity makes little difference to the size of the call graph when measured this way, with one major exception. In the sablecc-j benchmark, the number of call edges is 17925 in a context-insensitive analysis, but only 5175 in a 1-object-sensitive analysis. This could make a significant difference to the cost of a client analysis whose complexity depends on the number of edges in the call graph. The large difference is caused by the following pattern of code. The sablecc-j benchmark contains code to represent a parse tree, with many different kinds of nodes. Each kind of node implements a method called removeChild(). The code contains a large number of calls of the form this.getParent().removeChild(this). In a context-insensitive analysis, getParent() is found to possibly return any of hundreds of possible kinds of nodes. Therefore, each of these many calls to removeChild(this) results in hundreds of call graph edges. However, in a context-sensitive analysis, getParent() is analyzed in the context of the this pointer. For each kind of node, there is a relatively small number of kinds of nodes that can be its parent. Therefore, in a given context, getParent() is found

**Table 6.** Number of call edges in call graph originating from a benchmark (non-library) method

| Benchmark | CHA | insens. | object-sensitive | | | | call site | | | actually executed |
|---|---|---|---|---|---|---|---|---|---|---|
| | | | 1 | 2 | 3 | 1H | 1 | 2 | 1H | |
| compress | 456 | **270** | 270 | 270 | 270 | 270 | 270 | 270 | 270 | 118 |
| db | 940 | 434 | **427** | 427 | 427 | 427 | 434 | 427 | 434 | 184 |
| jack | 1936 | 1283 | 1251 | 1251 | 1251 | **1250** | 1276 | 1251 | 1276 | 833 |
| javac | 13146 | 10360 | **10296** | 10296 | 10296 | 10296 | 10318 | 10301 | 10318 | 2928 |
| jess | 4700 | 3626 | 3618 | 3618 | 3618 | **3571** | 3618 | 3618 | 3618 | 919 |
| mpegaudio | 1182 | 858 | **812** | 812 | 812 | 812 | 812 | 812 | 812 | 400 |
| mtrt | 925 | 761 | **739** | 739 | 739 | 739 | 746 | 746 | 746 | 484 |
| soot-c | 20079 | 14611 | 14112 | 14112 | 14112 | **13868** | 14185 | 14112 | 14185 | 2860 |
| sablecc-j | 24283 | 17925 | 5175 | 5140 | 5140 | **5072** | 5182 | 5140 | 5182 | 2326 |
| polyglot | 19898 | 11768 | 11564 | 11564 | 11564 | **11374** | 11566 | 11566 | 11566 | 5440 |
| antlr | 10769 | **9553** | 9553 | 9553 | 9553 | 9553 | 9553 | 9553 | 9553 | 4196 |
| bloat | 36863 | 18586 | 18143 | 18143 | | **17722** | 18166 | 18143 | 18166 | 477 |
| chart | 24978 | 9526 | 9443 | 9443 | | **9178** | 9443 | 9443 | | 2166 |
| jython | 13679 | 9382 | 9367 | 9367 | | **9307** | 9367 | 9365 | 9367 | 2898 |
| pmd | 29401 | 18785 | 18582 | 18582 | 18580 | **18263** | 18601 | 18599 | 18601 | 3879 |
| ps | 13610 | 11338 | 11292 | 11292 | 11292 | **10451** | 11298 | 11292 | 11298 | 705 |

to return only a small number of kinds of parent node, so each call site of removeChild() adds only a small number of edges to the call graph.

# 6   Virtual Call Resolution

Table 7 shows the number of virtual call sites for which the call graph contains more than one potential target method. Call sites with at most one potential target method can be converted to cheaper static instead of virtual calls, and they can be inlined, possibly enabling many other optimizations. Therefore, an analysis that proves that call sites are not polymorphic can be used to significantly improve run-time performance.

In the benchmarks written in an object-oriented style, notably javac, soot-c, sablecc-j, polyglot, bloat, and pmd, many more call sites can be devirtualized using object-sensitive analysis than context-insensitive analysis. In some cases, call-site-string analysis gives the same improvement, but never any more, and in soot-c and sablecc-j, the improvement from 1-object-sensitive analysis is much greater than from 1-call-site string analysis.

In sablecc-j, there are three sets of call sites that can be devirtualized using context-sensitive analysis. Any context-sensitive analysis is sufficient to devirtualize the first set of call sites. Devirtualization of the second set of call sites requires an object-sensitive analysis; an analysis using call sites as the context abstraction cannot prove them to be monomorphic. Devirtualization of the third set of call sites not only requires an object-sensitive analysis, but it also requires that abstract heap objects be modelled with context.

The first set of call sites are the calls to the removeChild() method mentioned in Section 5.2. Object sensitivity reduces the number of potential target methods at each of these call sites. At many of them, it reduces the number down to one, so the calls

**Table 7.** Total number of potentially polymorphic call sites in benchmark (non-library) code

| Benchmark | CHA | insens. | object-sensitive | | | | call site | | |
|---|---|---|---|---|---|---|---|---|---|
| | | | 1 | 2 | 3 | 1H | 1 | 2 | 1H |
| compress | 16 | **3** | 3 | 3 | 3 | 3 | 3 | 3 | 3 |
| db | 36 | 5 | **4** | 4 | 4 | 4 | 5 | 4 | 5 |
| jack | 474 | 25 | 23 | 23 | 23 | **22** | 24 | 23 | 24 |
| javac | 908 | 737 | **720** | 720 | 720 | 720 | 720 | 720 | 720 |
| jess | 121 | **45** | 45 | 45 | 45 | 45 | 45 | 45 | 45 |
| mpegaudio | 40 | 27 | **24** | 24 | 24 | 24 | 24 | 24 | 24 |
| mtrt | 20 | 9 | **7** | 7 | 7 | 7 | 8 | 8 | 8 |
| soot-c | 1748 | 983 | **913** | 913 | 913 | 913 | 938 | 913 | 938 |
| sablecc-j | 722 | 450 | 325 | 325 | 325 | **301** | 380 | 325 | 380 |
| polyglot | 1332 | 744 | 592 | 592 | 592 | **585** | 592 | 592 | 592 |
| antlr | 1086 | **843** | 843 | 843 | 843 | 843 | 843 | 843 | 843 |
| bloat | 2503 | 1079 | 962 | 962 | | **961** | 962 | 962 | 962 |
| chart | 2782 | 254 | 235 | 235 | | **214** | 235 | 235 | |
| jython | 646 | 347 | 347 | 347 | | **346** | 347 | 347 | 347 |
| pmd | 2868 | 1224 | 1193 | 1193 | 1193 | **1163** | 1205 | 1205 | 1205 |
| ps | 321 | 304 | 303 | 303 | 303 | **300** | 303 | 303 | 303 |

can be devirtualized. The same improvement is obtained with call-site-string context sensitivity.

The second set of call sites are calls to methods of iterators over lists. The sablecc-j benchmark contains several implementations of lists similar to those in the standard Java library. A call to iterator() on any of these lists invokes iterator() on the AbstractList superclass, which in turn invokes the listIterator() method specific to each list. The actual kind of iterator that is returned depends on which listIterator() was invoked, which in turn depends on the receiver object of the call to iterator(); it is independent of the call site of listIterator(), which is always the same site in iterator(). Therefore, calls to hasNext() and next() on the returned iterator can be devirtualized only with an object-sensitive analysis.

The third set of call sites are calls to methods such as toString() and equals() on objects stored in maps. As we explained in Section 5.1, object-sensitive modelling of abstract heap objects is required to distinguish the internal map entry objects in each separate use of the map implementation. The map entry objects must be distinguished in order to distinguish the objects that are stored in the maps. Therefore, devirtualization of these calls to methods of objects stored in maps requires an object-sensitive analysis that models abstract heap objects with context.

## 7   Cast Safety

We have used the points-to analysis results in a client analysis that proves that some casts cannot fail. A given cast cannot fail if the pointer that it is casting can only point to objects whose type is a subtype of the type of the cast. Table 8 shows the number of casts in each benchmark that cannot be statically proven safe by the cast safety analysis.

**Table 8.** Number of casts potentially failing at run time

| Benchmark | insens. | object-sensitive | | | | call site | | | ZCWL |
|---|---|---|---|---|---|---|---|---|---|
| | | 1 | 2 | 3 | 1H | 1 | 2 | 1H | |
| compress | **18** | 18 | 18 | 18 | 18 | 18 | 18 | 18 | 18 |
| db | 27 | 27 | 27 | 27 | **21** | 27 | 27 | 27 | 27 |
| jack | 146 | 145 | 145 | 145 | **104** | 146 | 145 | 146 | 146 |
| javac | 405 | 370 | 370 | 370 | **363** | 391 | 370 | 391 | |
| jess | 130 | 130 | 130 | 130 | **86** | 130 | 130 | 130 | 130 |
| mpegaudio | 42 | **38** | 38 | 38 | 38 | 40 | 40 | 40 | 42 |
| mtrt | 31 | **27** | 27 | 27 | 27 | 27 | 27 | 27 | 29 |
| soot-c | 955 | 932 | 932 | 932 | **878** | 932 | 932 | 932 | |
| sablecc-j | 375 | 369 | 369 | 369 | **331** | 370 | 370 | 370 | |
| polyglot | 3539 | 3307 | 3306 | 3306 | **1017** | 3526 | 3443 | 3526 | 3318 |
| antlr | 295 | 275 | 275 | 275 | **237** | 276 | 275 | 276 | 276 |
| bloat | 1241 | 1207 | 1207 | | **1160** | 1233 | 1207 | 1233 | 1234 |
| chart | 1097 | 1086 | 1085 | | **934** | 1070 | 1070 | | |
| jython | 501 | 499 | 499 | | **471** | 499 | 499 | 499 | 499 |
| pmd | 1427 | 1376 | 1375 | 1375 | **1300** | 1393 | 1391 | 1393 | |
| ps | 641 | 612 | 612 | 612 | **421** | 612 | 612 | 612 | 612 |

Context sensitivity improves precision of cast safety analysis in jack, javac, mpegaudio, mtrt, soot-c, sablecc-j, polyglot, antlr, bloat, chart, jython, pmd, and ps. Object sensitive cast safety analysis is never less precise and often significantly more precise than the call-site-string context sensitive variations. The improvements due to context sensitivity are most significant in the polyglot and javac benchmarks. In db, jack, javac, jess, soot-c, sablecc-j, polyglot, antlr, bloat, chart, jython, pmd, and ps, modelling abstract heap objects with receiver object context further improves precision of cast safety analysis.

The improvement is most dramatic in the polyglot benchmark, which contains a hierarchy of classes representing different kinds of nodes in an abstract syntax tree. At the root of this hierarchy is the Node_c class. This class implements a method called copy() which, like the clone() method of Object, returns a copy of the node on which it is called. In fact, the copy() method first uses clone() to create the copy of the node, and then performs some additional processing on it. The static return type of copy() is Object, but at most sites calling it, the returned value is immediately cast to the static type of the node on which it is called. In our analysis, the clone() native method is modelled as returning its receiver; that is, the original object and the cloned version are represented by the same abstract object. Therefore, given a program that calls clone() directly, the cast safety analysis correctly determines that the run-time type of the clone is the same as that of the original. However, in polyglot, the call to clone() is wrapped inside copy(), and the casts appear at sites calling copy(). When copy() is analyzed in a context-insensitive way, it is deemed to possibly return any of the objects on which it is called throughout the program, so the casts cannot be proven to succeed. In an object-sensitive analysis, however, copy() is analyzed separately in the context of each receiver object on which it is called, and in each such context, it returns only an object of the same type as that receiver object. Therefore, the cast safety analysis proves statically that the casts of the return value of copy() cannot fail.

The number of potentially failing casts in the polyglot benchmark decreases even more dramatically between the 1-object-sensitive and 1H-object-sensitive columns of Table 8, from 3307 to 1017. The majority of these casts are in the parser generated by JavaCUP. The parser uses a Stack as the LR parse stack. Each object popped from the stack is cast to a Symbol. The generated polyglot parser contains about 2000 of these casts. The Stack class extends Vector, which uses an internal elementData array to store the objects that have been pushed onto the stack. In order to prove the safety of the casts, the analysis must distinguish the array implementing the parse stack from the arrays of other uses of Vector in the program. Since the array is allocated in one place, inside the Vector class, the different array instances can only be distinguished if abstract heap objects are modelled with context. Therefore, modelling abstract heap objects with object sensitivity is necessary to prove that these 2000 casts cannot fail.

## 8   Related Work

The most closely related work is the evaluation of object-sensitive analysis by Milanova, Rountev, and Ryder [17, 18]. They implemented a limited form of object sensitivity within their points-to analysis framework based on annotated constraints [21] and built on top of the BANE toolkit [2]. In particular, they selected a subset of pointer variables (method parameters, the this pointer, and the method return value) which they modelled context-sensitively using the receiver object as the context abstraction. All other pointer variables and all abstract heap objects were modelled without context. The precision of the analysis was evaluated on benchmarks using version 1.1.8 of the Java standard library, and compared to a context-insensitive and to a call-site context-sensitive analysis, using call graph construction, virtual call resolution, and mod-ref analysis as client analyses. Our BDD-based implementation has made it feasible to evaluate object-sensitive analysis on benchmarks using the much larger version 1.3.1_01 of the Java standard library. Thanks to the better scalability of the BDD-based implementation, we have performed a much broader empirical exploration of the design space of object-sensitive analyses. In particular, we have modelled all pointer variables context-sensitively, rather than only a subset, we have used receiver object strings of length up to three, rather than only one, and we have modelled abstract heap objects context-sensitively.

Whaley and Lam [29] suggest several client analyses of the ZCWL algorithm, but state that "in-depth analysis of the accuracy of the analyses ... is beyond the scope of this paper." They do, however, provide some preliminary data about thread escape analysis and a "type refinement analysis" for finding variables whose declared type could be made more specific. In this paper, we have compared the precision of the ZCWL algorithm against object-sensitive and call-site-string context-sensitive analyses using several client analyses, namely call graph construction, virtual call resolution, and cast safety analysis.

Liang, Pennings and Harrold [16] evaluated the effect of context sensitivity on the size of pointed-to-by sets (the inverse of points-to sets), normalized using dynamic counts. Instead of using BDDs to allow their analyses to scale to benchmarks using the large Java standard library, they simulated the library with a hand-crafted model. Their results agree with our findings that context sensitivity improves precision for some benchmarks, and that a context-sensitive heap abstraction is important for precision. However, they found that call sites are sometimes more precise than receiver objects. This difference could be caused by several factors, including their different choice of benchmarks, their very different precision metric (pointed-to-by sets), or their simulation of the standard library.

Several context-sensitive points-to analyses other than the subset-based analyses studied in this paper have been proposed. Wilson and Lam [30] computed summary functions summarizing the effects of functions, which they then inlined into summaries of their callers. Liang and Harrold [15] proposed an equality-based context-sensitive analysis; its precision relative to subset-based context-sensitive analysis remains to be studied. Ruf [22] compared context-insensitive analysis to using "assumption sets" as the context abstraction, and concluded that on C benchmarks, context sensitivity had little effect on the points-to sets of pointers that are actually dereferenced. Like object sensitivity, the Cartesian Product Algorithm [1, 28] uses abstract objects as the context abstraction, but includes all method parameters as context, rather than only the receiver parameter. In the future, it would be interesting to empirically compare these additional variations of context-sensitive analysis with those studied in this paper.

## 9    Conclusions

We have performed an in-depth empirical study of the effects of variations of context sensitivity on the precision of Java points-to analysis. In particular, we studied object-sensitive analysis, context-sensitive analysis using call sites as the context abstraction, and the ZCWL algorithm. We evaluated the effects of these variations on the number of contexts generated, the number of distinct points-to sets constructed, and on the precision of call graph construction, virtual call resolution, and cast safety analysis.

Overall, we found that context sensitivity improved call graph precision by a small amount, improved the precision of virtual call resolution by a more significant amount, and enabled a major precision improvement in cast safety analysis.

Object-sensitive analysis was clearly better than the other variations of context sensitivity that we studied, both in terms of analysis precision and potential scalability. Client analyses based on object-sensitive analyses were never less precise than those based on call-site-string context-sensitive analyses or on the ZCWL algorithm, and in many cases, they were significantly more precise. As we increased the length of context strings, the number of abstract contexts produced with object-sensitive analysis grew much more slowly than with the other variations of context sensitivity, so object-sensitive analysis is likely to scale better. However, the number of equivalence classes of contexts was greater with object sensitivity than with the other variations, which indicates that object sensitivity better distinguishes contexts that give rise to differences in points-to sets.

Of the object-sensitive variations, extending the length of context strings caused very few additional improvements in analysis precision compared to 1-object-sensitive analysis. However, modelling abstract heap objects with context did improve precision significantly in many cases. Therefore, we conclude that 1-object-sensitive and 1H-object-sensitive analyses provide the best tradeoffs between precision and analysis efficiency. Our measurements of the numbers of abstract contexts and distinct points-to sets suggest that it should be feasible to implement an efficient non-BDD-based 1-object-sensitive analysis using current implementation techniques such as shared bit vectors. Efficiently implementing a 1H-object-sensitive analysis without BDDs will require new improvements in the data structures and algorithms used to implement points-to analyses, and we expect that our results will motivate and help guide this future research.

Although the ZCWL algorithm constructs call-site strings of arbitrary length, client analyses based on it were never more precise than those based on object-sensitive analysis. In many cases, analyses based on the ZCWL algorithm were even less precise than those based on 1-call-site-sensitive analysis. The key cause of the disappointing results of this algorithm was its context-insensitive treatment of calls within SCCs of the initial call graph — a large proportion of call edges were indeed within SCCs.

# References

1. O. Agesen. The Cartesian product algorithm. In *ECOOP '95*, volume 952 of *LNCS*, pages 2–51, 1995.
2. A. Aiken, M. Faehndrich, J. S. Foster, and Z. Su. A toolkit for constructing type- and constraint-based program analyses. In *Types in Compilation*, volume 1473 of *LNCS*, pages 78–96, 1998.
3. M. Berndl, O. Lhoták, F. Qian, L. Hendren, and N. Umanee. Points-to analysis using BDDs. In *Proceedings of PLDI 2003*, pages 103–114, 2003.
4. M. Burke, P. Carini, J. Choi, and M. Hind. Interprocedural pointer alias analysis. Technical Report RC 21055, IBM T. J. Watson Research Center, Dec. 1997.
5. DaCapo Benchmark Suite. `http://www-ali.cs.umass.edu/DaCapo/gcbm.html`.
6. J. Dean, D. Grove, and C. Chambers. Optimization of object-oriented programs using static class hierarchy analysis. In *ECOOP '95*, volume 952 of *LNCS*, pages 77–101, 1995.
7. B. Dufour. Objective quantification of program behaviour using dynamic metrics. Master's thesis, McGill University, June 2004.
8. M. Emami, R. Ghiya, and L. J. Hendren. Context-sensitive interprocedural points-to analysis in the presence of function pointers. In *Proceedings of PLDI 1994*, pages 242–256, 1994.
9. N. Heintze. Analysis of large code bases: the compile-link-analyze model. `http://cm.bell-labs.com/cm/cs/who/nch/cla.ps`, 1999.
10. M. Hind. Pointer analysis: haven't we solved this problem yet? In *Proceedings of PASTE 2001*, pages 54–61. ACM Press, 2001.
11. M. Hind, M. Burke, P. Carini, and J.-D. Choi. Interprocedural pointer alias analysis. *ACM Trans. Program. Lang. Syst.*, 21(4):848–894, 1999.
12. O. Lhoták. *Program Analysis using Binary Decision Diagrams*. PhD thesis, McGill University, Jan. 2006.
13. O. Lhoták and L. Hendren. Scaling Java points-to analysis using Spark. In *Compiler Construction, 12th International Conference*, volume 2622 of *LNCS*, pages 153–169, Apr. 2003.
14. O. Lhoták and L. Hendren. Jedd: a BDD-based relational extension of Java. In *Proceedings of PLDI 2004*, pages 158–169. ACM Press, 2004.

15. D. Liang and M. J. Harrold. Efficient points-to analysis for whole-program analysis. In *ESEC/FSE '99*, volume 1687 of *LNCS*, pages 199–215. Springer-Verlag / ACM Press, 1999.
16. D. Liang, M. Pennings, and M. J. Harrold. Evaluating the impact of context-sensitivity on andersen's algorithm for Java programs. In *PASTE 2005*. ACM Press, Sept. 2005.
17. A. Milanova, A. Rountev, and B. G. Ryder. Parameterized object sensitivity for points-to and side-effect analyses for Java. In *Proceedings of ISSTA 2002*, pages 1–11. ACM Press, 2002.
18. A. Milanova, A. Rountev, and B. G. Ryder. Parameterized object sensitivity for points-to analysis for Java. *ACM Trans. Softw. Eng. Methodol.*, 14(1):1–41, 2005.
19. E. M. Nystrom, H.-S. Kim, and W.-m. W. Hwu. Importance of heap specialization in pointer analysis. In *Proceedings of PASTE 2004*, pages 43–48. ACM Press, 2004.
20. N. Nystrom, M. R. Clarkson, and A. C. Myers. Polyglot: An extensible compiler framework for Java. In *Compiler Construction*, volume 2622 of *LNCS*, pages 138–152, 2003.
21. A. Rountev, A. Milanova, and B. G. Ryder. Points-to analysis for Java using annotated constraints. In *Proceedings OOPSLA 2001*, pages 43–55. ACM Press, 2001.
22. E. Ruf. Context-insensitive alias analysis reconsidered. In *Proceedings of the Conference on Programming Language Design and Implementation*, pages 13–22. ACM Press, 1995.
23. B. G. Ryder. Dimensions of precision in reference analysis of object-oriented programming languages. In *Compiler Construction*, volume 2622 of *LNCS*, pages 126–137. Springer, 2003.
24. M. Sharir and A. Pnueli. Two approaches to interprocedural data flow analysis. In S. S. Muchnick and N. D. Jones, editors, *Program Flow Analysis: Theory and Applications*, chapter 7, pages 189–233. Prentice-Hall, 1981.
25. O. Shivers. Control flow analysis in scheme. In *Proceedings of PLDI 1988*, pages 164–174.
26. SPEC JVM98 Benchmarks. http://www.spec.org/osg/jvm98/.
27. R. Vallée-Rai. Ashes suite collection. http://www.sable.mcgill.ca/ashes/.
28. T. Wang and S. F. Smith. Precise constraint-based type inference for Java. In *Proceedings of ECOOP 2001*, volume 2072 of *LNCS*, pages 99–117, 2001.
29. J. Whaley and M. S. Lam. Cloning-based context-sensitive pointer alias analysis using binary decision diagrams. In *Proceedings of PLDI 2004*, pages 131–144. ACM Press, 2004.
30. R. P. Wilson and M. S. Lam. Efficient context-sensitive pointer analysis for C programs. In *Proceedings of PLDI 1995*, pages 1–12. ACM Press, 1995.
31. J. Zhu and S. Calman. Symbolic pointer analysis revisited. In *Proceedings of PLDI 2004*, pages 145–157. ACM Press, 2004.

# Selective Runtime Memory Disambiguation in a Dynamic Binary Translator

Bolei Guo,[1] Youfeng Wu,[2] Cheng Wang,[2] Matthew J. Bridges,[1]
Guilherme Ottoni,[1] Neil Vachharajani,[1]
Jonathan Chang,[1] and David I. August[1]

[1] Department of Computer Science, Princeton University
[2] Programming Systems Lab, Intel Corporation
{bguo, mbridges, ottoni, nvacchar,
jcone, august}@princeton.edu
{youfeng.wu, cheng.c.wang}@intel.com

**Abstract.** Alias analysis, traditionally performed statically, is unsuited for a dynamic binary translator (DBT) due to incomplete control-flow information and the high complexity of an accurate analysis. Whole- program profiling, however, shows that most memory references do not alias. The current technique used in DBTs to disambiguate memory references, instruction inspection, is too simple and can only disambiguate one-third of potential aliases. To achieve effective memory disambiguation while keeping a tight bound on analysis overhead, we propose an efficient heuristic algorithm that strategically selects key memory dependences to disambiguate with runtime checks. These checks have little runtime overhead and, in the common case where aliasing does not occur, enable aggressive optimizations, particularly scheduling. We demonstrate that a small number of checks, inserted with a low-overhead analysis, can approach optimal scheduling, where all false memory dependences are removed. Simulation shows that better scheduling alone improves overall performance by 5%.

## 1 Introduction

Dynamic Binary Translators (DBTs) are used to provide binary compatibility across platforms. For efficient execution, the translated binary must be re-optimized for the target microarchitecture. This paper focuses on techniques that allow memory disambiguation to be performed in a DBT, enabling advanced optimizations, such as load/store reordering and redundant memory operation elimination, that rely on aliasing information. However, traditional static pointer/alais analysis [1, 2], is expensive both in time and memory, making it unsuitable for DBTs where contention for runtime resources with the program execution itself needs to be kept to a minimum. Additionally, for correctness, the analysis must know all control flows or it becomes overly conservative. Since control flows in DBTs are discovered on the fly as each new branch target is being translated, accurate pointer analysis would require recomputation, taking yet more time that is not available 3-5.

Given the difficulties of performing a full-fledged pointer analysis at runtime, most DBTs, such as Dynamo [3], Transmeta [4], and Daisy [5], do not perform pointer

A. Mycroft and A. Zeller (Eds.): CC 2006, LNCS 3923, pp. 65–79, 2006.

alias analysis except in the form of *instruction inspection*, a simple dependence test that disambiguates two memory references if they access either different memory regions or their addresses have the same base register and different offsets. While our whole-program profile of the SPECINT2000 benchmarks indicates that 97% of memory reference pairs do not alias, instruction inspection can only disambiguate one-third of them. Without a more sophisticated disambiguation mechanism, the optimizer has to conservatively assume dependences between the other memory references. These false dependences [1] greatly constrain the aggressiveness of various code transformations.

To provide better memory disambiguation for runtime optimizations while keeping a tight control over runtime analysis costs we only attempt to disambiguate specific memory references that actually hide optimization opportunities. This is in contrast to performing pointer analysis on all memory references. In particular, we design a simple heuristic algorithm that precisely selects memory dependences whose removal may result in shortened instruction schedules. It does so without having to recompute the dependence graph and compare the before-and-after schedules. Correctness is guaranteed by inserting runtime checks that dynamically compare the effective addresses of the memory references involved. To maximize the benefit of each runtime check, we perform a light-weight but effective pointer analysis to identify all memory dependences that can be safely removed either directly or indirectly by a single check. For this to work correctly, the runtime check must take into account different offsets of each memory reference, using dynamic address profiles to reduce misspeculation.

We evaluated our technique and experimental results show that only a small number of checks need to be inserted to yield performance gain. Specifically, our technique can remove more than twice as many false memory dependences as does instruction inspection and generate schedules close to the optimal schedules, where all false memory dependences are removed. Finally, this is done with very low analysis overhead.

In summary, the main contributions of this work are:

– An efficient heurisitic algorithm that precisely identifies memory dependences whose removal can benefit scheduling to the greatest extent.
– A light-weight pointer analysis that allows as many dependences as possible to be safely removed by a single runtime check.
– An evaluation of our technique that compares with baseline, instruction inspection and optimal scheduling.

We discuss related work in Section 2. Sections 3 and 4 present the heuristic dependence selection algorithm and the light-weight pointer analysis. Section 5 describes how the test condition for each runtime check is determined. Evaluation methodology and experimental results are discussed in Section 6. Finally, we conclude in Section 7.

## 2   Related Work

The idea of speculatively disambiguating memory references and relying on runtime tests to guard against misspeculation is not new. The work closest to ours is Nicolau's

---

[1] In this paper, "false dependence" refers to a dependence that does not occur at runtime, not anti-dependence or output dependence in the traditional data dependence terminology.

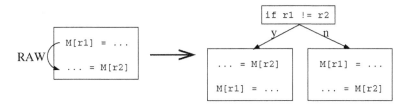

**Fig. 1.** Example of Runtime Memory Disambiguation

*run-time disambiguation* [6], where the compiler inserts branches that test for aliasing conditions. It relies on trace scheduling to schedule the on-trace path aggressively, assuming that the aliasing conditions are not met, and to insert compensation code in the off-trace path for correctness. This is illustrated by Figure 1. The original code on the left contains a read-after-write (RAW) memory dependence. However, if a check comparing the two addresses is inserted, then in the common case where the addresses are not equal, the load instruction can be moved above the store. Huang et al. [7] describe a similar technique targeting architectures that support conditional execution. Instead of explicit branches, it uses predication to guard the execution of the two paths. Fernandez et al. propose *speculative alias analysis* [8], which is more precise along the hot paths but may not be correct with respect to the whole control flow graph. Any optimization enabled by this analysis requires similar check-and-recovery mechanism.

In order to control the code growth resulting from the introduction of extra execution paths, it is important to narrow the set of runtime tests to those that are essential to performance gains. Fernandez et al. [8] does not provide any mechanism to do so. Nicolau [6] skips memory references that can be disambiguated statically with traditional alias analysis and memory references between whom there exist other types of dependences that cannot be removed by runtime disambiguation. Huang et al. [7] uses an iterative heuristic that, after each memory dependence is selected for runtime disambiguation, recomputes the critical path and the estimated execution time before and after removing a dependence for each of the remaining memory dependences. Unlike these two works, both of which are compiler techniques and therefore can afford the cost of a traditional alias analysis or an iterative heuristic, our technique has to meet the much tighter analysis budget in a runtime environment. Not only is our heuristic for selecting critical memory dependence more streamlined and efficient, but also we use light-weight pointer analysis to maximize the coverage of each runtime test.

Data speculation that moves loads above potentially aliasing stores also exists in other DBTs, but relies on special hardware in the target architecture for detecting and recovering from misspeculation. DAISY [5] has a special *load-verify* instruction. Placed at the original position of the speculative load, it reloads the value to compare with the speculatively loaded value and traps to the virtual machine manager if the two values differ. The drawback is that the extra loads executed consume memory bandwidth and energy. Transmeta [4] has a small cache called *alias buffer*, which records the addresses and sizes of speculative loads to compare with later stores for aliases. In this approach, the number of speculative loads is limited by hardware size and false positives may arise as the result of aliasing with unreachable stores. Our approach does not assume any hardware support and does not suffer from these problems. Neither of these two works performs analysis like ours to select the most beneficial loads for speculation.

## 3   Critical Memory Dependence Selection

### 3.1   Preliminary Selection

Before applying the heuristic algorithm to identify memory dependences critical to scheduling, several preliminary steps are taken to prepare a group of candidates.

1. **Trace selection:** We only want to disambiguate memory references in frequently executed code. Hot code identification often comes for free in DBTs as most of them are organized into two phases. The first phase translates blocks of code without optimization and inserts instrumentation to collect execution frequency information. The second phase forms hot regions from frequently executed blocks and applies optimizations to them. Unlike the profiling done in the compilers, which may suffer from the problem of unrepresentative input sets, the profile information collected by DBTs in the first phase is highly relevant to the optimizations done in the second phase. In most DBTs, the hot regions are single entry and multiple exit traces. In our evaluation, the average finishing rate, the probability the trace finishes execution in the last of its constituent blocks, is 88%.

2. **Instruction inspection:** Instruction inspection is performed on each trace to filter out memory reference pairs that definitely do not alias. We then build the dependence graphs of the traces and label each dependence edge with its latency.

3. **Alias profiling:** For those memory references in the traces that cannot be determined to be independent by instruction inspection, instrumentation is inserted to record the effective addresses accessed. The heuristic algorithm will not consider memory reference pairs that actually alias. We find that the aliasing behavior is highly stable throughout the lifetime of a program. That is, a very short inital profiling period yields essentially the same prediction of alias/non-alias as does whole-program profiling. For example, the length of the alias profiling period can be set to end after a trace finishes execution in its last block 50 times. The profiling overhead thus incurred is negligible.

   For the SPECINT2000 benchmarks, true aliases that can be filtered out this way are at most 3%. For other workloads, alias profiling might turn out to be more useful. In addition, the effective addresses collected by alias profiling are also useful later when guiding the determination of appropriate test conditions for the runtime checks. This is discussed in Section 5.

### 3.2   The Heuristic Algorithm

The goal of the heuristic algorithm is to narrow the number of runtime checks inserted per trace to just 1 or 2 and no more than 3 for the occasional large traces. Our experimental results indicate that this is sufficient to improve scheduling to close-to optimal. Given the small number of memory dependences that are to be removed, the kind of iterative algorithm proposed in [7], which involves recomputation of critical paths and estimated execution time, is not necessary. After removing only a couple of dependence arcs, we do not expect the memory dependences remaining on the new critial path to be drastically different from what has been there on the original critical path. In addition, we can simply use the latency of each dependence edge to approximate the difference between the execution time of the trace before and after the edge is removed. Based on these reasonings, the basic idea of our heuristic algorithm is to simply pick memory dependences that are responsibile for the largest latency on the original critical paths.

**Selecting Critical Base Address Pairs.** We start by grouping memory instructions according to their *base addresses*. This is done through simple syntactic inspection of the memory operands of each instruction. In the x86 ISA, memory addresses are specified by the expressions base_reg + index_reg * scale + offset, where scale and offset are constants. By base address, we refer to the part of the expression that involves registers, ignoring the constant offset. Memory instructions accessing constant addresses (i.e. no base addresses) are gathered in the same group.

The intuition behind this is the observation that a trace often contains multiple memory references with the same base address but different offsets. If the registers involved in the base address are not redefined in between these references or if it can be proven that the redefinitions always write the same values into those registers, then a single runtime check examining the runtime value of the base address can allow multiple memory dependences to be removed. For example, both the registers EBP (frame pointer) and ESP (stack pointer) are used as the base register and combined with various displacements to access stack locations. In compiler-generated code, stack references with either EBP or ESP as the base register almost never alias. Using a single runtime check that compares the positions pointed to by EBP and ESP and the proper test condition that takes into account all relevant displacements, we can often remove numerous dependences from a trace that cannot otherwise be disambiguated by instruction inspection because the base registers are different. Section 4 describes the analysis needed for proving runtime equality of two occurrences of a base address expression. Section 5.1 discusses how to handles multiple displacements from a base address.

In the next step, the algorithm traverses the dependence graph computed based on instruction inspection to do two things: 1) to identify critical paths, 2) for each pair of base addresses, to sum the latencies of all memory dependence arcs that are false dependences according to the alias profiling and whose source and destination instructions fall into the two groups of base addresses respectively. We use *Total_Latencies* to denote this value. Next, the algorithm computes another value similar to *Total_Latencies*, the only difference being that only memory dependences on the critical paths are considered. We call this value *Critical_Latencies*. Figure 2 (a) contains a small trace whose dependence graph is shown in Figure 2 (b). The dependence arcs are marked with latencies computed based on the machine model. Arcs with latencies in brackets are memory dependences, the rest are register dependences. Among the four memory instructions, there are three distinct base addresses: EDI, EDX*2, and EBX. In the dependence graph, memory instructions having the same base address are represented with the same symbol. Figure 2 (c) shows the values of *Total_Latencies* and *Critical_Latencies* for each base address pair.

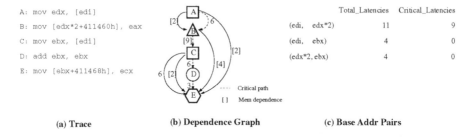

**Fig. 2.** Example of Target Memory Dependence Selection

The algorithm then selects for runtime disambiguation the pair of base addresses that has the largest non-zero **Critical_Latencies**. Ties are broken using **Total_Latencies**. The pair of base addresses with the next largest non-zero **Critical_Latencies** is also selected. At this point, for most traces, there are no more base address pairs responsible for latencies on the critical paths. For some very large traces, we allow a third pair to be selected. Beyond three pairs, our experience is that the extra number of runtime checks do not yield substantial performance gains. We refer to the selected base address pairs as **critical base addresses**. In the example shown in Figure 2, there is only one base address pair (EDI, EDX*2) responsible for latencies on the critical path and therefore it will be selected by the algorithm for runtime disambiguation.

**Generating Inputs to Pointer Analysis.** Because the registers involved in a base address may be redefined within a trace, we need to analyze the trace to determine whether a single runtime check is sufficient to validate assumptions about multiple occurrences of the base address. If not, priority is given to the earliest occurrences in the program order because oftentimes removing one memory dependence gives pointer analysis more accurate information about memory content and thereby helps unravel other memory dependences (details are given in Section 4). The earlier a memory dependence is removed, the more chances there are for it to help eliminate other dependences. For each selected critical base address pair, the heuristic algorithm identifies the earliest pair of memory instructions on the critical path with the corresponding base addresses. These are the inputs to the pointer analysis, which automatically considers the specified memory instruction pairs to be independent.

As an optimization, if there is an even earlier pair, though not on the critical path, it may be returned instead by the algorithm, but only if the registers involved in the address expressions are not redefined between this pair and the earliest pair on the critical path. This way we guarantee that the latter is always disambiguated, hence the critical path shortened. In Figure 2, the earliest memory dependence corresponding to the selected base address pair (EDI, EDX*2) is the edge $A \rightarrow B$, which is not on the critical path.

## 4   Light-Weight Pointer Analysis

Given the critical base address pairs returned by the heuristic algorithm, the goal of the pointer analysis is to identify two kinds of memory dependences:

**Directly covered dependences.** Memory references whose base addresses (which syntactically may or may not look the same as the critical base addresses) are guaranteed to evaluate to the same runtime value as the critical base addresses.

**Indirectly covered dependences.** Memory references that, though not accessing memory locations pointed to by the critical base addresses, may still be disambiguated as a result of more accurate pointer information when some false memory dependences have been removed.

The analysis achieves this by computing symbolically the set of possible values for each register and each memory location touched within a trace. Amme et al. design a intra-procedural data dependence analysis for assembly code by symbolic evaluation [9]. However, their algorithm does not keep track of memory contents and therefore loses crucial information and accuracy.

The key to the success of our analysis is not just to prove non-aliases, but to infer must-aliases such that information about the content of a memory location can be propagated from one memory reference to another. The fact that the traces are single-entry greatly increases the rate at which must-aliases can be proven since every use has exactly one reaching definition for both registers and memory locations. In addition, this control-flow property also keeps the analysis extremely light-weight because the size of any symbolic value set is always exactly 1 due to the absence of merge points.

Notice that this analysis only needs to be performed on traces for which the heuristic algorithm returns at least some memory dependences to recommend for runtime disambiguation. Also notice that we could have used this more sophisticated analysis in place of instruction inspection in the preliminary dependence selection phase to filter out more non-aliases. However, without some dependences assumed to be removed by runtime checks, the analysis is too constrained by inaccurate information about memory contents to offer significant benefit over instruction inspection. On top of that, the analysis will have to be run on all traces. Therefore we use instruction inspection instead, which is simpler and cheaper.

The remainder of this section first walks through a small example to show how the analysis works and then gives the formal definition of the analysis.

### 4.1 Walking Through an Example

In the trace shown in Figure 2, there are five pairs of ambiguous memory references: $A \rightarrow B$, $A \rightarrow E$, $B \rightarrow C$, $B \rightarrow E$, and $C \rightarrow E$. We show that all of them can be removed by inserting one runtime check.

The pointer analysis receives from the memory dependence selection algorithm the input instruction pair $(A, B)$, which can be assumed to be independent since a runtime check will be inserted to compare the values of EDI and EDX*2. The same check also directly removes the dependence between $B$ and $C$ because EDI remains unchanged between $A$ and $C$. Although syntactically the address referenced by instruction $E$ has nothing to do with EDI or EDX, interestingly the remaining three dependences involving it can still be eliminated in the presence of the check. Since $A$ and $B$ do not alias, we know that the content of the location pointed to by EDI is not overwritten by $B$, therefore the values loaded by $A$ and $C$ must be the same, that is, EBX == EDX right after $C$. After symbolically executing instruction $D$, EBX == EDX*2, hence the symbolic

```
//r1     = base1 + index1 * scale1 + offset1
//r2     = base2 + index2 * scale2 + offset2
//result = base  + index  * scale + offset

base   := r1
index  := r2
scale  := a
offset := b

if (base2 == NULL && index2 == NULL)
    index  := NULL
    offset += offset2 * a
else if (index2 == NULL)
    index  := base2
    offset += offset2 * a
else if (base2 == NULL)
    index  := index2
    scale  *= scale2
    offset += offset2 * a

if (index1 == index || index1 == NULL  || index == NULL)
    base   := base1
    scale  += scale1
    offset += offset1

if (base == index)
    base := NULL
    scale++
```

**Fig. 3.** Pseudo-code for Computing $r1 + r2 * a + b$

address referenced by $E$ is EDX*2 + 411468h with EDX*2 as base. This means that $B$ and $E$ definitely do not alias since they access the same base address with different offsets. The dependence between $A \rightarrow E$ and $C \rightarrow E$ are removed because their base addresses can be compared by the runtime check.

### 4.2   Symbolic Pointer Values

We use the same expression, base_reg + index_reg * scale + offset, to represent all symbolic values, pointers or non-pointers. Each register value in the expression is a pair (reg_name, def_site), where def_site is the id of the instruction that writes the value into the register. Either base_reg or index_reg can be omitted (we say that their value is NULL). The rule for arithmetics on the symbolic values is described by the pseudo-code in Figure 3, which computes $r1 + r2 * a + b$ where $r1$ and $r2$ are themselves symbolic expressions. It merges the two symbolic expressions if it can, otherwise it gives up and returns $r1 + r2 * a + b$.

### 4.3   Analysis Algorithm

The algorithm finishes in one pass over the instructions in the trace starting from the entry. At each memory instruction, it compares the symbolic address with those of all previous memory instructions to see whether aliases exist. Therefore the worst case complexity of the algorithm is quadratic in the number of instructions.

The algorithm maintains the following data structures.

1. *Reg_Values* – Maps each register to a symbolic expression describing the current value held in that register.

```
//Instruction t is a memory reference
addr_t := Inst_Addrs(t)

for each memory instruction s before t
    addr_s := Inst_Adds(s)
    if (may_alias(addr_s, addr_t))
        record dependence s->t
        if (is_store(t))
            Mem_Values(addr_s) := NULL

if (is_load(t))
    r := dest_reg(t)
    content_t := Mem_Values(addr_t)
    if (content_t != NULL)
        Reg_Values(r) := content_t
    else
        Reg_Values(r) := (r, t)
        Mem_Values(addr_t) := Reg_Values(r)
```

**Fig. 4.** Pseudo-code for Analyzing Memory Instructions

2. *Mem_Values* – Maps each symbolic memory address to a symbolic expression describing the current value stored at that address. If the analysis cannot infer any information about the content of that memory location, it will map the symbolic address to the value NULL.
3. *Inst_Addrs* – Maps each memory instruction to the symbolic address it references.

Figure 4 contains the pseudo-code for actions taken at memory instructions. At other instructions, the analysis simply does symbolic evaluation based on the semantics of the instruction.

The symbolic address of each memory instruction is compared with those of all memory instructions that come before it in the trace. Non-alias is determined if the base address parts of the two symbolic addresses are the same and the offsets are different. Must-alias is determined if both the base addresses and the offsets are the same. If the memory instruction is a store, the analysis removes the contents of all aliasing symbolic addresses recorded in the table *Mem_Values* and changes them to NULL. This is because the store might write to any of these aliasing locations, destroying the values held in there. If the memory instruction is a load, the analysis looks up the symbolic address up in *Mem_Values*. If it is mapped to a non-NULL value, this means that there is a previous must-alias instruction for which the analysis has recorded what value is in the memory location right after the instruction and this information has not been destroyed by any subsequent aliasing store. In this case, the destination register of the load can assume the value recorded in *Mem_Values*. Otherwise, the analysis can say nothing about the value loaded into the destination register, either because the value has been destroyed by aliasing stores or because the value is a live-in through memory. In this case, the analysis simply records in *Mem_Values* that the content of the memory location is whatever value that is currently in the destination register.

## 5   Inserting Runtime Checks

Runtime checks are inserted in the trace and scheduled together with other instructions. Instructions that do not depend on the checks can be scheduled past them, no compensation code is needed on the off-trace path. Instructions dependent on the checks but with no side-effects, i.e. loads and their uses, can also be scheduled past the checks. We rely on the trace scheduling algorithm [10] to insert proper compensation code at the split points.

## 5.1   Determining Test Conditions

Each memory reference is characterized by an address and a reference size, which together specify a range of memory addresses [address, address + size). A runtime check needs to test for the disjoint-ness of two memory ranges. Let $range1 = [a, b)$ and $range2 = [c, d)$, either $range1$ is below $range2$, which is captured by the condition $b <= c$, or $range1$ is above $range2$, which is captured by the condition $d <= a$. For each pair of critical base addresses $(base_a, base_b)$,

We separate the memory dependences directly covered by it into two groups to differentiate between these two situations. It turns out that just like the aliasing behavior, the relative positions of any two memory references are also highly stable throughout the lifetime of the program. This is not surprising as the two memory references may access different data structures whose locations in memory are fixed. As such, profiling can provide good guidance on deciding which group a memory dependence should go to. Indeed, we use the actual addresses recorded in the initial alias profiling phase for this purpose. Let $a \rightarrow b$ be a dependence directly covered by $(base_a, base_b)$ and suppose that instruction $a$'s base address is $base_a$ and instruction $b$'s base address is $base_b$. If the actual address range of $a$ is below the actual address range of $b$ according to the profile, then we put $a \rightarrow b$ in group I, otherwise we put it in group II.

Two checks are then generated, one for each group. Within each group, the check needs to be able to accommodate all the different offsets from a single base address. To do this, we introduce the concept of an ***extended range***, which contains all ranges relevant to a base address within either group. Suppose that there are $n$ dependences in group I (or group II) and that the $n$ instructions with $base\_a$ as base address are described by the (symbolic_address, size) pairs $(base_a + offset_1, size_1)$, ..., and $(base_a + offset_n, size_n)$. Then the extended range corresponding to $base_a$ in this group is $[base_a + min(offset_1, ..., offset_n), base_a + max(offset_1 + size_1, ..., offset_n + size_n))$. The extended range for $base\_b$ can be computed in the same fashion.

For example, in Figure 5, there are three memory dependences covered by same critical base address pair: no base address (instruction $A$, $B$, and $D$) and edx (instruction $C$). All memory references have a size of 4 bytes. The dependences $A \rightarrow C$ and $B \rightarrow C$ belong to group I as the effective address range of $A$ and $B$ are below that of $C$, and the dependence $C \rightarrow D$ belongs to group II. The extended range covering both $A$ and $B$ is $[301280h, 411464h + 4]$ and the extended range covering $C$ is $[edx, edx + 8 + 4]$.

```
A: 411464h
B: 301280h
C: edx + 8   (profiled addr: 560890h)
D: 62013Ch
```

**Fig. 5.** Determining Test Conditions

Therefore the test condition we generate for group I is $411464h + 4 <=$ edx. Similarly the test condition for group II is edx $+ 8 + 4 <= 62013Ch$.

# 6   Evaluation

## 6.1   Experimental Framework

We implemented selective runtime disambiguation algorithm in the Star Dynamic Binary Translator (StarDBT), a DBT framework currently being developed inside Intel for 32-bit x86. We evaluated our technique on an in-order VLIW simulator with stall-on-load semantics. The simulator models a 6-issue processor with 2 memory read ports, 2 memory write ports, 4 integer units, 1 floating point unit, and 1 branch unit. The configuration of the memory hierarchy is given in Table 1. The memory behavior of StarDBT itself is not simulated since the execution time spent in StarDBT code is a small fraction of the execution time of the entire program. Execution time is computed by summing of the static cycle counts generated from the instruction schedules and the miss penalties reported by a cache simulator.

The simulation is done online while StarDBT is translating and executing the program. StarDBT inserts instrumentation before each memory instruction to record the actual addresses in a data structure. Whenever the data structure is filled up, StarDBT jumps

**Table 1.** Memory Hierarchy

| Level | Write Policy | Allocation Policy | Floating Point Bypass | Associativity | Size | Latency |
|---|---|---|---|---|---|---|
| L1 | Write through | Read-only alloc | Yes | 4-way | 16KB | 1 cycle hit |
| L2 | Write back | Write alloc | No | 8-way | 128KB | 3 cycle hit |
| L3 | Write back | Write alloc | No | 12-way | 3MB | 10 cycle hit / 100 cycles miss |

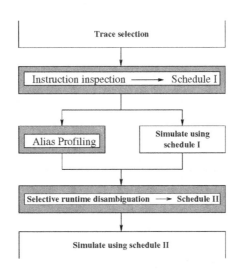

**Fig. 6.** Flow Chart of Simulation in StarDBT

out of the execution of the program and transfers control to the cache simulator, which then simulates the memory accesses in the order specified by the instruction schedules. Figure 6 contains the flow chart of the simulation process within StarDBT. After a trace is formed, the first schedule is computed based on dependence information generated from instruction inspection. Next, alias profiling is conducted, during which period the memory accesses of the trace are simulated based on the first schedule. At the end of alias profiling, our heuristic algorithm and light-weight pointer analysis are performed and a second schedule is generated if any runtime check is to be inserted. From that point on till the end of the program execution, memory accesses are simulated using the second schedule. The benchmarks we used is the SPECINT2000 benchmarks with ref input.

## 6.2  Precision Evaluation

Precision in this context is how finely our technique controls where to apply selective disambiguation and where to spend analysis effort. We also look at the misspeculation rate of the runtime checks to see whether the test conditions accurately capture the frequent cases.

In Table 2, the column "#Selected Traces" refers to traces for which the heuristic algorithm reports beneficial critical dependences, the column "#Optimized Traces" refers to traces that, with runtime checks inserted, indeed have schedules shorter than their original schedules. There are two interesting points. First, on average the selected traces are only 26% of the total traces. The rest simply do not have memory dependences on the critical path. This could happen if the memory dependence is not the only type of dependence between two instructions and there exists a chain of other dependences whose total latency is larger than the latency of the memory dependence. From this point, the heuristic algorithm is precise in that no check is ever inserted where it cannot possibly improve scheduling. Second, out of the selected traces, almost all (97%) have improved schedules with runtime checks inserted. The reason why some traces may fail to have shorter schedules is that not enough dependences are removed by the runtime checks. For example, there may be two critical paths of equal lengths in the original dependence graph and the checks can only remove dependences on one path, or too few dependences are removed to make up for the overhead of the runtime checks themselves. From this point, the heuristic algorithm is also precise because the critical base addresses it selects are such that the runtime checks for these addresses

**Table 2.** Precision Evaluation

| Benchmark | #Traces | #Selected Traces | #Optimized Traces | #Checks | Misspeculation |
|---|---|---|---|---|---|
| 164.gzip | 1558 | 364 | 362 | 636 | - % |
| 175.vpr | 1220 | 366 | 349 | 552 | 0.01% |
| 176.gcc | 14924 | 2251 | 2164 | 3124 | - % |
| 181.mcf | 174 | 50 | 50 | 76 | 0.01% |
| 186.crafty | 1431 | 175 | 173 | 263 | 1.51% |
| 197.parser | 2566 | 376 | 347 | 645 | 1.55% |
| 252.eon | 739 | 215 | 211 | 390 | 5.75% |
| 253.perlbmk | 9299 | 3093 | 2913 | 5217 | 0.36% |
| 254.gap | 1691 | 287 | 281 | 444 | 0.38% |
| 255.vortex | 3956 | 1734 | 1713 | 3990 | - % |
| 256.bzip2 | 963 | 247 | 241 | 359 | 0.85% |
| 300.twolf | 931 | 311 | 302 | 548 | 0.48% |

almost always cover enough dependences to yield actual performance gains, hence no work subsequently done in the pointer analysis and rescheduling is wasted.

For the traces that do have improved schedules, we go ahead and insert the runtime checks and recovery code. On average, only about 1.7 checks are inserted per optimized trace. If averaged over all traces that make up the program, about 0.4 checks are inserted per trace. Assuming pessimistically that with each check inserted the entire trace has to be duplicated, this translates to a rough estimation of a 40% code growth over the original translated binary. In reality, however, the code growth should be much smaller because checks are often inserted not at the entry of the trace but in the middle, therefore only the tail of the trace needs to be duplicated.

Misspeculation happens when a runtime check fails either because the initial alias profiling did not accurately predict the aliasing behavior of the whole program or because the test conditions fail to characterize all cases of disjoint-ness in their attempt to cover multiple displacements from base addresses. The misspeculation rate is measured in StarDBT by prolonging the initial alias profiling phase to span the entire execution of the program and evaluating the test conditions on the effective addresses collected by profiling. The last column in Table 2 gives the misspeculation rate as the percentage of the number of misspeculations over the total number of runtime checks performed dynamically.

### 6.3  Impact on Scheduling

To evaluate the impact of removed memory dependences on the quality of the instruction schedules, we compare the schedules generated with no disambiguation at all, with instruction inspection, and with our technique respectively to the optimal schedules, where all false memory dependences are removed. The quality of the schedules is measured as slowdown from the optimal schedules in static cycle counts. As we can see from Figure 7, without any memory disambiguation, the schedules generated assuming all memory references alias are really bad, with a geometric mean slowdown of 24.5%. With instruction inspection, the slowdown is reduced to 7.7%. And finally, our technique can almost close the gap and match the optimal scheduling (1.3% slowdown) just by inserting a small number of runtime checks.

### 6.4  Speedup from Improved Scheduling

We compare the actual performance gains, obtained respectively from instruction inspection only and from our technique, over baseline where no memory disambiguation is performed at all. The same online cache simulation mechanism is used to compute the execution time of baseline and instruction inspection. As shown in Table 3, our technique can disambiguate more than twice as many dependences as does instruction inspection, which amounts to 73% of all false memory dependences. This translates to a 5% increase in performance gains over baseline as the result of improved instruction scheduling alone. If combined with other optimizations such as redundant memory operation elimination and register promotion, we expect even bigger improvement.

### 6.5  Analysis Overhead

We measured the time spent in our analysis, which corresponds to the shaded boxes in Figure 6. It is a function of the number of traces and the size of the traces on which the

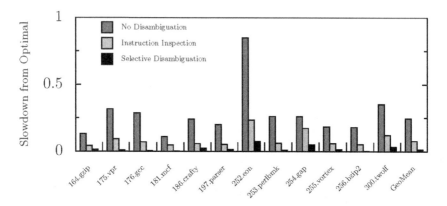

**Fig. 7.** Comparing with Optimal Scheduling

**Table 3.** Performance Gains over Baseline

| Benchmark | Instruction Inspection | | Selection Disambiguation | |
|---|---|---|---|---|
| | Deps Removed | Speedup | Deps Removed | Speedup |
| 164.gzip | 42% | 7.7% | 78% | 10.3% |
| 175.vpr | 30% | 16.9% | 80% | 23.3% |
| 176.gcc | 35% | 16.8% | 69% | 21.9% |
| 181.mcf | 34% | 5.6% | 79% | 9.9% |
| 186.crafty | 31% | 14.2% | 47% | 18.9% |
| 197.parser | 40% | 12.4% | 80% | 15.5% |
| 252.eon | 34% | 33.3% | 69% | 42.0% |
| 253.perlbmk | 32% | 15.8% | 76% | 20.0% |
| 254.gap | 17% | 6.9% | 57% | 16.6% |
| 255.vortex | 34% | 10.4% | 87% | 14.2% |
| 256.bzip2 | 47% | 13.2% | 75% | 17.2% |
| 300.twolf | 40% | 16.9% | 84% | 23.5% |
| Average | 35% | 14.2% | 73% | 19.3% |

**Table 4.** Analysis Time

| Benchmark | Execution Time (sec) | Analysis Time (sec) |
|---|---|---|
| 164.gzip | 125 | 0 |
| 175.vpr | 129 | 1 |
| 176.gcc | 122 | 3 |
| 181.mcf | 104 | 0 |
| 186.crafty | 112 | 0 |
| 197.parser | 144 | 1 |
| 252.eon | 92 | 5 |
| 253.perlbmk | 166 | 5 |
| 254.gap | 70 | 1 |
| 255.vortex | 105 | 9 |
| 256.bzip2 | 129 | 0 |
| 300.twolf | 191 | 1 |

light-weight pointer analysis and rescheduling are performed. Table 4 shows the analysis time together with the execution time of the benchmarks in StarDBT without our technique on a 3.2GHz Xeon with 2.5MB of cache and 2G of memory.[1] The analysis

---

[1] StarDBT does not yet run on in-order machines that we want to evaluate our technique on, hence the speedup through our technique could not be measured in the same way.

overhead is extremely low compared to the program execution time, so the performance gained through our technique will not be offset by the overhead of the technique itself.

## 7  Conclusion and Future Work

In this paper, we present a technique designed to provide sophisticated memory disambiguation in a dynamic binary translator at low cost. It precisely selects memory dependences whose removal by runtime disambiguation can result in shortened schedules. Simple analysis is applied to allow as many dependences to be removed by one runtime check as possible. We also use profile guidance to trim the actual test conditions of the runtime checks. Our experiments demonstrate that selective runtime memory disambiguation almost doubles the number of memory dependences removed by instruction inspection and improves the overall performance by 5% just from scheduling. In the future, we will investigate other optimizations such as redundant memory operation elimination and register promotion, which can make use of the disambiguation offered by our technique for further improvements.

## References

1. B.-C. Cheng and W. W. Hwu, "Modular interprocedural pointer analysis using access paths: design, implementation, and evaluation," in *ACM SIGPLAN Conference on Programming Language Design and Implementation*, pp. 57–69, 2000.
2. W. Landi and B. G. Ryder, "A safe approximate algorithm for interprocedural pointer aliasing," in *Proceedings of the ACM SIGPLAN '92 Conference on Programming Language Design and Implementation*, pp. 235–248, June 1992.
3. V. Bala, E. Deusterwald, and S. Banerjia, "Transparent dynamic optimization," Tech. Rep. HPL-1999-77, Hewlett Packard Labs, June 1999.
4. J. C. Dehnert, B. K. Grant, and J. P. Banning, "The transmeta code morphing software: using speculation, recovery and adaptive retranslation to address real-life challenges," in *Proceedings of the 1st International Symposium on Code Generation and Optimization*, pp. 15–24, March 2003.
5. K. Ebcioglu and E. R. Altman, "DAISY: Dynamic compilation for 100% architectural compatibility," in *Proceedings of the 24th International Symposium on Computer Architecture*, June 1997.
6. A. Nicolau, "Run-time disambiguation: Coping with statically unpredictable dependences," *IEEE Transactions on Computers*, vol. 38, pp. 663–678, May 1989.
7. A. S. Huang, G. Slavengurg, and J. P. Shen, "Speculative disambiguation: A compilation technique for dynamic memory disambiguation," *ACM SIGARCH Computer Architecture News Archive*, vol. 22, pp. 200–210, April 1994.
8. M. Fernandez and R. Espasa, "Speculative alias analysis for executable code," in *Proceedings of the 2002 International Conference on Parallel Architectures and Compilation Techniques*, pp. 222–231, September 2002.
9. W. Amme, P. Braun, and E. Zehendner, "Data dependence analysis of assembly code," Tech. Rep. 3764, INRIA, Rocquencourt, France, September 1999.
10. J. A. Fisher, "Trace scheduling: A technique for global microcode compaction," *IEEE Transactions on Computers*, vol. C-30, pp. 478–490, July 1981.

# Accurately Choosing Execution Runs for Software Fault Localization

Liang Guo, Abhik Roychoudhury, and Tao Wang

School of Computing, National University of Singapore, Singapore 117543
{guol, abhik, wangtao}@comp.nus.edu.sg

**Abstract.** Software fault localization involves locating the exact cause of error for a "failing" execution run – a run which exhibits an unexpected behavior. Given such a failing run, fault localization often proceeds by comparing the failing run with a "successful" run, that is, a run which does not exhibit the unexpected behavior. One important issue here is the choice of the successful run for such a comparison. In this paper, we propose a control flow based difference metric for this purpose. The difference metric takes into account the sequence of statement instances (and not just the set of these instances) executed in the two runs, by locating branch instances with similar contexts but different outcomes in the failing and the successful runs. Given a failing run $\pi_f$ and a pool of successful runs $S$, we choose the successful run $\pi_s$ from $S$ whose execution trace is closest to $\pi_f$ in terms of the difference metric. A bug report is then generated by returning the difference between $\pi_f$ and $\pi_s$. We conduct detailed experiments to compare our approach with previously proposed difference metrics. In particular, we evaluate our approach in terms of (a) effectiveness of bug report for locating the bug, (b) size of bug report and (c) size of successful run pool required to make a decent choice of successful run.

**Keywords:** Programming tools, Debugging.

## 1  Introduction

Debugging is an important program development activity. In the past few years, substantial research has been conducted to improve debugging tools by identifying the error cause of an observable error with higher degree of automation [3, 7, 11, 12, 13, 18]. These fault localization approaches compare the failing execution run, which exhibits the observable error, with one that does not. Most of the research in this topic has focused on how to compare the successful and failing execution runs. In this paper, we present a control flow based difference metric to choose a successful run from a pool for such a comparison; the pool of successful program runs could be constructed by picking successful runs from a test-suite of program inputs. Our difference metric measures "similarity" between execution runs of a program. Given a failing run $\pi_f$ and a pool of successful

A. Mycroft and A. Zeller (Eds.): CC 2006, LNCS 3923, pp. 80–95, 2006.

```
1.   while (lin[i] != ENDSTR) {
2.       m=...
3.       if (m >= 0) {
4.           ...
5.           lastm = m;
6.       }
7.       if ((m == -1) || (m == i)) {
8.           ...
9.           i = i + 1;
10.      }
11.      else
12.          i = m;
13.  }
14.  ...
```

**Fig. 1.** An example program fragment

runs $S$, we select the most similar successful run $\pi_s \in S$ in terms of the difference metric, and generate a bug report by returning the difference between $\pi_f$ and $\pi_s$.

Our difference metric considers branch instances with similar contexts but different outcomes in two execution runs, because these branch instances may be related to the cause of error. When these branch instances are evaluated differently from the failing run, certain faulty statements may not be executed — leading to disappearance of the observable error in the successful run. Consider the program fragment (from a faulty version of **replace** program in the Siemens benchmark Suite [6, 14] — simplified here for illustration) in Figure 1, where the bug fix lies in strengthening the condition in line 3 to if ((m >= 0) && (lastm != m)). This piece of code changes all substrings $s_1$ in string lin matching a pattern to another substring $s_2$, where variable i represents the index to the first un-processed character in string lin, variable m represents the index to the end of a matched substring $s_1$ in string lin, and variable lastm records variable m in last loop iterations. At the $i$th iteration, if variable m is not changed at line 2, line 3 is wrongly evaluated to true, and substring $s_2$ is wrongly returned as output, deemed by programmer as an observable "error". The execution of the $i$th iteration of this failing run $\pi_f$ could follow path $\langle 1, 2, 3, 4, 5, 7, 8, 9 \rangle$. In this case, a successful run $\pi_s$ whose $i$th iteration follows path $\langle 1, 2, 3, 7, 8, 9 \rangle$ can be useful for error localization. By comparing $\pi_f$ with $\pi_s$, we see that only the branch at line 3 is evaluated differently. Indeed this is the erroneous statement in this example, and was pinpointed by our method in the experiment. For programs whose erroneous statement is not a branch, our method will try to report the nearest branch for locating the error.

*Summary of Results.* The main results of this paper are as follows. We propose a control-flow based difference metric to compare execution runs (*i.e.* data flow in the runs is not taken into account). We take the view that the *difference* between two runs can be summarized by the *sequence* of comparable branch statement instances which are evaluated differently in the two runs. This difference metric is used to choose a successful run from a pool of successful runs for automated debugging. We return as *bug report* the branch statements whose instances (1) have similar contexts, and (2) are evaluated differently in the failing run and the selected successful run. We experimentally evaluate the quality of our bug report, the volume of our bug report, and the impact of successful run pool size on the quality of our bug report. We also share some experience in using our method for debugging real-life programs.

## 2    Related Work

In this section, we discuss work on localizing software errors. There have been a lot of techniques [1, 3, 7, 10, 11, 12, 13, 18] proposed for automatic program error localization by comparing successful and failing runs of the buggy program. These techniques compare different characteristics of execution runs, *e.g.* acyclic paths [13], potential invariants [11], executed statements [1, 7, 15], basic block profiling [12], program states [3, 18], predicates [10] or return value of methods [9]. Unlike our method, most of these works focus on how to compare successful and failing execution runs to generate accurate bug reports.

The focus of our method is to choose a successful run from a given pool of successful runs, provided we have access to the failing run. In other words, we do not (semi)-automatically generate the successful run. Generating a successful run (and a corresponding input) close to a given failing run has been studied in various papers [2, 5, 19], including our past work [17].

Our difference metric bears similarities to the notion of proximity between runs proposed by Zeller et al. in [3, 18]. Their approach compares program states with similar contexts for fault localization at some control locations. Through a series of binary search over the program state and re-executing (part of) the program from "mixed" states, a set of variables which may be responsible for the bug are mined and reported. However, these "mixed" states may be infeasible. Furthermore, it may be quite costly to compare program states and to re-execute the program several times.

The work of Renieris and Reiss [12] is related to ours. They have demonstrated through empirical evidence that the successful run which is "closest" to the failing run can be more helpful for error localization than a randomly selected successful run. However, [12] measures the proximity of two runs by comparing the *set* of basic blocks[1] executed in each run. Thus, they cannot distinguish between runs which execute exactly the same statements but in different order — consider the program `for (....){ if (...) S1 else S2 }` and the two execution runs $\langle S1, S2 \rangle$, $\langle S2, S1 \rangle$. We consider the *sequence* of statements executed in each run for determining proximity between two runs. Detailed experiments comparing our method with [12] are reported in Section 5.

---

[1] Actually a sorted sequence of the basic blocks based on execution counts is used; this is different from the execution sequence of the basic blocks in the failing run.

## 3    Measuring Difference Between Execution Runs

We elaborate on the difference metric used for comparing execution runs in this section. We consider each execution run of a program to be a sequence of *events* $\langle e_0, e_1, ..., e_{n-1} \rangle$ where $e_i$ refers to the $i$th event during execution. *Each event $e_i$ represents an execution instance of a line number in the program*; the program statement corresponding to this line number is denoted as $stmt(e_i)$. To distinguish events from different execution runs, we denote the $i$th event in an execution run $\pi$ as $e_i^\pi$, that is, the execution run appears as a superscript. We will drop the superscript when it is obvious from the context.

Our difference metric measures the difference between two execution runs $\pi$ and $\pi'$ of a program, by comparing behaviors of "corresponding" branch statement instances from $\pi$ and $\pi'$. The branch statement instances with differing outcomes in $\pi, \pi'$ are captured in $diff(\pi, \pi')$ – the difference between execution run $\pi$ and execution run $\pi'$. In order to find out "corresponding" branch instances, we have defined a notion of *alignment* to relate statement instances of two execution runs. Our alignment is based on *dynamic control dependence*. Given an execution run $\pi$ of a program, an event $e_i^\pi$ is *dynamically control dependent* on another event $e_j^\pi$ if $e_j^\pi$ is the last event before $e_i^\pi$ in $\pi$ where $stmt(e_i^\pi)$ is statically control dependent [4] on $stmt(e_j^\pi)$. Note that any method entry event is dynamically control dependent on the corresponding method invocation event. We use the notation $dep(e_i^\pi, \pi)$ to denote the event on which $e_i^\pi$ is dynamically control dependent in run $\pi$. We now present our definition of event alignment.

**Definition 1 (Alignment).** *For any pair of event $e$ in run $\pi$ and event $e'$ in run $\pi'$, we define $align(e, e') = true$ (e and e' are aligned) iff.*

1. *$stmt(e) = stmt(e')$, and*
2. *either $e, e'$ are the first events appearing in $\pi, \pi'$ or*
   *$align(dep(e, \pi), dep(e', \pi')) = true$.*

When a branch event $e_i^\pi$ cannot be aligned with any event from the execution $\pi'$, this should only affect alignments of events in $\pi$ which are transitively dynamically control dependent on $e_i^\pi$. In addition, the $i$th iteration of a loop in the execution $\pi$ will be aligned with the $i$th iteration of the same loop in the execution $\pi'$, in order to properly compare events from different loop iterations.

A simple illustration of alignment appears in Figure 2; here $\pi, \pi'$ and $\pi''$ represent three execution runs of the program segment in Figure 1 (page 81). In Figure 2, events along the same horizontal line are aligned. From this example, we can see that events in the $i$th loop iteration in run $\pi$ are aligned with events in the $i$th loop iteration in run $\pi'$.

According to the notion of alignment presented in Definition 1, for any event $e$ in $\pi$ there exists *at most* one event $e'$ in $\pi'$ such that $align(e, e') = true$. The difference between $\pi$ and $\pi'$ (denoted $diff(\pi, \pi')$) captures all branch event occurrences in $\pi$ which (i) can be aligned to an event in $\pi'$ and (ii) have different outcomes in $\pi$ and $\pi'$. Formally, the difference between two execution runs can be defined as follows.

| Execution Run | | | Alignment | | | | Difference | |
|---|---|---|---|---|---|---|---|---|
| $\pi$ | $\pi'$ | $\pi''$ | $\pi$ | $\pi'$ | | $\pi$  $\pi''$ | $diff(\pi, \pi')$ | $diff(\pi, \pi'')$ |
| $1_1$ | $1_1$ | $1_1$ | | | | | | |
| $2_2$ | $2_2$ | $2_2$ | | | | | | |
| $3_3$ | $3_3$ | $3_3$ | | | | | $\bullet$ | |
| $4_4$ | | $4_4$ | | | | | | |
| $5_5$ | | $5_5$ | | | | | | |
| $7_6$ | $7_4$ | $7_6$ | | | | | | $\bullet$ |
| $8_7$ | $8_5$ | | | | | | | |
| $9_8$ | $9_6$ | | | | | | | |
| | | $12_7$ | | | | | | |
| $1_9$ | $1_7$ | $1_8$ | | | | | | |
| $2_{10}$ | $2_8$ | $2_9$ | | | | | | |
| $3_{11}$ | $3_9$ | $3_{10}$ | | | | | | |
| $4_{12}$ | $4_{10}$ | $4_{11}$ | | | | | | |
| $5_{13}$ | $5_{11}$ | $5_{12}$ | | | | | | |
| $7_{14}$ | $7_{12}$ | $7_{13}$ | | | | | $\bullet$ | $\bullet$ |
| $8_{15}$ | | | | | | | | |
| $9_{16}$ | | | | | | | | |
| | $12_{13}$ | $12_{14}$ | | | | | | |
| $14_{17}$ | $14_{14}$ | $14_{15}$ | | | | | | |

**Fig. 2.** Example to illustrate alignments and difference metrics. The first three columns show the event sequences of three execution runs $\pi$, $\pi'$ and $\pi''$ of the program fragment in Figure 1 (page 81). Next two columns show alignments of $(\pi, \pi')$ and $(\pi, \pi'')$, where solid lines indicate aligned statement instances and dashed lines indicate unaligned statement instances. The last two columns show the difference between execution runs.

**Definition 2 (Difference Metric).** *Consider two execution runs* $\pi, \pi'$ *of a program. The difference between* $\pi, \pi'$, *denoted* $diff(\pi, \pi')$, *is defined as:*

$$diff(\pi, \pi') = \langle e_{i_1}^{\pi}, \ldots, e_{i_k}^{\pi} \rangle$$

*such that*

1. *each event* $e$ *in* $diff(\pi, \pi')$ *is a branch event occurrence drawn from run* $\pi$.
2. *the events in* $diff(\pi, \pi')$ *appear in the same order as in* $\pi$, *that is, for all* $1 \leq j < k$, $i_j < i_{j+1}$ *(event* $e_{i_j}^{\pi}$ *appears before event* $e_{i_{j+1}}^{\pi}$ *in* $\pi$ *).*
3. *for each* $e$ *in* $diff(\pi, \pi')$, *there exists another branch occurrence* $e'$ *in run* $\pi'$ *such that* $align(e, e')$=true *(i.e.* $e$ *and* $e'$ *can be aligned). Furthermore, the outcome of* $e$ *in* $\pi$ *is different from the outcome of* $e'$ *in* $\pi'$[2].
4. *all events in* $\pi$ *satisfying criteria (1) and (2) are included in* $diff(\pi, \pi')$.

*As a special case, if execution runs* $\pi$ *and* $\pi'$ *have the same control flow, then we define* $diff(\pi, \pi') = \langle e_0^{\pi} \rangle$.

Clearly we can see that in general $diff(\pi, \pi') \neq diff(\pi', \pi)$. The reason for making a special case for $\pi$ and $\pi'$ having the same control flow will be explained later in the section when we discuss comparison of differences.

Consider the example in Figure 2. The difference between execution runs $\pi$ and $\pi'$ is: $diff(\pi, \pi') = \langle 3_3, 7_{14} \rangle$, as indicated in Figure 2. This is because

---

[2] Since $e, e'$ can be aligned, they denote occurrences of the same branch statement.

branch instances $3_3, 7_{14}$ are aligned in runs $\pi$ and $\pi'$ and their outcomes are different in $\pi, \pi'$. If the branches at lines $3_3, 7_{14}$ are evaluated differently, we get $\pi'$ from $\pi$. Similarly, the difference between execution runs $\pi$ and $\pi''$ is: $diff(\pi, \pi'') = \langle 7_6, 7_{14} \rangle$.

Why do we capture branch event occurrences of $\pi$ which evaluate differently in $\pi'$ in the difference $diff(\pi, \pi')$ ? Recall that we want to choose a successful run for purposes of fault localization. If $\pi$ is the failing run and $\pi'$ is a successful run, then $diff(\pi, \pi')$ tells us which branches in the failing run $\pi$ need to be evaluated differently to produce the successful run $\pi'$. Clearly, if we have a choice of successful runs we would like to make minimal changes to the failing run to produce a successful run. Thus, given a failing run $\pi$ and two successful runs $\pi', \pi''$, we choose $\pi'$ over $\pi''$ if $diff(\pi, \pi') < diff(\pi, \pi'')$. This requires us to *compare* differences. How we do so is elaborated in the following.

**Definition 3 (Comparison of Differences).** *Let* $\pi, \pi', \pi''$ *be three execution runs of a program. Let*

$$diff(\pi, \pi') = \langle e_{i_1}^\pi, e_{i_2}^\pi, \ldots, e_{i_n}^\pi \rangle \quad and \quad diff(\pi, \pi'') = \langle e_{j_1}^\pi, e_{j_2}^\pi, \ldots, e_{j_m}^\pi \rangle$$

*We define* $diff(\pi, \pi') < diff(\pi, \pi'')$ *iff there exists an integer* $K \geq 0$ *s.t.*

1. $K \leq m$ *and* $K \leq n$
2. *the last $K$ events in* $diff(\pi, \pi')$ *and* $diff(\pi, \pi'')$ *are the same, that is,* $\forall 0 \leq x < K \quad i_{n-x} = j_{m-x}$.
3. *one of the following two conditions holds*
   - *either* $diff(\pi, \pi')$ *is a suffix of* $diff(\pi, \pi'')$, *that is,* $K = n < m$
   - *or the $(K+1)$th event from the end in* $diff(\pi, \pi')$ *appears later in $\pi$ as compared to the $(K+1)$th event from the end in* $diff(\pi, \pi'')$, *that is,* $i_{n-K} > j_{m-K}$.

Thus, given a failing run $\pi$ and two successful runs $\pi', \pi''$ we say that $diff(\pi, \pi') < diff(\pi, \pi'')$ based on a combination of the following criteria.

- Fewer branches of $\pi$ need to be evaluated differently to get $\pi'$ as compared to the number of branches of $\pi$ that need to be evaluated differently to get $\pi''$. This is reflected in the condition $K = n < m$ of Definition 3.
- The branches of $\pi$ that need to be evaluated differently to get $\pi'$ appear closer to the end of $\pi$ (where the error is observed), as compared to the branches of $\pi$ that need to be evaluated differently to get $\pi''$ . This is reflected in the condition $i_{n-K} > j_{m-K}$ of Definition 3.

To illustrate our comparison of differences, consider the example in Figure 2. Recall that $diff(\pi, \pi') = \langle 3_3, 7_{14} \rangle$, and $diff(\pi, \pi'') = \langle 7_6, 7_{14} \rangle$, as illustrated by the "•" in the last two columns of Figure 2. Comparing $\langle 3_3, 7_{14} \rangle$ with $\langle 7_6, 7_{14} \rangle$, we see that $\langle 7_6, 7_{14} \rangle < \langle 3_3, 7_{14} \rangle$ since statement instance $7_6$ occurs after statement instance $3_3$ in execution run $\pi$.

According to the comparison of differences in Definition 3, we favor last differing branch instances instead of early ones. This is because the early branch instances (where the two runs are different) are often not related to the error. For example, many programs check whether the input is legal in the beginning. If we favor early branch instances, we may get failing and successful runs which only differ in whether the input is legal for such programs. Comparing such runs is unlikely to produce a useful bug report.

*Comparing Runs with Identical Control Flow.* Using Definitions 2 and 3 we can see that if $\pi$ is the failing run, $\pi_1$ is a successful run with same control flow as that of $\pi$ (*i.e.* same sequence of statements executed by a different input) and $\pi_2$ is a successful run with control flow different from $\pi$ we will have $diff(\pi, \pi_2) < diff(\pi, \pi_1)$. As a result, our method for choosing a successful run will avoid successful runs with same control flow as that of the failing run. This choice is deliberate; we want to find a successful run with minimal difference in control flow from the failing run, but not with zero difference. Recall here that we construct bug report by comparing the control-flow of the selected successful run with the failing run. If the two runs have the same control flow, the bug report is null and hence useless to the programmer. In our experiments, we encountered few cases where there were some successful runs with same control flow as the failing run; these were not chosen due to our method of comparing differences between runs.

## 4    Experimental Setup

In order to experimentally validate our method for fault localization, we developed a prototype implementation and conducted detailed experiments. We have also implemented the Nearest Neighbor method with permutations spectrum, which performs best in [12], for a comparison with our method. We employed our prototype on the Siemens benchmark suite [6, 14] and used the evaluation framework in [12] to quantitatively measure the quality of bug reports generated by both methods. The Siemens suite has been used by other recent works on fault localization [3, 12]. In this section, we introduce the subject programs (Section 4.1) and the evaluation framework (Section 4.2).

### 4.1    Subject Programs

Table 1 shows the subject programs from the Siemens suite [6, 14] which we used for our experimentation. There are 132 buggy C programs in the Siemens suite, each of which is created from one of seven programs, by manually injecting defects. The seven programs range in size from 170 to 560 lines, including comments. The third column in Table 1 shows the number of buggy programs created from each of the seven programs. Various kinds of defects have been injected, including code omissions, relaxing or tightening conditions of branch statements, and wrong values for assignment statements.

In the experiments, we found that there was no input whose execution run observed the error, for two out of the 132 programs. Code inspection showed

**Table 1.** Description of the Siemens suite

| Subject Pgm. | Description | # Buggy versions |
|---|---|---|
| schedule | priority scheduler | 9 |
| schedule2 | priority scheduler | 10 |
| replace | pattern replacement | 32 |
| print_tokens | lexical analyzer | 7 |
| print_tokens2 | lexical analyzer | 10 |
| tot_info | information measure | 23 |
| tcas | altitude separation | 41 |

that, these two programs are syntactically different from, but semantically the same as correct programs. Actually, these two programs are not buggy programs, so we ruled out them from our experiments. We slightly changed some subject programs in our experiments. In particular, we rewrote all conditional expressions into *if* statements. This is because our prototype collects execution traces at the statement level, and cannot detect branches inside conditional expressions which are evaluated differently.

### 4.2 Evaluation Framework

In order to evaluate the effectiveness of a defect localizer, an evaluation framework has been proposed by Renieris and Reiss [12]. This framework assigns a score to each bug report to show the quality, defined as follows:

$$score = 1 - \frac{|DS_*|}{|PDG|} \tag{1}$$

where $PDG$ refers to the program dependence graph of the buggy program. Let $DS(n)$ be the set of nodes that can reach or be reached from nodes in the bug report by traversing at most $n$ directed edges in the PDG. Then $DS_*$ is the $DS(n)$ with the smallest $n$ which contains the observable error statement (or at least one error statement if there are more than one observable errors).

The score measures the percentage of code that can be ignored for debugging. Clearly, higher score indicates bug report with higher quality. Note that the score only measures the utility of the bug report for debugging, *it does not necessarily correlate a good quality bug report with a lean bug report*. To address this weakness, we conducted separate experiments to measure bug report size.

## 5   Experimental Results

We employed the prototype implementation of both our method and the Nearest Neighbor method with permutations spectrum (NN method) [12][3] to 130

---

[3] We used the accurate permutations spectrum for NN method and considered all failing runs which had *some* successful run with a different spectrum. So, we can study all the 130 programs compared to the 109 programs studied in [12] where certain programs were ruled out based on a coarser spectrum (coverage).

buggy programs from the Siemens suite. The NN method compares code coverage between a failing run and the "nearest" successful run from a pool of successful runs. Through the experiments, we validate our method by answering the following three questions.

- Is our method effective for fault localization?
- Is the size of generated bug report voluminous and overwhelming?
- How many successful runs are required available to make a decent choice of successful run?

In this section, we present experimental results for these questions.

## 5.1   Locating the Bug

In the Siemens benchmark suite, each buggy program $P$ comes with a large pool of inputs, some of which result in successful runs, and others result in failing runs. For each failing run $\pi_f$, there is a set of successful runs $Closest(\pi_f)$ which are closest to $\pi_f$, in terms of our difference metric or that of the NN method. The score for a failing run $\pi_f$ averages scores of comparing $\pi_f$ against each successful run $\pi_s$ in $Closest(\pi_f)$, $i.e.$

$$score(\pi_f) = \frac{\sum_{\pi_s \in Closest(\pi_f)} score(\pi_f, \pi_s)}{|Closest(\pi_f)|}$$

where the quantity $score(\pi_f, \pi_s))$ is defined in Equation (1) in Section 4.2. The score for a buggy program $P$ averages scores of all failing run $\pi_f$ of $P$, $i.e.$

$$pgm\_score(P) = \frac{\sum_{\pi_f \in Failing(P)} score(\pi_f)}{|Failing(P)|}$$

where $Failing(P)$ refers to the set of failing runs of program $P$. Our method differs from the NN method in which successful runs are selected for comparison, and (hence) which statements are reported in bug report.

Table 2(a) shows the distribution of $pgm\_score$ for two methods. Our method is shown as CF, an abbreviation for Control Flow based difference metric. As we can see, our method performs a little better than the NN method on the Siemens suite. Bug reports returned by our method achieved a score of 0.8 or better for more than 37% of all the buggy programs, while the NN method achieved a score of 0.8 or more for about 31% of the programs. Note that a bug report with score of 0.8 or more indicates that programmer needs to inspect at most 20% of a buggy program for fault localization using this bug report.

In the above experiments, we computed the score of program $P$ by averaging scores w.r.t. all $\pi_s$ and $\pi_f$. However, the programmer will often choose one closest successful run $\pi_s$ and one failing run $\pi_f$ for comparison. Is our method sensitive to the choice of $\pi_s$ and $\pi_f$? First, our method is not sensitive to the choice of closest successful run $\pi_s$ since any $\pi_s \in Closest(\pi_f)$ returns the same bug report, that is, $score(\pi_f, \pi_s)$ is the same for all $\pi_s \in Closest(\pi_f)$. Secondly, our method

**Table 2.** (a) Distribution of scores, and (b) Locating different kinds of errors, where each category has 77, 38 and 18 programs, respectively. Note that the sum of programs in each category is more than 130. This is because 3 programs have two bugs of different kinds, and are counted in two categories.

| Score | CF | NN |
|---|---|---|
| 0.9 - 1 | 23.1 | 10.8 |
| 0.8 - 0.89 | 13.8 | 20.0 |
| 0.7 - 0.79 | 8.5 | 20.8 |
| 0.6 - 0.69 | 10.8 | 13.8 |
| 0.5 - 0.59 | 14.6 | 10.8 |
| 0.4 - 0.49 | 9.2 | 10.0 |
| 0.3 - 0.39 | 6.2 | 2.3 |
| 0.2 - 0.29 | 9.2 | 3.1 |
| 0.1 - 0.19 | 2.3 | 0.8 |
| 0 - 0.09 | 2.3 | 7.7 |

(a)

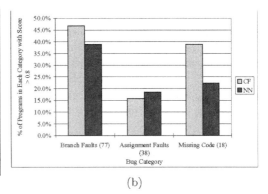

(b)

is less sensitive to the choice of failing run $\pi_f$ than the NN method. We validated this by computing variances w.r.t. choice of failing run for each fault program in our experiments. Given a set of failing runs $Failing(P)$ of a faulty program $P$, the variance of $P$ is defined as:

$$variance(P) = \frac{\sum_{\pi_f \in Failing(P)} (score(\pi_f) - pgm\_score(P))^2}{|Failing(P)|}$$

where $score(\pi_f)$ and $pgm\_score(P)$ are defined in the preceding. Using our method, we found that the score's variance was small (less than 0.01) for 56.6% of all 130 faulty programs. On the other hand, using the NN method, only 42.3% of 130 faulty programs had small variances (less than 0.01) in their scores.

Next we study the effectiveness of our technique in locating different kinds of errors. We classified all the errors in the faulty programs into three categories: *Assignment Faults*, *Branch Faults* and *Missing Code*, where *Assignment Faults* refer to errors in assignment and return statements, *Branch Faults* refer to errors in conditional branch statements and *Missing Code* refers to errors due to missing program statements. Table 2(b) shows percentage of faulty programs in each category where the bug reports got a score of 0.8 or better. We see that our method was more effective in locating branch faults. For almost half of the programs with branch faults, our method got a score of at least 0.8; this is not surprising since the difference metric returned by our method contains only branch statements with different outcomes in failing and successful runs. For the same reason, our method did not fare as well in locating faulty assignments. Since we report only branches in the bug report, the programmer has to follow dependencies from these branches to the faulty assignment – thereby reducing the score of our bug report. In presence of "missing code" errors, our method may report branch statements on which missed code would have been (transitively) control dependent.

## 5.2   Size of Bug Report

In the above experiments, we used scores to measure the quality of bug report according to the evaluation framework in Section 4.2. *The reader should note that there is a fundamental difference between the bug report statements and the statements that a programmer should inspect for debugging according to the evaluation framework.* Clearly, measuring the amount of code to be inspected for debugging (captured by the bug report score) is important. However, we feel that measuring the bug report size is also important. If the programmer is overwhelmed with a voluminous bug report (*e.g.* 50 statements for a 500 line program), he/she may not even get to the stage of identifying which code to inspect using the bug report.

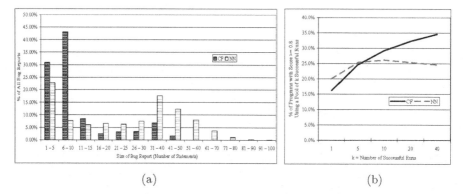

(a)                                    (b)

**Fig. 3.** (a) Size of bug report and (b) Impact of successful run pool-size

Figure 3(a) shows sizes of bug reports produced by our method and NN method. We can see the bug reports produced by our method are relatively small. For example, more than 80% (40%) of bug reports in all the 130 faulty programs contained less than 15 statements using our method (NN method). Considering that programs in the Siemens suite are relatively small, reports with more than 15 statements may be too voluminous. The choice of the cutoff number 15 is not crucial as can be seen in Figure 3(a); similar trends are observed for any small cut-off number on the bug report size.

Recall from Table 2(a) that our method and NN method produced roughly the same scores – 37 % (31 %) of all the 130 programs produced a score of 0.8 or more with our (NN) method. However, if we study these buggy programs which produced a high score (of 0.8 or more) with the two methods — we see that bug report in 83% of them had less than 15 statements for our method, compared to only 28% for the NN method.

## 5.3   Size of Successful Run Pool

In the Siemens suite, each faulty program has a large set of test inputs (1000 – 5000). The successful run pool is constructed out of these inputs. How many successful runs are required for the programmer to make a decent choice of successful run? We study this in the following.

Given a program $P$, we selected the failing run $\pi_f$ whose score $score(\pi_f)$ (using both our method and NN method) is closest to the score of the program $pgm\_score(P)$) (again using both our and NN methods). The selected failing run $\pi_f$ was used to study both our method and the NN method. We did not conduct experiments w.r.t. all failing runs because it was too expensive.

Next, for every successful run $\pi_s$ in the available pool of the Siemens suite, we computed the difference between $\pi_f$ and $\pi_s$, generated a bug report by comparing $\pi_f$ and $\pi_s$, and computed $score(\pi_f, \pi_s)$ (refer Equation (1)). After all successful runs were processed, their differences were sorted in ascending order. Let $\pi_i$ be the successful run with $i$th smallest difference w.r.t. $\pi_f$. The *parameterized mean score* of a faulty program $P$ for a successful run pool-size of $k$ is:

$$par\_score(P, k) = \sum_{i=1}^{n} score(\pi_f, \pi_i) \cdot p(i, k) \qquad p(i, k) = \frac{^{n-i}C_{k-1}}{^{n}C_k}$$

where $\pi_f$ is the failing run chosen in $P$ as mentioned above, $n$ is the number of available successful runs in Siemens suite, and $p(i, k)$ is defined above. Here $^{n}C_k$ denotes a well-known quantity — the number of ways of choosing $k$ items from $n$ distinguishable items. Clearly, $p(i, k)$ denotes the probability that the $i$th-closest successful run of the failing run is chosen as the nearest successful run of a failing run from a pool of $k$ different successful runs. Hence $par\_score(P, k)$ captures the statistical expectation of the score obtained for failing run $\pi_f$ using any pool of $k$ successful runs. Calculating the parameterized mean score $par\_score(P, k)$ allows us to avoid exhaustively enumerating the score of $P$ for different successful run pools of size $k$.

Figure 3(b) presents the parameterized mean scores for different values of $k$, the successful run pool size. We see that both our method and NN method made a decent choice of successful run from a pool of 5 runs and thereby achieved a score of at least 0.8 in 25% of the 130 faulty programs. However, as the pool size increases to 40, our method achieved a score of 0.8 or more for larger number of faulty programs (for 35% of faulty programs). This is not the case for the NN method, which in fact needed even larger pool sizes.

## 5.4   Threats to Validity

In our experiments, we used the evaluation framework of Section 4.2 to measure the quality of bug report. However, the score computed by the framework of Section 4.2 may not accurately capture the human efforts for fault localization in practice. First, the framework assumes that the programmer can find the error when he/she reads the erroneous statements. This assumption may not hold for non-trivial bugs, where the programmer has to analyze program states. Secondly, the evaluation framework requires the programmer to perform pure breadth-first search for fault localization starting from statements in the bug report. However, the programmer usually has some understanding of the buggy program, and he/she can prune some irrelevant statements from bug report.

There are also threats to the validity of the study on successful run pool size. In this experiment, we chose one failing run for each faulty program, instead of studying all failing runs. Thus, if we chose some other failing run, the *parameterized mean score* for a pool of $k$ successful runs may change. We expect that such changes will not be significant (though it is possible), because the variances w.r.t. all failing runs were small for most faulty programs.

# 6    Experience and Discussion

In this paper, we present a control flow based difference metric to compare execution runs. This difference metric can be used to choose a successful run from a pool of program inputs, and compare the given failing run with the chosen successful run for fault localization. Our experiments with the Siemens suite indicate that our difference metric produces bug reports which are small in size and effective in fault localization.

One important issue in a method like ours is the choice of the successful run pool. In the last section, we reported experiments to measure the required size of the successful run pool. However, even for a given pool-size many choices of the pool are possible. So, how do we construct the pool? There are two solutions to this problem. One possibility is to have a pre-defined large set of program inputs *Inp*; this set of test-cases might have been generated using some notion of coverage. Now given a failing run, we find out which of the inputs in *Inp* produces a successful run — thereby getting a pool of successful runs. In our experiments with the Siemens suite, we followed this approach by using the pre-defined pool of inputs provided with each benchmark. Another way of constructing the successful run pool is to use the input for the given failing run. We can slightly perturb this failing input to generate a set of program inputs; we then classify which of these perturbed inputs produce a successful run — thereby getting a pool of successful runs. The main drawback of this approach is that it relies too much on the programmer's intuition in deciding what to perturb in the failing input. Although automatic techniques such as Delta Debugging [19] exist, they cannot be used for arbitrary programs. This is because these approaches construct an input by removing part of the erroneous input. *This is indeed suitable for debugging programs like compilers, web-browsers — where the program input is a large file. However, for other programs* (e.g. *programs with integer inputs*) *this approach may be problematic.*

We now conclude the paper by sharing some experience in this regard that we gained by debugging a widely used Unix utility – the *grep* program. The correct version of *grep* has 13,286 lines, without header files. The *grep* program searches text files for a pattern and prints all lines that contain that pattern. Faulty versions of the *grep* program and test cases are provided at [16]. For the sake of illustrating our point about the successful run pool, here we only report our experience in

```
1.   char ch[2];
2.   ch[0] = c;
3.   ch[1] = '\0';
4.   if (strcoll (ch, lo) <= 0 && strcoll (hi, ch) <= 0)
5.   { ...
```

**Fig. 4.** Fragment of a faulty version of the *grep* program

debugging a particular failing run of a particular buggy version. Figure 4 presents a faulty version of **grep**, where the branch in line 4 should be if (strcoll (lo, ch) <= 0 && strcoll (ch, hi) <= 0). We consider the failing run corresponding to the input grep -G '[1-5\]' grep1.dat. This failing run contains 800,738 statement instances. This run did not return all lines which contain numbers between 1 and 5 in the grep1.dat file — an observable error.

When we ran our debugging method against 35 selected successful runs from the given test inputs of *grep* (provided in [16]) we got a bug report containing 11 statements. A line very close to the faulty branch statement in Figure 4 was included in the report; the score of the bug report is 0.977. This means that programmer needs inspecting about 100 lines in the worst case, considering that the *grep* program has many blank lines. In practice, some statements contained in the bug report may be pruned, depending on programmer's understanding of the program. This will lead to ever fewer statements for inspection.

On the other hand, if we perturb the failing input to get various sub-intervals of [1-5] as the first argument of *grep*, only the following five are encountered as successful inputs.

$$\text{grep} - \text{G } '[i - i\backslash]' \text{ grep1.dat} \qquad i \in \{1, 2, 3, 4, 5\}$$

When we applied our debugging method to this pool of five successful runs we observed the following. (1) Depending on the choice of the successful run, there was substantial variation in the bug reports and their scores (the score varied from 0.288 – 0.998). Thus choosing a successful run seems to be important even if the successful run pool is manually generated using programmer's intuition. (2) The difference corresponding to the chosen successful run produced a bug report of 15 statements, which included the buggy statement (thereby obtaining a nearly perfect score 0.998).

Thus, the score was slightly better than the score produced using the test input pool provided with the *grep* program. However, significant intuition was needed to manually construct the successful input pool for a specific failing run. In practice, we feel that the choice of successful run will always benefit from the programmer's intuition. However fault localization methods — such as the one described in this paper — can substantially increase the degree of automation in this debugging task.

*Future Work.* In terms of future work, we note that our prototype implementation currently has limitations w.r.t. tracing overheads. Since our difference metric uses more information (traces of the failing and successful runs) than the NN method (which uses sets of statements in the two runs), therefore the issue of tracing overheads becomes important. Indeed, it was costly to collect and store execution traces using our prototype. To make our method scalable to large programs, sophisticated instrumentation techniques (*e.g.* [8]) need to be employed. We are currently working in this direction.

## Acknowledgments

This work was partially supported by a Public Sector Research Grant from Agency of Science Technology and Research (A*STAR), Singapore.

## References

1. T. Ball, M. Naik, and S. K. Rajamani. From symptom to cause: localizing errors in counterexample traces. In *ACM SIGPLAN-SIGACT symposium on Principles of programming languages (POPL)*, pages 97–105, 2003.
2. S. Chaki, A. Groce, and O. Strichman. Explaining abstract counterexamples. In *ACM SIGSOFT Symp. on the Foundations of Software Engg. (FSE)*, 2004.
3. H. Cleve and A. Zeller. Locating causes of program failures. In *ACM/IEEE International Conference on Software Engineering (ICSE)*, 2005.
4. J. Ferrante, K.J. Ottenstein, and J.D. Warren. The program dependence graph and its use in optimization. *ACM Transactions on Programming Languages and Systems*, 9(3):319–349, 1987.
5. A. Groce. Error explanation with distance metrics. In *Tools and Algorithms for the Construction and Analysis of Systems (TACAS)*, pages 108–122, 2004.
6. M. Hutchins, H. Foster, T. Goradia, and T. Ostrand. Experiments on the effectiveness of dataflow- and controlflow-based test adequacy criteria. In *ACM/IEEE International Conference on Software Engineering (ICSE)*, pages 191–200, 1994.
7. J. A. Jones, M. J. Harrold, and J. Stasko. Visualization of test information to assist fault localization. In *ACM/IEEE International Conference on Software Engineering (ICSE)*, pages 467–477, 2002.
8. J. R. Larus. Whole program paths. In *ACM SIGPLAN Conference on Programming Language Design and Implementation (PLDI)*, pages 259–269, 1999.
9. B. Liblit, A. Aiken, A. Zheng, and M. I. Jordan. Bug isolation via remote program sampling. In *ACM SIGPLAN Conference on Programming Language Design and Implementation (PLDI)*, 2003.
10. B. Liblit, M. Naik, A. Zheng, A. Aiken, and M. Jordan. Scalable statistical bug isolation. In *ACM SIGPLAN Conference on Programming Language Design and Implementation (PLDI)*, 2005.
11. B. Pytlik, M. Renieris, S. Krishnamurthi, and S. P. Reiss. Automated fault localization using potential invariants. *CoRR*, cs.SE/0310040, Oct, 2003.
12. M. Renieris and S. P. Reiss. Fault localization with nearest neighbor queries. In *Automated Software Engineering (ASE)*, pages 30–39, 2003.
13. T. W. Reps, T. Ball, M. Das, and J. R. Larus. The use of program profiling for software maintenance with applications to the year 2000 problem. In *ACM SIGSOFT Symp. on the Foundations of Software Engg. (FSE)*, 1997.

14. G. Rothermel and M. J. Harrold. Empirical studies of a safe regression test selection technique. *IEEE Transactions on Software Engineering*, 24, 1998.
15. J. Ruthruff, E. Creswick, M. Burnett, C. Cook, S. Prabhakararao, M. Fisher II, and M. Main. End-user software visualizations for fault localization. In *ACM Symposium on Software Visualization*, pages 123–132, 2003.
16. http://www.cse.unl.edu/~galileo/sir.
17. T. Wang and A. Roychoudhury. Automated path generation for software fault localization. In *ACM/IEEE International Conference on Automated Software Engineering (ASE)*, pages 347–351, 2005.
18. A. Zeller. Isolating cause-effect chains from computer programs. In *ACM SIGSOFT Symposium on the Foundations of Software Engineering (FSE)*, pages 1–10, 2002.
19. A. Zeller and R. Hildebrandt. Simplifying and isolating failure-inducing input. *IEEE Transactions on Software Engineering*, 28, 2002.

# Demonstration: On-Line Visualization and Analysis of Real-Time Systems with TuningFork

David F. Bacon[1], Perry Cheng[1], Daniel Frampton[2],
David Grove[1], Matthias Hauswirth[3], and V.T. Rajan[1]

[1] IBM T.J. Watson Research Center
[2] Department of Computer Science, The Australian National University
[3] Università della Svizzera Italiana

**Abstract.** TuningFork is an online, scriptable data visualization and analysis tool that supports the development and continuous monitoring of real-time systems. While TuningFork was originally designed and tested for use with a particular real-time Java Virtual Machine, the architecture has been designed from the ground up for extensibility by leveraging the Eclipse plug-in architecture. This allows different client programs to design custom data formats, new visualization and analysis components, and new export formats. The TuningFork views allow the visualization of data from time scales of microseconds to minutes, enabling rapid understanding and analysis of system behavior.

## 1 Introduction

When designing and developing system software of significant complexity, meeting performance goals is as important and challenging as correctness. In the case of a real-time system, coarse-grained performance characteristics such as overall throughput alone are not enough to verify responsiveness or determine the causes of failure. The ability to measure and visualize fine-grained events is necessary for determining correctness and analyzing why the system misbehaved.

The large volume of data often generated by these systems is hard to understand without visualization. In production systems where downtime is unacceptable, online monitoring and analysis can be useful for problem determination and resolution. During development, a real-time system must be tested for performance regression automatically and a useful analysis tool must also support scripting commands.

In the accompanying presentation we will demonstrate *TuningFork*, an online, scriptable, and re-configurable data visualization and analysis tool for the development and continuous monitoring of real-time systems. TuningFork is an Eclipse plug-in using the Rich Client Platform (described at `www.eclipse.org`), and itself exports a plug-in architecture that allows user-defined data stream formats, stream filters, and visualizations. Because TuningFork is still under rapid development, it is not yet available for download.

TuningFork is a combination of known and novel techniques and visualizations, but it is the whole that is greater than the sum of the parts. TuningFork's

A. Mycroft and A. Zeller (Eds.): CC 2006, LNCS 3923, pp. 96–100, 2006.

features include a real-time centered design that adapts to data loss and event reordering due to resource constraints in the traced system, the ability to handle very large volumes of data online with a running system, an adaptive data summarization framework allowing even more past data to be viewed, the ability to play the data in forward and reverse, plugin-based extensibility of trace formats and views, a composable data stream abstraction that allows creation of new synthetic events, and the ability to run the same system in batch mode with a scripting language.

Novel views include the "oscilloscope" view that presents interval data in a sequence of "time strips". With a large LCD display, this allows 2-3 seconds of data to be visualized at $10\mu s$ resolution, or 20-30 seconds of data at 10ms resolution, with user-selectable continuously variable time scales. When play mode is off, data can be viewed down to the nanosecond scale. Furthermore, a statistical superimposition facility allows the overall behavior of huge amounts of periodic high-resolution data to be visualized (hence the oscilloscope analogy).

The demonstration will show how TuningFork is used to diagnose run-time anomalies in real-time behavior in Metronome, our real-time garbage collector for Java implemented in the IBM J9 virtual machine product. The various views allow the identification of a failure to meet a high-level response-time specification using a time-strip animation, followed by identification of the cause using a histogram which categorizes different atomic sections of the garbage collector, and culminating in the identification of the precise point of failure in the execution of the program using the oscilloscope view. We will also show how to evaluate memory policy using a spatial view that shows the physical or logical state of the heap.

## 2    Architecture

At the high level, TuningFork's architecture consists of a thin client-side layer which transmits application or JVM events and the server-side TuningFork visualization application which we simply call TuningFork. The client is instrumented at various points to collect special information and send the data in an application-specific *feed* to TuningFork via a socket or to a file for post-mortem analysis. Although our primary client of TuningFork is a JVM, any system that emits trace files in the specified format is a suitable target for TuningFork.

At the high-level, the feed is broken into *chunks* which are the units of network transmission to TuningFork. Certain initial chunks describe overall properties as well as the format of the rest of the feed. The event chunks are the most interesting and constitute the bulk of the feed. Each event chunk includes a chunk identifier so that TuningFork can obtain the appropriate interpreter plug-in for that application. Since the client application may be multi-threaded, the data feed is broken into feedlets and each event chunk contains data only from one feedlet.

Because TuningFork is fundamentally a time-based tool, all events have a time stamp, typically the value of a cycle counter which on current architectures provides nanosecond-scale resolution. In order to present a globally time-ordered view of events to the rest of TuningFork, data from different feeds are merged into a single global feed by making data at a certain time visible only after all feeds have reached that point in time.

Because TuningFork is built on top of the Eclipse Rich Client Platform, it is simple for the application developer to export application-specific portions such as an *event chunk interpreter* to TuningFork via the plug-in architecture. The application also can export *filters* which convert events to non-application-specific streams. These streams can then be composed into figures for visualization.

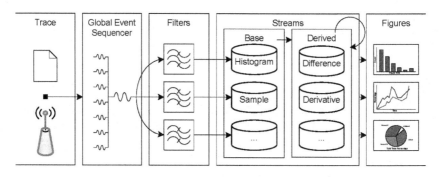

**Fig. 1.** TuningFork Architecture

## 2.1 Streams

In a real-time system, many quantities of interest are time-series data. Because TuningFork can be used to monitor an online system or large post-mortem trace files, the volume of data will generally exceed the memory capacities of Tuning-Fork. The traditional method of implementing a ring buffer is simple but has the disadvantage of losing data that is older than the size of the buffer, making diagnosis of certain problems difficult and understanding of long-term trends impossible. In addition, computation and display of data streams is complicated by requiring a constant awareness of this possibiliy.

This problem is greatly reduced by continuing to use a stream abstraction so that a stream appears to be a function whose domain is an ever-increasing time range and whose range is dependent on the particular stream. For example, a stream representing memory usage would map time values to bytes while a stream representing interrupt handler execution would map to time intervals. However, depending on memory pressure, the precision of older data may be continuously degraded by aggregated data into a collection of statistics.

The functional aspect of streams simplifies the computational model by allowing standard mathematical functions like addition, differentiation, and smoothing via convolution. Streams are initially created by applying filters to the events that enter the system. For example, a "used memory" filter would generate pairs of values $(t, m)$ which are used to create the used memory stream which logically consists of the function $memory(t)$ and the range $[t_{start}, t_{end}]$. A new stream, *allocation rate*, can be created by applying the differentiation filter to the "used memory" stream.

Certain operators will take operand streams of different types. For example, one can take a value stream (e.g. used memory) and a time interval stream (e.g. time intervals when the garbage collector is off) and create a value stream which shows only used memory when the garbage collector is off.

Other base types include categories which is useful for understanding the relationship of a set of quantities. For example, we might have a categry-value stream which would show the duration of each GC pause and the type of activity the colletor was performing in that time interval. A histogram of such a stream would then show not only the average and maximum pause time but also what the collector was doing during those pauses.

## 2.2 Figures

At the heart of TuningFork are the visualization components, called *figures*. Figures are responsible for taking streams of data and displaying them to the user. The figure architecture has been designed for extensibility, device-independent rendering, and high performance to allow the display of live data feeds with high data rates.

Visualizations are typically composed of several common reused subcomponents. Histograms, axes, legends, and time series plots may occur many times within different visualizations, albeit with minor differences in display characteristics. This approach is important because of our goal of allowing the user to extend the system by plugging in custom views.

In order to facilitate the rapid development of new visualization components, TuningFork introduces two key design features: a high-level drawing interface tailored to on-line visualization, and *painters*. The high level interface allows device-independent drawing; we currently have both an SWT implementation for the user interface, and a PDF implementation for printing functionality. The programming interface includes simple painting functionality for basic shapes. Painters build on top of this simple interface to provide more complex, data-dependent visualization components such as axes, histograms, and time series plots.

Within this design framework, the role of a figure becomes to divide the visualization display into different areas, determine the precise data that needs to be drawn, and delegate drawing to various painter implementations. Additionally, the figure contains all state regarding the display settings for the visualization component. This can be accessed both through a host eclipse view, and via the programmatic *conductor* interface.

## 2.3 Conductor

The interactive visualization and analysis of TuningFork is very powerful. However, there is also a need for automated analysis, in particular for such tasks as regression testing where the results of the analysis must be fed into automated tools that report performance anomalies and automatically create work items in the product development database.

Such text-based analyses are typically written as entirely separate tools. However, the modular stream processing, filtering, and transformation facilities in TuningFork are extremely useful for building such analyses. In order to minimize code duplication, facilitate the creation of automated analyses, and to provide a more productive environment for power users, TuningFork includes the *conductor* – a lightweight scripting environment.

It is possible to perform nearly all visualization operations from within the conductor, such as connecting to traces, opening figures, performing analysis, and exporting PDF files. Additionally, due to the pluggable nature of the application, it is possible to run the conductor outside of the graphical user interface, an important capability for automated testing. This allows the creation of tools produce purely textual results for use in larger programmatic systems, and for the creation of visualizations of exceptional conditions that can be uploaded into a web-based graphical database.

## 3   Comparisons and Conclusions

TuningFork has drawn on many sources of inspiration (space constraints unfortunately do not permit formal citations), particularly the work of Tufte on visual display of quantitative information. It is perhaps most similar to the *PV Program Visualizer* (Kimmelman et al), which can visualize very large event traces without loading the complete trace into memory. It provides an animated visualization of the information in a sliding window over the trace. PV supports temporal vertical profiling, integrating information from hardware, operating system, native libraries and native applications. It mainly focuses on visualizing events, states, and the corresponding source code, but can also visualize the value of a metric over time.

Much prior visualization work has focused on parallel systems and their complex behavior, including Paradyn (Miller et al), Jumpshot (Zaki et al), Pablo (Reed et al), and others. Real-time behavior presents its own unique challenges, but shared with such systems a need to coordinate the time scales of many independent parts running on potentially distributed or unsynchronized clocks.

TuningFork is a comprehensive tool for visualization and analysis tool for real-time systems. TuningFork allows visualization of real-time events as they are happening, and provides views that allow data to be visualized across a very wide range of time scales, while still providing a high degree of resolution. Our experience has shown that the broad range of visualization capability promotes a deep understanding of the detailed behavior of real-time systems at both macro and micro time-scales.

# Data-Flow Analysis as Model Checking Within the jABC

Anna-Lena Lamprecht[1], Tiziana Margaria[1], and Bernhard Steffen[2]

[1] Service Engineering for Distributed Systems, Universität Göttingen, Germany
alamprec@stud.informatik.uni-goettingen.de, margaria@cs.uni-goettingen.de
[2] Chair of Programming Systems, Universität Dortmund, Germany
steffen@cs.uni-dortmund.de

**Abstract.** This paper describes how the jABC, a generic framework for library-based program development, and two of its plugins - the Model Checker and a flow graph converter - form a framework for intraprocedural data-flow analysis via model checking. Based on functionalities provided by the Soot program analysis platform, the converter generates graph structures from Java classes. Data flow analyses are then expressed as formulas in the modal $\mu$-calculus. Executing the analysis is carried out by checking the validity of the formulas on the flow graph.

The tool demonstration will illustrate the interplay of the involved components, which elegantly provides a fully integrated implementation of Data-Flow Analysis as Model Checking in a software development environment.

## 1 Introduction

Static program analysis [8, 3, 1] aims at reliably approximating information about the actual run-time behavior of programs. It consists of two major steps: control-flow analysis, mainly used to generate a control flow graph that is used for the next step, and data-flow analysis (DFA), for collecting information about the program that might be of use for optimization or validation. Classical data-flow analyses use iterative algorithms, which compute a particular property for a given program, and can be characterized as follows [11, 10]:

DFA-algorithm for a property :
programs $\rightarrow$ program points satisfying the property

Model checking [2, 6], a technique for the automatic identification of states in a finite system that satisfy a specific modal or temporal formula, can be used for DFA with appropriate input [11, 10]:

model checker:
modal formulas $\times$ model $\rightarrow$ states satisfying the argument formula

Thus, if we have a model checker at our disposal and want to check a new program property, specifying a new DFA simply means writing a new formula.

A. Mycroft and A. Zeller (Eds.): CC 2006, LNCS 3923, pp. 101–104, 2006.

This is significantly different from traditional DFA specifications in terms of DFA frameworks or equational systems, as it allows to directly describe the desired outcome as temporal formula, rather than the way how it may be computed (in terms of transfer functions and the like).

During the tool demonstration we will illustrate the interplay of the involved components, which elegantly provides a fully integrated implementation of Data-Flow Analysis as Model Checking (DFA-MC) in a software development environment.

## 2   Data-Flow Analysis Via Model Checking

The connection between data-flow analysis and model checking described above implies what is required for DFA-MC [10, 11]: instead of programs we need models of programs, and instead of different DFA-algorithms for different properties we need a model checker and different modal formulas.

*From Programs to Program Models.* Slight variants of Kripke transition systems [6] work well for modeling sequential imperative programs for data flow analysis purposes, as they are able to concisely express the implied predicate transformer scheme [10, 11, 9].

Two variants are available in our framework. The first is closely related to the classical control flow graphs (CFGs), i.e. the nodes of the graph structure represent the statements and the predicates, while the edges represent the control flow (conditional or unconditional branching). The second, which we will use during our demonstration, is that the statements are pushed from the nodes into the outgoing edges. Thus, nodes express the predicates or results of the considered analysis, and edges labelled with the statements express the nodes' interdependencies. Pushing the statements downwards (i.e. into the outgoing edges), like it is done here, results in a *precondition* model.

Formally, a precondition program model $P$ is a quintuple $(S, Act, \rightarrow, B, \lambda)$, where

1. $S$ is a finite set of nodes or program states.
2. $Act$ is a set of actions (i.e. the possible statements of the programming language).
3. $\rightarrow \subseteq S \times Act \times S$ is a set of labeled transitions, which define the control flow of $P$.
4. $B$ is a set of atomic propositions.
5. $\lambda$ is a function $\lambda : S \rightarrow 2^B$ that labels states with subsets of $B$.

Due to the similarities between control flow graphs and these program models, the latter can be generated analogously to the former. As we will see later, our framework generates its models directly from control flow graphs.

*How to write Modal Specifications.* In contrast to traditional DFA specifications in terms of DFA frameworks or equational systems, which specify *how* a certain information about the program is computed (how specifications), DFA specifications via temporal formulas allow us to directly describe *what* we want to compute (what specifications). E.g., one describes a dead variable analysis directly as an analysis, which checks for a variable whether it is guaranteed to be redefined before any future use, rather than as a propagation of values keeping track of usage information (see [10, 11, 9] for details). This does not only simply the specification of new DFAs, but also simplifies the corresponding correctness and completeness proofs. Formally, these DFA specifications can intuitively be written in variations of CTL or in the modal mu calculus ([2]).

## 3   The jABC Framework

The Java-based *jABC* picks up the principles that have already been used in the C++-based Agent Building Center (ABC) since 1993 [4] and combines them with new ideas. The jABC is a commercial product as well as a student experimentation platform [7].

The typcial feature of the jABC framework is the usage of a graphical, high-level programming layer, where hierarchical directed graphs can be constructed from special components, called SIBs (Service Independent Building Blocks), that represent a unit of source code encoding a particular functionality. It is possible to define what programs do and in what order just by building such graphs from SIBs. Thus, an application designer does not necessarily have to have knowledge about "real" programming, provided some programming experts have developed an appropriate set of SIBs before.

Several plugins and extensions are available. Three of them, that form the main constituents of DFA-MC framework, are

- the **Model Checker**, which we will consider as a black box in the following, just as typical users of our method do,
- the **UnitGraph2SibGraph** plugin, which allows us to generate SIB-Graphs from Java-programs based on Soot functionality. Soot creates control flow graphs from Java source code, which can then be enriched by fetching information from the nodes of the CFGs in order to generate SIBGraphs, the input format for the Model Checker.
- the **Formula Builder**, which supports the convenient specification of temporal formulas. In particular, it supports the high-level specification of temporal properties, which are then translated into the mu-calculus.

Based on these ingredients, we were able to fully integrate the Data-Flow Analysis as Model Checking framework in the jABC software development environment. In this application of the jABC, SIBs are used in a particularly fine-granular form: we use a SIB per Jimple statement.

## 4   Conclusion

We illustrated our framework for the intraprocedural data-flow analysis of Java programs by means of model checking. Characteristic for our approach was the underlying framework architecture of the jABC which allowed us to modularly realize the required functionality.

Currently, each formula has to be checked separately (including the adaption of the parameters by hand), making the analysis process quite arduous. We are therefore planning to develop a bit-vector functionality for the model checking plugin, and we are in the course of extending the model checker plugin to capture pushdown systems, which would directly provide us with the power of interprocedural analysis.

There are other plugins and extensions of the jABC which can be applied in the context of our DFA-MC framework. One example is the *jETI* (Java Electronic Tool Integration Platform) System [5], which can enable the framework to be executed remotely.

**Acknowledgements.** Many thanks to Marco Bakera, Clemens Renner and Marc Njoku for programming and technical support.

# References

1. A. Aho and J. Ullman. *Principles of Compiler Design.*, volume 3. Addison-Wesley, 1979.
2. E. Clarke, O. Grumberg, and D. Peled. *Model Checking.*, volume 3. The MIT Press, 2001.
3. M. Hecht. *Flow Analysis of Computer Programs (Programming Languages Ser. Volume5).* Elsevier Science Ltd, 1977.
4. T. Margaria. Components, features, and agents in the abc. In M. Ryan, J. Meyer, and H. Ehrich, editors, *Objects, Agents, and Features*, volume 2975 of *Lecture Notes in Computer Science*, pages 154–174. Springer, 2003.
5. T. Margaria, R. Nagel, and B. Steffen. jeti: A tool for remote tool integration. In N. Halbwachs and L. Zuck, editors, *TACAS*, volume 3440 of *Lecture Notes in Computer Science*, pages 557–562. Springer, 2005.
6. M. Müller-Olm, D. Schmidt, and B. Steffen. Model-checking: A tutorial introduction. In A. Cortesi and G. Filé, editors, *SAS*, volume 1694 of *Lecture Notes in Computer Science*, pages 330–354. Springer, 1999.
7. R. Nagel. Java abc framework. http://jabc.cs.uni-dortmund.de, July 2005.
8. F. Nielson, H. Nielson, and C. Hankin. *Principles of Program Analysis.* Springer, 1999.
9. D. Schmidt and B. Steffen. Program analysis *as* model checking of abstract interpretations. In G. Levi, editor, *SAS*, volume 1503 of *Lecture Notes in Computer Science*, pages 351–380. Springer, 1998.
10. B. Steffen. Data flow analysis as model checking. In T. Ito and A. Meyer, editors, *TACS*, volume 526 of *Lecture Notes in Computer Science*, pages 346–365. Springer, 1991.
11. B. Steffen. Generating data flow analysis algorithms from modal specifications. *Sci. Comput. Program.*, 21(2):115–139, 1993.

# The CGiS Compiler—A Tool Demonstration

Philipp Lucas*, Nicolas Fritz*, and Reinhard Wilhelm

Compiler Design Lab, Saarland University, Saarbrücken, Germany
{phlucas, cage, wilhelm}@cs.uni-sb.de

**Abstract.** The CGiS programming language is designed to open up the parallel performance possibilities of graphics processing units (*GPUs*) to general purpose programmers. This tool demonstration paper sums up the ideas behind CGiS and the compiler framework and shows its usage.

## 1 Introduction

Graphics processing units (*GPUs*), the processors used by standard graphics hardware in PCs, underwent a fast and incessant development in the past few years. Designed to execute small programs determining the pixel colours in an image, they make use of parallel execution units. Such programs can also be used for non-graphics related general purpose programming on GPUs (*GPGPU*) [6].

Scientists have developed various parallel algorithms on GPUs and experienced performance gains for several kinds of algorithms with high algebraic density. But nearly all of such applications were implemented using the GPU's assembly language or languages with a very low level of hardware abstraction, or the programmer had to interact with the graphics API to program the GPU. Recently more general purpose programming languages for GPUs have emerged (BROOK for GPUs, SH, CGiS [1, 8, 4]). In this tool demonstration paper we introduce GPGPU and the compiler for our language, CGiS.

In Section 2, we briefly describe GPUs as targets for general purpose programming. In Section 3, we describe the programming language and the usage of CGiS. Section 4 gives an outlook into future development.

## 2 GPUs

We give a very short introduction without using the terminology of the graphics world. For further information on features of current GPUs, the reader should consult the documentation of APIs [9, 12] or homepages of vendors (ATI, NVIDIA, 3Dlabs).

Because of their legacy, GPUs have a number of features distinguishing them from usual CPUs. They are built around a pipeline model of graphics operations, eventually transforming geometry data into screen pixels. The latter part of the pipeline, which works on single pixels, is implemented with parallel execution

---

* Supported by DFG grant WI 576/10-3.

A. Mycroft and A. Zeller (Eds.): CC 2006, LNCS 3923, pp. 105–108, 2006.

pipelines, which have become programmable in recent years. The processor provides the usual arithmetical instructions on single-precision floating-point four-vectors and some special computer graphics instructions. It is this part with programmable, relatively simple and slow but parallel processing units[1] that is used in general purpose programming. A wide variety of applications have been ported to GPUs, from image synthesis [10] and linear algebra [7] to database operations [5] and cryptography [2].[2]

The main restrictions of GPUs lie in the memory model and the support for control flow. Sections of memory are used either for reading or for writing during the execution of a program. This can be switched by the controlling application after a GPU program (hereafter: *kernel*) has completed its execution, or the data have to be copied from write-memory into read-memory. Thus, only a streaming kind of execution is possible. Newer GPUs offer restricted dynamic control flow, whereas only straight-line control flow was available before. The restriction concerns the nesting level of conditionals and the maximal iteration count of loops, which are bounded.[3] In general, only naturally parallel algorithms without complex control flow can benefit from GPUs; but those which can take advantage of the massive raw floating point power can outperform current CPUs.

The restrictions of this memory model and the number of outputs pose the main difficulties to a compiler writer. Only in the newest generation of NVIDIA's GPUs, each of the programs running in parallel can output more than one four-vector (upto four such vectors). Functions have to be split at appropriate points, such that only few values need to be passed between the different kernels [3, 11]. Also, the severe limits on the control flow (if supported it at all) pose a difficulty to compilers. But it is exactly this combination of restricted features with powerful capabilities which makes high-level GPU languages desirable.

# 3    CGiS

A CGiS program [4] describes the computation as a sequence of parallel executions of functions over streams of data, where each function operates on a single element of each stream. Figure 1 gives an example of the general layout of a CGiS program. More elaborate examples and a detailed explanation can be found in [4].

The usage of CGiS is illustrated in Figure 2. The programmer writes the code to be executed on the GPU in CGiS. The compiler generates the kernels and directing C++ code for the platform independent graphics API OpenGL [12], as well as all necessary code to switch between kernels, to realign the streams and to transfer data. The user interfaces with the generated code by giving pointers to input data, starting the computation and receiving the output data.

---

[1] For example, the current NVIDIA chip *GeForce 7800* features 24 lanes at about 400 MHz and a memory bandwidth of more than 38 GB/s to 256 MB RAM.

[2] See [6] for pointers to other applications.

[3] To enable the programer to write general loops in CGiS, the language allows to annotate loops with a guaranteed *maximal* number of iterations.

```
PROGRAM vector_add;
INTERFACE // Declare streams.
extern inout float4 in_out_data<_>;
extern in float4 in_data<_>;
CODE // Declare element functions.
function add(in float4 a, in float4 b, out float4 c){
    c = a + b;
}
CONTROL // Perform parallel computation on streams.
forall(float4 io in in_out_data; float4 i in in_data){
    add(io,i,io);
}
```

**Fig. 1.** A small CGiS program, computing the sum of two vectors of unspecified length

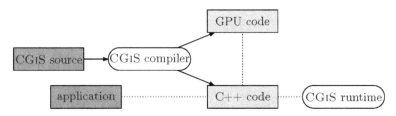

**Fig. 2.** Basic usage pattern of CGiS. Dotted lines denote linkage, solid arrows denote in- or output. The left rectangles denote user-provided sources, the other rectangles are the output of the CGiS compiler. The ellipses stand for the CGiS base system components. There is no direct connection between the application and the GPU.

The GPU is invisible to the programmer and to the end user. The programmer interacts only with the CGiS runtime system. For the user, the use of the GPU is invisible, because the program computes in off-screen memory space.

With each GPU generation, new features become available. The compiler generates code using features of a desired generation. Thus, the GPU code needs a GPU of the chosen kind or a newer model.[4] Currently, the main focus of the CGiS compiler is on the NV30 generation of GPUs. We have begun upgrading our compiler to the newer, more powerful NV40 generation.

The generated C++ code is independent of operating system or windowing system. All such differences are either abstracted away in the runtime library of CGiS (such as the procedure of creating an invisible window and an OpenGL context) or are part of OpenGL proper and thus in itself platform independent. Thus, the generated code can be compiled and run on any system with the runtime and an appropriately powerful GPU. Currently, the CGiS runtime is available for Windows and Linux (i386), though we expect it to be adaptable trivially to other systems with the Windows or X window model and OpenGL support. The main prerequisite for porting is the availability of current OpenGL

---

[4] The programmer may generate code for various GPU architectures, the best fitting of which is to be used at run-time of the application.

drivers. NVIDIA drivers are developed also for Solaris and FreeBSD on i386 and for other processors with Windows, Linux or MacOS.

## 4   Future Work

When the adaption to the NV40 architecture is completed, we will focus on the development of a general analysis and optimisation framework in the compiler. At present very few optimisations are implemented. Then we will develop other back-ends to support newer generations of GPUs. We also plan to create a general library for linear algebra functions and a visualisation framework.

## References

1. I. Buck, T. Foley, D. Horn, J. Sugerman, K. Fatahalian, M. Houston, and P. Hanrahan. Brook for GPUs: Stream computing on graphics hardware. In *Proceedings of SIGGRAPH*, 2004.
2. D. L. Cook, J. Ioannidis, A. D. Keromytis, and J. Luck. CryptoGraphics: Secret key cryptography using graphics cards. In *Proceedings of the RSA Conference*, pages 334–350, February 2005.
3. T. Foley, M. Houston, and P. Hanrahan. Efficient partitioning of fragment shaders for multiple-output hardware. In *Proceedings of Graphics Hardware*, August 2004.
4. N. Fritz, P. Lucas, and P. Slusallek. CGiS, a new language for data-parallel GPU programming. In B. Girod, H.-P. Seidel, and M. Magnor, editors, *Proceedings of "Vision, Modeling, and Visualization"*, pages 241–248, 2004.
5. N. K. Govindaraju, B. Lloyd, W. Wang, M. Lin, and D. Manocha. Fast computation of database operations using graphics processors. In *SIGMOD*, 2004.
6. General-purpose computation using graphics hardware. http://www.gpgpu.org, 2005.
7. J. Krüger and R. Westermann. Linear algebra operators for GPU implementation of numerical algorithms. In *Proceedings of SIGGRAPH*, 2003.
8. M. D. McCool, Z. Qin, and T. S. Popu. Shader metaprogramming. In *Eurographics Workshop on Graphics Hardware*. ACM, 2002. Revised version.
9. Microsoft. DirectX 9.0 C++ reference. http://msdn.microsoft.com/library/en-us/directx9_c/directx/graphics/reference/reference.asp, August 2005.
10. T. J. Purcell, C. Donner, M. Cammarano, H. W. Jensen, and P. Hanrahan. Photon mapping on programmable graphics hardware. In *Proceedings of the SIGGRAPH/Eurographics Workshop on Graphics Hardware*, 2003.
11. A. Riffel, A. E. Lefohn, K. Vidimce, M. Leone, and J. D. Owens. Mio: Fast multipass partitioning via priority-based instruction scheduling. In *Proceedings of Graphics Hardware*, August 2004.
12. M. Segal and K. Akeley. *The OpenGL Graphics System: A Specification (Version 2.0)*, 2004.

# Loop Transformations in the Ahead-of-Time Optimization of Java Bytecode

Simon Hammond and David Lacey

University of Warwick

**Abstract.** Loop optimizations such as loop unrolling, unfolding and invariant code motion have long been used in a wide variety of compilers to improve the running time of applications. In this paper we present a series of experimental results detailing the effect these techniques have on the running time of Java applications following ahead of time optimization.

We also detail the optimization tools and transformations developed for this paper which extend the SOOT framework discussed in a number of previous papers on the subject.

Our experimentation, conducted on the SciMark 2.0 benchmarking suite, demonstrates that when optimized using the techniques mentioned, Java applications can benefit from performance improvements of up to 20%.

We finish with a discussion of the results obtained, including results on how the optimizations affect JIT compilation and class size and proceed to argue that ahead-of-time loop unrolling and unfolding optimization may have a role to play in improving the performance of Java applications, particularly in scientific applications.

## 1 Introduction

Improving the running time of programs through the optimizing phase of a compiler is a well established practice with a long history of well developed techniques and tools.

The success of optimizing compilers depends heavily upon the architecture that the final object code will be run on and architectures have changed since initial work in the field. One aspect of this phenomenon is that hardware architecture has become more complex but another aspect, and the one of interest here, is that in many cases the object code of a compiler is bytecode that is to be run on virtual machines such as the Java Virtual Machine.

Optimizing compiler designers face a couple of new issues when the target architecture is a virtual machine. Firstly, there is the question of whether the interpretive layer will affect the effectiveness of the optimizations. Secondly, when using a virtual machine we have the opportunity to compile and optimize at run-time and indeed this is what modern *just in time* (JIT) compiling virtual machines do.

The fact that compilation and optimization can happen at run time naturally leads to new thinking in compiler design. Do we need to perform ahead of time

A. Mycroft and A. Zeller (Eds.): CC 2006, LNCS 3923, pp. 109–123, 2006.

optimizations at all? One could argue that all optimizations can be deferred to run time and this would make the initial compiler design much simpler. One added advantage of this approach is that we have more information around at run time (*e.g.* profiling information) which can help us. However, it can also be argued that the static analysis required for some optimizations is too expensive to perform at run-time and should be performed beforehand. Another argument is that the interpretive layer slows down the program so much that optimizing the code is not worth it and that if one really wants speed then one should compile down to native code anyway - so called "way ahead of time" compilation.

All these possibilities have led to a lack of interest in traditional optimization of bytecode and despite much discussion about what the optimization architecture should be there is an underlying question to address. It is the authors' opinion that the discussion would be better informed if the following question was answered:

> Do traditional ahead-of-time compiler optimizations applied to bytecode cause significant performance increasing in running-time when executed on current (optimizing) JVMs?

*i.e.* given the current state of the art in JITs, does optimizing the bytecode still help? Is it still relevant? This is the question that this paper contributes towards answering. It builds on earlier work (particularly that of the SOOT optimization framework) and Section 4 details this earlier work that contribute toward answering this question. This paper provides a fully detailed study into a selection of traditional loop optimizations and the conclusion of the paper can be summarized as:

- Traditional ahead of time loop optimizations (in particular, loop unfolding and unrolling) applied to Java bytecode increase the run-time performance of the tested benchmark programs by up to 20%, with an average increase of approximately 4-5%

In the rest of this paper, Section 2 will give the methodology and decisions made when performing our tests. The numerical results of the testing will be given in Section 3 along with an analysis of these results. Finally, Sections 4 and 5 give the background to and a summary of the paper respectively.

## 2    Optimizations, Methodology and Testing

The research presented here is an empirical study of optimization. It is essential to such an endeavor that we identify the parameters of the experiments we carry out. In this case we can identify four main factors that affect the results:

- The benchmark suite used for testing.
- The optimizations used.
- The underling hardware architecture.
- The Java Virtual Machine (JVM) that executes the bytecode.

Each of the following sub-sections will describe the approach we took when considering each of these factors.

## 2.1   The Benchmarks

For the purposes of experimentation we used two benchmarking suites. The first was the command line version of the SciMark 2.0 benchmarking suite [19]. The second was the SPECjvm98 suite of benchmarks [3].

Table 1. Benchmark Description

| Benchmark | Description |
|---|---|
| FFT | Performs a one-dimensional forward transform of 4000 complex numbers. |
| SOR | Performs Jacobi Successive Over-relaxation on a 100x100 grid |
| Monte Carlo | Approximates the value of Pi through integration of a quarter circle |
| Sparse Matrix Multiplication | Performs a matrix multiplication of a 1000x1000 square matrix containing 5000 non-zero elements |
| LU | Computes the LU Factorization of a dense 100x100 matrix using partial pivoting. |
| Compress | Lempel-Ziv Compressor/Decompressor |
| Jess | A Java Expert Shell |
| DB | An in memory database |
| JavaC | A JDK 1.0.2-complaint Java Compiler |
| MPEGAudio | Performs MPEG-3 Audio Compression |
| MTRT | A dual-threaded version ray tracing algorithm |
| Jack | A Java Parser Generation which has since become the JavaCC Project |

Table 1 lists the benchmark suites optimized for this paper. We decided to choose a range of benchmarks across two benchmarking suites to ensure that the optimizations tested during our research provided benefits to a number of applications rather than a niche set of code. The SciMark 2.0 suite provides code mainly from scientific applications, these were chosen since they suited the type of optimization we were testing.

To obtain a average performance indicator for our benchmarks we averaged the benchmarks over 50 successive runs of the benchmarking suites.

Both benchmarks provide pre-compiled class files which have been compiled using the Sun Microsystems JDK 1.2 compiler.

## 2.2   Optimizations

We implemented three optimizations as intra-procedural transformation extensions to the SOOT Framework [21], a framework for analyzing and optimizing Java bytecode. This framework has an established and widely used set of tools for experimentation and research and as such was a natural choice.

All of the optimizations developed as part of our experiments were implemented as intra-procedural transformations in the Jimple intermediate representation [23] provided by the SOOT framework.

The three main optimizations implemented for this paper were:

- Loop Unrolling
- Loop Unfolding
- Loop Invariant Code Motion

The rest of this sub-section is dedicated to explaining each of these optimization techniques. Although brief descriptions are given, the techniques used are quite generic and more in depth explanations can be found in a number of books on the subject of compilation and optimization [1, 13, 16].

We choose to apply the loop invariant code motion transformation first as this removed redundant invariant statements prior to unfolding and unrolling. If invariant statements did exist they were hoisted before the unfolding and unrolling transformations to reduce the total size of the unfolded and unrolled copies of the loop.

Unfolding and unrolling are not commutative in that unfolding an unrolled loop leads to more copies of the loop being made. Although the unfolding factor can be altered to take this into account, we chose to apply the unfolding transformation before the unrolling process.

**Loop Unrolling.** Loop unrolling replaces the main body of a loop with several copies, adjusting the loop control code such that new body executes the same instructions as the original loop but with a smaller proportion of execution spent on evaluating the control. Since, by completing the unrolling process, we have changed the body of the loop to execute more than one original iteration on each iteration of the new loop we introduce a *epilogue* to the loop to handle 'odd' iterations which cannot be processed in the new unrolled loop [1]. The epilogue is created by placing a copy of the original loop at the end of the unrolled loop so that when execution is finished in the optimized code the epilogue can 'mop' up the remaining iterations.

Unrolling has two main benefits, firstly the transformation usually results in a smaller proportion of time being spent evaluating the control code of the loop since each iteration in the 'new' loop is executing the unrolling factor more iterations of the original. Secondly, the unrolling transformation opens multiple iterations to further optimization using techniques such as common sub-expression elimination [17]. Although common sub-expression elimination is not conducted by our optimization tool, the unrolled code may introduce opportunities for the just-in-time compiler to further optimize the code at runtime.

The level of benefit that the unrolling transformation provides is determined by the *unrolling factor* - i.e. the number of copies of the loop that replace the original body. For very small loops with simple control code a high unrolling factor can be used as the unrolled code is likely to fit into a cache line. For large complex loops small unrolling factors, usually 2, should be used as the unrolled loop can become too large to cache efficiently.

**Original:**

```
for(int  i  =  0;  i < 10;  i++) {
    a = a * 2;
}
```

**Transformed:**

```
for(int  i  =  0;  i < 10;  i = i + 2) {
    a = a * 2;
    a = a * 2;
}
```

**Fig. 1.** Unrolling applied to a simple loop

Due to the increase in the code size of a loop following unrolling the optimization can have detrimental effects on performance by making the code too large to fit into cache lines in the processor. When this occurs cache blocks may need to be transfered resulting in slower execution.

For our transformation we used a generic unrolling algorithm [16] to process single-basic block loops with simple control code. The unrolling factor used in our tool was set to 2 to limit the effect that larger loops would have on the caching of our benchmark programs.

The transformation was also developed to use a relatively conservative approach to unrolling in that it would only unroll loops without branching statements in their main body. This restriction was imposed because branching within loop bodies results in jump statements being fed through to the processor pipeline, as the unrolling process was meant to remove jump instructions by reducing the number of times the loop needed to jump to the start, allowing branches to be unrolled would be unlikely to result in a performance improvement.

We also chose a relatively simple approach to finding induction variables for the unrolling process. The tool was designed to only unroll loops with locally defined induction variables that are not compared to the result of a method return within the loop guard. These restrictions were created because the dynamic-class loading feature in Java allowed classes loaded at runtime to interfere with non local variables in a manner that could not be determined at optimization time. Since our transformation was intra-procedural we could not determine whether the return value of a method at runtime was constant therefore, induction variables compared against method returns could have behaved in a manner that would have meant the transformation resulting in different behaviour to the input.

**Loop Unfolding.** Loop unfolding, or *loop peeling*, removes a number of the first iterations of a loop and places them before the main body to form a *prologue*[18]. Extra control code is often introduced to ensure the overall number of iterations executed does not differ from the original loop code.

Original:

```
for ( i  =  0;  i  <  10;  i++) {
    a  =  a  *  2;
}
```

Transformed:

```
a  =  a  *  2;
a  =  a  *  2;
for ( i =2;  i  <  10;  i  =  i++) {
    a  =  a  *  2;
}
```

**Fig. 2.** Unfolding applied to a simple loop

Unfolding has two main benefits, firstly it allows the earlier iterations of the loop to execute without requiring the processor to follow jump instructions back to the beginning of the loop, improving the ability of the code to be pipelined and secondly, opening the earlier iterations to further optimizations such as common sub-expression elimination.

In a similar manner to unrolling, unfolding can increase the overall size of the application code which can affect how the application will be cached. For large loops unfolding will create a sizable epilogue which may make the method difficult to cache. The impact of unfolding is usually determined by the *unfolding factor* - i.e. the number of copies of the loop placed in the prologue. Large unfolding factors can increase the size of the code considerably disrupting cache behaviour and may, in the case of Java, prevent the JIT compilation process if the JVM decides that the code is too large to compile on the fly.

We decided to use an unfolding factor of 8 to create a balance between unfolding enough iterations for the optimization to be useful yet keeping the factor small enough to prevent excessive increases in code size. Our unfolding transformation also used conservative approaches to deducing induction variables for the same reasons outlined in the unrolling optimization description. We did however allow the unfolding transformation to unfold loops with branches in the main body. The purpose of this decision was to permit optimizations to be carried out across the unfolded iterations with the possibility of reducing the number of branches through optimization on the branch conditions.

**Loop Invariant Code Motion.** Loop invariant code motion is applied to code within loops that does not change on each iteration of the loop [2], this is code whose execution is independent of the loop induction variable.

The transformation works by finding expressions using only constants or variables that are defined from outside the loop. Given that these values will not change on each iteration of the loop, any expression that uses only these values will also be unchanged by each iteration or change in a pre-determined manner. A generic algorithm is explained in [1].

When loop invariant code has been found it can be removed from the loop by hoisting. The hoisting process takes invariant statements and places them outside of the loop making adjustments to ensure the value assigned to any variables resulting from the invariant expression will be the same. For instance, if a variable increases by a value of 2 on each iteration of the loop then hoisting will set this variable to have a value of 2 multiplied by the number of iterations added immediately following the execution of the loop.

| Original: | Transformed |
|---|---|
| ```int a = 0;```<br>```int b = 0;```<br>```int c = 10;``` | ```int a = 0;```<br>```int b = 0;```<br>```int c = 10;``` |

```
Original:                           Transformed
int  a  =  0;                       int  a  =  0;
int  b  =  0;                       int  b  =  0;
int  c  =  10;                      int  c  =  10;

for ( i  =  0;  i  <  10;  i++) {   for ( i  =  2;  i  <  10;  i  =  i++) {
    a  =  a  +  2;                      a  =  a  +  2;
    b  =  c  *  2;                  }
}                                   b  =  c  *  2;
```

**Fig. 3.** Loop invariant code motion applied to a simple loop

Loop invariant code motion usually results in faster execution of loops because the redundant code is eliminated from being executed multiple times saving processor resources.

Our transformation used a conservative approach to finding invariant code by only searching for locally defined variables as potential candidates for invariance since any method calls from inside the loop could have changed field level values potentially resulting in an unsafe transformation.

## 2.3   The Hardware and Environment

We ran our benchmarks on two different architectures to check whether the results obtained would show similar trends and whether the underlying architecture of the processor would change the benefit the optimizations could bring.

Our first machine was a Pentium 4 2.4Ghz machine configured with 1Gb of RAM running Microsoft Windows XP Service Pack 2. The Pentium processor used in this machine contains two 16kb L1 caches one allocated to data entries and one to instruction entries.

Our second machine was an Apple G4 Powerbook equipped with a 1.5Ghz G4 Processor and 512Mb of RAM running Apple OSX Tiger. The G4 processor uses two 32kb L1 caches allocated to data and instruction.

## 2.4   The Java Virtual Machines

On the Windows XP Machine, we used the standard Sun Microsystems Java Standard Edition (J2SE) Version 1.5.0 without any extra configuration. On the Apple Powerbook machine we used the standard Apple 1.4.2 Virtual Machine.

Since we are interested in the relationship between the ahead of time optimizations and the optimizing compilation in the JVM, for the SciMark 2.0 Benchmarks we decided to experiment with both the Client and Server just in time compiler included with the standard virtual machine. The Client compiler is configured to carry out a smaller amount of class file analysis during startup in an effort to reduce the loading time of Java applications. Since less analysis is being carried out on the bytecode a smaller number of transformations can be conducted during execution.

The Server compiler takes an alternative strategy seeking to spend longer conducting analysis during startup with the assumption that the application is likely to execute for a longer period of time. As more analysis is carried out a larger number of transformations are available during execution.

The exact details of the compilers provided with the Sun and Apple Virtual Machines go far beyond the remit of this paper, we refer the reader to the respective vendor websites for up-to-date information and features.

## 3    Results

In this section we present our results and offer an analysis on the figures shown. Tables 2 and 3 show the performance change following our optimizations. The figures shown represent speedup which is computed as a factor of the time taken to compute the unoptimized code. A speedup for less than 1 indicates a performance degradation, a speedup of greater than 1 represents an improvement.

The aim of our experiments was to examine whether, through the use of traditional loop optimizations, the performance of Java applications could be improved. As the reader can see in the results tables, the effect of these optimizations is somewhat varied depending on the type of application being optimized.

The application that gained the most through optimization was the LU Factorization application included in the SciMark 2.0 suite. The results showed a 14% improvement on the Intel system and 20% improvement on the Apple G4 System. If we examine the source code of the LU application we notice a reasonably large number of loops which contain only a few instructions. Since the unrolling

**Table 2.** SciMark 2.0 Benchmark Result (Higher Result is Higher Performance)

| | Pentium 4 | | G4 | |
|---|---|---|---|---|
| SciMark 2.0 Benchmark | Client JIT | Server JIT | Client JIT | Server JIT |
| FFT | 1.17x | 1.12x | 1.05x | 1.04x |
| SOR | 1.00x | 1.03x | 1.01x | 1.01x |
| Monte Carlo | 0.97x | 0.99x | 1.01x | 1.02x |
| Sparse Matrix Multiplication | 1.01x | 1.09x | 0.97x | 0.97x |
| LU | 1.14x | 1.08x | 1.20x | 1.20x |

**Table 3.** SPECjvm98 Benchmark Result (Higher Result is Higher Performance)

| SPECjvm98 Benchmark | Pentium 4 | Apple G4 |
|---|---|---|
| Compress | 0.99x | 1.04x |
| Jess | 1.10x | 1.08x |
| DB | 1.02x | 1.03x |
| JavaC | 1.06x | 1.03x |
| MPEGAudio | 1.00x | 1.02x |
| MTRT | 0.93x | 0.95x |
| Jack | 1.14x | 1.11x |

and unfolding of these loops produced a larger speedup than other benchmarks this indicates that the optimization of Java loops, like fully compiled languages, is best aimed at smaller, simple loops. Some of the benchmarks suffered from a performance degradation due to the transformations. The most notable of these was the MTRT ray-tracing benchmark from the SPECjvm98 benchmarks which suffered a 7% performance degradation on the Pentium 4 architecture.

Overall, the impact of the optimizations on many of the benchmarks was mixed but generally beneficial. Some benchmarks responded to optimization very well producing more efficient code that executed faster across a range of hardware platforms and virtual machines and other applications responded poorly. At the time of writing we have no firm conclusions about the nature of code that benefits or suffers from these transformations. However, the tool that applied the transformations did so indiscriminately on all loops that it could (given the innate conservative nature of the tool). A more guided transformation phase taking into account, for example, the size of the loop may lead to better results.

### 3.1   Architectural Considerations

The purpose of selecting an Intel Pentium 4 processor based machine and an Apple G4 processor based machine was to examine whether alternative virtual machines and architectures would alter the performance benefits of the optimizations presented.

As the reader can see from Table 2 the benefits vary slightly between the two machines. However, the overall average performance increase for the Pentium 4 and G4 architecture are roughly the same at 4.9% and 4.4% respectively.

Due to the fact that we are optimizing loops whose performance is largely down to efficient caching mechanisms we can attribute some of the variations in specific benchmarks to the different cache layouts offered by the two architectures.

Of course, hardware factors may be reduced by the effect of the bytecode running on an interpreter in the JVM. Nevertheless, there are two reasons why hardware factors may "show through": Firstly, in the case of caching, the fetching of bytecode instructions in a small loop will only take up a relatively small part of the data-cache leaving the rest for the program data and, secondly, we expect most of the critical code in these loops to be JIT compiled and therefore be run directly on the hardware anyway.

Another potential source for differences in the results comes from the varying number of registers available on the processors used for testing. The RISC based G4 architecture contains more registers than the Pentium and therefore may be able to hold more variables within the processor reducing the number of cache transfers required. This facility may lessen the impact of the optimizations on smaller loops as all the variables will be within registers thus reducing the speed improvement offered by more efficient usage of cache following unrolling.

### 3.2   The Client Versus Server Just-In-Time Compiler

For the SciMark 2.0 Benchmarks presented in Table 2 we decided to experiment with both the Client and Server just in time compiler included with the standard virtual machine. As one might expect, on both architectures the benchmarks ran faster with the Server JIT than the Client JIT. Despite this there was little difference in the percentage speedups caused by the optimizations. On the G4 architecture the speedups were identical and on the Pentium 4 architecture the average were similar at 5.8% for the Client and 6.2% for the Server. These results indicate that the difference in underlying optimization architecture for current JITs do not affect the beneficial effects of the loop transformations.

### 3.3    Overhead of the SOOT Framework

The overhead of converting the Java bytecode input to the SOOT Jimple Intermediate Representation and back out to bytecode introduces some penalties due to the complexities of creating the representation and re-generating the input from this. In the original paper introducing SOOT [21] Vallee-Rai *et al.* claimed that this overhead was between 1% and 2% of program execution time.

**Table 4.** Effect on performance after being parsed by SOOT Framework but no optimizations applied

| Benchmark | Speedup |
|-----------|---------|
| FFT | 0.96x |
| SOR | 0.98x |
| Monte Carlo | 1.00x |
| Sparse Matrix | 0.99x |
| LU | 1.00x |

Table 4 shows the potential impact on performance of the benchmarking applications being input to the SOOT framework and emitted without any optimizations being applied. The output of the framework is likely to be different to the input bytecode due to the conversion of the input into an intermediate representation that does not have an exact one-to-one mapping between a virtual machine bytecode and an element of the representation.

Experiments conducted on our benchmarks by reading the bytecode into the optimization tool and emitting it without completing any transformation are shown in Table 4. We believe that our results are broadly representative of the data provided by Vallee-Rai *et al.*

### 3.4    Cost of Performing the Optimizations

The main aim of this paper is to evaluate the effectiveness of the optimizing transformations under consideration. As such, the development of the analysis and transformation tool was not undertaken with compilation performance in mind. However, for the sake of completeness, Table 5 shows the time and memory required for the optimization tool to process the benchmark classes on the same Pentium 4 machines that was used in to execute the benchmarks.

**Table 5.** Time and memory requirements for optimization

| Benchmark | Memory Required (Mb) | Time Required (Seconds) |
|---|---|---|
| FFT | 22.236 | 9.01 |
| SOR | 23.688 | 11.08 |
| Monte Carlo | 17.160 | 3.36 |
| Sparse Matrix | 19.904 | 5.14 |
| LU | 18.102 | 4.24 |

The figures shown in Table 5 are unrepresentative of the resources that the analysis and transformation would need in a industry standard developed compiler. As such, it is hard to judge whether the transformations could be performed at runtime in a JIT compiler. However, given the analysis required for the transformations this seem unlikely.

Instead, we would claim that in situations such as this, where the optimization process may be lengthy, ahead of time optimization, or possibly ahead of time analysis, could provide a mechanism for communicating information to the just in time compiler as a guide to which optimizations could be used in each section of code. A recent study on the use of inter-procedural side effect analysis [14] demonstrated that when code was analyzed ahead of time and the information communicated to the just in time compiler a performance improvement of up to 20% could be achieved.

### 3.5   Effect of Optimization on Bytecode Size

Due to the fact that unrolling and unfolding optimizations result in copies of the loop body being replicated either before or into the loop the size of the code is expected to increase. Table 6 shows the increase in code size of the SciMark 2.0 benchmarking suite when unrolling and unfolding optimizations are applied. Due to the use of the SOOT framework a small increase in code size is attributable to using the Jimple intermediate representation which does not provide an exact mapping between input bytecodes and the bytecodes emitted.

The transformation tool will unfold a loop first by a factor of 8 and then unroll with a factor of 2. Furthermore, the tool only acts conservatively and will not unroll loops nested within another. Given this, we can expect that every loop transformed will have its size increased by a factor of 10.

**Table 6.** Size of bytecode before and after optimization

| Benchmark | No Optimizations | Optimized | Percent Increase |
|---|---|---|---|
| FFT | 2718 bytes | 3630 bytes | 33.55% |
| SOR | 580 bytes | 1176 bytes | 102.76% |
| Monte Carlo | 547 bytes | 622 bytes | 13.71% |
| Sparse Matrix | 510 bytes | 668 bytes | 30.98% |
| LU | 2166 bytes | 4482 bytes | 106.92% |

## 3.6    The Relationship Between AOT Optimization and JIT Compilation at Runtime

In this section we aim to investigate how the ahead of time optimization process changes the JIT compilation that occurs at runtime. Our work for this section centres on the SciMark 2.0 benchmarks. Table 7 shows that following optimization the number of bytes compiled by the Just-In-Time compiler at runtime for the Client JVM on the Pentium P4 architecture. It can be seen from the table that every benchmark has a rise in the amount of code compiled. However, this is to be expected due to the increase in bytecode size described in the previous section. It seems a reasonable assumption that given a bigger class file the JVM will compile more bytes of code.

The optimizations in this paper target loops in the program and these are the parts of the program one expects to be JIT compiled. If after the optimization the same loops are compiled then it may be reasonable to expect all the bytes added to the class file by unrolling and unfolding to be JIT compiled as well. In this case, we would expect the program size increase to be roughly the same as the increase in the number of extra bytes compiled at run-time. Table 8 shows that this is not the case. In fact there seems to be no correlation between the increase in code size and the increase in amount of JIT compilation.

The FFT, Monte Carlo and LU factorization benchmarks show behaviour where the JIT compilation increase is less than the increase in bytecode size. This is perhaps due to the fact that not all the code added by the transformations is processed by the JIT. Despite this, both FFT and LU factorization show large increases in running time performance.

The SOR and Sparse Matrix transformations show an even more unusual phenomenon where the JIT compiles more code after the transformation than the

**Table 7.** Number of Bytes Compiled by the Client Just-In-Time Compiler at Runtime

| | Bytes Compiled | | Percentage |
|---|---|---|---|
| Benchmark | No optimization | optimized | Increase |
| FFT | 614 bytes | 963 bytes | 56.84% |
| SOR | 148 bytes | 884 bytes | 497% |
| Monte Carlo | 66 bytes | 76 bytes | 15% |
| Sparse Matrix | 96 bytes | 362 bytes | 277% |
| LU | 542 bytes | 982 bytes | 81% |

**Table 8.** Comparison between size increase and JIT compilation increase

| Benchmark | Program Size Increase | Extra Bytes Compiled |
|---|---|---|
| FFT | 912 bytes | 349 bytes |
| SOR | 596 bytes | 736 bytes |
| Monte Carlo | 75 bytes | 10 bytes |
| Sparse Matrix | 158 bytes | 266 bytes |
| LU | 2316 bytes | 440 bytes |

transformation added. Somehow, the re-arrangement of code has caused the JIT to fire more often.

These results give us no clear correlation between the transformations and the effect they have on the amount of work the JIT will do at run time. It is possible that the results may be clearer if more fine grained information was known about the JIT (in particular, if it were known exactly which pieces of code were compiled or optimized). However, the tools available for the JVMs used in this experiment could not provide this information.

## 4   Background and Related Work

The work in this paper builds on other work that perform optimizations on Java bytecode. The main systems the authors are aware of are Briki [5] (although this is mainly a JIT compilation framework), Cream [6], Jax [20] and SOOT [21, 22]. The tool developed for this paper was built on top of SOOT. With the exception of Jax (whose main purpose was code compression) all of these systems report beneficial effects on performance when transforming Java bytecode ahead of time. As far as we are aware none of these systems include loop unrolling or unfolding in their transformation sets. However, forms of loop invariant code motion are applied by some tools (including the SOOT framework).

Other related systems are optimizing compilers that compile Java to native code [9, 12] and bytecode manipulation tools [7, 15].

Descriptions of all three optimizations can be found in standard compiler texts [1, 13, 16]. Loop unrolling and unfolding has been investigated on several architectures (for example [2, 8, 10, 11]) but as far as we are aware has not been investigated on platforms where a bytecode machine is used.

## 5   Conclusions and Future Work

The main contribution of this paper is the creation of a tool to perform certain optimizing transformations and a detailed investigation to determine whether traditional loop optimizations (in particular loop unrolling and unfolding) provide performance benefits on current JVMs when applied to bytecode.

The results average out with the transformations causing a 4-5% perfomance increase. Some benchmarks responded very well with up to a 20% increase and the worst performance degradation was a 7% decrease in performance. Overall the figures suggest that these AOT transformations are beneficial to the efficiency of Java programs.

In addition to the main results about performance increases, we can observe the following from the experiments:

– Although there are some variations in individual benchmarks, the trends of performance increase are the same across the hardware architectures tested
– Although there are some variations in individual benchmarks, the trends of performance increase are the same across the types of JIT tested

- The overhead of the SOOT framework is in line with earlier reported work.
- The effect of the transformations on the amount of code that is JIT compiled is unpredictable though increased performance can occur even with less than expected JIT compilation.

These results together lend support to the argument that, in some sense, the AOT optimization process is independent of the underlying run-time architecture including the JVM. However, individual cases can vary and the relationship between the transformations and JIT compilation is still not understood and could well still be an important factor in the effectiveness of the transformations. Further investigation into this relationship seems warranted.

As mentioned earlier in the paper, it may be possible for these transformations to be integrated into JIT compilation though the program analysis required may be too costly. A method of communicating ahead of time analysis to the JIT such as suggested in [14] may work in this context.

The tool developed for the purposes of this paper is quite conservative in its application of the transformations and also applies them uniformly without taking into account any context such as the size of the loop being transformed. It is possible that a more aggressive or more guided tool would produce more reliably beneficial results and this should be investigated further. Furthermore, the factors of unrolling and unfolding have been fixed for the reported experiments here, taking values that have worked well on other platforms. The performance effect of these parameters in Java is still to be fully investigated.

Often, the loop optimizations here are described as being successful due to their exploitation of cache behavior. Given that these transformations can be beneficial even when executed on a JVM, it may be the case that other loop transformations that affect cache behavior (*e.g.* loop tiling, strip mining, loop fusion etc.) would also benefit on Java code, particularly in scientific applications. A survey of these types of transformation can be found in [2].

# References

1. Andrew W. Appel. *Modern Compiler Implementation in Java*. Cambridge Press, 2002.
2. David F. Bacon, Graham Susan L., and Oliver J. Sharp. Compiler Transformations for High-Performance Computing. *ACM Computing Surveys*, 26(4):345–420, 1994.
3. SPEC JVM98 Client Benchmarks. World Wide Web, http://www.spec.org/osg/jvm98/.
4. J M Bull, L A Smith, L Pottage, and R Freeman. Benchmarking java against c and fortran for scientific applications. In *Proceedings of the 2001 joint ACM-ISCOPE conference on Java Grande*, pages 97–1005. ACM Press, 2001.
5. M Cierniak and W Li. Just in time optimizations for high performance java programs. *Concurrency: Practice and Experience*, 1997.
6. L. R. Clausen. A java bytecode optimizer using side effect analysis. *Concurrency: Practuce and Experience*, 1997.
7. Geoff A. Cohen, Jeffrey S. Chase, and David L. Kaminsky. Automatic program transformation with joie. In *Proceedings of the USENIX 1998 Annual Technical Conference*, pages 167–178. USENIX Association, 1998.

8. Jack W Davidson and Sanjay Jinturkar. An agressive approach to loop unrolling. Technical report, University of Virginia, 2001.
9. Jeffrey Dean, Greg De Fouw, David Grove, Vassily Litvino, and Craig Chambers. Vortex: An optimizing compiler for object-oriented languages. In *Proccedings OOPSLA '96 Conference on Object-Oriented Programming Systems, Languages and Applications*, volume 31, pages 83–100. ACM Sigplan, 1996.
10. J. J. Dongarra and A. R. Hinds. Unrolling loops in fortran. *Software Practice and Experience*, 9(3):219–226, 1979.
11. J.R. Ellis. *Bulldog: A Compiler for VLIW Architectures*. MIT Press, 1987.
12. Robert Fitzgerald, Todd B Knoblock, Erik Ruf, Bjarne Steensgaard, and David Tarditi. Marmot: an optimizing compiler for java. Technical report, Microsoft Research, 1998.
13. D. Grune, H. Bal, C. Jacobs, and K. Langendoen. *Modern Compiler Design*. John Wiley and Sons, 2000.
14. Anatole Le, Ondřej Lhoták, and Laurie Hendren. Using inter-procedural side-effect information in JIT optimizations. In R. Bodik, editor, *Compiler Construction, 14th International Conference*, volume 3443 of *LNCS*, pages 287–304, Edinburgh, April 2005. Springer.
15. Han Bok Lee and Benjamin G. Zorn. A tool for instrumenting java bytecodes. In *The USENIX Symposium on Internet Technologies and Systems*, pages 73–82, 1997.
16. Steven S. Muchnick. *Advanced Compiler Design and Implementation*, pages 559–563. Morgan Kaufmann, 1997.
17. B.V.Mohan Kirshna Reddy. A work bench for loop transformation. Master's thesis, Indian Institute of Technology, Kanpur, May 2001.
18. Litong Song and Krishna Kavi. What can we gain by Unfolding Loops? *SIGPLAN Not.*, 39(2):26–33, 2004.
19. SciMark 2.0 Benchmarking Suite. World Wide Web, http://math.nist.gov/scimark2/.
20. Frank Tip, Chris Laffra, Peter F. Sweeney, and David Streeter. Practical experience with an application extractor for java. Technical Report RC 21451, IBM Research, 1999.
21. R. Vallee-Rai, C. Phong, G. Etienne, H. Laurie, L. Patrick, and S. Vijay. Soot - a Java bytecode optimization framework, 1999.
22. Raja Vallee-Rai, Etienne Gagnon, Laurie J. Hendren, Patrick Lam, Patrice Pominville, and Vijay Sundaresan. Optimizing Java Bytecode Using the Soot Framework: Is It Feasible? In *Computational Complexity*, pages 18–34, 2000.
23. Raja Vallee-Rai and Laurie J. Hendren. Jimple: Simplifying Java Bytecode for Analyses and Transformations.

# Hybrid Optimizations:
# Which Optimization Algorithm to Use?

John Cavazos[1], J. Eliot B. Moss[2], and Michael F.P. O'Boyle[1]

[1] Member of HiPEAC,
Institute for Computing Systems Architecture (ICSA),
School of Informatics, University of Edinburgh,
Edinburgh, UK
[2] Department of Computer Science,
University of Massachusetts, Amherst,
Amherst, MA, USA

**Abstract.** We introduce a new class of compiler heuristics: *hybrid optimizations*. Hybrid optimizations choose dynamically at compile time which optimization algorithm to apply from a set of different algorithms that implement the same optimization. They use a *heuristic* to predict the most appropriate algorithm for each piece of code being optimized. Specifically, we construct a hybrid register allocator that chooses between linear scan and graph coloring register allocation. Linear scan is more efficient, but sometimes less effective; graph coloring is generally more expensive, but sometimes more effective. Our setting is Java JIT compilation, which makes optimization algorithm efficiency particularly important.

Our hybrid allocator decides, based on features of a method, which algorithm to apply to that method. We used supervised learning to induce the decision heuristic. We evaluate our technique within Jikes RVM [1] and show on average it outperforms graph coloring by 9% and linear scan by 3% for a typical compilation scenario. To our knowledge, this is the first time anyone has used heuristics induced by machine learning to select between different optimization algorithms.

## 1 Introduction

Compiler writers constantly invent new optimization algorithms to improve the state of the art. They frequently arrive at significantly different algorithms for a particular compiler optimization. Often, however, there is no clear winner among the different algorithms. Each algorithm has situations in which it is preferable to the other algorithms. For example, many different register allocation algorithms have been invented that achieve either a good running time performance [8, 6, 10, 2], possibly at the expense of increased allocation time, or a reduction in allocation time [13, 16] at the expense of performance. Two register allocation algorithms that differ in these seemingly mutually exclusive goals are graph coloring and linear scan.

Graph coloring is an aggressive technique for allocating registers, but is computationally expensive due to its use of the interference graph, which can have a worst-case size that is quadratic in the number of live ranges. Linear scan (LS), on the other hand, does not build an interference graph, but instead allocates registers to variables in a

A. Mycroft and A. Zeller (Eds.): CC 2006, LNCS 3923, pp. 124–138, 2006.
© Springer-Verlag Berlin Heidelberg 2006

greedy fashion by scanning all the live ranges in a single pass. It is simple, efficient, and produces a relative good packing of all the variables of a method into the available physical registers. Graph coloring can sometimes lead to more effective packing of the registers, but it can be much more expensive than linear scan.[1]

We invent a new class of optimization heuristics, *hybrid optimizations*. Hybrid optimizations assume that one has implemented two or more algorithms for the same optimization. A hybrid optimization uses a heuristic to choose the best of these algorithms to apply in a given situation. Here we construct a hybrid register allocator that chooses between two different register allocation algorithms, graph coloring and linear scan. The goal is to create an allocator that achieves a good balance between two factors: trying to find a good packing of the variables to registers (and thereby achieving good running time performance) and trying to reduce the overhead of the allocator.

We discuss how we use supervised learning to construct a hybrid allocator. The induced heuristic should be significantly cheaper to apply than register allocation itself; thus we restrict ourselves to using properties (features) of a method that are cheap to compute or have already been computed in a previous compilation phase.

The contributions of the paper are:

1. To our knowledge, this is the first time anyone has used properties of code to construct automatically (using machine learning) a heuristic function that selects between different optimization algorithms.
2. We can construct an allocator that is as good as always using graph coloring with a significant reduction in allocation/compilation time.

## 2    Motivation

We measured the time to run GC and LS for the case of 24 registers (12 volatile (callee-save) registers and 12 non-volatile (caller-save) registers) on a PowerPC processor. Figure 1 shows scatter plots of the running time versus method size (expressed in number of instructions). Both graphs omit outliers that have very large running times. LS's running time is consistent and fairly linear. GC's time is in the same general region, but is worse and does not have as clear a linear relationship with method size (this is to be expected, given the overhead of constructing an interference graph in the GC algorithm).

Table 1 gives statistics on the measured running times of GC and LS. The second column gives the average time to allocate registers in units of microseconds per (low-level intermediate code) instruction. GC is nearly 7 times slower than LS on this measure. However, if we exclude a small number of methods that took more than 1 second to schedule (outliers), then the ratio is 1.7. This shows that a small percentage of methods strongly bias GC's average running time. A possible strategy to ameliorate this is to predict when applying GC will benefit a method over LS, and run GC only in those cases. This is exactly the goal of a hybrid optimization. A hybrid optimization will reduce

---

[1] Poletto et al. [13] show data where graph coloring can be as much as 1000 times more expensive than linear scan as the size of the live variables grows.

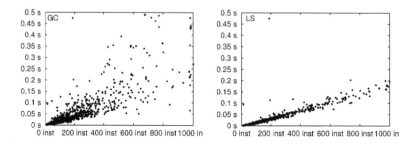

**Fig. 1.** Algorithm running time versus method size for GC and LS. Each point represents a method, where x-axis is size of method and y-axis is time to allocate.

**Table 1.** Average running time to allocate with GC and LS in microseconds ($\mu$s) per instruction

| Algorithm | ($\mu$s) / Inst | ($\mu$s) / Inst Without Outliers |
|---|---|---|
| GC | 1241 | 300 |
| LS | 183 | 176 |

compilation effort, using an efficient algorithm most of the time, but will use a more effective, but expensive, optimization algorithm seldomly, when it deems the additional benefit is worth the effort. This trade-off is especially interesting if compilation time is important, such as in a JIT (just-in-time) compilation environment.

## 3   Problem and Approach

We want to construct a heuristic that with high effectiveness predicts which alloca-tion algorithm is most beneficial to apply. We opted not to construct a hybrid allocator by hand, but instead to try to induce a choice function automatically using *supervised learning* techniques.

Developing and fine-tuning a hybrid allocator manually requires experimenting with different features (i.e., combinations of features of the method). Fine-tuning heuristics to achieve suitable performance is therefore a tedious and time-consuming process. Machine learning, if it works, is thus a desirable alternative to manual tuning.

Our approach uses a technique called *rule induction* to induce a hybrid allocator that is based on the features of the method. Rule induction heuristics are typically faster to induce than using other machine learning techniques, [2] they are more understandable than heuristics learned using other techniques (e.g., neural networks and decision trees), and are easier to make work (than unsupervised learning).

The first step in applying supervised learning to this problem requires phrasing the problem as a classification problem. For this task, this means that each method is rep-resented by a training instance and each training instance is labeled with respect to

---

[2] Our technique induces heuristics in seconds on one desktop computer. Stephenson et al. [15] report taking days to induce heuristics on a cluster of 15 to 20 machines.

whether graph coloring achieves enough additional benefit (fewer spills) over linear scan to warrant applying it.

### 3.1  Features

What properties of a method might predict which allocation algorithm to use? One can imagine that certain properties of a method's interference graph might predict whether or not to use graph coloring. However, building the interference graph often dominates the overall running time of the graph coloring algorithm. Since we require cheap-to-compute features, we specifically choose not to use properties of the interference graph.

Instead, we use features that have previously been computed for other compilation phases. For instance, we use features summarizing the control flow graph, *CFG*, such as statistics pertaining to regular (non-exceptional) versus exceptional edges.[3] We also use features that describe liveness information, such as the number of variables that are live in and out of a block. We also try other cheap-to-compute features that we thought might be relevant. Computing these features requires a single pass over the method.

**Table 2.** Features of a method

| Features | Meaning |
|---|---|
| In/Out Edges | Number of CFG In/Out Edges |
| Exception In/Out | Number of CFG Exceptional In/Out Edges |
| Live on Entry/Exit | Number of edges live on entry/exit |
| Intervals | Number of live intervals |
| Virtual Registers | Number of virtual registers |
| Insts per block | Number of instructions per blocks |
| Insts per method | Number of instructions in method |
| Blocks per method | Number of blocks in method |

The features can be grouped into three different categories. The first set of features pertains to edges in the control flow graph. These features include regular CFG edges and exceptional CFG edges. The second set of features pertains to the live intervals. We provide features for statistics describing the number of intervals (roughly, "variables") that are live going in and out of the blocks. This set also includes features for the number of live intervals and virtual registers. [4] The third set of features describes statistics about sizes of blocks and the total number of instructions and blocks in the method. See Table 2 for a complete list of the features. These features were either pre-computed or as cheap to compute as we can imagine while offering some useful information. These features work well so we decided not to refine them further. Our domain knowledge allowed us to develop a set of features that on our first attempt produced highly-predictive heuristics.

---

[3] Exceptional edges represent control flow if an exception is raised.

[4] Virtual registers refers to user-defined variables and compiler generated temporaries that we would like to allocate to machine registers.

We present all of the features (except number of instructions and blocks) in several forms, such as minimum, maximum, total, and mean. This allows the learning algorithm to generalize over many different method sizes.

It might be possible that a smaller set of features would perform nearly as well. However, calculating features and evaluating the heuristic functions takes less than 0.1% of compile time (a negligible fraction of compile time) in our experiments, so we did not explore this possibility. In addition, rule induction automatically finds the set of most significant features, so we did not need to eliminate features manually. One final observation is that these features are machine independent and should be useful across a wide range of systems. For instance, we performed experiments varying the number of available registers and found this set of features worked well across all configurations we evaluated.[5]

## 3.2 Generating Training Instances

We have constructed a set of features and now take the next step, generating training instances. Each training instance consists of a vector of feature values, plus a boolean classification label, i.e., *LS* (Linear Scan) or *GC* (Graph Coloring), depending on which algorithm is best for the method.

After the Java system compiles and optimizes each Java method, the last phase involves presenting the method for register allocation. As we allocate the variables in the method to registers we can compute the features in Table 2. We instrument both a graph coloring allocator and a linear scan allocator to print into a trace file, for each method, raw data for forming a training instance.

Each raw datum consists of the features of the method that make up the training instance and statistics used to calculate the label for that instance. For the particular step of computing the features of a method, we can use either algorithm since the features are not algorithm specific. However, computing the final statistics used for labeling requires allocating the method with both graph coloring and linear scan. These statistics include the time to allocate the method with each allocation algorithm, and the number of additional spills incurred by each algorithm. We discuss the use of these statistics for labeling each training instance in Section 3.3.

We obtain the number of spills for a method by counting the number of loads and stores added to each block after register allocation and multiplying this by the number of times each basic block executes. We obtain basic block execution counts by profiling the application. We emphasize that these steps take place in an instrumented compiler, run over a benchmark suite, and all happen *off-line*. Only the heuristics produced by supervised learning are part of the production compiler and these heuristics are fast.

## 3.3 Labeling Training Instances

We label an instance based on two different thresholds, a *cost threshold* and a *benefit threshold*. The cost threshold pertains to the time it takes to allocate registers with each

---

[5] The exact heuristic *functions* may vary. For rather larger registers (24 or more), graph coloring only rarely beats linear scan, while for small sets (4 or 8) graph coloring is even more important than the medium size case we consider here (12).

algorithm. The benefit threshold pertains to the number of spill loads and stores incurred by each allocation algorithm. We use spills as an indirect method to measure the benefit of an allocation algorithm instead of using the direct metric of a method's running time. Measuring running time of an individual method is hard to do reliably, whereas measuring dynamic spill count is easy to do and does not change between runs. Our results show that this indirect metric works well.

For the experiments in this paper we use the following procedure to label the training instances. We label an instance with "GC" (prefer graph coloring) if the number of spills using linear scan minus the number of spills using graph coloring on the same method is greater than some threshold (Spill_Threshold). We label an instance with "LS" (prefer linear scan) if there is no spill benefit by allocating the method with graph coloring. We also label an instance with "LS" if the cost of using graph coloring is above a threshold (Cost_Threshold) more than the cost of applying linear scan. Those instances where there is no clear benefit, in terms of spills or cost, in using graph coloring or linear scan are discarded and not considered for learning. They do not provide useful guidance and only push rule induction to try to make inconsquential fine distinctions. Figure 2 depicts this algorithm for labeling.

```
if (LS_Spill − GC_Spill > Spill_Threshold)
    Label as GC;
else if (LS_Spill - GC_Spill <= 0)
    Label as LS;
else if (LS_Cost/GC_Cost > Cost_Threshold)
    Label as LS;
else
    { // No Label (discard instance) }
```

**Fig. 2.** Procedure for labeling instances with GC and LS

We experimented with different threshold values for the spill benefit and cost threshold. Varying these threshold values gave us a variety of different heuristic functions. We report results for the best heuristic function found from 6 heuristic functions explored.

### 3.4   Learning Algorithm

An important rule in applying machine learning successfully is to try the simplest learning methodology that might solve the problem. We chose the supervised learning technique called *rule set induction*, which has many advantages over other learning methodologies. The specific tool we use is Ripper [9].

Ripper generates sets of if-then rules that are more expressive, more compact, and more human readable (hence good for compiler writers) than the output of other learning techniques, such as neural networks and decision tree induction algorithms. We analyze one of the induced if-then rule sets in Section 3.5.

### 3.5   A Sample Induced (Learned) Heuristic

As we mentioned, rule sets are easier to comprehend and are often compact. It is also relatively easy to generate code from a rule set that can be used to build a hybrid allocator.

Table 3 shows a rule set induced by our training data. If the right hand side condition of any rule (except the last) is met, then we will apply GC on the method; otherwise the hybrid allocator predicts that GC will not benefit the method and it applies LS. The numbers in the first two columns give the number of training examples that are correctly and incorrectly classified by the rule.

**Table 3.** Induced Heuristic Generated By Ripper

```
( 20/ 9) GC ← avgLiveOnExitBB >= 3.8  ∧  avgVirtualRegsBB >= 13
( 22/13) GC ← avgLiveOnEntryBB >= 4  ∧  avgCFGInEdgesBB >= 1.4  ∧  avgLiveOnExitBB >= 5.5  ∧
              numberInsts <= 294
( 10/ 5) GC ← avgLiveOnExitBB >= 4.3  ∧  maxLiveOnEntry <= 13
( 12/ 2) GC ← avgLiveOnExitBB >= 3.7  ∧  maxLiveOnEntry >= 9      ∧  numVirtualRegs >= 895  ∧
              maxLiveIntervals >= 38   ∧  maxLiveIntervals <= 69
(1815/78) LS ←
```

In this case we see that liveness information and the number of virtual registers are the most important features, with the rest offering some fine tuning. For example, the first if-then rule predicts that it is beneficial to use graph coloring on methods consisting blocks with a high average number of live intervals exiting the block and a high average number of virtual registers in the block. Note that for this training set a large percentage of methods ($1815 + 78 = 1893$ of $1986 = 95\%$) were predicted not to benefit from graph coloring. As we see in Section 6.2, determining the feature values and then evaluating rules like this sample one does not add very much to compilation time, and takes much less time than actually allocating the methods.

### 3.6   Integration of the Induced Heuristic

After training, the next step is installing the heuristic function in the compiler and applying it *online*. When the optimizer invokes register allocation on a method, we first compute our features for the method. We then call the heuristic function, passing the features. If the heuristic functions says to use graph coloring, we do so, otherwise we apply linear scan. If a method is re-optimized, as sometimes happens in adaptive compilation, the heuristic will be applied again, to the new code, and may make a different decision.

We include in our reported timings of allocation the cost of computing features and invoking the heuristic function. These costs are quite small compared with running the allocation algorithms.

## 4   Experimental Infrastructure

We implemented our register allocation algorithms in Jikes RVM, a Java virtual machine with JIT compilers, provided by IBM Research [1]. The system provides a linear scan allocator in its optimizing compiler. In addition, we implemented a Briggs-style graph coloring register allocator [5].

We experiment with Jikes RVM in an adaptive scenario, which is a typical scenario for compiling Java programs. In this scenario, the compiler identifies and optimizes only frequently executed (*hot*) methods at progressively higher levels of optimization [3]. This is the typical compilation scenario of a Java JIT compiler. It achieves most of the benefit of optimizing all methods, but with much lower compilation cost.

Our specific target architecture is the PowerPC. We ran our experiments on an Apple Macintosh system with two 533 MHz G4 processors, model 7410. This is an aggressive superscalar architecture whose microarchitecture is representative of the state of the art in processor implementations. We motivated this work allocating 24 registers, the number available on a PowerPC. We present results for allocating 12 registers (6 volatile and 6 non-volatile), which corresponds to AMD, ARM, and many embedded processors in wide-spread use.

## 4.1  Benchmarks

We examine 7 programs drawn from the SPECjvm98 suite [14] for the experiments in this paper. We detail these benchmarks in Table 4. We ran these benchmarks with the largest data set size (called 100).

**Table 4.** Characteristics of the SPECjvm98 benchmarks

| Program | Description |
|---------|-------------|
| compress | Java version of 129.compress from SPEC 95 |
| jess | Java expert system shell |
| db | Builds and operates on an in-memory database |
| javac | Java source to bytecode compiler in JDK 1.0.2 |
| mpegaudio | Decodes an MPEG-3 audio file |
| raytrace | A raytracer working on a scene with a dinosaur |
| jack | A Java parser generator with lexical analysis |

# 5   Evaluation Methodology

As is customary in evaluating a machine learning technique, our learning methodology was leave-one-out cross-validation: given a set of $n$ benchmark programs, in training for benchmark $i$ we train (develop a heuristic) using the training set (the set of instances) from the $n - 1$ *other* benchmarks, and we apply the heuristic to the test set (the set of instances from benchmark $i$). This makes sense in our case for two reasons. First, we envision developing and installing of the heuristic "at the factory", and it will then be applied to code it has not "seen" before. Second, while the end goal is to develop a single heuristic, it is important that we test the overall procedure by developing heuristics many times and seeing how well they work. The leave-one-out cross-validation procedure is a commonly used way to do this. Another way is repeatedly to choose about half the programs and use their data for training and the other half for testing. However, we want our heuristics to be developed over a wide enough range of benchmarks that we are likely to see all the "interesting" behaviors, so leave-one-out may be more realistic in that sense.

To evaluate a hybrid allocator on a benchmark, we consider three kinds of results: *spill loads, total running time*, and *benchmark running time*.

*Spill loads* refers to the additional number of loads (read memory accesses) incurred by the allocation algorithm. Spill loads give an indication of how well the allocator is able to perform its task. Memory accesses are expensive, and although the latency of some additional accesses can be hidden by overlapping with execution of other instructions, the number of spill loads is highly correlated with application running time. We do not count spill stores because their latency can be mostly hidden with *store buffers*. (A store buffer is an architectural feature that allows computation to continue while a store executes. Store buffers are typical in modern architectures.)

*Total time* refers to the running time of the program including compile time. We compare our hybrid allocator to always using linear scan and always using graph coloring. Since timings of our proposed system include the cost of computing features and applying the heuristic function, this (at least indirectly) substantiates our claim that the cost of applying the heuristic at run time is low. (We also supply measurements of those costs in Section 6.2.)

*Running time* refers to the running time of the program without compilation time. This measures the change in execution time of the allocated code, compared with always using linear scan and always using graph coloring. This validates not only the heuristic function but also our instance labeling procedure, and by implication the spill model we used to develop the labels.

The goal of the hybrid allocator is to achieve application running time close to always applying graph coloring, while reducing compilation time to substantially less than applying graph coloring to every method. If these two objectives are met, a hybrid allocator should reduce total time compared to always applying either graph coloring or linear scan.

# 6  Experimental Results

We aimed to answer the following questions: How *effective* is the hybrid allocator in obtaining best application performance compared to graph coloring? How *efficient* is our hybrid allocator compared to allocating all methods with linear scan? We ask these questions on the SPECjvm98 benchmark suite. We then consider how much time it takes to apply the hybrid heuristic in the compiler.

We answer the first question by comparing the running time of the application, with compilation time removed. We address the second by comparing total time which includes time spent compiling including allocating. Since we are using adaptive optimization in a JIT compiler, *total time* is the key measure of overall importance.

We requested that the Java benchmark iterate 26 times garbage collecting between iterations. The first iteration will cause the program to be loaded, compiled, and allocated according to the allocation algorithm. The remaining 25 iterations should involve no compilation; we use the *best* of the 25 runs as our measure of application performance.

Section 6.1 discusses the benefit of our allocators with respect to reducing spills. Section 6.2 discusses the cost of using the hybrid heuristic. Finally, Section 6.3

discusses the effect of using hybrid allocators in reducing program execution (running and total) time.

## 6.1  Spill Loads

Before looking at execution times on an actual machine, we consider the quality of the induced hybrid allocator (compared with always applying either graph coloring or linear scan) in terms of the number of spill loads added by register allocation. Spill loads predict whether a method will benefit from the additional effort of applying the more expensive graph coloring allocator.

Spill loads are used in the labeling process, thus we hoped that our hybrid allocator would perform well on the spill load metric. Comparing the allocators against spill loads allows us to validate the learning methodology, independently of validating against the actual performance on the target machine.

We calculate the dynamic number of spill loads added to each method by multiplying the number of spill loads added to each block by the number of times that block is executed (as reported by profiling information). Then we sum the number of dynamic spill loads added to each block. We obtain the dynamic number of spills loads for the entire program by summing the number of dynamic spill loads added to each method. More precisely, the performance measure for program $P$ is:

$$\text{SPILLS}_\pi(P) = \sum_{M \in P} \sum_{b \in M} (\# \text{ Executions of } b) \cdot (\text{spill loads added to } b \text{ under allocator } \pi)$$

where $M$ is a method, $b$ is a basic block in that method, and $\pi$ is hybrid, graph coloring, or linear scan.

**Table 5.** Spill loads for hybrid and linear scan relative to graph coloring

| Register Allocator | jack | db | javac | mpeg-audio | ray-trace | com-press | jess | geo. Mean |
|---|---|---|---|---|---|---|---|---|
| HYBRID | 1.07 | 1.00 | 1.04 | 1.49 | 1.05 | 2.01 | 1.33 | 1.25 |
| LS | 1.07 | 1.20 | 1.07 | 2.13 | 1.55 | 2.01 | 1.42 | 1.44 |

Table 5 shows the spill loads for each allocator as a ratio to spill loads produced by our graph coloring algorithm. These numbers are given as geometric means over the 7 SPECjvm98 benchmarks. We see improvements for the hybrid allocator over linear scan. These improvements do not correspond exactly to measured execution times, which is not surprising given that the number of spill loads is not an exact measure of performance on the architecture. What the numbers confirm is that the induced heuristic indeed improves the metric on which we based its training instances. Thus, supervised learning was able to solve this learning problem. Whether we get improvement on the real machine is concerned with how predictive reducing spill loads (i.e., the spill model) is to benchmark performance. The hybrid allocator was able to reduce the number of spills obtained by linear scan by 19%. In Section 6.3, we see that reducing the number of dynamic spill loads leads to an average reduction in running time of 5% for hybrid allocation over linear scan for our set of benchmarks.

## 6.2   The Cost of Evaluating a Hybrid Heuristic

Table 6 gives a breakdown of the compilation costs of our system, and statistics concerning the percentage of methods and instructions allocated with each allocator. The costs are given as geometric means over the 7 benchmarks.

**Table 6.** Cost breakdowns: GCM/GCI = GC allocated methods/instructions; LSM/LSI = LS allocated methods/instructions; $f$ = time to evaluate features and heuristic function; $a$ = time spent allocating methods; $c$ = compile time excluding allocation time

| Allocator | GCM | GCI | LSM | LSI | $f/a$ | $f/c$ | $a/c$ |
|---|---|---|---|---|---|---|---|
| GC | 100.00% | 100.00% | 0.00% | 0.00% | 0.00% | 0.00% | 21.26% |
| HYBRID | 2.42% | 9.53% | 97.58% | 90.47% | 1.20% | 0.09% | 7.31% |
| LS | 0.00% | 0.00% | 100.00% | 100.00% | 0.00% | 0.00% | 3.41% |

Here are some interesting facts revealed in the table. First, the fraction of methods and of instructions allocated with GC drops significantly for our hybrid scheme. Second, the fraction of instructions allocated with GC, which tracks the relative cost of allocation fairly well, is about 4 times as big as the fraction of methods allocated with GC, implying that the hybrid allocator tend to use GC for longer methods. This makes sense in that longer methods probably tend to benefit more from graph coloring.

Third, the cost of calculating the heuristic, as a percentage of compilation time, is less than 0.1%. Finally, we obtain a factor of 3 reduction in allocation time compared with GC (applying graph coloring to every method).

## 6.3   Effectiveness and Efficiency

We now consider the quality of the hybrid heuristic induced for adaptive optimization. Figure 3(a) shows the impact of the hybrid allocation and GC on application running time, presented relative to LS. Here there is little variation between graph coloring and hybrid allocation across the benchmarks, with GC doing well at 5% and the hybrid allocator doing just as well. Given the lower cost of the hybrid allocator to run, it is preferable to running GC all the time. The results are fairly consistent across the benchmarks, though some benchmarks improve more than others.

As Figure 3(a) shows we can effectively select dynamically the methods where graph coloring improves over linear scan with our hybrid heuristic. The hybrid allocator is effective, but what happened to efficiency?

Figure 3(b) shows the total time of the hybrid allocator and GC (always performing graph coloring), relative to LS (always performing linear scan). The average for the total time graph shows an improvement using the hybrid allocator over either always using linear scan or always using graph coloring. Using the hybrid allocator we can achieve up to an 15% improvement over linear scan for compress with an average improvement of 3%. Using graph coloring, we can also achieve a substantial improvement on some benchmarks over linear scan, but we also incur a significant degradation on some programs (up to 22% for mpegaudio) over linear scan. However, by selective applying

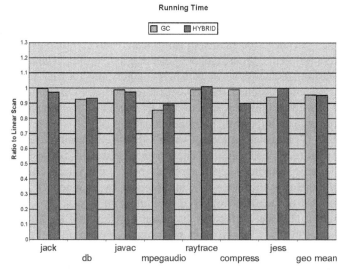

(a) Running Time Using Hybrid versus Graph Coloring relative to Linear Scan

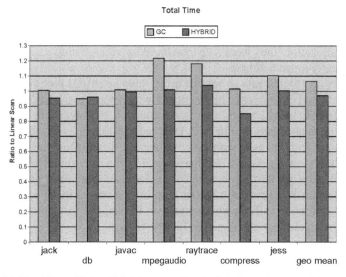

(b) Total Time Using Hybrid versus Graph Coloring relative to Linear Scan

**Fig. 3.** Efficiency and Effectiveness Using Hybrid Allocator with Adaptive Compiler

GC only when it is beneficial we can reduce total time by 9% on average using hybrid allocator over graph coloring. The improvement in total time of hybrid allocation over graph coloring shows we were able to cut the compilation effort (and therefore total time) significantly.

## 7    Related Work

Lagoudakis et al. [11] describe an idea of using features to choose between algorithms for two different problems, order statistics selection and sorting. The authors used reinforcement learning to choose between different algorithms for each problem. For the order statistics selection problem, the authors choose between Deterministic Select and Heap Select. For sorting, they choose between Quicksort and Insertion Sort. The hybrid algorithms were able to outperform each individual algorithm.

Cavazos et al. [7] describe an idea of using supervised learning to control whether or not to apply instruction scheduling. They induced heuristics that used features of a basic block to predict whether scheduling would benefit that block. Using the induced heuristic, they were able to reduce scheduling effort by as much as 75% while still retaining about 92% of the effectiveness of scheduling all blocks.

Monsifrot et al. [12] use a classifier based on decision tree learning to determine which loops to unroll. They looked at the performance of compiling Fortran programs from the SPEC benchmark suite using g77 for two different architectures, an Ultra-SPARC and an IA64, where their learned scheme showed modest improvement.

Stephenson et al. [15] used genetic programming to tune heuristic priority functions for three compiler optimizations within the Trimaran IMPACT compiler. For two optimizations they achieved significant improvements. However, these two pre-existing heuristics were not well implemented. For instance, turning off data prefetching completely is preferable and reduces many of their significant gains. For the third optimization, register allocation, they were able to achieve on average only a 2% improvement over the manually tuned heuristic.

Bernstein et al. [4] describe an idea of using three heuristics for choosing the next variable to spill, and choosing the best heuristic with respect to a cost function. This is similar to our idea of using a hybrid allocator to choose which algorithm is best based on properties of the method being optimized. Their technique applies all the spill heuristics and measures the resultant code with the cost function. Their technique results in about a 10% reduction in spills and a 3% improvement in running time. Our technique, on the other hand, does not try each option, but instead uses features of the code to make a prediction. By making a prediction using simple properties of the code, our heuristics are more efficient while still remaining effective. In fact, our technique could be used as an alternative to the cost function used in their work.

## 8    Conclusions

Choosing *which* optimization algorithm to apply among different optimization algorithms that differ in efficiency and effectiveness can avoid potentially costly compiler optimizations. It is an important open problem. We consider here the particular case of register allocation, with the possible choices being linear scan, graph coloring , and a hybrid allocator that chooses between these two algorithms. Since many methods do not gain additional benefit from applying graph coloring over linear scan, a hybrid allocator applies graph coloring only to a subset of the methods. We demonstrated that for an aggressive optimizing compiler (in a typical adaptive scenario) it is possible to induce a function automatically that is competent at making this choice: we obtain the effectiveness benefit of graph coloring and the efficiency benefit of linear scan.

Sometimes (only rarely) it is beneficial to perform graph coloring in a JIT, depending on how long the program runs, etc. Since it is only rarely worthwhile, that emphasizes the need for our heuristic to decide when to apply it. The general approach we took here should apply in other optimization situations.

Supervised learning worked well for this learning task. In addition, the learning algorithm we use produces understandable heuristics. As with any machine learning technique, devising the appropriate features is critical. Choosing which register allocation algorithm to apply turns out to require only simple, cheap-to-compute features.

We conclude that machine learning shows promise for developing heuristics for choosing between multiple algorithms for the same optimization task. A useful direction for future exploration is more expensive, rarely helpful, yet sometimes essential, optimizations, such as redundant load and store elimination.

## References

1. B. Alpern, C. R. Attanasio, J. J. Barton, M. G. Burke, P.Cheng, J.-D. Choi, A. Cocchi, S. J. Fink, D. Grove, M. Hind, S. F. Hummel, D. Lieber, V. Litvinov, M. F. Mergen, T. Ngo, J. R. Russell, V. Sarkar, M. J. Serrano, J. C. Shepherd, S. E. Smith, V. C. Sreedhar, H. Srinivasan, and J. Whaley. The Jalapeño virtual machine. *IBM Systems Journal*, 39(1):211–238, Feb. 2000.
2. A. Appel and L. George. Optimal spilling for CISC machines with few registers. In *Proceedings of the ACM SIGPLAN '01 Conference on Programming Language Design and Implementation*, pages 243–253, Snowbird, Utah, June 2001. Association of Computing Machinery.
3. M. Arnold, S. Fink, D. Grove, M. Hind, and P. F. Sweeney. Adaptive optimization in the Jalapeño JVM. In *ACM SIGPLAN Conference on Object-Oriented Programming Systems, Languages, and Applications (OOPSLA)*, pages 47–65, Minneapolis, MN, Oct. 2000. ACM Press.
4. D. Bernstein, D. Q. Goldin, M. C. Golumbic, Y. Mansour, I. Nahshon, and R. Y. Pinter. Spill code minimization techniques for optimizing compilers. In *SIGPLAN '89 Conference on Programming Language Design and Implementation*, pages 258–263, Portland, Oregon, June 1989. ACM Press.
5. P. Briggs, K. D. Cooper, K. Kennedy, and L. Torczon. Coloring heuristics for register allocation. In *Proceedings of the ACM SIGPLAN 1989 Conference on Programming language design and implementation*, pages 275–284. ACM Press, June 1989.
6. P. Briggs, K. D. Cooper, and L. Torczon. Improvements to graph coloring register allocation. *ACM Transactions on Programming Languages and Systems (TOPLAS)*, 16(3):428–455, May 1994.
7. J. Cavazos and J. E. B. Moss. Inducing heuristics to decide whether to schedule. In *Proceedings of the ACM SIGPLAN '04 Conference on Programming Language Design and Implementation*, pages 183–194, Washington, D.C., June 2004. ACM Press.
8. G. J. Chaitin. Register allocation and spilling via graph coloring. In *Proceedings of the ACM SIGPLAN '82 Conference on Programming Language Design and Implementation*, pages 98–101, Boston, Massachusetts, June 1982. ACM Press.
9. W. W. Cohen. Fast effective rule induction. In *Proceedings of the Twelfth International Conference on Machine Learning*, pages 115–123, Lake Tahoe, CA, Nov. 1995. Morgan Kaufmann.

10. L. George and A. W. Appel. Iterated register coalescing. *ACM Transactions on Programming Languages and Systems*, 18(3):300–324, May 1996.
11. M. G. Lagoudakis and M. L. Littman. Algorithm selection using reinforcement learning. In *Proceedings of the 17th International Conference on Machine Learning*, pages 511–518, Stanford, CA, June 2000. Morgan Kaufmann.
12. A. Monsifrot and F. Bodin. A machine learning approach to automatic production of compiler heuristics. In *Tenth International Conference on Artificial Intelligence: Methodology, Systems, Applications (AIMSA)*, pages 41–50, Varna, Bulgaria, September 2002. Springer Verlag.
13. M. Poletto and V. Sarkar. Linear scan register allocation. *ACM Transactions on Programming Languages and Systems*, 21(5):895–913, Sept. 1999.
14. Standard Performance Evaluation Corporation (SPEC), Fairfax, VA. *SPEC JVM98 Benchmarks*, 1998.
15. M. Stephenson, S. Amarasinghe, M. Martin, and U.-M. O'Reilly. Meta optimization: Improving compiler heuristics with machine learning. In *Proceedings of the ACM SIGPLAN '03 Conference on Programming Language Design and Implementation*, pages 77–90, San Diego, Ca, June 2003. ACM Press.
16. O. Traub, G. Holloway, and M. D. Smith. Quality and speed in linear-scan register allocation. In *Proceedings of the ACM SIGPLAN '98 Conference on Programming Language Design and Implementation*, pages 142–151, Montreal, Canada, June 1998. ACM Press.

# A Fresh Look at PRE as a Maximum Flow Problem

Jingling Xue[1] and Jens Knoop[2]

[1] Programming Languages and Compilers Group, School of Computer Science and
Engineering, University of New South Wales, Sydney, NSW 2052, Australia
[2] Technische Universität Wien, Institut für Computersprachen,
Argentinierstraße 8, 1040 Wien, Austria

**Abstract.** We show that classic PRE is also a maximum flow problem, thereby
revealing the missing link between classic and speculative PRE, and more importantly, establishing a common high-level conceptual basis for this important compiler optimisation. To demonstrate this, we formulate a new, simple unidirectional
bit-vector algorithm for classic PRE based only on the well-known concepts of
availability and anticipatability. Designed to find a unique minimum cut in a flow
network derived from a CFG, which is proved simply but rigorously, our algorithm is simple and intuitive, and its optimality is self-evident. This conceptual
simplicity also translates into efficiency, as validated by experiments.

## 1 Introduction

Partial redundancy elimination (PRE) is a compiler optimisation that eliminates computations that are redundant on some but not necessarily all paths in a program. As
a result, PRE encompasses both global common subexpression elimination and loop-
invariant code motion. Over the years, PRE has also been extended to perform other
optimisations at the same time, including strength reduction [8, 12, 16, 18], global value
numbering [3] and live-range determination [21]. For these reasons, PRE is regarded as
one of the most important optimisations in optimising compilers.

As a code transformation, PRE eliminates a partially redundant computation at a
point by inserting its copies on the paths that do not already compute it prior to the point,
thereby making the partially redundant computation fully redundant. PRE problems
come in two flavours: *classic PRE* and *speculative PRE*. Classic PRE, as described in
the seminal work [22], inserts a computation at a point only if the point is *safe* (or
*down-safe*) for the computation, i.e., only if the computation is fully anticipatable at the
point. On the other hand, speculative PRE may insert a computation at a point even if
the computation is partially but not necessarily fully anticipatable at the point. If the
computation cannot cause an exception and if the execution frequencies of the flow
edges in a CFG are available, speculative PRE may find transformations missed by
classic PRE, thereby removing more redundancies in dynamic terms than classic PRE.

In the case of classic PRE, Knoop, Rüthing and Steffen invented an optimal unidirectional bit-vector formulation of the problem [17, 19]. This algorithm, known as Lazy
Code Motion (LCM), was later recasted to operate in static single assignment (SSA)
form [15]. Subsequently, a number of alternative formulations have been proposed
[7, 8, 9, 23]. While LCM and other earlier algorithms [8, 9] find code insertion points by

A. Mycroft and A. Zeller (Eds.): CC 2006, LNCS 3923, pp. 139–154, 2006.

modelling the optimisation as a code motion transformation, the latter ones [7, 23] avoid this by identifying code insertion points directly. Apparently, a search for a conceptual basis upon which an optimal formulation of classic PRE can be both developed and understood more intuitively has been the driving force behind these research efforts. Up to now, however, this conceptual basis has been elusive. All existing algorithms are developed and reasoned about at the low level of individual program paths.

While classic PRE is profile-independent, speculative PRE is profile-guided. Given a weighted CFG, where the weights of the flow edges represent their execution frequencies, we have shown previously that speculative PRE is a maximum flow problem [26]. Finding an optimal transformation on a CFG amounts to finding a special minimum cut in a flow network derived from the CFG. Furthermore, different optimal transformations on a CFG may result if the weights of the flow edges in the CFG differ.

In this paper, we show for the first time that classic PRE is also a maximum flow problem. This is the key to the main contribution of our paper: to provide a uniform approach for classic and speculative PRE. The insight behind this finding lies in the following assumption made about classic PRE [17, 19]: all control flow edges are nondeterministic, or equivalently, have nonzero execution frequencies. We show that finding the optimal transformation for a CFG amounts to finding a unique minimum cut in a flow network derived from the CFG. Since all insertions in a CFG must be safe in classic PRE (as mentioned above), this unique minimum cut is invariant of the execution frequencies of the flow edges in the CFG. This establishes the connection and highlights the main difference between classic and speculative PRE. More importantly, our finding provides a common high-level conceptual basis upon which an optimal formulation of PRE can be more systematically and intuitively developed and proved. *Every PRE algorithm, if being optimal, must find the unique minimum cut on a flow network that is derived from a CFG.* As a result, tedious and non-intuitive reasoning that has been practised at the lower level of control flow paths is dispensed with.

Based on this insight, we have developed a new, simple algorithm for classic PRE. Our formulation, applicable to standard basic blocks, consists of solving four unidirectional bit-vector data-flow problems based only on the well-known concepts of availability and anticipatability. Designed to find a unique minimum cut in a flow network derived from a CFG, which is proved simply but rigorously, our data-flow equations reason positively about the global properties computed without using logical negations. Such a formulation is intuitive and its optimality self-evident. This conceptual simplicity also translates into efficiency, as demonstrated by our experimental results.

The rest of this paper is organised as follows. Section 2 gives the background information. Section 3 shows that classic PRE is a maximum flow problem. We do so constructively by giving an algorithm, MIN-PRE, that consists of solving three data-flow problems and invoking a min-cut algorithm to find a unique minimum cut in a flow network derived from a CFG. Section 4 compares and contrasts classic and speculative PRE when both are viewed as maximum flow problems. In Section 5, we derive from MIN-PRE a simple algorithm, called SIM-PRE, for classic PRE by solving four data-flow problems only. Section 6 discusses some experimental results. Our simple algorithm uses fewer bit-vector operations than three algorithms across 22 SPECcpu2000 benchmarks on two platforms. Section 7 reviews the related work and concludes.

## 2    Background

A control flow graph (CFG), $G = (N, E, W)$, is a weighted directed graph, where $N$ is the set of basic blocks (or nodes), $E$ the set of control flow edges and $W : N \cup E \mapsto \mathbb{IN}$. Given a node or edge $x$, $W(x)$ represents its execution frequency (under an arbitrary input). In addition, *ENTRY* $\in N$ denotes its *entry block* and *EXIT* $\in N$ its *exit block*, which are both empty. Furthermore, every block is assumed to lie on some path from *ENTRY* to *EXIT*. Let pred$(G, n)$ be the set of all *immediate predecessors* of a block $n$ in $G$ and succ$(G, n)$ the set of all *immediate successors* of a block $n$ in $G$.

**Assumption 1.** *For every $G = (N, E, W)$, we have the following tautology:*

$$\forall n \in N : \sum_{m \in \text{pred}(G,n)} W(m, n) = \sum_{m \in succ(G,n)} W(n, m)$$

As in [17, 19], we consider a non-SSA intermediate representation, where each statement has the form $v = e$ such that $v$ is a variable and $e$ a single-operator expression. As is customary, we assume that local common subexpression elimination (LCSE) has already been applied to all basic blocks. Given an expression $e$, the following three local predicates associated with a block $n$ are used in the normal manner. $\text{ANTLOC}_n$ is true if $e$ is locally anticipatable on entry to block $n$ (i.e., block $n$ contains an upwards exposed computation of $e$). $\text{COMP}_n$ is true if $e$ is locally available on exit from block $n$ (i.e., block $n$ contains a downwards exposed computation of $e$). $\text{TRANSP}_n$ is true if block $n$ does not contain any modification to $e$. PRE is a global optimisation. So only the upwards and downwards exposed computations of $e$, called the *PRE candidates*, will be considered. A block can contain at most two PRE candidate computations. It is important to be reminded that $\text{ANTLOC}_n$ and $\text{COMP}_n$ can both be true in block $n$, in which case, either a common PRE candidate of $e$ is locally available and anticipatable simultaneously, implying that $\text{TRANSP}_n = true$ or two distinct PRE candidates of $e$ are locally available and anticipatable, respectively, implying that $\text{TRANSP}_n = false$.

A PRE transformation for an expression is realised by replacing all redundant computations of the expression by a new temporary that is initialised correctly at suitable program points. We adopt the definition of PRE as used in LCM [19] except that we will make use of edge insertions as in [7, 23, 26] rather than node insertions; these insertions serve to make all the partially redundant computations fully redundant. Therefore, we do not have to split *critical edges*, i.e., the edges leading from nodes with more than one immediate successor to nodes with more than one immediate predecessor.

The fundamental assumption in classic PRE as stated clearly in LCM [17, 19] is that all control flows in a CFG are nondeterministic. Equivalently, we have:

**Assumption 2.** *Given $G = (N, E, W)$. In classic PRE, $\forall x \in (N \cup E) : W(x) > 0$.*

A directed graph $F = (V, A)$ is a *flow network* if it has two distinguished nodes, a *source* $s$ and a *sink* $t$, in $V$ and a nonnegative *capacity* (or *weight*) for each edge in $A$. Let $S$ and $T = V - S$ be a partition of $V$ such that $s \in S$ and $t \in T$. We denote by $(S, T)$ the set of all (directed) edges with tail in $S$ and head in $T$: $(S, T) = \{(n, m) \in A \mid n \in S, m \in T\}$. A *cut* separating $s$ from $t$ is any edge set $(C, \overline{C})$, where $s \in C$, $\overline{C} = V - C$ is the complement of $C$ and $t \in \overline{C}$. The *capacity* of this cut is the sum of the capacities of all *cut edges* in the cut. A *minimum cut* is a cut separating $s$ from $t$ with minimum capacity. The *max-flow problem* consists of finding a flow of maximum value from the source $s$ to the sink $t$. The max-flow min-cut theorem of [10] dictates that such a flow exists and has a value equal to the capacity of a minimum cut.

# 3   Classic PRE as a Maximum Flow Problem

In classic PRE, only safe insertions are used as discussed previously. Based on this safety constraint and Assumption 2, we show that classic PRE on a CFG is a maximum flow problem and a special minimum cut on a flow network derived from the CFG leads to the construction of the unique (lifetime) optimal transformation for the CFG — the uniqueness was known earlier in [17, 19]. These results provide a common high-level conceptual basis for developing, understanding and reasoning about PRE algorithms.

In Section 3.1, MIN-PRE is presented and illustrated by an example. In Section 3.2, we give an intuitive explanation why classic PRE is a maximum flow problem. In Section 3.3, we see that the optimality proof in this context is straightforward.

## 3.1   MIN-PRE

In classic PRE, a computation of an expression $e$ is said to be *redundant* (partially or fully) if it can be eliminated by using safe code insertions of the form $t_e = e$, where $t_e$ is a new temporary. A computation of $e$ is said to *generate* some redundancies if it can cause another computation of $e$ (both may be identical, as in a loop) to be redundant.

To shed the light on the nature of classic PRE on a CFG, we specify such a transformation for an expression $e$ by using the following three sets (as in the GCC compiler):

DELETE gives the set of blocks where the upwards exposed computations of $e$ are redundant (partially or fully). Every such computation will be replaced by a new temporary $t_e$. Note that a computation of $e$ that is downwards but not also upwards exposed cannot be redundant (i.e., removable using safe code insertions only).

COPY gives the set of all *copy blocks* where the downwards exposed computations of $e$ generate redundancies in the blocks given in DELETE but these computations themselves (when they are also upwards exposed) are not redundant. Such a computation will be replaced by $t_e$ and preceded by a *copy* insertion of $t_e = e$. Note that a computation of $e$ that is upwards but not also downwards exposed cannot generate any redundancies (i.e., cause other computations to be redundant).

INSERT gives the set of edges, called *insertion edges*, on which $t_e = e$ will be inserted, thereby making all partially redundant computations of $e$ fully redundant.

This definition distinguishes clearly the different roles that the three different code modifications play in a PRE transformation. As we shall see shortly, DELETE and INSERT are so closely related that both can be built simultaneously. However, more information about redundancy-generating computations is needed in order to build COPY.

A transformation is *correct* if every use of $t_e$ is identified with a definition of $t_e = e$ in every execution path. The total number of computations of $e$ eliminated by a

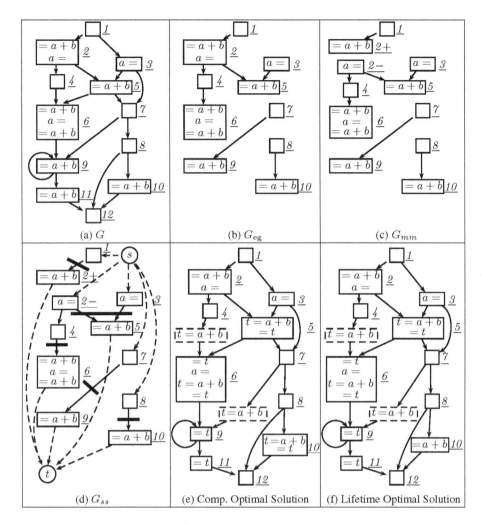

**Fig. 1.** A running example

transformation in $G = (N, E, W)$ is given by $\sum_{b \in \text{DELETE}} W(b) - \sum_{e \in \text{INSERT}} W(e)$. A transformation is *computationally optimal* if this term is maximised and is *lifetime optimal* (or *optimal* for short) if the live ranges of all definitions of $t_e$ are also minimised.

Our running example is given in Figure 1. An optimal PRE algorithm will take as input the CFG shown in Figure 1(a) and produce as output the transformed CFG as shown in Figure 1(f). The optimal transformation for the example is specified by:

$$
\begin{aligned}
\text{DELETE} &= \{6, 9, 11\} \\
\text{COPY} &= \{5, 6\} \\
\text{INSERT} &= \{(4, 6), (7, 9)\}
\end{aligned}
\tag{1}
$$

Figure 2 gives a mincut-based algorithm, MIN-PRE, for classic PRE by modelling it as a maximum flow problem. The reader is invited to read the algorithm since it is made to be self-contained. Below we explain its steps and illustrate them by our example.

We start with a weighted CFG, $G = (N, E, W)$, where the weights of its blocks and flow edges are their execution frequencies. In the example given in Figure 1(a), we do not actually show the weights. As we shall see later, the optimal transformation in classic PRE is independent of the weights in a CFG. In Steps 1 and 2, we compute the standard global properties, availability and anticipatability, on $G$. Based on this information, in Step 3, we derive an important subgraph $G_{eg}$ from $G$. $G_{eg}$ contains every *essential edge* $(m, n) \in E$ such that $\mathsf{ESS}(m, n) = \overline{\mathsf{AVAILOUT}_m} \cdot \mathsf{ANTIN}_n$ holds and its two incident nodes $m, n \in N$. Figure 1(b) depicts this subgraph for the running example. By definition, the following two properties about $G_{eg}$ are true.

**Lemma 1.** *Let $n$ be a node in $G$ such that $\mathsf{ANTLOC}_n = true$. If the upwards exposed computation in $n$ is not fully redundant, then $n$ is always included in $G_{eg}$.*

Note that $n$ in the above lemma may also be contained in $G_{eg}$ even if $n$ is fully redundant, in which case, $n$ must have at least one outgoing edge that is essential.

In Figures 1(a) and (b), we see that $G_{eg}$ contains block 2, 5, 6, 9 and 10 but not 11.

**Lemma 2.** *For every computationally optimal transformation, its $\mathsf{INSERT}$ must be a subset of the edge set $E_{eg}$ of $G_{eg}$.*

*Proof.* By Assumption 2, a transformation whose $\mathsf{INSERT}$ contains $(m, n) \notin E_{eg}$ such that $\mathsf{AVAILOUT}_m = true$ ($\mathsf{ANTIN}_n = false$) cannot be computationally optimal (safe). □

*Thus, $G_{eg}$ is the fundamental subgraph of $G$ where code insertions are to be made to make all the partially redundant computations (i.e., those that are removable by using safe code insertions only) in $G$ fully redundant.*

In Step 4, we obtain a multi-source, multi-sink flow network, $G_{mm}$, from $G_{eg}$. Figure 1(c) depicts this network for our example, where block 2 has been split (conceptually). Note that $N_{eg}^{ss} = \{2\}$. Intuitively, an insertion of $t = a + b$ that makes the upwards exposed computation $a + b$ in block 6 fully redundant must be made "below" block 2. Hence, the conceptual split. Note that the sources and sinks are: $S_{mm} = \{1, 2-, 3, 7, 8\}$ and $T_{mm} = \{2+, 5, 6, 9, 10\}$. By construction, $S_{mm} \cap T_{mm} = \emptyset$ holds. Finally, $\mathcal{N}$ ($\mathcal{E}$) relates the nodes (edges) in $G_{mm}$ to those in $G$. We have $\mathcal{N}(2+) = \mathcal{N}(2-) = 2$ and $\mathcal{N}(n) = n$ for other nodes $n$. As a result, $\mathcal{E}(1, 2+) = (1, 2)$, $\mathcal{E}(2-, 4) = (2, 4)$, $\mathcal{E}(2-, 5) = (2, 5)$ and $\mathcal{E}(m, n) = (m, n)$ for other edges.

By construction, the following two lemmas about the structure of $G_{mm}$ are immediate. Lemma 3 says that every sink in $G_{mm}$ contains an upwards exposed computation (which cannot be fully redundant since at least one of its incoming edges is essential). The correctness of this lemma can be verified in Figure 1(c). Lemma 4 gives the key reason why classic PRE can be more efficiently solved by data-flow analysis only and also reveals its difference with speculative PRE (Section 4).

**Lemma 3.** *Let $n$ be a node in $G_{mm}$. Then $n \in T_{mm}$ iff $\mathsf{ANTLOC}_{\mathcal{N}(n)} = true$.*

*Proof.* Follows from the construction of $G_{eg}$ and the derivation of $G_{mm}$ from $G_{eg}$ by means of the conceptual split as conducted in Step 4 of MIN-PRE. □

(1) Compute global availability on $G$:

$$\text{AVAILIN}_n = \begin{cases} false & \text{if } n = ENTRY \\ \displaystyle\prod_{m \in pred(G,n)} \text{AVAILOUT}_m & \text{otherwise} \end{cases}$$

$$\text{AVAILOUT}_n = \text{COMP}_n + \text{AVAILIN}_n \cdot \text{TRANSP}_n$$

(2) Compute global anticipatability on $G$:

$$\text{ANTOUT}_n = \begin{cases} false & \text{if } n = EXIT \\ \displaystyle\prod_{m \in succ(G,n)} \text{ANTIN}_m & \text{otherwise} \end{cases}$$

$$\text{ANTIN}_n = \text{ANTLOC}_n + \text{ANTOUT}_n \cdot \text{TRANSP}_n$$

(3) Define $G_{eg} = (N_{eg}, E_{eg}, W_{eg})$ as a subgraph of $G$:
$N_{eg} = \{n \in N \mid \exists\, m \in N : \text{ESS}(m,n) \vee \exists\, m \in N : \text{ESS}(n,m)\}$
$E_{eg} = \{(m,n) \in E \mid \text{ESS}(m,n)\}$
where $\text{ESS}(m,n) = \overline{\text{AVAILOUT}_m} \cdot \text{ANTIN}_n$ for all $(m,n) \in E$.

(4) Derive a multi-source, multi-sink network $G_{mm} = (N_{mm}, E_{mm}, W_{mm})$ from $G_{eg}$ as follows. A *source (sink)* is a node without predecessors (successors). Let $N_{eg}^{ss} = \{n \in N_{eg} \mid \text{ANTLOC}_n \wedge \overline{\text{TRANSP}_n} \wedge pred(G_{eg}, n) \neq \emptyset \wedge succ(G_{eg}, n) \neq \emptyset\}$. For every such a *source-sink node* $n \in N_{eg}^{ss}$, containing instructions $I_1, \dots, I_p$, such that $I_k$ is the first modification to expression $e$, replace $n$ by two new nodes $n+$ and $n-$, where $n+$ contains $I_1, \dots, I_{k-1}$ and $n-$ contains $I_k, \dots, I_p$, such that the incoming (outgoing) edges of $n$ in $G_{eg}$ are now directed into (out of) $n+$ ($n-$) and no edges exist between $n+$ and $n-$. (If $I_k$ is of the form $h = e$ such that $e$ is upwards exposed, and also modified by $h$, i.e., the LHS of $I_k$, then split conceptually $h = e$ into $h' = e; h = h'$ before splitting $n$.) Let $S_{mm} = \{n \in N_{mm} \mid pred(G_{mm}, m) = \emptyset\}$ and $T_{mm} = \{n \in N_{mm} \mid succ(G_{mm}, m) = \emptyset\}$. Let $\mathcal{N} : N_{mm} \mapsto N$ such that $\mathcal{N}(n+) = \mathcal{N}(n-) = \mathcal{N}(n) = n$. Let $\mathcal{E} : E_{mm} \mapsto E$ such that $\mathcal{E}(m,n) = (\mathcal{N}(m), \mathcal{N}(n))$.

(5) Derive a single-source, single-sink flow network $G_{ss} = (N_{ss}, E_{ss}, W_{ss})$ from $G_{mm}$ as follows. Introduce two new nodes, $s$ and $t$, add an edge with weight $\infty$ from the *source* $s$ to every node in $S_{mm}$ and an edge with weight $\infty$ from every node in $T_{mm}$ to the *sink* $t$.

(6) Find a unique minimum cut, $\mathcal{E}^{-1}(\mathcal{C}_\Lambda) = (\Lambda, \overline{\Lambda})$, in $G_{ss}$, as follows:

(a) Apply any min-cut algorithm to find a maximum flow $f$ in $G_{ss}$.
(b) Let $G_{ss}^f = (N_{ss}, E_{ss}^f, W_{ss}^f)$ be the residual network induced by $f$ [5], where
$E_{ss}^f = \{(u,v) \in E_{ss} \mid W_{ss}(u,v) - f(u,v) > 0\}$
$W_{ss}^f = E_{ss}^f \mapsto \mathbb{N}$, where $W_{ss}^f(u,v) = W_{ss}(u,v) - f(u,v)$
(c) Let $\overline{\Lambda} = \{n \in N_{ss} \mid \text{there is a path from } n \text{ to sink } t \text{ in } G_{ss}^f\}$ and $\Lambda = N_{ss} \setminus \overline{\Lambda}$.
(d) Let $\mathcal{C}_\Lambda = \mathcal{C}_\Lambda^{ins} \uplus \mathcal{C}_\Lambda^{copy}$, where $\mathcal{C}_\Lambda^{copy} = \{(m,n) \in \mathcal{C}_\Lambda \mid \forall\, p \in pred(G,n) : (p,n) \in \mathcal{C}_\Lambda\}$.

(7) Solve the "live range analysis for $t_e$" in $G$:

$$\text{LIVEOUT}_n = \begin{cases} false & \text{if } n = EXIT \\ \displaystyle\sum_{m \in succ(G,n)} (\text{LIVEIN}_m \cdot ((n,m) \notin \mathcal{C}_\Lambda)) & \text{otherwise} \end{cases}$$

$$\text{LIVEIN}_n = \text{ANTLOC}_n + \text{LIVEOUT}_n \cdot \text{TRANSP}_n$$

(8) Define the optimal transformation as follows:
$\text{DELETE} = \{n \in N \mid \text{ANTLOC}_n \wedge \text{UE-REDUND}_n\}$
$\text{COPY} = \{n \in N \mid \text{COMP}_n \wedge \text{LIVEOUT}_n \wedge (\overline{\text{TRANSP}_n} \vee \overline{\text{UE-REDUND}_n})\}$
$\text{INSERT} = \mathcal{C}_\Lambda^{ins}$
where $\text{UE-REDUND}_n = (\{(m,n) \in E \mid m \in pred(G,n)\} \not\subseteq \mathcal{C}_\Lambda^{copy})$ for all $n \in N$.

**Fig. 2.** A mincut-based algorithm, MIN-PRE, for classic PRE on $G = (N, E, W)$

**Lemma 4.** *For every* $n \in N_{mm} \setminus (S_{mm} \cup T_{mm})$, *the following statement is true:*

$$\sum_{m \in pred(G_{mm}, n)} W(m, n) \leqslant \sum_{m \in succ(G_{mm}, n)} W(n, m) \tag{2}$$

*Proof.* For every $n \in N_{mm} \setminus (S_{mm} \cup T_{mm})$, we must have $n \in G_{eg}$. It suffices to show that all outgoing edges of $n$ in $G$ are included in $G_{mm}$, i.e., $\forall\ m \in succ(G, n)$ : $(n, m) \in N_{mm}$. By Lemma 3, $\mathsf{ANTLOC}_n = false$. Since $n \notin S_{mm}$, then there must exist an incoming edge $(p, n)$ of $n$ in $G_{mm}$ such that $\mathsf{ESS}(p, n) = true$, i.e., $\mathsf{AVAILOUT}_p = false$ and $\mathsf{ANTIN}_n = true$. When $\mathsf{AVAILOUT}_p = false$, we have $\mathsf{AVAILIN}_n = false$. Note that $\overline{\mathsf{ANTLOC}_n} \wedge \mathsf{ANTIN}_n \implies \mathsf{TRANSP}_n$. Furthermore, $\overline{\mathsf{ANTLOC}_n} \wedge \mathsf{TRANSP}_n \implies \overline{\mathsf{COMP}_n}$. Thus, $\mathsf{AVAILOUT}_n = false$ and $\mathsf{ANTOUT}_n = true$. When $\mathsf{ANTOUT}_n = true$, by definition, we have $\forall\ m \in succ(G, n) : \mathsf{ANTIN}_m = true$. Hence, $\forall\ m \in succ(G, n) : \mathsf{ESS}(n, m) = \overline{\mathsf{AVAILOUT}_n} \wedge \mathsf{ANTIN}_m = true$, implying that $\forall\ m \in succ(G, n) : (n, m) \in N_{mm}$. $\square$

In Step 5, we obtain a single-source, single sink flow network $G_{ss}$ from $G_{mm}$ in the normal manner. In Step 6, we find a unique minimum cut $\mathcal{E}^{-1}(\mathcal{C}_\Lambda)$ on $G_{ss}$ by applying the "Reverse" Labelling Procedure of [10], where $\overline{\Lambda}$ is the smallest possible (Lemma 8). Figure 1(d) depicts $G_{ss}$ for our example, together with the following minimum cut:

$$\begin{aligned}
\mathcal{C}_\Lambda &= \{(1, 2), (2, 5), (3, 5), (4, 6), (7, 9), (8, 10)\} \\
\mathcal{C}_\Lambda^{\mathrm{ins}} &= \{(4, 6), (7, 9)\} \\
\mathcal{C}_\Lambda^{\mathrm{copy}} &= \{(1, 2), (2, 5), (3, 5), (8, 10)\}
\end{aligned} \tag{3}$$

Such a partition of $\mathcal{C}_\Lambda$ into $\mathcal{C}_\Lambda^{\mathrm{ins}}$ and $\mathcal{C}_\Lambda^{\mathrm{copy}}$ is significant due to the fundamentally different roles they play in defining DELETE, COPY and INSERT given in Step 8. According to their definitions in Step 6(d), $\mathcal{C}_\Lambda^{\mathrm{ins}}$ ($\mathcal{C}_\Lambda^{\mathrm{copy}}$) includes a cut edge $(m, n)$ iff some but not all (all) incoming edges of $n$ in the original CFG, $G$, are cut edges.

In order to define DELETE, we need to know if a computation is redundant or not. This is trivial for downwards but not also upwards exposed computations.

**Lemma 5.** *Let $n$ be a node in $G$ such that* $\mathsf{COMP}_n = true$. *If* $\mathsf{TRANSP}_n = false$, *then the downwards exposed computation in $n$ is not redundant.*

To check if an upwards exposed computation is redundant or not, we apply Lemma 6, which makes use of the predicate $\mathsf{UE}\text{-}\mathsf{REDUND}_n$ introduced at the end of Step 8.

**Lemma 6.** *Let $n$ be a node in $G_{mm}$, where $n' = \mathcal{N}(n)$ is the corresponding node in $G$. Then* $\mathsf{UE}\text{-}\mathsf{REDUND}_{n'} = false$ *iff the upwards exposed computation in $n'$ is not redundant (i.e., not removable by using safe code insertions only).*

*Proof.* To prove "$\implies$", we note that MIN-PRE finds the minimum cut $(\Lambda, \overline{\Lambda})$ by applying the "Reverse" Labelling Procedure of [10] to $G_{ss}$. Therefore, $n$ must be a sink in $G_{mm}$, which implies $\mathsf{ANTLOC}_{n'} = true$ by Lemma 3. Let $X$ be the set of all nodes in $G_{mm} \setminus (S_{mm} \cup T_{mm})$ lying on a path from a source in $G_{mm}$ to $n$. By Lemma 4, $\mathsf{UE}\text{-}\mathsf{REDUND}_{n'} = false$, i.e., all incoming edges of $n'$ in $G$ are included in $\mathcal{C}_\Lambda^{\mathrm{copy}}$ iff $\forall\, p \in X : \sum_{m \in pred(G_{mm}, p)} W(m, p) = \sum_{m \in succ(G_{mm}, p)} W(p, m)$. To prove "$\impliedby$", we know that $n'$ must be contained in $G_{\mathrm{eg}}$ by Lemma 1. By Lemma 3, $n$ is a sink node in $G_{mm}$. By Lemma 4, the upwards exposed computation in $n'$ is not redundant iff $\forall\, p \in X : \sum_{m \in \mathrm{pred}(G_{mm},p)} W(m,p) = \sum_{m \in \mathrm{succ}(G_{mm},p)} W(p,m)$. A combination of the results proved so far concludes the proof.                                                              □

Looking at Step 8, we find that $\mathcal{C}_\Lambda^{\mathrm{copy}}$ is sufficient for defining DELETE (Lemmas 5 and 6) while $\mathcal{C}_\Lambda^{\mathrm{ins}}$ is sufficient for defining INSERT. However, Lemmas 5 and 6 do not tell us if a computation that is not redundant generates any redundancies or not. This means that some extra information is required in order to define COPY completely.

A naive solution is to copy at *all* blocks containing non-redundant computations:

$$\mathrm{COPY}^{\mathrm{all}} = \{n \in N \mid \mathrm{COMP}_n \wedge (\overline{\mathrm{TRANSP}_n} \vee \overline{\mathrm{UE\text{-}REDUND}_n})\} \tag{4}$$

Then, $\mathrm{COPY}^{\mathrm{all}}$, together with DELETE and INSERT given in Step 8, will yield a computationally optimal transformation (as implied by the proof of Theorem 1). In terms of LCM, this transformation corresponds to ALCM (Almost LCM) [17, 19].

For the running example, such a computationally optimal transformation is:

$$\begin{aligned}
\mathrm{DELETE} &= \{6, 9, 11\} \\
\mathrm{COPY}^{\mathrm{all}} &= \{5, 6, 10\} \\
\mathrm{INSERT} &= \{(4, 6), (7, 9)\}
\end{aligned} \tag{5}$$

where DELETE and INSERT are the same as in (1). This results in the transformed code in Figure 1(e). However, the definition of $t$ in block 10 is only used in that block. Such a copy operation should be avoided since the live range of $t$ is unnecessarily introduced. The downwards exposed computations of this kind are known to be *isolated* [17, 19]. In Step 7, we solve a third data-flow problem so that $\mathrm{COPY} \subseteq \mathrm{COPY}^{\mathrm{all}}$ is defined in Step 8 with all these isolated blocks being excluded. Note that a copy is required in a block $n$ if it contains a downward exposed computation, which generates redundancies and is not upwards exposed (i.e., $\mathrm{COMP}_n \wedge \mathrm{LIVEOUT}_n \wedge \overline{\mathrm{TRANSP}_n}$ (Lemma 5)) or if it contains an upward exposed computation, which generates redundancies and is not redundant itself (i.e., $\mathrm{COMP}_n \wedge \mathrm{LIVEOUT}_n \wedge \overline{\mathrm{UE\text{-}REDUND}_n}$ (Lemma 6)).

This problem can be understood as one of solving the live variable analysis for temporary $t_e$ on the transformed CFG realised by DELETE and INSERT and $\mathrm{COPY}^{\mathrm{all}}$. By comparing $\mathrm{COPY}^{\mathrm{all}}$ and COPY, we see that we include a block in COPY by also requiring $t_e$ to be live on exit from that block. This guarantees that the downwards exposed computation of $e$ in such a block must generate some redundancies.

Consider Figure 1(e), $\mathrm{LIVEOUT}_5 = \mathrm{LIVEOUT}_6 = \mathit{true}$ but $\mathrm{LIVEOUT}_{10} = \mathit{false}$. Hence, COPY includes only blocks 5 and 6. The final transformation is given in (1), which results in the optimally transformed code shown in Figure 1(f).

*Remark.* If we apply the (normal) Labelling Procedure of [10] in Step 6 of MIN-PRE, $(\Lambda, \overline{\Lambda})$ will be found such that $\overline{\Lambda}$ is the largest. The PRE transformation obtained using such a cut will correspond to the Busy Code Motion (BCM) as described in [17, 19].

### 3.2   (Full) Availability as the Single Commodity

Consider classic PRE carried out optimally on a CFG $G$ for an expression $e$. All (partially or fully) redundant computations of $e$, which must be upwards exposed, as identified by DELETE, are *consumers* of the value of $e$. All downwards exposed computations of $e$ that generate redundancies and are not redundant themselves, as identified by COPY, are *producers* of the value of $e$. Classic PRE can be modelled as a single-commodity maximum flow problem. The value of $e$ (i.e., the commodity) is to be routed from the existing producers to the existing consumers under the condition that $e$ must be (fully) available at the consumers. To achieve this full availability, new producers, as identified by INSERT, can be introduced in $G$, or precisely, $G_{ss}$ under the safe constraint that only the existing consumers can receive the value of $e$. The cost of introducing these new producers (i.e., the number of computations of $e$ incurred) is equal to the maximum flow on $G_{ss}$. In order to be computationally optimal, their placements are the cut edges of a minimum cut as implied in the proof of Theorem 1. In the optimal transformation, new producers must be installed according to the unique minimum cut found by applying essentially the "Reverse" Labelling Procedure of [10] to $G_{ss}$.

### 3.3   Optimality

First of all, we recall Lemma 10 from [14] on the structure of all minimum cuts.

**Lemma 7.** *If* $(A, \overline{A})$ *and* $(B, \overline{B})$ *are minimum cuts in an s-t flow network, then* $(A \cap B, \overline{A \cap B})$ *and* $(A \cup B, \overline{A \cup B})$ *are also minimum cuts in the network.*

This lemma implies immediately that a unique minimum cut $(C, \overline{C})$ exists such that $\overline{C}$ is the *smallest*, i.e., that $\overline{C} \subset \overline{C'}$ for every other minimum cut $(C', \overline{C'})$. Note that $\subset$ is strict. In addition, this lemma is valid independently of any maximum flow that one may use to enumerate all maximum cuts for the underlying network.

In fact, for the minimum cut $(\Lambda, \overline{\Lambda})$ found by MIN-PRE, $\overline{\Lambda}$ is the smallest.

**Lemma 8.** *Let* $S_{cut}$ *be the set of minimum cuts in* $G_{ss} = (N_{ss}, E_{ss}, W_{ss})$. *Consider the minimum cut* $(\Lambda, \overline{\Lambda})$ *in* $G_{ss}$ *found by MIN-PRE. Then:*

$$\overline{\Lambda} \subseteq \overline{C} \text{ for all } (C, \overline{C}) \in S_{cut} \tag{6}$$

*where the equality in* $\subseteq$ *holds iff* $\overline{\Lambda} = \overline{C}$.

*Proof.* By Assumption 2, $G_{ss}$ is an $s$-$t$ flow network with positive edge capacities only. In Step 6 of MIN-PRE, we find the minimum cut $(\Lambda, \overline{\Lambda})$ by applying essentially the "Reverse" Labelling Procedure of [10]. Its construction ensures that (6) holds with respect to the maximum flow $f$ used. Lemma 7 implies that this "smallest minimum cut" is independent of the maximum flow $f$. Hence, (6) is established.                    □

**Theorem 1.** *The transformation found by MIN-PRE is (lifetime) optimal and unique.*

*Proof.* Consider an expression $e$ in $G = (N, E, W)$. Let $LO$ denote the transformation found by MIN-PRE, which is represented by DELETE, INSERT and COPY. Let a lifetime optimal transformation be represented by $\text{DELETE}_T$, $\text{INSERT}_T$ and $\text{COPY}_T$. By Lemma 6, $\text{DELETE} = \text{DELETE}_T$. By also applying Lemma 6 and noting that $n \in$ COPY iff it generates redundancies in DELETE, we must have $\text{COPY} = \text{COPY}_T$. Recall that $\mathcal{E}^{-1}(\mathcal{C}_\Lambda) = (\Lambda, \overline{\Lambda})$ is the minimum cut found by MIN-PRE in its Step 6, where $\mathcal{C}_\Lambda = \mathcal{C}_\Lambda^{\text{ins}} \uplus \mathcal{C}_\Lambda^{\text{copy}}$. By Lemma 2, $\mathsf{INSERT}_T$ must be drawn from the edges of $G_{\text{eg}}$. Clearly, $\mathcal{E}^{-1}(\mathcal{C}_\Lambda^{\text{copy}} \uplus \mathsf{INSERT}_T)$ must be a cut since $T$ cannot be valid otherwise. Furthermore, $\mathcal{E}^{-1}(\mathcal{C}_\Lambda^{\text{copy}} \uplus \mathsf{INSERT}_T)$ must be a minimum cut. Otherwise, $LO$ constructed using a minimum cut will cause fewer computations of $e$ to be evaluated. Let $\mathcal{E}^{-1}(\mathcal{C}_\Lambda^{\text{copy}} \uplus \mathsf{INSERT}_T) = (\Lambda', \overline{\Lambda'})$. By Lemma 8, $\overline{\Lambda} \subseteq \overline{\Lambda'}$. Thus, the equality in $\overline{\Lambda} \subseteq \overline{\Lambda'}$ must hold. Otherwise, the live ranges of $t_e = e$ in $LO$ will be better than those in $T$. Hence, $LO = T$ is lifetime optimal, which is unique since $(\Lambda, \overline{\Lambda})$ is.    $\square$

## 4    Classic PRE vs. Speculative PRE

In [26], we formulated speculative PRE as a maximum flow problem. This work shows that classic PRE is also a maximum flow problem. We recognise immediately that the fundamental difference between the two optimisations lies only in Step 2 of MIN-PRE. In the case of speculative PRE, we will compute partial anticipatability rather than full anticipatability. As a result, two seemingly different PRE problems are unified.

We compare and contrast classic and speculative PRE by using Figures 1 and 3. In Figure 3(a), our example CFG $G$ is annotated with two different edge profiles. Figures 3(b) and 3(c) depict (identically) the flow network $G_{ss}^{\text{spre}}$ obtained by applying MIN-PRE to $G$ except that partial anticipatability is computed in its Step 2. Compared to $G_{ss}$ in Figure 1(d) in classic PRE, $G_{ss}^{\text{spre}}$ has two more edges: $(3,7)$ and $(7,8)$.

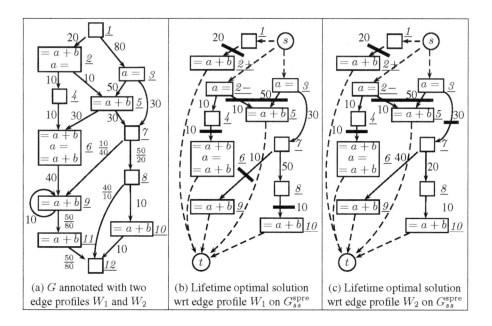

(a) $G$ annotated with two edge profiles $W_1$ and $W_2$

(b) Lifetime optimal solution wrt edge profile $W_1$ on $G_{ss}^{\text{spre}}$

(c) Lifetime optimal solution wrt edge profile $W_2$ on $G_{ss}^{\text{spre}}$

**Fig. 3.** Profile-sensitivity of speculative PRE. In (a), the CFG from Figure 1(a) is annotated with two different edge profiles. If an edge is labelled by $x$, $W_1(e) = W_2(e) = x$. If an edge label is $\frac{x}{y}$, $W_1(e) = x$ and $W_2(e) = y$. The optimal solutions for $W_1$ and $W_2$ are given in (b) and (c).

The difference between classic and speculative PRE translates into the structural difference between $G_{mm}$ and $G_{mm}^{\mathrm{spre}}$, from which $G_{ss}$ and $G_{ss}^{\mathrm{spre}}$ are derived. Lemma 4 that is valid for $G_{mm}$ in classic PRE is not valid for $G_{mm}^{\mathrm{spre}}$ in speculative PRE. For example, block 8 in $G_{ss}^{\mathrm{spre}}$ given in Figure 3(b) or 3(c) is one such a counterexample node. As a result, $G_{ss}^{\mathrm{spre}}$ is generally an arbitrary flow network, implying that speculative PRE needs to be solved optimally using a min-cut algorithm. In addition, speculative PRE is profile-sensitive. Different execution profiles can result in different optimal transformations as illustrated in Figures 3(b) and 3(c). In both cases, only the execution frequencies on edges $(7, 8)$ and $(7, 9)$ are different. Note that the solution shown in Figure 3(b) is the same as the one found in classic PRE (Figure 1(d)). In speculative PRE, the benefit of an optimal transformation depends on the accuracy of the profiling information used. More computations may be evaluated if the profiling information used is completely inaccurate. On the other hand, classic PRE is profile-independent and thus conservative. Never will more computations be evaluated in the transformed code. Due to Lemma 4, different profiles always result in the same optimal transformation, as implied in Theorem 1. The reader can verify that MIN-PRE will return exactly the same minimum cut in Figure 1(d) for the two execution profiles given in Figure 3(a).

## 5   SIM-PRE: A Simple Mincut-Motivated Algorithm

Due to the special structure of $G_{mm}$, and consequently, $G_{ss}$, as identified in Lemma 4, we can find the unique minimum cut $\mathcal{E}^{-1}(\mathcal{C}_\Lambda) = \mathcal{C}_\Lambda^{\mathrm{ins}} \uplus \mathcal{C}_\Lambda^{\mathrm{copy}} = (\Lambda, \overline{\Lambda})$ found in Step 6 of MIN-PRE by solving one data-flow problem. Based on MIN-PRE, we have developed a simple and efficient algorithm, called SIM-PRE and given in Figure 4, for

---

(1) Compute global availability on $G$:

(2) Compute global anticipatability on $G$:

(3) Compute global availability perceived to be done on the transformed CFG:

$$\mathcal{TG}\text{-AVAILIN}_n = \begin{cases} false & \text{if } n = ENTRY \\ \text{AVAILIN}_n + \text{ANTIN}_n \cdot \sum_{m \in pred(G,n)} \mathcal{TG}\text{-AVAILOUT}_m & \text{otherwise} \end{cases}$$

$$\mathcal{TG}\text{-AVAILOUT}_n = \text{COMP}_n + \mathcal{TG}\text{-AVAILIN}_n \cdot \text{TRANSP}_n$$

(4) Compute a restricted form of partial anticipatability on the transformed CFG:

$$\mathcal{TG}\text{-PANTOUT}_n = \begin{cases} false & \text{if } n = EXIT \\ \mathcal{TG}\text{-AVAILOUT}_n \cdot \sum_{m \in succ(G,n)} \mathcal{TG}\text{-PANTIN}_m & \text{otherwise} \end{cases}$$

$$\mathcal{TG}\text{-PANTIN}_n = \text{ANTLOC}_n + \mathcal{TG}\text{-PANTOUT}_n \cdot \text{TRANSP}_n$$

(5) Define the optimal transformation as follows:

DELETE $= \{n \in N \mid \text{ANTLOC}_n \wedge \mathcal{TG}\text{-AVAILIN}_n\}$

COPY $= \{n \in N \mid \text{COMP}_n \wedge \mathcal{TG}\text{-PANTOUT}_n \wedge (\overline{\text{TRANSP}_n} \vee \overline{\mathcal{TG}\text{-AVAILIN}_n})\}$

INSERT $= \{(m, n) \in E \mid \overline{\mathcal{TG}\text{-AVAILOUT}_m} \wedge \mathcal{TG}\text{-AVAILIN}_n\}$

---

**Fig. 4.** A mincut-motivated algorithm, SIM-PRE, for classic PRE on $G = (N, E, W)$

classic PRE by solving four data-flow problems. Steps 1 and 2 remain the same. In Step 3, we solve a data-flow problem in $G$ but the problem can be understood as one of computing global availability on the optimally transformed graph, $G_{\mathrm{opt}}$, of $G$. The two global properties, $\mathcal{TG}\text{-AVAILIN}_n$ and $\mathcal{TG}\text{-AVAILOUT}_n$, are defined for the entry and exit of every block $n$ in $G_{\mathrm{opt}}$. $\mathcal{TG}\text{-AVAILOUT}_n$ is computed in the normal manner. In the case of $\mathcal{TG}\text{-AVAILIN}_n$, an expression $e$ is available on entry to block $n$ in $G_{\mathrm{opt}}$ if it is already available in $G$. In addition, if $e$ is available along some incoming edges of block $n$ but not along some others $(m, n)$ in $G_{\mathrm{opt}}$ and if $e$ is (fully) anticipatable on entry to $n$ in $G$, then $(m, n) \in \mathcal{C}_\Lambda^{\mathrm{ins}}$ must be an insertion edge. After $t_e = e$ has been made on all these insertion edges, $\mathcal{TG}\text{-AVAILIN}_n = true$ will hold. Hence, we have:

$$\text{UE-REDUND}_n = \mathcal{TG}\text{-AVAILIN}_n \tag{7}$$

which leads directly to:

$$\begin{aligned}
\mathcal{C}_\Lambda^{\mathrm{ins}} &= \{(m, n) \in E \mid \overline{\mathcal{TG}\text{-AVAILOUT}_m} \wedge \mathcal{TG}\text{-AVAILIN}_n\} \\
\mathcal{C}_\Lambda^{\mathrm{copy}} &= \bigcup\nolimits_{n \in N: \text{ANTLOC}_n \wedge \overline{\text{UE-REDUND}_n}} \{(m, n) \in E \mid m \in pred(G, n)\}
\end{aligned} \tag{8}$$

To define COPY, we do not use the "live variable analysis" given in Step 7 of MIN-PRE. Instead, we solve a different data-flow problem, which is simpler for two reasons. First, we do not need to compute the predicate $(m, n) \in \mathcal{C}_\Lambda$ on flow edges. Second, the meet operator will use fewer bit-vector operations than before. This problem can be understood as one of computing partial anticipatability for an expression $e$ on the transformed graph $G_{\mathrm{opt}}$ but only at the points where $e$ is available in $G_{\mathrm{opt}}$. (Note that $\mathcal{TG}\text{-PANTIN}_n$, which is not used, can be true on entry to block $n$ if $\text{ANTLOC}_n = true$.)

**Theorem 2.** *The transformation found by SIM-PRE is lifetime optimal.*

*Proof.* Let *LO* be the transformation found by MIN-PRE, which is represented by DELETE, INSERT and COPY and *SIM* the transformation found by SIM-PRE, which is represented by $\text{DELETE}_{SIM}$, $\text{INSERT}_{SIM}$ and $\text{COPY}_{SIM}$. By Lemma 4, (7) and (8) hold. By Lemmas 5 and 6, $\text{DELETE} = \text{DELETE}_{SIM}$ and $\text{INSERT} = \text{INSERT}_{SIM}$. By definition, $\mathcal{TG}\text{-PANTOUT}_n = true$ iff $t_e$ is live on exit from $n$. So $\mathcal{TG}\text{-PANTOUT}_n = \text{LIVEOUT}_n$. Thus, $\text{COPY} = \text{COPY}_{SIM}$. This means that *LO=SIM*. $\square$

## 6   Experimental Results

We evaluate the efficiencies of SIM-PRE and three other algorithms (denoted by LCM-DS, LCM-DS+COPY and E-Path) in terms of the total number of bit-vector operations performed on benchmark programs. All algorithms are implemented in GCC 3.4.3 and invoked to operate at its RTL (Register Transfer Language). We have applied the four algorithms to all 22 C/C++/FORTRAN SPECcpu2000 benchmarks compiled on two different platforms: Intel Xeon and SUN UltraSPARC-III. Due to architectural differences, the RTL representations on two platforms are drastically different.

LCM-DS denotes the GCC's implementation of a variant of LCM that was described in [9]. This algorithm assumes that the result of an expression is always available in a distinct temporary. Therefore, COPY is not computed. Since this assumption is not

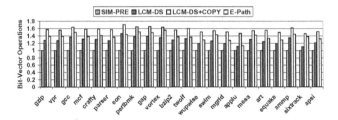

**Fig. 5.** A comparison of four algorithms on Xeon

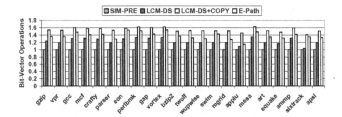

**Fig. 6.** A comparison of four algorithms on UltraSPARC-III

valid for RTL, GCC does a brute-force search on a CFG to compute COPY for each expression separately. There is no way to translate these graph traversal operations into equivalent bit-vector operations. Therefore, LCM-DS+COPY denotes the algorithm formed by combining LCM-DS and the 4th data-flow analysis used in SIM-PRE for computing COPY. E-Path is a recent new algorithm presented in [7].

SIM-PRE, LCM-DS+COPY and E-Path each solve four data-flow problems while LCM-DS solves only three (as discussed above). The first two problems, availability and anticipatability, are all the same. These algorithms differ only in how the remaining problem(s) are formulated. The efficiency of an algorithm is measured in terms of the number of bit-vector operations performed by all data-flow problems in an algorithm.

All algorithms are implemented using the bit-vector routines provided by GCC and operate on the same set of PRE candidate expressions used by GCC. A PRE candidate expression is always the RHS of an assignment, where the LHS is a virtual register. The RHS expressions that are constants or virtual registers are excluded (since no computations are involved). So are any expressions such as call expressions with side effects.

Figure 5 gives the (normalised) bit-vector operations consumed by four algorithms on Xeon. In LCM-DS (and LCM-DS+COPY), the data-flow equations for computing EARLIEST and LATER are expensive due to the excessive use of logical negations and somewhat complex equations employed. In E-Path, the equations used in the last two data-flow problems are more complex than those in SIM-PRE. In particular, the meet operators in $Eps\_in_i$ and $SA\_out_i$ are more expensive to evaluate. Figure 6 gives our experimental results on UltraSPARC-III. In both computer platforms, SIM-PRE requires fewer bit-vector operations than each of the other three algorithms. The key reason for SIM-PRE's efficiency is that the equations in solving its last two data-flow problems are simpler. Since these two problems are formulated to find a unique minimum cut for a CFG, we reason positively about the two global properties without using logical negations. So the number of bit-vector operations used are reduced.

## 7  Related Work and Conclusions

LCM [17, 19] and its extensions [8, 15] find code insertion points by modelling the optimisation as a code motion transformation as suggested in [6]. This approach is characterised by a few concepts, such as *earliest*, *latest* and *isolated*, that are not inherent in the PRE problem itself. Alternatively, some formulations of classic PRE [7, 23] avoid these concepts by identifying code insertion points directly. The driving force behind the development of these different formulations has probably been the insatiable desire to find a good conceptual basis upon which an optimal formulation of classic PRE can be easily developed, understood and reasoned about. However, in all existing formulations of classic PRE, data-flow equations are still cleverly but ad hocly designed. Their optimality is usually not obvious to their users and their proofs tedious and non-intuitive since the proofs have always been conducted at the low level of individual paths. This work provides a common high-level conceptual basis upon which an optimal formulation of PRE can be developed and proved. All optimal algorithms must find one way or another the unique minimum cut on a flow network $G_{ss}$ derived from a CFG.

Classic PRE has been extended to perform other important optimisations, including strength reduction [8, 12, 16, 18], global value numbering [3], live-range determination [21], code size reduction [24], redundant load/store elimination [21] and data speculation [20]. Its scope has also been extended by means of code restructuring [2].

The earliest papers on speculative PRE can be found in [11, 13]. There are three computationally optimal algorithms for speculative PRE [1, 4, 25]. Later we also developed a lifetime optimal algorithm [26]. This work shows that both seemingly different problems are inherently related and can be unified under a common conceptual basis.

PRE is an important optimisation in optimising compilers and also serves as a classic classroom example for iterative and worklist data-flow analysis. The results and insights presented in this work are expected to be valuable in both settings.

## References

1. R. Bodik. *Path-Sensitive Value-Flow Optimizations of Programs*. PhD thesis, University of Pittsburgh, 1999.
2. R. Bodik, R. Gupta, and M. L. Soffa. Complete removal of redundant computations. In *Proceedings of the ACM SIGPLAN '98 Conference on Programming Language Design and Implementation*, pages 1–14, 1998.
3. P. Briggs and K. D. Cooper. Effective partial redundancy elimination. In *Proceedings of the ACM SIGPLAN '94 Conference on Programming Language Design and Implementation*, pages 159–170, 1994.
4. Q. Cai and J. Xue. Optimal and efficient speculation-based partial redundancy elimination. In *1st IEEE/ACM International Symposium on Code Generation and Optimization*, pages 91–104, 2003.
5. T. H. Cormen, C. E. Leiserson, and R. L. Rivest. *Introduction to Algorithms*. Cambridge, Mass.: MIT Press, 1990.

6. D. M. Dhamdhere. A fast algorithm for code movement optimisation. *SIGPLAN Not.*, 23(10):172–180, 1988.

7. D. M. Dhamdhere. E-path_pre: partial redundancy elimination made easy. *SIGPLAN Not.*, 37(8):53–65, 2002.

8. V. M. Dhaneshwar and D. M. Dhamdhere. Strength reduction of large expressions. *Journal of Programming Languages*, 3:95–120, 1995.

9. K.-H. Drechsler and M. P. Stadel. A variation on Knoop, Rüthing, and Steffen's lazy code motion. *SIGPLAN Notices*, 28(5):29–38, 1993.

10. L. R. Ford and D. R. Fulkerson. *Flows in Networks*. Princeton University Press, 1962.

11. R. Gupta, D. A. Berson, and J. Z. Fang. Path profile guided partial redundancy elimination using speculation. In *Proceedings of the 1998 International Conference on Computer Languages*, pages 230–239, 1998.

12. M. Hailperin. Cost-optimal code motion. *ACM Transactions on Programming Languages and Systems*, 20(6):1297 – 1322, 1998.

13. R. Horspool and H. Ho. Partial redundancy elimination driven by a cost-benefit analysis. In *8th Israeli Conference on Computer System and Software Engineering*, pages 111–118, 1997.

14. T. C. Hu. *Integer Programming and Network Flows*. Addison-Wesley, 1970.

15. R. Kennedy, S. Chan, S.-M. Liu, R. Lo, and P. Tu. Partial redundancy elimination in SSA form. *ACM Transactions on Programming Languages and Systems*, 21(3):627–676, 1999.

16. R. Kennedy, F. C. Chow, P. Dahl, S.-M. Liu, R. Lo, and M. Streich. Strength reduction via SSAPRE. In *Proceedings of the 7th International Conference on Compiler Construction*, pages 144–158, London, UK, 1998. Springer-Verlag.

17. J. Knoop, O. Rüthing, and B. Steffen. Lazy code motion. In *Proceedings of the ACM SIGPLAN '92 Conference on Programming Language Design and Implementation*, pages 224–234, 1992.

18. J. Knoop, O. Rüthing, and B. Steffen. Lazy strength reduction. *Journal of Programming Languages*, 1(1):71 – 91, 1993.

19. J. Knoop, O. Rüthing, and B. Steffen. Optimal code motion: Theory and practice. *ACM Trans. Program. Lang. Syst.*, 16(4):1117–1155, 1994.

20. J. Lin, T. Chen, W.-C. Hsu, P.-C. Yew, R. D.-C. Ju, T.-F. Ngai, and S. Chan. A compiler framework for speculative analysis and optimizations. In *Proceedings of the ACM SIGPLAN '03 Conference on Programming Language Design and Implementation*, pages 289–299, 2003.

21. R. Lo, F. Chow, R. Kennedy, S.-M. Liu, and P. Tu. Register promotion by sparse partial redundancy elimination of loads and stores. *SIGPLAN Not.*, 33(5):26–37, 1998.

22. E. Morel and C. Renvoise. Global optimization by suppression of partial redundancies. *Commun. ACM*, 22(2):96–103, 1979.

23. V. K. Paleri, Y. N. Srikant, and P. Shankar. A simple algorithm for partial redundancy elimination. *SIGPLAN Not.*, 33(12):35–43, 1998.

24. O. Rüthing, J. Knoop, and B. Steffen. Sparse code motion. In *Conference Record of the 27th Annual ACM SIGPLAN-SIGACT Symposium on Principles of Programming Languages (Boston, Massachusetts)*, pages 170 – 183. ACM, New York, 2000.

25. B. Scholz, R. N. Horspool, and J. Knoop. Optimizing for space and time usage with speculative partial redundancy elimination. In *Proceedings of the 2004 ACM SIGPLAN/SIGBED Conference on Languages, Compilers, and Tools for Embedded Systems*, pages 221–230, 2004.

26. J. Xue and Q. Cai. Profile-guided partial redundancy elimination using control speculation: a lifetime optimal algorithm and an experimental evaluation. Technical Report UNSW–CSE–TR–0420, School of Computer Science and Engigeering, University of New South Wales, Jul. 2004.

# Performance Characterization of the 64-bit x86 Architecture from Compiler Optimizations' Perspective

Jack Liu and Youfeng Wu

Intel Corporation,
2200 Mission Blvd, Santa Clara, CA
{jack.liu, youfeng.wu}@intel.com
http://www.intel.com/

**Abstract.** Intel Extended Memory 64 Technology (EM64T) and AMD 64-bit architecture (AMD64) are emerging 64-bit x86 architectures that are fully x86 compatible. Compared with the 32-bit x86 architecture, the 64-bit x86 architectures cater some new features to applications. For instance, applications can address 64 bits of virtual memory space, perform operations on 64-bit-wide operands, get access to 16 general-purpose registers (GPRs) and 16 extended multi-media (XMM) registers, and use a register-based argument passing convention. In this paper, we investigate the performance impacts of these new features from compiler optimizations' standpoint. Our research compiler is based on the Intel Fortran/C++ production compiler, and our experiments are conducted on the SPEC2000 benchmark suite. Results show that for 64-bit-wide *pointer* and *long* data types, several SPEC2000 C benchmarks are slowed down by more than 20%, which is mainly due to the enlarged memory footprint. To evaluate the performance potential of 64-bit x86 architectures, we designed and implemented the LP32 code model such that the sizes of *pointer* and *long* are 32 bits. Our experiments demonstrate that on average the LP32 code model speeds up the SPEC2000 C benchmarks by 13.4%. For the register-based argument passing convention, our experiments show that the performance gain is less than 1% because of the aggressive function inlining optimization. Finally, we observe that using 16 GPRs and 16 XMM registers significantly outperforms the scenario when only 8 GPRs and 8 XMM registers are used. However, our results also show that using 12 GPRs and 12 XMM registers can achieve as competitive performance as employing 16 GPRs and 16 XMM registers.

## 1 Introduction

In year 2003, AMD first introduced the AMD64 Opteron processor family that extends the existing 32-bit x86 architecture to 64-bit. In the following year, Intel announced that the Intel Extended Memory 64 Technology (EM64T) would be added to a series of IA-32 processors, which includes the Pentium 4 and Pentium M processors. Both AMD's AMD64 architecture and Intel's EM64T architecture allow applications to access up to one terabyte of memory address space. In addition, 64-bit Windows and Linux operating systems running on 64-bit x86 processors are supported by Microsoft, Red Hat and SuSE. Intel's 64-bit extension technology software

A. Mycroft and A. Zeller (Eds.): CC 2006, LNCS 3923, pp. 155 – 169, 2006.

developer's guide [1] details the EM64T architecture and the programming model. With the advent of 64-bit x86-compatible processors, it is imperative to understand its performance potential and its capability. Although the experiments of this study are done on the EM64T machine, we believe many of the results and insights can be applied to the AMD64 machine. (Note that EM64T and AMD64 are nearly binary compatible with each other, except for some of the instructions like AMD's 3DNOW and Intel's SSE3.)

The 64-bit x86 architecture furnishes many advantages over the 32-bit x86 architecture. The main advantages include: (1) 64-bit pointers over 32-bit pointers. 64-bit pointer allows applications to get access to one terabyte address space directly; (2) 64-bit-wide general purpose registers (GPRs) over 32-bit-wide GPRs. The 64-bit-wide GPR allows 64-bit integer operations to be executed natively; and (3) 16 GPRs and 16 XMM registers over 8 GPRs and 8 XMM registers. With more registers, more values can be put into registers instead of in memory, and thus improve the performance. However, on the other side, we noticed that the 64-bit x86 architecture does not favor all the applications. For instance, within the 64-bit environment, some system vendors run 32-bit applications to report the peak performance, and a prior experiment [15] discusses several SPEC benchmarks whose 32-bit code can run substantially faster than their 64-bit counterparts can.

In this paper, we evaluate how these new features provided by the 64-bit x86 architecture can affect applications' performance from compiler optimizations' perspective. The contributions of this paper are threefold. First, we implemented the LP32 code model that supports 32-bit-wide *long* and *pointer* data types, and measured the performance impact of the LP32 code model. Secondly, we compared the performance difference using two different argument passing conventions. Lastly, we studied the sensitivities of applications' performances with respect to the number of allocatable registers.

The rest of the paper is organized as follows. In Section 2, we describe the infrastructure of the experimental framework. In Section 3, we evaluate the performance impact of the LP32 code model. In Section 4, we compare the register-based argument passing convention with the stack-based argument passing convention. In Section 5, we evaluate how applications' performances are improved with more allocatable registers. In Section 6, we briefly describe how the other 64-bit x86 features can improve application's performance. Finally, we conclude our study in Section 7.

## 2   Experimental Framework

In this section, we first give an overview of the 64-bit x86 architecture, and then illustrate how we set up the experimental infrastructure, which include how we construct a research compiler and how we characterize the performance impact of the 64-bit x86 architecture's new features.

### 2.1   Overview of the 64-bit x86 Architecture

The 64-bit x86 architecture is an extension of the 32-bit x86 architecture: it increases the virtual linear address space from 32 bits to 64 bits, and supports physical address space to 40 bits. The 64-bit x86 architecture supports three operating modes: (1)

*legacy mode*, which enables 32-bit operating system to run 32-bit software, (2) *compatibility mode*, which enables 64-bit operating system to run 32-bit legacy software without any modification, and (3) *64-bit mode*, which enables the 64-bit operating system to run 64-bit software that can get access to the 64-bit flat linear address space. Only software running on 64-bit mode can get access to the extended registers, and directly address up to one terabyte of memory space.

Evolved from the IA-32 architecture, the 64-bit x86 architecture doubled the number of GPRs and XMM registers from 8 to 16, respectively. In addition, the width of GPRs is extended from 32 bits to 64 bits. Equipped with more registers, the argument passing convention is changed considerably: instead of passing arguments through stack, now six GPRs and six XMM registers are dedicated to pass arguments [8].

In spite of rendering attractive new features, the 64-bit architecture comes at the cost of enlarging memory footprint. In both Linux and Windows operating systems, the size of *pointer* data type is widened from 32 bits to 64 bits, and in Linux operating system, the size of *long* data type is widened from 32 bits to 64 bits. Enlarged data types could degrade the performance of pointer intensive applications, because now they have bigger memory footprint that causes more cache misses. As another side effect of 64-bit address, occasionally sign extensions are required to perform address computations through 32-bit signed operands. In addition, the code size could increase due to a set of prefixes are introduced when extended registers or 64-bit register operands are referred. We will present additional details in the following related sections. In this paper, we conducted all the experiments on a Dell Precision Workstation 370 MiniTower containing a 3.8 GHz Intel Pentium 4 processor. The system's detail configuration is listed in Table 1.

**Table 1.** Hardware system configuration

| Processor | one 3.8 GHz Intel Pentium 4 Prescott |
|---|---|
| L1 Trace cache | 12K micro-ops, 8-way set associative<br>6 micro-ops per line |
| L1 Data cache | 16KB, 4-way set associative<br>64B line size, write-through |
| L2 Unified cache | 8-way, Sectored, 1MB unified L2 Cache<br>64 byte line size |
| Data TLB | fully associative, 4K/2M/4M pages, 64 entries |
| Instruction TLB | 4-way associative, 4K pages, 64 entries |
| System chipset | Intel® E7520 Chipset |
| System bus speed | 800 MHz system bus |
| Main memory | 3GB, 400MHz, DDR2 NECC SDRAM memory |

## 2.2 Methodology on Performance Characterization

We used a research compiler to generate different executables to reflect the interested 64-bit x86 architectural features. Once the executables were generated, we applied a set of performance profiling tools to study the performance characteristics. The following sections described the tools and the operating system that we used in this study.

### 2.2.1  Overview of the Intel Compiler

Our research compiler is based on Intel's 9.0 version Fortran and C++ production compiler that supports many Intel architectures. A high-level overview of the Intel compiler infrastructure is given in Figure 1. In this study, we used options "-*O3* –*xP* – *ipo* –*prof_use*" to compile all the benchmarks. Here option –*xP* specifies that the compilation is targeting for a Prescott family processor, option –*ipo* enables the use of inter-procedural optimization, and option –*prof_use* enables the use of profiling information during compilation. Since we started this study, a few new optimizations and enhancements have been implemented to the product Intel compiler. For this reason, our research compiler may not demonstrate the best performance, and thus we only present relative performance numbers in the experimental result sections.

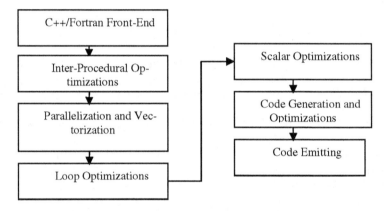

**Fig. 1.** A high-level overview of the Intel compiler architecture

Throughout this study, we conducted our experiments using the SPEC CPU2000 benchmark suite, which consists of twelve integer benchmarks (CINT2000) and fourteen floating-point benchmarks (CFP2000). In this paper, we refer all the SPEC2000 benchmarks that are written in C as SPEC2000 C benchmarks.

### 2.2.2  Profiling Tools

Intel's Pentium 4 processor provides a rich set of performance-monitoring counters that can be used for performance tuning [5][17]. In this study, we used emon, a low-level and low overhead performance tool, to collect the L2 cache references from the performance-monitoring counters by monitoring event *BSQ_cache_reference*. This event counts the number of second level cache loads and read-for-ownership (RFO) as seen by the bus unit. RFO happens when memory writes that miss must read the rest of the cache line to merge with new data.

Besides emon, we used *pin* [4] to collect the dynamic instruction distribution information. Pin is a dynamic instrumentation system developed at Intel Corporation. It provides a rich set of APIs so that users can write tools to analyze an application at the instruction level. Here we used a modified version of *insmix*, one of the pintools provided by pin, to the collect dynamic instruction information.

### 2.2.3 Operating System

We conducted all our experiments on the Enterprise Linux operating system with kernel 2.6.9-5. We chose Linux operating system, because it provides us the flexibility to modify the kernel to support the LP32 code model.

To support the LP32 code model in this study, we modified the operating system kernel by specifying the value of macro *TASK_SIZE* to *0x100000000UL* within file asm-x86_64/processor.h. In this manner, user applications' spaces are allocated within the lower 32-bit address space. (Note that modifying the value of TASK_SIZE to support the LP32 code model might not be the best approach. We adopted this approach to serve our evaluation purpose only.)

## 3  Performance Characterization of the LP32 Code Model

Under the 64-bit processor environment, the sizes of *long* and *pointer* data types by default are 64 bits on Linux operating system. In this study, we implemented the LP32 code model so that the sizes of *long* and *pointer* are 32 bits. To illustrate the differences among different modes, Figure 2 depicts how the address of variable *j* is stored into the *i*-th element of array *a*, *a[i]* = *&j*, in 64-bit mode, compatibility mode, and the LP32 code model, respectively.

```
48 63 05 00 00 00 00      movslq i(%rip), %rax
48 c7 04 c5 00 00 00      movq   $j, a(,%rax,8)
                          (a)


a1 00 00 00 00            movl   i, %eax
c7 04 85 00 00 00 00      movl   $j, a(,%eax,4)
                          (b)


8b 05 00 00 00 00         movl   i(%rip), %eax
67 c7 04 85 00 00 00 00   movl   $j, a(,%eax,4)
                          (c)
```

**Fig. 2.** Different code sequences in different modes used to perform assignment "*a[i]* = *&j*". (a) Instruction sequence generated in 64-bit mode. (b) Instruction sequence generated in compatibility mode. (c) Instruction sequence generated in the LP32 code model.

As depicted in Figure 2(a) and Figure 2(b), the differences between compatibility mode and 64-bit mode are threefold: (1) application memory footprint is increased for larger pointer; (2) sign extension operation is required to compute the 64-bit address; and (3) code size is increased because of prefixes. In Figure 2(c), address-size prefix *0x67* is required to specify that the effective address size is 32 bits. (In 64-bit mode, the default effective address size is 64 bits; in compatibility mode, the default effective address size is 32 bits.) In this section, we study how the aforementioned modes could affect the SPEC2000 C benchmarks' performance.

### 3.1  Implementation Challenges

We encountered numerous challenges during the implementation of the LP32 code model. The first challenge was how to guarantee that the user stack are allocated in the lower 32-bit address space. A quick work around is described in Section 2.2.3 by modifying the operating system kernel. Once that was resolved, we need to solve the compatibility issue: external functions do not understand the LP32 code model.

One solution is to provide a group of LP32 compatible libraries. In this study, we implemented a set of wrappers for those external functions that will read/write the user-defined *pointer-* or *long-type* data directly or indirectly. Across all the SPEC2000 C benchmarks, we experienced few such kind of external functions; typical instances are *time()*, *fstat()*, and *times()*. Note that the performances of these functions do not affect our characterization results.

## 3.2  Experimental Results

Figure 3 shows the normalized execution time (with respect to base compilation in 64-bit mode) of the *ILP32 code model*, compatibility mode, and the LP32 code model. The ILP32 code model is the result of the auto ilp32 optimization, which will be elaborated in Section 3.3. On average, the LP32 speedups the performance across all the SPEC C benchmarks by 13.4%. Without otherwise stated, we use geometric mean to calculate the average values.

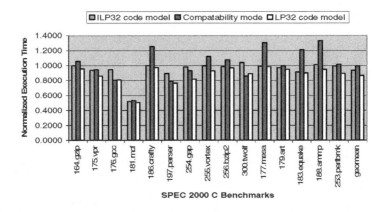

**Fig. 3.** The normalized execution time in the ILP32 code model, compatibility mode, and the LP32 code model for the SPEC2000 C benchmarks

Figure 4 gives the normalized L2 cache miss ratio for the SPEC2000 C benchmarks in the LP32 code model. Since the out-of-order execution engine of the 64-bit x86 processor can effectively hide many of stalls incurred by cache misses, the purpose of this figure is not to correlate with Figure 3 directly, but to provide us some insights on how the LP32 code model can reduce the cache miss ratio. Notice that the L2 cache miss ratio of benchmark 183.equake is increased by more than 20%. This is because in the LP32 code model, the absolute numbers of L2 cache accesses and L2 cache misses are reduced, yet the number of L2 cache accesses is reduced more.

Across the SPEC2000 C benchmarks, 181.mcf gains the most speedup, by almost 50%. This is understandable because 181.mcf is a memory-bound benchmark, and

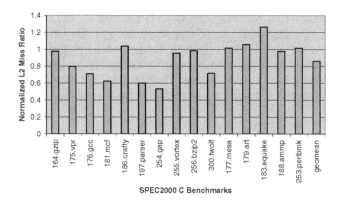

**Fig. 4.** The normalized L2 cache miss ratio for the SPEC2000 C benchmarks in the LP32 code model

many of the cache optimization techniques can improve its performance greatly. However, not all the performance loss in 64-bit mode is due to enlarged memory footprint. Benchmark 254.gap exemplifies our argument. Compiled in the LP32 code model, the 254.gap benchmark demonstrates a 20% speedup. We observed that the performance of this benchmark is dominated by a garbage collection function named *CollectGarb()*. This function will be invoked when the internal memory pool is exhausted. In compatibility mode, *CollecGarb()* is invoked 74 times, as opposed to 132 times in 64-bit mode. This is because some objects allocated within 254.gap require more memory space in 64-bit mode than in compatibility mode, and thus the internal memory pool is used up more quickly. In fact, the execution time of 254.gap can be reduced by almost 10% if we double the memory space allocated to its internal memory pool.

### 3.3   Related Work

For 32-bit applications, the LP32 code model is an effective approach to reduce the memory footprint, and leverage the new hardware features. However, in practice, it requires tremendous engineering effort to maintain a separate set of libraries and part of the kernel layer support.

To reduce the enlarged memory footprint in 64-bit mode, gcc compiler and pathcc compiler can generate 32-bit executables if users specify *–m32* compilation option, yet at the cost that these executables can only be executed in compatibility mode. To overcome this limitation, Intel compiler provides auto ilp32 optimization, which can represent the sizes of pointer and long data type values in 32 bits, and the applications can use all the new features of the 64-bit x86 architecture. However, the current optimization scope of the auto ilp32 optimization is limited: it only considers pointers within objects allocated by *malloc()* function, and its effectiveness relies on the accuracy of the points-to analysis. The auto ilp32 optimization can be regarded as a trade-off solution between the *–m32* mode and the LP32 code model.

Recently, Lattner and Adve use pointer compression technique to reduce the memory space consumed by 64-bit pointers for linked list data structure [9]. The idea is to allocate dynamically created linked list objects in the contiguous memory space, and replace the original 64-bit pointers with 32-bit integer values that can be used as off-sets. The original pointer value can be calculated through this offset and the starting address of the memory pool. This approach requires whole program analysis and introduces run-time overhead for pointer compression and decompression. Similar approach is adopted by Intel's open runtime platform [10] that compresses 64-bit-wide pointers in a similar way for applications written in Java language.

# 4   Register Argument Passing Convention

Argument passing convention specifies how arguments are passed from caller function to callee function. In compatibility mode, arguments are passed through stack. In 64-bit mode, leveraged with doubled registers, six GPRs are dedicated to pass integer arguments, and six XMM registers are dedicated to pass floating-point arguments [8]. The major benefit of register argument passing convention is to reduce the stack accesses, and thus improve the performance, especially for call-intensive applications.

In this section, we compare the performance difference between the stack-based argument passing convention and the register-based argument passing convention in 64-bit mode.

## 4.1   Implementation Challenges

In this study, we implemented two argument passing schemes within the compiler: (1) arguments are passed through registers, which is the default convention in 64-bit mode; and (2) arguments are passed through stack, which is the default convention in compatibility mode. For the purpose of performance study, we implemented the later convention scheme for the compilation in 64-bit mode.

To emulate the stack-based argument passing convention in the 64-bit environment, it is compiler's responsibility to maintain the convention compatibility between caller and callee functions: if the callee function is an *external* function that is not processed by compiler (i.e., library functions), then the arguments should be passed through registers at the call site. Likewise, if the caller function is an external function, then the callee function should expect the arguments are passed through registers. Under other scenarios, arguments are passed through stack. To preserve the compatibility, we relied on the information provided by the inter-procedural optimization (IPO), which will process all the user-defined functions before argument passing convention code is generated.

Empirical study shows that only a handful of functions within the SPEC2000 need to use the default convention, and most of these functions are called by external function *qsort()*, which is a library function that  will call user-defined functions for data comparisons. Execution time profiling information shows that these functions do not have noticeable performance impact.

## 4.2   Experimental Results

Figure 5 shows the normalized execution time (with respect to the base compilation using register argument passing convention) when the stack-based argument passing convention is applied for the SPEC2000. On average, the CINT2000 is slowed down by 0.86%, and almost no noticeable slowdown for the CFP2000. On the contrary, we can see that some of the benchmarks actually have better performance with stack-based convention. For example, benchmark 300.twolf has an almost 4% speedup. However, 300.twolf is a *volatile* benchmark, and it is difficult to reproduce the result consistently.

Curious by the marginal performance difference, we suspected that the advantages of using registers to pass arguments were mainly obscured by the aggressive function inlin-ing optimization, which potentially eliminates many of the function calls. To confirm our hypothesis, we turned off function inlining and partial function inlining optimizations by specifying compilation option *"–ip-noinlining –ip-no-pinlining"*. The normalized execution time without functional inlining or partial inlining for the SPEC2000 is given in Figure 6. We can see a clear performance difference: the CINT2000 has a 7.4% performance slowdown and the CFP2000 has a 1.2%

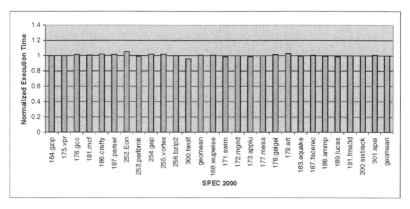

**Fig. 5.** The normalized execution time when the stack-based argument passing convention for the SPEC2000

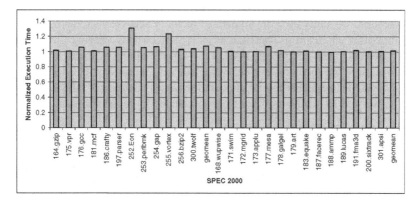

**Fig. 6.** The normalized execution time when the stack-based argument passing convention for the SPEC2000 with function inlining and partial inlining being turned off

performance slowdown. Among all the benchmarks, 252.eon and 255.vortex slow down the most, by 31% and by 23%, respectively. For 252.Eon benchmark, the number of dynamic function calls is increased by a factor of 86 if the function inlining optimization is turned off.

### 4.3  Related Work

To our best knowledge, there is no direct performance comparison between these two different argument passing conventions. Hubička [3] hypothesized that the register argument passing convention could improve the performance. However, our experiment shows that the performance impact is very limited, given that most of function calls have been eliminated by a sophisticated function inlining optimization.

## 5  Performance Improvement with More Registers

Register allocation has long been considered as one of the most important optimization techniques conducted by modern compilers. Alleviated with more registers, compiler can keep more values in registers without going through the memory system, and thus speed up application's performance. The 64-bit x86 architecture provides 16 GPRs (including the stack pointer register) and 16 XMM registers, which is twice as many registers that IA-32 architecture provides.

However, introducing more registers also brings in new challenges. First, the code size could be enlarged. Whenever an extended register or a 64-bit operand is refered, the REX prefix is required as the first opcode byte of the instruction [16]. These extra REX prefixes increase instruction size, and thus code size. Second, more caller-saved registers could affect performance. In the IA-32 processor, there are total 11 caller-saved registers (including 3 GPRs and 8 XMM registers). The number is more than doubled in the 64-bit x86 architecture, which has total 25 caller-saved registers (including 9 GPRs and 16 XMM registers). Saving more caller- and callee-saved registers could degrade performance, and increase the code size.

In this section, we study how the number of memory accesses is reduced with more registers, and how applications' performances are affected by varying the number of allocable registers in 64-bit mode. Instead of experimenting with all the different combinations, here we focus on two set of register configurations: (1) *REG_8*, where 8 GPRs and 8 XMM registers can be allocated by register allocator, and (2) *REG_12*, where 12 GPRs and 12 XMM registers can be allocated by register allocator.

### 5.1  Implementation Challenges

We conducted this study by adjusting the number of available registers can be allocated by the register allocator within the compiler. The register allocation algorithm implemented by the research compiler is an extension of the Chaitin-Briggs style graph coloring algorithm [6][7].

It is a straightforward process to setup the number of available registers for the register allocator. However, in 64-bit mode, register *R8* and register *R9* will be used to pass the fifth and the sixth integer arguments, respectively. To comply with the argument passing convention, when the available GPRs do not include R8 and R9, we have to deploy R8 and R9 specifically for integer argument passing purpose only, if they are required.

## 5.2 Experimental Results

Figure 7 gives the normalized execution time (with respect to the base compilation using 16 GPRs and 16 XMM registers) with the REG_8 and REG_12 register configurations for the SPEC2000 benchmarks. On average, with the REG_8 configuration, the CINT2000 exhibits a 4.4% slowdown, and the CFP2000 exhibits a 5.6% slowdown; with the REG_12 configuration, the CINT2000 is slowed down by 0.9%, and the CFP2000 is slowed down by 0.3%. Clearly, these results show that REG_12 already works well for most of the SPEC2000 benchmarks.

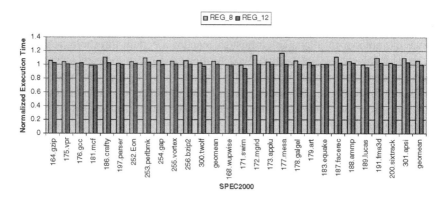

**Fig. 7.** The normalized execution time for the SPEC2000 benchmarks with the REG_8 and REG_12 configurations

Note that REG_8 slightly outperforms REG_12 on 176.gcc benchmark. In addition, for 181.mcf and 300.twolf benchmarks, the fewer the registers, the better the performances are. (We do not pursue the cause further, since the improvement with fewer registers is only within the 2% range.)

In addition to performance, the normalized dynamic number of memory accesses (including stack accesses) for the CINT2000 and CFP2000 is shown in Fig. 8. On average, with the REG_8 configuration, the memory references are increased by 42% for the CINT2000 and by 78% for the CFP2000; with the REG_12 configuration, the memory references are increased by 14% for CINT2000 and by 29% for the CFP2000.

Overall, for the SPEC2000 benchmark suite, we can see the trend that when the number of available registers is increased from 8 to 12, the memory accesses are reduced dramatically, and moderate performance improvement is achieved. However, with more than 12 registers, although the memory accesses are further reduced, the performance is barely improved.

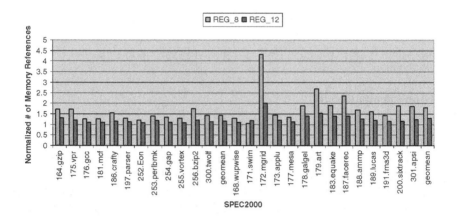

**Fig. 8.** The normalized number of memory accesses for the SPEC2000 benchmarks with the REG_8 and REG_12 configurations

Once the number of allocatable registers reaches a certain threshold, results show that the performance cannot be improved further even given more registers. We suspected that this phenomenon is due to the powerful out-of-order execution engine of the x86 core. In addition, comprehensive compiler optimization techniques can reduce the register pressure by folding some of the memory load instructions into other instructions as operands.

### 5.3   Related Work

An abundant research has been conducted on register allocation. Optimal, or near-optimal, register allocation algorithms [11][13][14] are also proposed for IA-32 architecture. Most of the prior works only demonstrate how the amount of spill code can be reduced and how efficient the solvers are (while compared with an exponential approach). However, not much work has been done on experimenting with the recent SPEC benchmark suite to demonstrate how the additional registers could improve the application's performance.

Luna et al. [2] experimented with different register allocators on AMD64 platform. Their studies show that with more registers, a fast linear scan based register allocation algorithm [18] could produce competitive performance code with graph coloring based algorithm. It is interesting for us to evaluate the performance of a linear scan approach with different number of registers on the SPEC2000. In addition, Luna et al. show that the code size could be increased by 17% due to REX prefixes.

Experimented on an out-of-order MIPS processor, Govindarajan et al. [12] propose an instruction scheduling algorithm to reduce the spill code. Their experiment on SPEC95 floating-point benchmarks show that their technique could reduce the average number of spill code by 10.4% and 3.7%, respectively, and on average the performance is improved by 3.2%. Note that MIPS architecture has 32 GPRs, as compared with 16 GPRs supported by the 64-bit x86 architecture.

# 6   Other 64-bit x86 Architecture Features

One important feature of the 64-bit x86 architecture is that the width of GPR is increased from 32 bits to 64 bits. In this study, we do not explicitly investigate the effectiveness of wider GPRs. From our experience, *197.crafty* is the only benchmark that gains most of the benefit, a 20% speedup, from 64-bit-wide GPRs. This is because 197.crafty performs intensive arithmetic operations on *long long* type data. Without 64-bit GPRs, sequences of 32-bit operations will be expanded to perform simple 64-bit operations. The example depicted in Fig. 9 illustrates this point.

```
movl   i, %edx              movq   i(%rip), %rdx
movl   4+i, %ecx            addq   j(%rip), %rdx
addl   j, %edx              movq   %rdx, k(%rip)
adcl   4+j, %ecx
movl   %edx, k
movl   %ecx, 4+k
        (a)                         (b)
```

**Fig. 9.** Example illustrating the code generations for assignment "k = i + j", where k, i and j are long long data type variables. (a) Instructions generated in compatibility mode. (b) Instructions generated in 64-bit mode.

In this example, it takes three 64-bit instructions to perform a 64-bit add operation "$k = i + j$" in 64-bit mode. However, it requires six 32-bit instructions to do the same task in compatibility mode: two load instructions are used to load the 64-bit value of variable *i* to two 32-bit registers, two add instructions are used to perform a 64-bit add operation using 32-bit operands, and two store instructions to store the 64-bit value to variable *k*.

In addition, the 64-bit x86 architecture introduces a new instruction-pointer relative-addressing mode, which can reduce the number of load-time relocations for position-independent code while accessing global data. A prior work [3] demonstrates that relative-addressing mode can reduce the performance loss significantly for position-independent code from 20% down to 6%.

# 7   Conclusions and Future Works

With the emerging of the 64-bit x86 architecture, it is imperative to understand its capability and its limitation. In this study, we evaluate several interesting new features of the 64-bit x86 architecture using a production level research compiler and conducting our experiments on the SPEC2000 benchmark suite.

The most noticeable change from 32-bit x86 to 64-bit x86 is that the size of pointer is increased from 32 bits to 64 bits. Experimenting on the SPEC2000 C benchmarks, we observe that the widened *pointer* and *long* data types could slow down an application's performance by as much as 50%. Prior studies on IA-32 processors [19][20] show that the number of data cache misses plays a critical role on modern database management systems (DBMS). The situation is even more severe in the 64-bit x86 processors that inherit larger memory footprint. It is interesting to see how the LP32 code model can help here. Besides studying 64-bit pointer, we also evaluate how the register-based argument passing convention could improve performance. Experiments show that the performance gain is imperceptible if an aggressive function inlining optimization is performed. Finally, we evaluate how the double sized register file could improve the performance. Experimental results show that using 12 GPRs and 12 XMM registers can achieve almost the same performance as using 16 GPRs and 16 XMM registers can.

The above observations point our future research to the following three areas: (1) investigate how to reduce memory footprint in the 64-bit x86 processors on DBMS; (2) investigate and improve the performance of linear scan register allocation [18]; and (3) study the interaction between register allocation and instruction scheduling in the 64-bit x86 processors.

## Acknowledgements

We thank Suresh Siddha for the advice on modifying the Linux kernel to support the LP32 code model, Somnath Ghosh for explaining the auto ilp32 optimization implemented in the Intel production compiler, Robert Cohn for the help in resolving a couple of PIN issues due to the modified Linux kernel, Thomas Johnson for the suggestions on using the emon tool, and Jin Lee for providing us the experimental machine. We also thank many anonymous reviewers for their helpful comments on earlier drafts of this paper.

## References

[1] Intel Corporation, Santa Clara. "64-bit Extension Technology Software Developer's Guide Volume 1&2" Order Number 300834, 300835

[2] Daniel Luna, Mikael Pettersson, and Konstantinos Sagonas. "Efficiently compiling a functional language on AMD64: the HiPE experience," PPDP '05: Proceedings of the 7th ACM SIGPLAN international conference on Principles and practice of declarative programming, 2005, pages 176--186

[3] Jan Hubička, "Porting GCC to the AMD64 architecture," In Proceedings of the GCC Developers Summit, pages 79--105, May 2003

[4] Chi-Keung Luk, Robert Cohn and et al. "Pin: building customized program analysis tools with dynamic instrumentation," In proceedings of the ACM SIGPLAN 2005 Conference on Programming language design and implementation, Pages 190—200, 2005

[5] Brinkley Sprunt. "Pentium 4 Performance-Monitoring Features," IEEE Micro, Vol 22, Num 4, 2002, Pages 72—82

[6] G. J. Chaitin. "Register allocation & spilling via graph coloring," SIGPLAN '82: Proceedings of the 1982 SIGPLAN symposium on Compiler construction, 1982, Pages 98—101

[7] P. Briggs, K. D. Cooper, K. Kennedy and L. Torczon. "Coloring heuristics for register allocation," PLDI '89: Proceedings of the ACM SIGPLAN 1989 Conference on Programming language design and implementation, pages 275—284

[8] Ed. J. Hubička, A. Jaeger and M. Mitchell. "System V Application Binary Interface: AMD64 Architecture Processor Supplement." Available from www.x86-64.org.

[9] Chris Lattner and Vikram S. Adve. "Transparent Pointer Compression for Linked Data Structures," In Proceedings of Memory System Performance Workshop, 2005

[10] Ali-Reza Adl-Tabatabai et al., "Improving 64-Bit Java IPF Performance by Compressing Heap References," In Proceedings of CGO, pages 100—111, March 2004

[11] David Koes and Seth Copen Goldstein. "A Progressive Register Allocator for Irregular Architectures," In Proceedings of CGO, pages 269--280, 2005

[12] R. Govindarajan, Hongbo Yang, Jose Nelson Amaral, Chihong Zhang and Guang R. Gao. "Minimum Register Instruction Sequencing to Reduce Register Spills in Out-of-Order Issue Superscalar Architectures," IEEE Transaction on Computers, 52(1), January 2003.

[13] Timothy Kong and Kent D. Wilken. "Precise register allocation for irregular architectures," In Proceedings of the 31st annual ACM/IEEE international symposium on Microarchitecture, pages 297—307, 1998

[14] Andrew W. Appel and Lal George. "Optimal spilling for CISC machines with few registers," In proceedings of the ACM SIGPLAN 2001 conference on Programming language design and implementation, pages 243—253, 2001

[15] Kirill Kochetkov, "SPEC CPU2000. Part 19. EM64T in Intel Pentium 4," June 2005. Available from http://www.digit-life.com/articles2/cpu/insidespeccpu2000-part-j.html.

[16] Intel Corporation, Santa Clara. "IA-32 Intel® Architecture Software Developer's Manual, Volume 1: Basic Architecture," 2005. Order Number 253665.

[17] Intel Corporation, Santa Clara. "IA-32 Intel® Architecture Software Developers Manual, Volume 3: System Programming Guide," 2005. Order Number 253668.

[18] Massimiliano Poletto and Vivek Sarkar, "Linear scan register allocation," ACM Transactions on Programming Languages and Systems, 21(5), pages 895—913, 1999

[19] Anastassia Ailamaki, David J. DeWitt, Mark D. Hill, David A. Wood, "DBMSs on a Modern Processor: Where Does Time Go?" Proceedings of 25th International Conference on Very Large Data Bases, pages 266—277, September 1999, Edinburgh, Scotland, UK

[20] Kimberly Keeton, David A. Patterson and et al., "Performance characterization of a Quad Pentium Pro SMP using OLTP workloads," In Proceedings of the 25th annual international symposium on Computer architecture, pages 15—26, 1998

# Lightweight Lexical Closures
# for Legitimate Execution Stack Access

Masahiro Yasugi, Tasuku Hiraishi, and Taiichi Yuasa

Graduate School of Informatics, Kyoto University, Japan
{yasugi, hiraisi, yuasa}@kuis.kyoto-u.ac.jp

**Abstract.** We propose a new language concept called "L-closures" for a running program to legitimately inspect/modify the contents of its execution stack. L-closures are lightweight lexical closures created by evaluating nested function definitions. A lexical closure can access the lexically-scoped variables in the creation-time environment and indirect calls to it provide legitimate stack access. By using an intermediate language extended with L-closures in high-level compilers, high-level services such as garbage collection, check-pointing, multithreading and load balancing can be implemented elegantly and efficiently. Each variable accessed by an L-closure uses private and shared locations for giving the private location a chance to get a register. Operations to keep coherency with shared locations as well as operations to initialize L-closures are delayed until an L-closure is actually invoked. Because most high-level services create L-closures very frequently but call them infrequently (e.g., to scan roots in garbage collection), the total overhead can be reduced significantly. Since the GNU C compiler provides nested functions, we enhanced GCC at relatively low implementation costs. The results of performance measurements exhibit quite low costs of creating and maintaining L-closures.

## 1   Introduction

Implementing sophisticated machine code generators for a variety of platforms is not easy work. Therefore, many compiler writers for high-level languages use C as an almost portable and machine-independent intermediate language; that is, they write only translators from high-level languages into C.

Most compiled C programs use execution stacks for efficiency. Upon a function call, a stack frame is allocated not only for parameters and local variables of the function but also for the return address, the previous frame pointer, the callee-save registers and `alloca`-ed spaces. Efficient support for some high-level run-time services (such as garbage collection, self-debugging, stack-tracing, check-pointing, migration, continuations, multi-threading and/or load balancing) requires inspecting/modifying the contents of execution stacks. In C, however, once a function is called, the callee cannot efficiently access the caller's local variables. Some local variables may have the values in callee-save registers, and *pointer*-based accesses interfere with many compiler optimization techniques. In addition, the stack frame layout is machine-dependent and direct stack manipulation by the running C program via forged pointers is illegal in essence, because

A. Mycroft and A. Zeller (Eds.): CC 2006, LNCS 3923, pp. 170–184, 2006.

the data of stack frames are not application-level data (values) but *meta-level* data for execution. Illegal access will also open security issues.

For example, to implement garbage collection (GC), the collector needs to be able to find all roots, each of which holds a reference to an object in the garbage-collected heap. In C, a caller's pointer variable may hold an object reference, but it may be sleeping in the execution stack. Even when using direct stack manipulation, it is difficult for the collector to distinguish *roots* from other elements in the stack. *Stack maps* may be used, but they are not inherent C data and need special compiler support. For this reason, conservative collectors[1] are usually used with some limitations. When a *copying collector* is used to implement GC, it needs to be able to accurately scan all *roots* since the objects are moved between semi-spaces and all root pointers should refer to the new locations of objects. Accurate copying collection can be performed by using translation techniques based on "structure and pointer"[2, 3], but translating local variables into structure fields invalidates many compiler optimization techniques.

This problem motivates researchers to develop new powerful and portable intermediate languages, such as C--[4, 5]. C-- is a portable assembly language (lower-level than C) but it has the ability to access the variables sleeping in the execution stack by using the C-- runtime system to perform "stack walk". Thus, C-- can be used as an intermediate language to implement high-level services such as garbage collection.

This paper proposes yet another intermediate language, which is an extended C language with a new language concept called "L-closures" for a running program to legitimately inspect/modify the contents of its execution stack (i.e., the values of data structures and variables). L-closures are lightweight lexical closures created by evaluating nested function definitions. A lexical closure can access the lexically-scoped variables in the creation-time environment and indirect calls to it provide legitimate stack access. Compared to C--, our approach more elegantly supports high-level services, and needs quite low implementation costs by reusing the existing compiler modules and related tools such as linkers.

The rest of this paper is organized as follows: Section 2 presents our motivating example. In Sect. 3, we show the design of the proposed language features (*closures* and *L-closures*), where we propose a semantical separation of nested functions from ordinary top-level functions. Section 4 proposes our implementation model for L-closures. Section 5 presents our current implementation based on GCC. The results of performance measurement are discussed in Sect. 6. The results exhibit quite low costs of creating and maintaining L-closures. Section 7 discusses the costs and applications of L-closures together with the related work, and shows that many high-level services can be implemented by translating into the extended C language.

# 2   A Motivating Example

Let us consider a high-level program which recursively traverses binary tree nodes and creates an associative list with the corresponding search data. Such a

```
Alist *bin2list(Bintree *x, Alist *rest){
  Alist *a = 0; KVpair *kv = 0;
  if(x->right) rest = bin2list(x->right, rest);
  kv = getmem(&KVpair_d);                 /* allocation */
  kv->key = x->key; kv->val = x->val;
  a = getmem(&Alist_d);                   /* allocation */
  a->kv = kv; a->cdr = rest;
  rest = a;
  if(x->left) rest = bin2list(x->left, rest);
  return rest;
}
```

**Fig. 1.** A motivating example: tree-to-list conversion

```
typedef void *(*move_f)(void *);

                  /* scan0 is an L-closure pointer. */
Alist *bin2list(lightweight void (*scan0)(move_f),
                Bintree *x, Alist *rest){
  Alist *a = 0; KVpair *kv = 0;
  /* scan1 is an L-closure, and pass it on the following calls. */
  lightweight void scan1(move_f mv){  /* nested function */
    x = mv(x); rest = mv(rest);         /* roots scans */
    a = mv(a); kv = mv(kv);             /* roots scans */
    scan0();                            /* for older roots */
  }
  if(x->right) rest = bin2list(scan1, x->right, rest);
  kv = getmem(scan1, &KVpair_d);        /* allocation */
  kv->key = x->key; kv->val = x->val;
  a = getmem(scan1, &Alist_d);          /* allocation */
  a->kv = kv; a->cdr = rest;
  rest = a;
  if(x->left) rest = bin2list(scan1, x->left, rest);
  return rest;
}
```

**Fig. 2.** Scanning GC roots with L-closures (nested functions)

high-level program may be translated into a C program shown in Fig. 1. Here, getmem allocates a new object in heap, and a copying collector needs to be able to scan all *root* variables such as x, rest, a and kv even when bin2list is being recursively called.

In the proposed intermediate language, a program with copying GC can be elegantly expressed as in Fig. 2. Allocator getmem may invoke the copying collector with L-closure scan1 created by evaluating the nested function definition. The copying collector can indirectly call scan1 which performs the movement (copy) of objects using roots (x, rest, a and kv) and indirectly calls L-closure scan0 in a nested manner.[1] The actual entity of scan0 may be another instance of scan1 in the caller. By repeatedly invoking L-closures until the bottom of the stack is reached, all roots in the entire execution stack can be scanned.

---

[1] Alternatively, scan1 may return scan0 to eliminate tail calls.

In Fig. 2, `bin2list`'s variables (`x`, `rest`, `a` and `kv`) should have chances to get (callee-save) registers. However, if we employ the typical Pascal-style implementation for L-closures, `bin2list` must perform memory operations (much slower than register operations) to access these variables because `scan1` also accesses the values of these variables in the stack memory usually via a static chain. Note that the same problem arises in translation techniques for stack-walking based on "structure and pointer" [2, 3].

Our goal is to reduce these costs of *maintaining* L-closures (i.e., to enable register allocation) by using a new implementation policy for L-closures. The policy also reduces the costs of *creating* L-closures but accepts higher invocation costs. Because most high-level services create L-closures very frequently but call them infrequently (e.g., to scan roots in garbage collection), the total overhead can be reduced significantly.

## 3    Design

Pascal and many modern programming languages other than C (such as Lisp, Smalltalk, and ML) permits a function defined within another (nested or top-level) function. We employ Pascal-style nested functions for our extended C language. It can access the lexically-scoped variables in the creation-time environment and a pointer to it can be used as a function pointer to indirectly call the lexical closure (that is, a pair of the nested function and its environment). A lexical closure is (logically) created every time the control arrives at the nested function definition in the same way as local variable definitions. Since a closure is created on the stack, unlike garbage-collected languages, the pointer to a closure cannot be used after the exit of the block where the nested function is defined.

We propose a semantical separation of nested functions from ordinary top-level functions, which enables a significant performance improvement by using different calling sequences for nested functions. For this purpose, we introduce a language concept called **closures**, which have almost the same roles as ordinary (top-level) functions but which are not regarded as ordinary functions. We extend the language syntax with a keyword `closure` in the same way as keyword `lightweight` in Fig. 2. A program which passes a closure pointer as an ordinary function pointer will produce a type error, and vice versa.[2]

We also introduce a new language concept called **L-closures** other than ordinary functions and other than *closures*. We extend the syntax with a keyword `lightweight` as in Fig. 2. That is, there are two types of lexical closures, and each type has the following goals and limitations:

**Closures** are intended to employ the Pascal-style implementation (i.e., static chains). *Closures* do not keep interoperability with ordinary top-level functions. The owner function of *closures* involves substantial costs of maintaining *closures*. *Closures* have moderate creation/invocation costs. These costs are the same as the corresponding costs for techniques based on "structure and pointer."

---

[2] In practice, coercing function pointers into closure pointers may be permitted.

**L-closures** are intended to employ the implementation policy for aggressively minimizing costs of creating and maintaining L-closures by accepting higher invocation costs. L-closures do not keep interoperability with ordinary top-level functions (and *closures*). L-closures are callable only from within the owner function and its descendants in the caller-callee relation. (e.g., not callable from different threads)

We can choose an adequate type according to a situation. For example, L-closures should be used to implement most of the high-level services discussed in Sect. 2 and Sect. 7, because those L-closures are rarely called and minimizing the creation/maintenance costs is desired.

## 4   Implementation Models

In this section, we propose recommended implementation models for closures and L-closures.

We can implement a *closure* with a stack-allocated pair of pointers. The pointer pair consists of the actual nested function and the environment (static chain). The *closure* pointer can refer to the pair. When a caller indirectly calls a closure, it already distinguish the closure pointer from ordinary function pointers by compile-time looking at the type of the pointer, then it loads the static chain (the second element of the pointer pair) into the static chain register and calls the actual nested function (the first element of the pointer pair). Note that we cannot use the pointer pair directly as a two-word closure pointer, since C permits interoperability between the generic `void *` type and any other pointer type.

To minimize costs of creating L-closures, the initialization of an L-closure is delayed until it is actually called. This means that the creation cost of L-closures is virtually zero (similar to carefully-implemented exception handlers.)

To minimize costs of maintaining L-closures, if a function $f$ has a nested function $g$ of L-closure type and $g$ accesses $f$'s local variable (or parameter) $x$, $x$ uses *two* locations, namely a *private* location and a *shared* location, for giving the private location a chance to get a (callee-save) register by reducing interference with the existing optimizers and register allocators. Note that $x$ does not use a private location if the address of $x$ is taken, or if a nested function accessing $x$ is not of L-closure type. In addition, if $g$ has a nested function $g_2$, $g_2$'s access to $f$'s variable is accounted to be $g$'s access regardless of $g_2$'s type.

The similar technique (but incomplete in terms of lazy pre/post-processing) can be expressed in extended C with nested functions as in Fig. 3 for the function `bin2list` in Fig. 2. The function `bin2list`, which owns a nested function `scan1`, introduces private variables (such as `p_x` and `p_a`) and uses the private ones except for the function calls. Upon a function call, `bin2list` saves the private values into the shared variables (such as `x` and `a`) as *pre-processing*. When the control is returned, it restores the private values from the shared variables as *post-processing*. This technique gives the private variable a chance to get a register. However, this technique cannot omit pre/post-processing even if `scan1`

```
Alist *bin2list(void (*scan0)(move_f), Bintree *x, Alist *rest){
  Alist *a = 0; KVpair *kv = 0;
  /* scan1 is a lexical closure, and pass it on the following calls. */
  void scan1(move_f mv){              /* nested function */
    x = mv(x); rest = mv(rest);       /* roots scans */
    a = mv(a); kv = mv(kv);           /* roots scans */
    scan0();                          /* for older roots */
  }
  /* private variables */
  Bintree *p_x = x, Alist *p_rest = rest, *p_a = a; KVpair *p_kv = kv;
  if(p_x->right){
    x = p_x, rest = p_rest, a = p_a, kv = p_kv;  /* pre-processing */
    Alist *_r = bin2list(scan1, p_x->right, p_rest);
    p_x = x, p_rest = rest, p_a = a, p_kv = kv,  /* post-processing */
    p_rest = _r;
  }
  {
    x = p_x, rest = p_rest, a = p_a, kv = p_kv;  /* pre-processing */
    KVpair *_r = getmem(scan1, &KVpair_d);       /* allocation */
    p_x = x, p_rest = rest, p_a = a, p_kv = kv;  /* post-processing */
    p_kv = _r;
  }
  p_kv->key = p_x->key; p_kv->val = p_x->val;
  {
    x = p_x, rest = p_rest, a = p_a, kv = p_kv;  /* pre-processing */
    Alist *_r = getmem(scan1, &Alist_d);         /* allocation */
    p_x = x, p_rest = rest, p_a = a, p_kv = kv;  /* post-processing */
    p_a = _r;
  }
  p_a->kv = p_kv; p_a->cdr = p_rest;
  p_rest = p_a;
  if(p_x->left){
    x = p_x, rest = p_rest, a = p_a, kv = p_kv;  /* pre-processing */
    Alist *_r = bin2list(scan1, p_x->left, p_rest);
    p_x = x, p_rest = rest, p_a = a, p_kv = kv,  /* post-processing */
    p_rest = _r;
  }
  return p_rest;
}
```

**Fig. 3.** Adding private variables and pre-processing and post-processing in C. This is not the real code but shown for explanation purpose only.

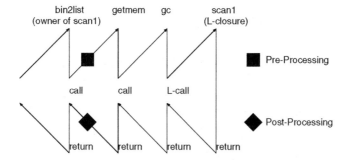

**Fig. 4.** Usual pre-processing and post-processing

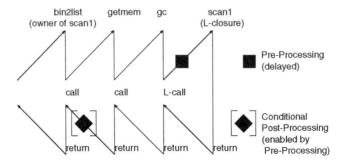

**Fig. 5.** Delayed pre-processing and conditional post-processing performed only if the L-closure is actually called

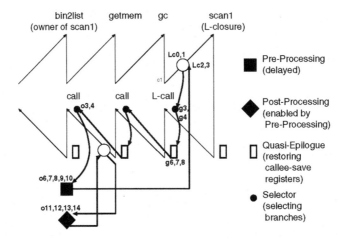

**Fig. 6.** (Non-local) temporary return to the owner of the L-closure to be called for correct pre-processing. Annotated numbers correspond to those in Fig 7.

is not actually called. The control flow on pre-processing and post-processing at the time when **scan1** is being called by **gc** can be depicted as in Fig. 4.

To overcome this problem, we propose *delayed pre-processing* and *conditional post-processing* as in Fig. 5. The pre-processing is delayed until the call to the L-closure, and the conditional post-processing is dynamically enabled by pre-processing. *Pre-processing* (indicated by filled squares) consists of the following steps: (1) initializing all L-closures (function-pointers and static chains), (2) copying private values into shared locations, and (3) enabling post-processing (by changing return addresses). Performing pre-processing more than once[3] is avoided (i.e., pre-processing is also conditional) by checking if the conditional post-processing is already enabled. *Post-processing* (indicated by filled diamonds) simply copies values from shared locations into private locations.

---

[3] In the case of recursive calls of an L-closure.

```
bin2list: // owner of scan1
o0  : ...
o1  : call getmem with selector o3.
o2  : ...
o3  : /* selector for o1 */
o4  : if (L-closure to be called is in this frame) jump to pre-processing o6.
o5  : else jump to quasi-epilogue o18.
o6  : /* pre-processing for o1 */
o7  : copy values from private locations to shared locations.
o8  : initialize all L-closures (function-pointers and static chains).
o9  : save and modify o1's return address to enable post-processing o11.
o10 : continue the L-call according to on-stack info.
o11 : /* post-processing for o1 */
o12 : save the return value.
o13 : copy values from shared locations to private locations.
o14 : continue the actual return.
o15 : ...
o16 : /* selector for modified return addresses */
o17 : continue the L-call according to on-stack info.
o18 : /* quasi-epilogue */
o19 : restore callee-save registers.
o20 : temp-return to the selector for the previous frame.

gc:  // caller of scan1 (= scan)
g0  : ...
g1  : L-call scan with selector g3.
g2  : ...
g3  : /* selector for g1 */
g4  : jump to quasi-epilogue g6.
g5  : ...
g6  : /* quasi-epilogue */
g7  : restore callee-save registers.
g8  : temp-return to the selector for the previous frame.

L-call f:
Lc0 : save f and registers.
Lc1 : temp-return to the selector for the previous frame.
Lc2 : restore f and registers.
Lc3 : setup static chain for f and jump to f.
```

**Fig. 7.** pseudo code and calling steps

Since we give each private location a chance to get a callee-save register, restoring callee-save registers (including the frame pointer but excluding the stack pointer) before pre-processing is required for correct pre-processing. Such restore can be performed by *quasi-epilogues* during non-local temporary return to the owner function as in Fig. 6.

The pseudo code for Fig. 6 is shown in Fig. 7. A call to L-closure scan1 (*L-call* to scan1 at g1 in Fig. 7) starts a non-local temporary return to the owner function (Lc0, Lc1); firstly, it temporarily returns to the *selector* for the previous frame (e.g., g3 for gc). Each *selector* (e.g., o3) selects a pre-processing branch (e.g., o4, o6) if the *current* frame is the owner of the L-closure to be called; otherwise, a quasi-epilogue branch (e.g., o18) is selected. Note that the quasi-epilogue branch is always taken for the functions without L-closures (e.g., g3, g4 and g6) to continue the non-local temporary return after restoring callee-save registers (e.g., g7, g8).

The pre-processing (o6,o7,o8,o9) can be performed using the *current* frame with restored callee-save registers. After pre-processing, the control is actually transfered to the L-closure (o10, Lc2, Lc3).

Each *temporary return* finds a selector for the previous frame based on the return address for the frame; after enabling post-processing by modifying return address, it finds a selector which continues the L-call without performing further pre-processing (o16, o17).

The solid arrows for L-call to scan1 in Fig. 6 corresponds to the following steps in Fig. 7: g1, L-call (Lc0, Lc1), g1, selector (g3, g4), quasi-epilogue (g6, g7, g8), ..., o1, selector (o3, o4), pre-processing (o6, o7, o8, o9, o10), L-call(Lc2, Lc3), and scan1.

Fig. 6 also illustrates that the enabled post-processing intercepts the ordinary return. The solid arrows for the return to bin2list corresponds to the steps: getmem, post-processing (o11, o12, o13, o14), and o1.

This implementation policy for L-closures effectively decouples L-closures from their owner function, and makes the owner function's variable access faster.

# 5   Implementation Based on GCC

This section presents our implementation based on the GNU C compiler[6]. We enhanced GCC-3.2 to implement closures and L-closures for IA-32 and SPARC.

GCC uses an intermediate representation in Register Transfer Language (RTL) to represent the code being generated, in a form closer to assembly language than to C. An RTL representation is generated from the abstract syntax tree, transformed by various passes (such as data flow analysis, optimization and register allocation) and then converted into assembly code.

GCC has its own nested functions as an extention to C. They keep interoperability with ordinary top-level functions by using a technique called "trampolines"[7]. Trampolines are code fragments generated on the stack at runtime to indirectly enter the nested function with a necessary environment. Therefore, GCC's approach involves more creation costs than *closures*.

*Closures* are implemented as was mentioned in Sect. 4. We use the stack-allocated pointer pairs instead of GCC's trampolines. A pair is initialized to hold the address of the actual nested function and the static chain. To call a closure, the caller first loads the static chain (the second element of the pointer pair) into the static chain register[4] and calls the actual nested function (the first element of the pointer pair). All of these are implemented by extending only the RTL generation scheme.

On the other hand, L-closures are implemented by (1) extending the RTL generation scheme, (2) extending the assembly code generation scheme, and (3) adding short runtime assembly code. In the implementation of L-closures, we accept loss of implementation simplicity to obtain reusability (portability) and efficiency. For reusability, our implementation employs the existing RTL without modification or extension. With this approach, most existing optimizers

---

[4] In GCC, static_chain_rtx holds the RTL expression of the static chain register.

**Table 1.** Implementation costs as patches to GCC

| Closures | | L-Closures (+ Closures) | | | (lines) |
|---|---|---|---|---|---|
| RTL | RTL | IA-32(i386) | i386 asm | SPARC(sparc) | sparc asm |
| 320 lines | 973 | 212 | 105 | 181 | 148 |

do not need modification or extension. We also minimize the extension on the assembly code generation scheme; we rather extend the RTL generation scheme if possible.

Table 1 summarizes the number of patch lines to implement *closures* and/or *L-closures* as patches to GCC. For example, the implementation of L-closure on IA-32 requires 973 line patch for RTL generation, 212 line patch for supporting selectors and quasi-epilogues, and 105 line assembly runtime code. The RTL generation part is shared with SPARC.

Since details of our implementation heavily depend on GCC internals, we only outline our implementation. We simply generate selector code and quasi-epilogue code at assembly-level by modifying the existing epilogue generation routines. Note that we assume the use of a register window for SPARC at this implementation. The pre/post-processing code is first generated as RTL code and transformed by usual optimization and register allocation phases. For the correct optimization in RTL, we employ a "virtual" control-flow edge for control transfer performed by assembly-level code such as between selector code and pre-processing code or between post-processing code and the original return point.

Our real implementation combines all selectors for each function into a single selector with all possible branches. It also employs intra-function code sharing among pre/post-processing code fragments for different call points and exploits the runtime code fragments for common tasks in pre/post-processing and quasi-epilogues. These improvements on code size produce complex code.

We do not have serious errors to use the unchanged GNU debugger to debug the generated code with L-closures; for example, the back-tracing works well. However, some execution status cannot be obtained correctly.

## 6    Performance Measurements

Without having nested functions, the speed of C programs will not change with our extended compiler. To measure costs of creating and maintaining lexical closures, we employed the following programs with nested functions for several high-level services and compared them with the corresponding plain C programs:

**BinTree (copying GC)** creates a binary search tree with 200,000 nodes, with a copying-collected heap.

**Bin2List (copying GC)** converts a binary tree with 500,000 nodes into a linear list, with a copying-collected heap.

**fib(36) (check-pointing)** calculates the 36th Fibonacci number recursively, with a capability of capturing stack state for check-pointing (see Fig. 8).

```
int cpfib(lightweight void (*save0)(), int n)
{
    int pc = 0;                 /* pseudo program counter */
    int s = 0;
    lightweight void save1(){ /* nested function */
        save0();                /* saving caller's state */
        save_pc(pc);            /* saving pc state */
        save_int(n);            /* saving variable state */
        save_int(s);            /* saving variable state */
    }
    if (n <= 2) return 1;
    pc = 1;   /* inc program counter before call */
    s += cpfib(save1, n-1);
    pc = 2;   /* inc program counter before call */
    s += cpfib(save1, n-2);
    return s;
}
```

**Fig. 8.** Capturing state with L-closures

**fib(36) (load balancing)** calculates the 36th Fibonacci number, on a load-balancing framework based on lazy partitioning of sequential programs[8].

**Pentomino/nqueens(13) (load balancing)** perform backtrack search for all possible solutions to the Pentomino puzzle/the N-queens problem ($N$=13), on the load-balancing framework.

Note that nested functions are never invoked in these measurements, that is, garbage collection, check-pointing and task creation do not occur.

We measure the performance on 1.05GHz UltraSPARC-III and 3GHz Pentium 4 using -O2 optimizers. Table 2 summarizes the results of performance measurements, where "no closures" means the plain C program without the high-level services (i.e., using no closures nor additional closure parameters for every function call). "Trampolines" means the use of GCC's conventional nested functions. In some programs, especially those creating nested functions frequently,

**Table 2.** Performance Measurements

| S:SPARC | | Elapsed time in seconds (relative time to "no closures") | | | | | | |
|---|---|---|---|---|---|---|---|---|
| P:Pentium | | no closures | | Trampoline | | Closure | | L-closure |
| BinTree | S | 0.180 | (1.00) | 0.240 | (1.33) | 0.226 | (1.26) | 0.190 | (1.06) |
| copying GC | P | 0.150 | (1.00) | 0.165 | (1.10) | 0.167 | (1.11) | 0.150 | (1.00) |
| Bin2List | S | 0.289 | (1.00) | 0.322 | (1.14) | 0.292 | (1.01) | 0.290 | (1.00) |
| copying GC | P | 0.139 | (1.00) | 0.141 | (1.01) | 0.139 | (1.00) | 0.139 | (1.00) |
| fib(36) | S | 0.56 | (1.00) | 2.76 | (4.93) | 0.81 | (1.45) | 0.60 | (1.07) |
| check pointing | P | 0.170 | (1.00) | 0.468 | (2.75) | 0.260 | (1.52) | 0.170 | (1.00) |
| fib(36) | S | 0.57 | (1.00) | 2.46 | (4.31) | 0.91 | (1.60) | 0.68 | (1.19) |
| load balancing | P | 0.168 | (1.00) | 0.400 | (2.38) | 0.346 | (2.06) | 0.283 | (1.68) |
| Pentomino | S | 3.16 | (1.00) | 5.75 | (1.82) | 4.66 | (1.47) | 3.44 | (1.09) |
| load balancing | P | 1.80 | (1.00) | 2.10 | (1.17) | 2.06 | (1.14) | 1.92 | (1.07) |
| nqueens(13) | S | 0.470 | (1.00) | 1.022 | (2.17) | 0.806 | (1.71) | 0.592 | (1.26) |
| load balancing | P | 0.316 | (1.00) | 0.426 | (1.35) | 0.423 | (1.34) | 0.464 | (1.47) |

the speed of the conventional nested functions is less than half. In contrast, L-closures exhibits good performance. The relative times to the plain C are considerably closer to 1.00.

However, there are two exceptional results in Table 2: fib(36) and N-queens (load balancing) on Pentium 4. In these results, unimportant variables are allocated to registers. Since Pentium 4 has only a few callee-save registers and performs explicit save/restore of callee-save registers, the penalty of wrong allocation is serious. Our technique using private locations increases the number of allocation candidates, and increases not only good allocation opportunities but also wrong allocation opportunities. On the other hand, our technique is quite effective on SPARC which has more callee-save registers and performs lazy save/restore with the register window.

# 7   Discussion

## 7.1   Costs of L-Closures

Like translation techniques based on "structure and pointer"[2, 3], closures and L-closures need more code space for additional infrequently-invoked procedures than annotation-based implementations. Grouping infrequently-used procedures (plus code fragments in the case of L-closures) into a different code segment will improve locality for the instruction cache.

To scan the execution stack with $n$ frames by the program in Fig. 2, additional $n$ frames are needed for nested invocation of L-closures. If this is a problem, standard techniques for eliminating tail calls can solve the problem. For its time complexity, the number of *temporary returns* is $O(n^2)$. If this is a problem, we should employ another L-closure policy which always converts unconverted part of the entire stack into the pre-processed stack each time an L-closure is invoked, where only the first conversion involves $O(n)$ temporary returns in this case.

The results of performance measurements does not indicated that the cost of additional closure parameters is serious. If we can find L-closures by using *tags* like *exception handlers*, this additional cost can be eliminated.

## 7.2   High-Level Services: Related Work

There are at least four schemes for implementing high-level services on top of C compilers: (1) Using direct stack manipulation in C neglecting legitimacy and portability[1], (2) Providing special service routines and using the routines for the translators into C[9], (3) Using elaborate translation techniques in the translators into C[2, 3, 10, 11, 12, 13], or (4) Extending C compilers and using the extended features for the translators into the extended C[14, 15]. Our approach employs the fourth implementation scheme.

**Capturing/Restoring Stack State.** By using nested functions, stack state can be captured without returning to the callers.[5] Figure 8 shows a C function

---

[5] Restoring a previously-captured state is much easier and does not need nested functions. For restoring, different versions of C functions can be used for efficiency.

with a nested function for capturing the stack state. The program uses a pseudo program counter to record the current program point and saves all parameters/local variables. This technique can be applied to check pointing, migration and first-class continuations.

Porch[10] is a translator that transforms C programs into C programs supporting portable checkpoints. They introduce source-to-source compilation techniques for generating code to save and recover from such portable checkpoints automatically. To save the stack state, the program repeatedly returns and legitimately saves the parameters/local variables until the bottom of the stack is reached. During restoring, this process is reversed.

**Multi-threads: Latency Hiding.** We can implement high-level language threads realized by a language system by using L-closures. To implement multiple threads, every function has its own nested function to continue its equivalent computation and save the pointer to the nested function to be called later to early execute the thread's unprocessed computation (continuation). The explicit continuation is provided by the nested function ane explicitly passed like a *continuation-passing style*.

Concert[11], OPA[12] use similar translation techniques to support suspension and resumption of multiple threads on a single processor with a single execution stack (e.g., for latency hiding). They create a new child thread as an ordinary function call and if the child thread completes its execution without being blocked, the child thread simply returns the control to the parent thread. But in case of the suspension of the child thread, the C functions for the child thread legitimately saves its (live) parameters/local variables into heap-allocated frames and simply returns the control to the parent thread. When a suspended thread become runnable, it may legitimately restore necessary values from the heap-allocated frames.

StackThreads/MP[14] allows the frame pointer to walk the execution stack independently of the stack pointer. When the child thread is blocked, it can transfer the control to an arbitrary ancestor thread without copying the stack frames to heap. StackThreads/MP employs the unmodified GNU C compiler and implements non-standard control flows by a combination of an assembly language postprocessor and runtime libraries.

**Load Balancing.** To realize efficient dynamic load balancing by transferring tasks among computing resources in fine-grained parallel computing such as search problems, load balancing schemes which lazily create and extract a task by splitting the present running task, such as *Lazy Task Creation* (LTC)[16], are effective. In LTC, a newly created thread is directly and immediately executed like a usual call while (the *continuation* of) the oldest thread in the computing resource may be stolen by other idle computing resources. Usually, the idle computing resource (*thief*) randomly selects another computing resource (*victim*) for stealing a task.

Compilers (translators) for multithreaded languages generate low-level code. In the original LTC[16], assembly code is generated to directly manipulate the execution stack. Both translators for Cilk[13] and OPA[12] generate C code. Since it is illegal and not portable for C code to directly access the execution stack, the Cilk/OPA translators generate two versions (fast/slow) of code; the fast version code saves values of live variables in a heap-allocated frame upon call (in the case of Cilk) or return (in the case of OPA) so that the slow version code can continue the rest of computation based on the heap-allocated saved *continuation*.

A message passing implementation[17] of LTC employs a polling method where the *victim* detects a task request sent from the *thief* and returns a new task created by splitting the present running task. This techniques enables OPA[12], StackThreads/MP[14] and Lazy Threads[15] to support load balancing.

We can generate an LTC-based load balancing program where callers' variables are accessed by using L-closures[8]. We can also perform *backtracking* by using L-closures. Here "backtracking" means not only to backtrack to a point where a new choice for the search can be made but also to undo the side effect of the previous examined choices as in a sequential backtrack search.

## 8  Conclusions

This paper has proposed a new language concept called "L-closures" for legitimate execution stack access. L-closures can be used to implement a wide variety of high-level services and can be implemented efficiently in terms of creation/maintenance costs by accepting higher invocation costs. We implemented L-closures based on GCC while reusing the existing optimizers.

The results of performance measurements exhibit quite low costs of creating and maintaining L-closures. Because most high-level services create L-closures very frequently but call them infrequently (e.g., to scan roots in garbage collection), the total overhead can be reduced significantly.

L-closures have roles similar to exception handlers, but they are sometimes more useful since they allow the control to return to the calling point.

Future work includes the implementation of various high-level languages by using our extended C language with L-closures as an intermediate language. We are also developing a transformation-based implementation of L-closures, which will be useful for the system where GCC-based compilers cannot be used.

**Acknowledgments.** We would like to thank Dr. Tatsurou Sekiguchi for his comments on improving the paper. This work was supported in part by MEXT Grant-in-Aid for Exploratory Research (17650008).

## References

1. Boehm, H.J., Weiser, M.: Garbage collection in an uncooperative environment. Software Practice & Experience **18**(9) (1988) 807–820
2. Hanson, D.R., Raghavachari, M.: A machine-independent debugger. Software – Practice & Experience **26**(11) (1996) 1277–1299

3. Henderson, F.: Accurate garbage collection in an uncooperative environment. In: Proc. of the 3rd International Symposium on Memory Management. (2002) 150–156

4. Jones, S.P., Ramsey, N., Reig, F.:  C--: a portable assembly language that supports garbage collection. In: International Conference on Principles and Practice of Declarative Programming. (1999)

5. Ramsey, N., Jones, S.P.: A single intermediate language that supports multiple implementations of exceptions. In: Proc. of the ACM SIGPLAN 2000 Conference on Programming Language Design and Implementation. (2000) 285–298

6. Stallman, R.M.: Using the GNU Compiler Collection. Free Software Foundation, Inc. for gcc-3.2 edn. (2002)

7. Breuel, T.M.: Lexical closures for C++. In: Usenix Proceedings, C++ Conference. (1988)

8. Yasugi, M., Komiya, T., Yuasa, T.: An efficient load-balancing framework based on lazy partitioning of sequential programs. In: Proceedings of Workshop on New Approaches to Software Construction. (2004) 65–84

9. Taura, K., Yonezawa, A.: Fine-grain multithreading with minimal compiler support – a cost effective approach to implementing efficient multithreading languages. In: Proc. of Conference on Programming Language Design and Implementation. (1997) 320–333

10. Strumpen, V.: Compiler technology for portable checkpoints. http://theory.lcs.mit.edu/~porch/ (1998)

11. Plevyak, J., Karamcheti, V., Zhang, X., Chien, A.A.: A hybrid execution model for fine-grained languages on distributed memory multicomputers. In: Supercomputing'95. (1995)

12. Umatani, S., Yasugi, M., Komiya, T., Yuasa, T.:  Pursuing laziness for efficient implementation of modern multithreaded languages. In: Proc. of the 5th International Symposium on High Performance Computing. Number 2858 in Lecture Notes in Computer Science (2003) 174–188

13. Frigo, M., Leiserson, C.E., Randall, K.H.: The implementation of the Cilk-5 multithreaded language. ACM SIGPLAN Notices (PLDI'98) **33**(5) (1998) 212–223

14. Taura, K., Tabata, K., Yonezawa, A.: StackThreads/MP: Integrating futures into calling standards. In: Proceedings of ACM SIGPLAN Symposium on Principles & Practice of Parallel Programming (PPoPP). (1999) 60–71

15. Goldstein, S.C., Schauser, K.E., Culler, D.E.: Lazy Threads: Implementing a fast parallel call. Journal of Parallel and Distributed Computing **3**(1) (1996) 5–20

16. Mohr, E., Kranz, D.A., Halstead, Jr., R.H.: Lazy task creation: A technique for increasing the granularity of parallel programs. IEEE Transactions on Parallel and Distributed Systems **2**(3) (1991) 264–280

17. Feeley, M.: A message passing implementation of lazy task creation. In: Proceedings of International Workshop on Parallel Symbolic Computing: Languages, Systems, and Applications. Number 748 in Lecture Notes in Computer Science, Springer-Verlag (1993) 94–107

# Polyhedral Code Generation in the Real World

Nicolas Vasilache, Cédric Bastoul, and Albert Cohen

ALCHEMY Group, INRIA Futurs and LRI, Université Paris-Sud XI

**Abstract.** The polyhedral model is known to be a powerful framework to reason about high level loop transformations. Recent developments in optimizing compilers broke some generally accepted ideas about the limitations of this model. First, thanks to advances in dependence analysis for irregular access patterns, its applicability which was supposed to be limited to very simple loop nests has been extended to wide code regions. Then, new algorithms made it possible to compute the target code for hundreds of statements while this code generation step was expected not to be scalable. Such theoretical advances and new software tools allowed actors from both academia and industry to study more complex and realistic cases. Unfortunately, despite strong optimization potential of a given transformation for e.g., parallelism or data locality, code generation may still be challenging or result in high control overhead. This paper presents scalable code generation methods that make possible the application of increasingly complex program transformations. By studying the transformations themselves, we show how it is possible to benefit from their properties to dramatically improve both code generation quality and space/time complexity, with respect to the best state-of-the-art code generation tool. In addition, we build on these improvements to present a new algorithm improving generated code performance for strided domains and reindexed schedules.

## 1 Introduction

Compiler performance has long been quantified through the number of processed code lines per time unit. Compile time used to be (almost) linear in the code length. In order to find the best possible optimizations, present day compilers must rely on higher complexity methods. A striking example is the polyhedral model. Many advances in program restructuring have been achieved through this model which considers each instance of a statement as an integer point in a convenient space [17]. Most of the underlying methods, as data dependence analysis [9, 23], transformation computation [21, 12] or code generation [16, 25] exhibit worst-case exponential complexity.

It is not easy to conclude about the scalability of such techniques. The literature is full of algorithms with high complexity which present a very good practical behavior (the *simplex* algorithm is probably the most famous [7]). Polyhedral code generation has an intrinsic worst-case complexity of $3^{n\rho}$ polyhedral operations (themselves associated with NP-complete problems), where $n$ is the

A. Mycroft and A. Zeller (Eds.): CC 2006, LNCS 3923, pp. 185–201, 2006.

number of statements, and $\rho$ the maximum loop depth. Nevertheless, input programs are not randomly generated. Most of the time, human-written codes show simple control, loop nests with low depth and which enclose few statements. Such properties make it possible to regenerate, through the whole source-to-polyhedra-to-source framework, well known benchmark codes with hundreds of statements per static control compute kernel (in the SPECfp2000 benchmarks) in an acceptable amount of time [3].

Complex transformations may be automatically computed by a given optimizing compiler [5, 21, 4, 12] or discovered by a programmer with the help of an optimization environment [22, 6]. Their application diminishes the input program regularity and lead to a challenging code generation problem. The challenge may come either from the ability to compute any solution (because of a complexity explosion) or from the ability to find a satisfactory solution (because of a high resulting control overhead). To solve these problems *in practice*, a new experiment-driven study was necessary, starting from the best state-of-the-art code generation tool [3]. We analyzed in depth a complex optimizing transformation sequence of the SPECfp2000 benchmark Swim that has been found by an optimization expert with the help of the URUK framework [6]. Our goal was to find properties of the transformations themselves that may be exploited to defer the complexity problem, and to improve the generated code quality.

To validate our approach, we studied and applied our methods to other complex problems that have been submitted by various teams from both industry and academia. Each of them uses its own strategy to compute transformations, which encourage the search for common transformation properties. QR has been provided by Reservoir Labs Inc. which develop the high level R-Stream compiler [14]. Classen has been submitted by the FMI laboratory of the University of Passau which develop the high level parallelization tool LooPo [19, 12]. DreamupT3 has been supplied by the RNTL Project DREAM-UP between Thales Research, Thomson R&D and École des Mines de Paris [13]. General properties of these reference problems are shown in Figure 1. They proved to be quite different, spanning all typical sources of complexity in polyhedral code generation: each benchmark has its own reason to be challenging, e.g. high statement number for Swim, deep loop nests for Classen, big values that need multi-precision arithmetic to be to manipulated with DreamupT3.

The paper is organized as follows. Section 2 introduces the polyhedral representation and transformation model, then presents the associated code generation problem. Section 3 positions our paper among related works. Section 4 investigates algorithmic scalability challenges and our solutions, driven by

| | Reference problems | | | |
|---|---|---|---|---|
| Properties | Swim | QR | Classen | DreamupT3 |
| Statement number | 199 | 10 | 8 | 3 |
| Maximum loop depth | 5 | 3 | 8 | 2 |
| Number of parameters | 5 | 2 | 1 | 0 |
| Scheduling dimensionality | 11 | 7 | 7 | 1 |
| Maximum coefficient value | 60 | 5 | 4 | 1919 |

**Fig. 1.** General properties of reference problems

experimental evaluations of the four reference benchmarks. Section 5 addresses additional code generation challenges associated with code size reduction and efficiency; in particular, it presents the first modulo-condition elimination technique that succeeds for a large class of real-world schedules while avoiding code bloat due to multi-versioning.

## 2   Overview of the Polyhedral Framework

This section presents both a quick overview of the polyhedral framework and notations we use throughout the paper. A more formal presentation of the model may be found in [24]. One usually distinguishes three steps: one first has to represent an input program in the formalism, then apply a transformation to this representation, and finally generate the target (syntactic) code.

Our introductory example is a polynomial multiplication kernel. The syntactic form is shown in Figure 2(a). It only deals with control aspects of the program, and we refer to the two computational statements (array assignments) through their names, $S1$ and $S2$. To bypass the limitations of such representation (e.g. weak data dependence analysis, restriction to simple transformations), the polyhedral model is closer to the execution itself by considering *statement instances*. For each statement we consider the *iteration domain*, where every statement instance belongs. The domains are described using affine constraints that can be extracted from the program control. For example, the iteration domain of statement $S1$, called $\mathcal{D}_{S1}$, is the set of values $(i)$ such that $2 \le i \le n$ as shown in Figure 2(b); a matrix representation is used to represent such constraints: $A \cdot \boldsymbol{x} + A_p \cdot \boldsymbol{p} \ge \boldsymbol{0}$, where $A$ is the *iteration matrix*, $\boldsymbol{x}$ is the *iteration vector* (composed of the loop counters), $A_p$ is the *parameter matrix* and $\boldsymbol{p}$ is the *parameter vector* (composed of the unknown constants and the scalar 1). In our example, $\mathcal{D}_{S1}$ is characterized by $\begin{bmatrix} 1 \\ -1 \end{bmatrix} \cdot (i) + \begin{bmatrix} 0 & -2 \\ 1 & 0 \end{bmatrix} \cdot \begin{pmatrix} n \\ 1 \end{pmatrix} \ge \boldsymbol{0}$.

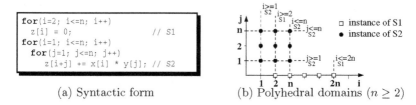

(a) Syntactic form                    (b) Polyhedral domains $(n \ge 2)$

**Fig. 2.** A polynomial multiplication kernel and its polyhedral domains

In this framework, a transformation is a set of *affine scheduling functions* written $\theta(\boldsymbol{x}) = T \cdot \boldsymbol{x} + T_p \cdot \boldsymbol{p}$. Each statement has its own scheduling function which maps each run-time statement instance to a logical execution date. In our polynomial multiplication example, an optimizer may notice a locality problem and discover a good data reuse potential over array $\mathbf{z}$, then suggest $\theta_{S1}(i) = (i)$ and $\theta_{S2} \begin{pmatrix} i \\ j \end{pmatrix} = (i + j + 1)$ to achieve better locality (see e.g., [4] for a method to compute such functions). The intuition behind such transformation is to execute consecutively the instances of $S2$ having the same $i + j$ value (thus accessing the same array element of $z$) and to ensure that the initialization of each element is executed by $S1$ just before the first instance of $S2$ referring this element. A transformation is applied in the polyhedral model by using the transformation formula shown in Figure 3(a) [3], where $t$ is the *time-vector*, i.e. the vector of the scheduling dimensions. The resulting polyhedra for our example are shown in Figure 3(b) with the additional dimension $t$.

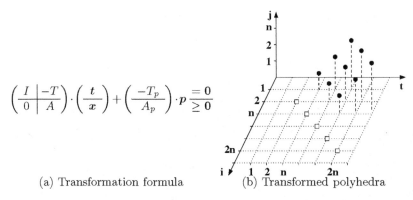

$$\left(\begin{array}{c|c} I & -T \\ \hline 0 & A \end{array}\right) \cdot \left(\begin{array}{c} t \\ x \end{array}\right) + \left(\begin{array}{c} -T_p \\ A_p \end{array}\right) \cdot p \begin{array}{c} = 0 \\ \geq 0 \end{array}$$

(a) Transformation formula    (b) Transformed polyhedra

**Fig. 3.** General transformation formula and its application

Once the transformation has been applied in the polyhedral model, one needs to generate the target code. The best syntax tree construction scheme consists in a recursive application of domain projections and separations [25, 3]. The final code is deduced from the set of constraints describing the polyhedra attached to each node in the tree. In our example, the first step is a projection onto the first dimension $t$, followed by a separation into disjoint polyhedra as shown on the top of Figure 4(a). This builds the first loop level of the target code (the loops with iterator $t$ shown in Figure 4(b)). The same process is applied onto the first two dimensions (on the bottom of Figure 4(a)) to build the second loop level and so on. The final code is shown in Figure 4(b) (the reader may care to verify that this solution does exploit at its best the temporal reuse of array $z$). Note that the separation step for two polyhedra needs three operations: $\mathcal{D}_{S1} - \mathcal{D}_{S2}$, $\mathcal{D}_{S2} - \mathcal{D}_{S1}$ and $\mathcal{D}_{S2} \cap \mathcal{D}_{S1}$, thus for $n$ statements the worst-case complexity is $3^n$.

## 3    Related Work

The history of code generation in the polyhedral model shows a constant growth in transformation complexity, from basic schedules for a single statement to general affine transformations for wide code regions. In their seminal work, Ancourt and Irigoin limited transformations to unimodular functions (the $T$ matrix presented in Section 2 has determinant 1 or $-1$) and the code generation process was applicable for only one domain at once [1]. Several works succeeded in relaxing the unimodularity constraint to invertibility (the $T$ matrix has to be

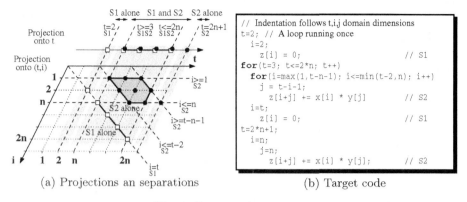

(a) Projections an separations          (b) Target code

**Fig. 4.** Target code generation

invertible), enlarging the set of possible transformations [8, 20]. A further step has been achieved by Kelly et al. by considering more than one domain and multiple scheduling functions at the same time [16]. All these methods relied on the Fourier-Motzkin elimination method [27] to build the target code. Quilleré et al. showed how to use polyhedral operations based on the Chernikova Algorithm [18] instead, to benefit from its practical efficiency to handle bigger problems [25]. Recently, a new transformation policy has been proposed to allow general non-invertible, non-uniform, non-integral affine transformations [3]. Such freedom allowed to apply polyhedral techniques to much larger programs with very sophisticated transformations, and led to novel complexity, scalability and code quality challenges we discuss in this paper.

## 4   Code Generation Scalability

This section analyzes three important properties of affine schedules used in real-world program generation problems, then for each property, proposes an algorithmic solution to improve scalability.

### 4.1   Scalar Dimensions

There are many ways to specify a given transformation (or a given sequence of transformations) using affine schedules. Basically we can divide them in two families. The first kind, mono-dimensional schedules, describe the execution order thanks to functions with only one dimension. The second kind, multi-dimensional schedules, use several dimensions to express the ordering. Most of the time, the original domains are parametric, i.e., are bounded by (statically) unknown constants. For the first kind, this variety amounts to manipulating non-affine expressions. This is not the case with multi-dimensional schedules, when using at least as many dimensions as the original domain [10]. Moreover, using additional dimensions to explicitly order different statements onto a given dimension makes transformation manipulation easier [15, 6]. As a result, multi-dimensional schedules with more dimensions than original domains are quite often used to specify transformations. Figure 5 shows an example of a loop interchange transformation applied to the example in Figure 2(a) that may be achieved thanks to different schedules. $\rho(S)$ is the depth of the original statement, i.e., the number of dimensions of its original iteration domain.

| Scheduling policy | $\theta_{S1}$ | $\theta_{S2}$ |
|---|---|---|
| Mono-dimensional | $(i)$ | $(n + j * n + i)$ |
| $\rho(S)$-dimensional | $(i)$ | $(n + j, i)^T$ |
| $(2 * \rho(S) + 1)$-dimensional | $(0, i, 0)^T$ | $(1, j, 0, i, 0)^T$ |

(a) Possible schedules for loop interchange

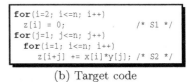

```
for(i=2; i<=n; i++)
    z[i] = 0;                    /* S1 */
for(j=1; j<=n; j++)
    for(i=1; i<=n; i++)
        z[i+j] += x[i]*y[j]; /* S2 */
```

(b) Target code

**Fig. 5.** Loop interchange for polynomial multiplication using different schedules

Unified transformation frameworks like UTF [15] or URUK [6] are good example of multi-dimensional schedule policies. Both ask for $(2\rho(S)+1)$ dimensions which allow them to be much more flexible. Nevertheless, using additional dimensions has a cost. In time: we will see that each dimension needs costly polyhedral operations (projection/separation/sorting). In space: each dimension implies (1) a new column in the constraint matrix, (2) as many rows as new constraints and (3) a new level in the generated code tree.

Most of the time, additional dimensions are *scalar*, i.e. they are constant for every scheduling functions. Because polyhedral operations on such dimensions are trivial, we systematically *remove them from the constraint matrix*, storing the scalar values in ad-hoc vectors. In the following, scalar dimensions will be implicitly stripped away from the schedule matrices. Polyhedral operations as usual with the additional provision that, before each separation step, we order the polyhedra according to the appropriate scalar vector components. Further steps of the code generation algorithm are applied onto lists of polyhedra having the same values for these components.

This optimization benefits from schedule properties without impacting expressiveness. It may dramatically reduce the number of polyhedral operations, improving both time and space complexity. Moreover, it also reduces the cost (in time and space) of every single polyhedral operation, by reducing matrix size. In practice, the actual benefits depend on the transformation policy: the more the constant scalar dimensions, the better the results. Also, this step has a very low complexity and thus does not degrade computation time even in worst

| Benchmark | Scalar ratio | Time | | | Space | | |
|---|---|---|---|---|---|---|---|
| | | Original(s) | Scalar(s) | Speedup | Original(KB) | Scalar(KB) | Reduction |
| Swim | 6/11 | 41.20 | 10.33 | 3.99× | 17480 | 8128 | 2.15× |
| QR | 4/7 | 19.47 | 2.44 | 7.98× | 3012 | 988 | 3.05× |
| Classen | 3/7 | 1.12 | 0.69 | 1.62× | 1092 | 672 | 1.62× |
| DreamupT3 | 0/1 | 0.49 | 0.49 | 1.00× | 160 | 160 | 1.00× |

**Fig. 6.** Experimental results for scalar dimension removal

case scenarios. Figure 6 shows the results when applying this optimization to our reference code generation problems. The scalar ratio gives the number of scalar dimensions with respect to the total number of dimensions, showing that the different teams which provided their problems do use scalar dimensions. This results into significant time and space improvement, except for the last program.

## 4.2  Node Fusion

When specifying transformations for a program with many statements, often is the case the processing is similar for several statements, at least for some dimensions. For instance, applying a given transformation (same schedules) to some statements of a given loop nest (same domains) allow to consider only one statement block. The modified version of the Quilleré algorithm [3] is given in Figure 7 and exploits the similarities of the transformations on certain dimensions for different statements.

```
CodeGeneration: builds an AST (Abstract Syntax Tree) scanning a list of polyhedra
Input:
  node: flat AST holding the domains to scan
  context: static context (known constraints met by the parameters)
  depth: the nesting level
Output: An AST scanning the polyhedra in the lexicographic order

  AST ←
  while node has successors
1   Intersect node.domain with the context
2   Project intersected domain on the depth outermost dimensions and on parameters
3   node ← node.next

  if nodes have scalar values at depth and they are different
4   Sort nodes according to their scalar values at depth
5 worklist ← partition nodes by scalar values

  foreach job in worklist
6   fusedlist ← Fuse nodes of job with the same projected intersected domain
7   separatedlist ← Apply Quilleré's separation step to fusedlist
8   sortedlist ← Sort separatedlist according to the lexicographic order
    foreach ASTnode in sortedlist
      if ASTnode.domain dimensionality > depth
9       ASTnode.inner = CodeGeneration(ASTnode.node, context, depth+1)
10      Enqueue ASTnode to AST

  return AST
```

**Fig. 7.** Code generation algorithm

Steps 4 and 5 create work-lists that fully take advantage of the detection of scalar dimensions described in Section 4.1. Step 6 examines nodes of each job of the work-list and tries to fuse them into sub-work-lists to reduce the number of elements given to the Quilleré algorithm as much as possible. Node fusion occurs at current depth on the projected domains and is guaranteed to exploit similarities between schedules at each nesting level independently. The complexity gain of Steps 4, 5 and 6 is difficult to quantify as it depends on the shape of the generated code itself and transformation similarities across different statements.

Considering a simple case with $n$ statements in a loop nest level that can be blocked into $c$ chunks of $s_c$ statements with same scalar components. Suppose each chunk can further be blocked into $b_c$ blocks of $l_{b_c} \leq s_c$ statements with same projected domain. This translates to $\sum_{b_c} (\text{Quilleré}(l_{b_c}))$ instead of Quilleré $(n)$ which stands for a call to the Quilleré separation algorithm that has a worst-case complexity of $3^n$. Furthermore, Step 8 also benefits from the reduction above and allows for $\sum_{b_c} (\text{Sort}(l_{b_c}))$ instead of Sort $(n)$ which stands for a call to a function sorting $n$ polyhedra that also has an exponential worst case complexity. Experimental results are summarized in Figure 8. As expected, this technique is quite useful for large problems like `Swim`.

| Benchmark | Time | | | Space | | |
|---|---|---|---|---|---|---|
| | Original(s) | Fused(s) | Speedup | Original(KB) | Fused(KB) | Reduction |
| Swim | 41.20 | 5.90 | 6.98× | 17480 | 5048 | 3.46× |
| QR | 19.47 | 19.17 | 1.02× | 3012 | 2992 | 1.01× |
| Classen | 1.12 | 1.03 | 1.09× | 1092 | 1060 | 1.03× |
| DreamupT3 | 0.49 | 0.49 | 1.00× | 160 | 160 | 1.00× |

**Fig. 8.** Experimental results on node fusion

## 4.3   Domain Iterators

It is well known that code generation is easier when restricting the problem to invertible schedules [29, 25]. CLooG was the first tool to seamlessly manage non-invertible schedules, at the cost of additional recursion steps, polyhedral projections and larger matrix sizes in Quilleré's algorithm [2, 3]. For scalability reasons, we propose to detect non-singularity conditions and refine the recursive AST traversal automatically. Indeed, when considering invertible transformations, the value of the original domain iterators (used, e.g., in the statement bodies) according to the target space iterators can be efficiently obtained via matrix inversion (instead of recursive polyhedral projections).

Let $\theta(\boldsymbol{x}) = T \cdot \boldsymbol{x} + T_p \cdot \boldsymbol{p}$ be a schedule transformation where $T$ is invertible, and consider an iteration domain $\mathcal{D} : A \cdot \boldsymbol{x} + A_p \cdot \boldsymbol{p} \geq 0$. The transformed domain $\mathcal{T}$ (see Figure 3(a)) can be broken down into two distinct components:

- a polyhedron to scan (Figure 9) obtained by projecting $\mathcal{T}$ on time iterators and parameters only;
- an *inverted scatter matrix* (ISM) that associates, locally to each statement, the expression of the domain iterators as invertible functions of time iterators and parameters. When $T$ is non-unimodular, $T^{-1}$ has rational coefficients. Let $(d_{i,j})$ be the denominators of $T^{-1}$, by taking $\lambda_i = \text{lcm}(d_{i,\bullet})$ we define $\Lambda = \text{Diag}(\lambda_i)$ as the diagonal matrix where the diagonal element of the $i^{th}$ line is $\lambda_i$. The left multiplication of the matrix representation of $\mathcal{T}$ (Figure 3(a)) by $(\Lambda T^{-1} | 0)$ yields an integral matrix, the ISM in Figure 10.

$$\mathcal{T} \perp \left( \begin{array}{c|c|c} t & 0 & 0 \\ \hline 0 & 0 & p \end{array} \right)$$

$$\left( \Lambda T^{-1} \mid -\Lambda \right) \left( \begin{array}{c} t \\ x \end{array} \right) - \Lambda T^{-1} T_p p = 0$$

**Fig. 9.** Simplified time-extended domain

**Fig. 10.** ISM to recover the domain iterators

The benefits brought to the separation algorithm are threefold and contribute to possibly exponential complexity gains:

- it is straightforward to write domain iterators as expressions of time iterators and parameters from Figure 10 instead of performing costly polyhedral projections on each domain iterator;
- the column number of each polyhedron to scan is reduced by the number of domain iterators (potentially half the original size if there are no parameters);
- the height of the generated AST is reduced on each path to every statement by the same amount above. However the paths subject to reduction are linear and save no branches from the original AST but still save polyhedral projections.

The `Swim` benchmark has invertible schedules only (this is a strong assumption of the URUK framework [6]), but this is not the case for the other benchmarks. We could therefore evaluate this optimization to `Swim` only, yielding 36% reduction in code generation time and 57% reduction in memory usage. We are working on extending this domain iterator elimination technique to all kinds of non-invertible schedules, combining Gaussian elimination steps with polyhedral projections.

### 4.4   If Conditional Hoisting

Under complex transformation sequences, the top-down part of Quilleré's code generation algorithm [25] yields `if` conditionals that greatly hamper the quality of the generated code and thus, its execution time. Figure 11 exhibits this behavior on a basic example: generating a code for scanning the polyhedra of Figure 11(a) using the algorithm in Figure 7 would lead to the code in Figure 11(b). This figure shows internal guards leading to a high control-overhead.

The approach presented in [25] for removing inner `if` conditionals and generating the better code in Figure 11(c) consists of a backtracking call to the separation procedure. Although it proved successful at performing its primary task, its side effects can yield unnecessary computation and code bloating. The aforementioned algorithm lacks the capability of factorizing similar conditionals. Examine a node at depth $d$ after the separation phase. Assume the separation has generated an inner conditional $c$ which depends only on the $i$, $i < d$, first dimension iterators. During the backtracking called on depth $d$, the algorithm in [25, 3] performs separation regardless of the condition $c$. Therefore, costly polyhedral operations have been made while only a separation at depth $i$ was necessary. Focusing only on conditionals also avoids to version triangular loops which may not execute only for specific values of the outer loop counters. For

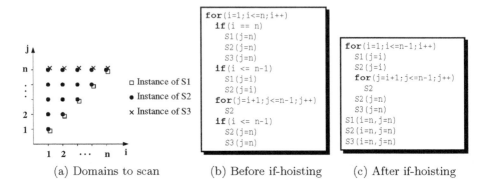

(a) Domains to scan        (b) Before if-hoisting        (c) After if-hoisting

**Fig. 11.** Removing internal guards with if-hoisting

instance, in Figure 11(c) the $j$-loop does not iterate for $i = n - 1$; removing this negligible control overhead would increase code size by 50%.

Our solution boils down to a depth-first traversal of the AST, fetching all the conditionals of subsequent domains for the current nesting level, *factorizing* them by performing polyhedral separation (intersection and difference) *on conditionals relevant to the current depth only*, and intersecting these newfound conditionals with the current domain, duplicating the underlying AST structure. The algorithm, which intervenes as a post pass after separation guarantees no unnecessary cuts are performed and therefore avoids unnecessary code explosion. Figure 12 shows the duplication factor results on the four reference benchmarks, i.e., the number of computational statements in the generated code divided by the number of statements in the polyhedral representation, a reasonable metric for code quality [2]. These results show strong code size reductions can be achieved through our improved if-hoisting phase. The relatively low duplication factor for Swim (2.5) is also a very good indication of the applicability and scalability of polyhedral techniques to larger optimization and parallelization problems. Eventually, to better isolate the effect of this optimization, the last row (Figure 12) reports results for the simple one-statement matrix multiplication, applying three-dimensional tiling and shifting through the URUK framework [6]. It incurs major (yet unavoidable) code bloat, but our technique reduces it by a factor of 2.5.

| Benchmark | Original dup. factor | if-hoisting dup. factor | Reduction |
|-----------|---------------------|-------------------------|-----------|
| Swim | 2.5 | 2.5 | 1 |
| QR | 107 | 35 | 3 |
| Classen | 11.5 | 9.6 | 1.2 |
| DreamupT3 | 23.3 | 4 | 5.8 |
| MxM | 175 | 69 | 2.5 |

**Fig. 12.** Experimental results with if-hoisting

# 5   Code Quality

Beyond code generation performance, addressing real-world problems raises generated code quality issues that may not directly emerge from smaller, academic examples. This section investigates two of them: extending code generation to implement a smarter loop unrolling strategy, and building on this extension to achieve a major step in code generation for strided domains and reindexed schedules.

## 5.1   Enabling Strip-Mining for Unrolling

In most cases, loop unrolling can be implemented as a combination of *strip-mining* and *full unrolling* [28]. Strip-mining itself may be implemented in several ways in a polyhedral setting. Following our earlier work in [6] and calling $b$ the strip-mining factor, we choose to model a strip-mined loop by dividing the iteration span of the outer loop by $b$ instead of leaving the bounds unchanged and inserting a non-unit stride $b$:

```
for(i=ℓ(x); i<=u(x); i++)
```
$\xrightarrow{\text{strip-mine}(b)}$
```
for(t1=⌈ℓ(x)/b⌉; t1<=⌊u(x)/b⌋; t1++)
    for(t2=max(ℓ(x),b*t1); t2<=min(u(x),b*t1+b-1); t2++)
```

This design preserves the convexity of the polyhedra representing the transformed code, alleviating the need for specific stride-recognition mechanisms (based, e.g., on the Hermite normal form).

In Figure 13(b) we can see how strip-mining by a factor of 2 the original code of Figure 13(a) yields an internal loop with non-trivial bounds. It can be very useful to unroll the innermost loop to exhibit register reuse (a.k.a. register tiling), relax scheduling constraints and diminish the impact of control on useful code. However, unrolling requires to cut the domains so that `min` and `max` constraints disappear from loop bounds. Our method is adapted the one presented for hoisting `if` conditionals; the difference lies in the selection of conditionals. For the purpose of if-hoisting (see Section 4.4), we just had to pick the constraints that did not concern the node at current depth. Here we focus on finding conditionals (lower bound and upper bound) for the current depth, *such that their difference is a non-parametric constant*: the unrolling factor. Hoisting these conditionals actually amounts to splitting the outer strip-mined loop into a kernel part where the inner strip-mined loop will be fully unrolled, and a remainder part

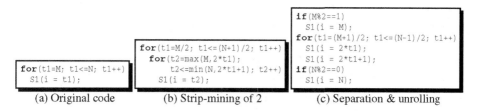

| (a) Original code | (b) Strip-mining of 2 | (c) Separation & unrolling |

**Fig. 13.** Strip-mining and unrolling transformation

(not unrollable) spanning at most as many iterations as the strip-mining factor. In our example, the conditions associated with a constant trip-count (equal to 2) are t2>=2*t1 and t2<=2*t1+1 and are associated with the kernel, separated from the prologue where 2*t1<M and from the epilogue where 2*t1+1>N. This separation leads to the more desirable form of Figure 13(c).

Finally, instead of implementing loop unrolling in the intermediate representation of our framework, we delay it to the code generation phase and perform full loop unrolling in a lazy way, avoiding the added (exponential) complexity on the separation algorithm. This approach relies on a preliminary strip-mine step that determines the amount of partial unrolling.

## 5.2   Removing Modulo Conditions

When the transformed domains $\mathcal{T}$ (see Figure 3(a)) are $\mathbb{Z}$-polyhedra (a.k.a. lattice polyhedra), the generated code shows modulo conditions. The modulo guards guarantee that only the iterations that belong to the original domain are scanned in the generated code. For instance, if the ISM of a statement $S$ (see section 4.3) that gives the value of the original domain iterators (e.g., $i$) according to the transformed space iterators (e.g., $t$) gives $2i = t$, the execution of the statement $S$ will be guarded with if (t%2 == 0). This situation happens either when the transformation matrices $T$ are not unimodular or when the original domains $\mathcal{D}$ are $\mathbb{Z}$-polyhedra, e.g., in some kinds of strip-mined loops[1]. Both cases boil down to the same code generation problem. For space reasons, we will only detail our solution in the case of invertible, non-unimodular schedules.

The consequence of generating modulo guards is to introduce a high control overhead. Many works focused on finding solutions to avoid them. The first idea was to compute an appropriate loop stride. At first it was done using the Hermite Normal Form [20, 29, 8, 26], but this was limited to only one domain, then by considering the transformation expression itself [16, 2], but some guards cannot be removed in this way. More recent methods suggest to use strip-mining for one domain [11], or to find equivalent transformations with convenient additional dimensions when this is possible [12], or to unroll the loops according to a convenient unroll factor in the case where modulo guards depend on only one loop counter [12]. Here we give a general algorithm to drastically reduce the number of modulo guards inside the loops and even void them all in the *loop kernels*.

Consider a simple example with two statements, where S1 has the one-dimensional schedule $2t_1 - 5$ and S2 has the one-dimensional schedule $3t_1$. In other words, the rate of S1 is 50% higher than S2 and is shifted ahead by 5 iterations. This example is derived from the low-level scheduling and code generation for a software-pipelined FIR filter, where one functional unit (a multiplier in S1) is needed at a 50% higher rate than a another one (an adder in S2), and S2 depends on S1. Due to the combined reindexing (factors 2 and 3 in the schedule) and shifting (by 5 iterations), traditional techniques to avoid modulo expressions cannot be applied [2], and existing code generators yield the inefficient code of

---

[1] Although one may express strip-mining with convex polyhedra only, see Section 5.1.

```
(...)
// software pipeline kernel
for (t1=5; t1<=2*N-2; t1++)
  if ((t1-5)%3 == 0)
    S2(i = (t1-5)/3);
  if (t1%2 == 0)
    S1(i = t1/2);
(...)
```

```
// prologue
S2(0);
// kernel code with S1 and S2 synchronized modulo 6
for (t1=1; t1<=floord(N-4,3); t1++)
  S1(i = 3*t1); S2(i = 2*t1-1); // t2%6 = 0
  S1(i = 3*t1+1);               // t2%6 = 2
  S1(i = 3*t1+2);               // t2%6 = 3
  S2(i = 2*t1);                 // t2%6 = 4
// epilogue
for (t1=ceild(N-3,3); t1<=floord(N-1,3); t1++)
  for (t2=6*t1; t2<=2*N-2; t2++)
    if ((-t2+5)%3 == 0)
      S2(i = (t2-5)/3);
    if (-t2%2 == 0)
      S1(i = t2/2);
```

**Fig. 14.** Traditional code genera-  **Fig. 15.** Our solution for the software-pipelined
tion    kernel

Figure 14. Our technique eliminates modulo expressions completely from the kernel part (the hot path) of the generated code, without code bloat, and generates the much more efficient version in Figure 15. On this simple example, our technique achieves a 67% reduction in generated code execution-time, with respect to the more naive one with modulo expressions.

In the general case, the main problem resides in the lower bound of the scattered domain [8, 26, 29] whose value *modulo the stride factor* must be known in order to exhibit a regular pattern in the loop body. This lower bound can be viewed as a *pattern alignment synchronization barrier* for S1 and S2. Indeed, parametric schedules with non-unit stride factors may generate as many different loop body patterns as the least common multiplier of these strides; notice these patterns are *not* identical (in general) up to loop body "rotations". The only solution to thoroughly eliminate modulo conditions is multi-versioning, but it results in severe code bloat for stride factors over 2 or 3.

Our approach consists in forcing *pattern synchronization* by strip-mining the original loop by a factor that is yet to determine. This amounts to extracting a prologue and an epilogue from the unrollable kernel, yielding the much more efficient solution of Figure 15. Using this method, the prologue and epilogue still contain internal modulo conditions whereas the kernel (where the vast majority of the execution time is spent) can be unrolled. This approach is effective on a large class of "well-behaved" schedules. We will argue at the end of this section that the other "ill-behaved" schedules are intrinsicly code-bloating if modulo expression elimination is to be attempted.

The previous case having the sole purpose of stating the problem simply, we now outline the general algorithm. This step takes place after the separation, if-hoisting, and lazy unrolling steps. From the *Inverse Scatter Matrix* (ISM) shown in Figure 10, we can derive that the $i^{th}$ original loop iterator $x_i$ corresponding to a given statement $S$ can be expressed thanks to the $i^{th}$ line of its ISM formula: $\lambda_i \cdot x_i = \left( \sum_j (k_{i,j} \cdot t_j) + C \right)$, where $C$ is the constant parametric part. It follows, a modulo condition that rules the execution of $S$ is $\left( \sum_j (k_{i,j} \cdot t_j) + C \right)$

mod $\lambda_i = 0$. Let us first assume that $C$ is known at compile time. The point is to statically determine the values of $(k_{i,j} \cdot t_j)$ mod $\lambda_i$ for all $i$ and $j$ to be able to remove all the modulo guards. For that purpose, for each node of the AST at depth $j$, the time dimension $t_j$ will be unrolled by the least common multiplier over all statements under this node (at depth $j$) of

$$\text{lcm}_j = \lcm_{\{i|k_{i,j}\neq 0\}} \left(\lambda_i/\gcd(k_{i,j},\lambda_i)\right).$$

Unrolling by this factor yields as many instances of $t_j$ for which we statically know the value modulo $\lambda_i$. For a given loop node at depth $d$, the least common multiplier of all such unrolling factors yields the global unrolling factor $\text{lcm}_j$ that is *necessary* for static elimination of all internal modulo conditions. To enable unrolling, a new time dimension is introduced by strip-mining by $\text{lcm}_j$. This new dimension scans the same points as the old time dimension, with the additional property that its first iteration is divisible by $\text{lcm}_j$, thus achieving the required *synchronization of all statements to a statically known pattern*. Building on the strip-mining method introduced in Section 5.1, the strip-mined loop is actually split into a prologue, a so-called *zero-aligned kernel*, and an epilogue. By construction, the zero-aligned kernel has the important property that *its outer strip-mined loop scans multiples of $\text{lcm}_j$ only*. Thanks to this property, and having fully unrolled the inner strip-mined loop, we may *statically evaluate* the remainder of the division of the *inner strip-mined loop's iterator* by $\text{lcm}_j$. Applying this systematically to all depths where $\text{lcm}_j$ is greater than 1 allows all modulo conditions to be removed *from the zero-aligned kernel only*.

```
RemoveModuloGuards: removes modulo conditionals from loop kernels
Input:
  node: AST root node
  depth: the depth of the modulo conditional
Output: an AST without modulo conditionals in loop nest kernel

  nodelist ← empty list
  while node has successors
    if node is a for loop
1     compute lcm_depth
      if lcm_depth > 1
2       kernel.inner ← new time dimension between t_depth and  t_depth+1 with constraints
          lcm_depth × t_depth ≤ t_new ≤ lcm_depth × t_depth + (lcm_depth − 1)
3       Update all the statement informations (domains and ISMs) with the new dimension
4       Strip-mine and partition node.domain in prologue, zero-aligned kernel, and epilogue
5       Enqueue prologue, kernel and epilogue to nodelist
6       Unroll kernel with respect to t_new
7       RemoveModuloGuards(kernel.inner.inner, depth+2)
      else
8       RemoveModuloGuards(node.inner, depth+1)
    else node is a statement
9     Prune node off the AST if needed
    node ← node.next

  return nodelist
```

**Fig. 16.** RemoveModuloGuards Algorithm

The algorithm in Figure 16 describes how to introduce new time dimensions and unroll them so as to eliminate modulo conditions. Step 9 is actually not trivial. When reaching the leaves of the AST, we need to determine which modulo guards have been simplified, which ones are still necessary and which ones have become unfeasible. Having strip-mined (and unrolled) by the factor $\text{lcm}_{\text{depth}}$, we have forced newly created time iterators on the path to the innermost kernel to be divisible by $\lambda_i$. If all the components of an ISM line $i$ are divisible by $\lambda_i$, then the modulo condition is always true and needs not to be printed. If all the components are divisible by $\lambda_i$ but not the constant part, the modulo condition is always false and the statement should be pruned. In the last case, the modulo condition for line $i$ needs to be printed, but at least its expression simpler (and faster to evaluate) than it would have been without strip-mining and unrolling.ˑ

Had we wished to fully unroll and had we used versioning, we could have generated an unreasonable number of versions (up to the factorial of $\text{lcm}_{\text{depth}}$). Our algorithm manages to fully unroll the kernel only, where most computation time is spent, while the prologues and epilogues (with modulo conditions) hold at most $\text{lcm}_{\text{depth}} - 1$ iterations.

When the value of *constant parametric shift component C* modulo $\text{lcm}_{\text{depth}}$ is not statically known, it is impossible to statically determine an interleaving pattern. Synchronizing the values of time iterators modulo $\text{lcm}_{\text{depth}}$ does not help and even leads to the insertion of internal modulo conditions. Nonetheless, one can argue on the interest of schedules that do not exhibit a regular pattern: the interleaving of statements itself totally changes with the values of parameters, hence is intrinsicly tied to multi-versioning.

## 6    Putting It All Together

Let us combine all the previous optimizations and summarize the total improvements in code generation time, memory usage and generated code size. To further stress the scalability of our tool, we added a more complex optimization of the `Swim` benchmark, called `Swim+`, in its most general setting with 5 parameters (without context).

| Benchmark | Time | | | Space | | | Code size | | |
|---|---|---|---|---|---|---|---|---|---|
| | Orig.(s) | Opt.(s) | Speedup | Orig.(KB) | Opt.(KB) | Reduction | Orig.(Lines) | Opt.(Lines) | Reduction |
| Swim | 41.20 | 2.41 | 17.09× | 17480 | 2380 | 7.34× | 830 | 764 | 1.09× |
| Swim+ | 1219.67 | 21.62 | 56.41× | 322624 | 22180 | 14.55× | 17791 | 12041 | 1.48× |
| QR | 19.47 | 2.42 | 8.05× | 3012 | 988 | 3.05× | 4733 | 1432 | 3.33× |
| Classen | 1.12 | 0.25 | 4.48× | 1092 | 272 | 4.01× | 130 | 105 | 1.24× |
| DreamupT3 | 0.49 | 0.20 | 2.45× | 160 | 160 | 1.00× | 382 | 68 | 5.62× |

**Fig. 17.** Summary of experimental results

## 7    Conclusion

The polyhedral model is a powerful framework to reason about high level loop transformations. Recently, new algorithms made it possible to compute the target code for hundreds of statements while this code generation step was expected not to be scalable. Unfortunately, these improvements allowed the exploration of larger, more complex optimization and parallelization problems, which in turn raised several scalability and code quality challenges.

We presented scalable code generation methods that make possible the application of complex program transformations to real-world computation kernels with up to 199 statements. By studying the transformations themselves, we show how it is possible to benefit from their properties to dramatically improve both code generation quality and space/time complexity. Moreover, building on these algorithmic improvements, we proposed a new algorithm to generate more efficient (conditional-free) code for strided domains and reindexed schedules.

We believe these improvements — implemented in the latest versions of the CLooG [3] and WRaP-IT/URUK [6] frameworks — will initiate an other virtuous cycle towards allowing polyhedral techniques to bring dramatic improvements in the effectiveness of optimizing and parallelizing compilers.

# References

1. C. Ancourt and F. Irigoin. Scanning polyhedra with DO loops. In *3rd ACM SIGPLAN Symposium on Principles and Practice of Parallel Programming*, pages 39–50, june 1991.
2. C. Bastoul. Efficient code generation for automatic parallelization and optimization. In *ISPDC'03 IEEE Intl. Symp. on Parallel and Distributed Computing*, pages 23–30, Ljubljana, october 2003.
3. C. Bastoul. Code generation in the polyhedral model is easier than you think. In *PACT'13 IEEE Intl. Conf. on Parallel Architecture and Compilation Techniques*, pages 7–16, Juan-les-Pins, september 2004.
4. C. Bastoul and P. Feautrier. Improving data locality by chunking. In *CC'12 Intl. Conf. on Compiler Construction, LNCS 2622*, pages 320–335, Warsaw, april 2003.
5. P. Boulet, A. Darte, G.-A. Silber, and F. Vivien. Loop parallelization algorithms: From parallelism extraction to code generation. *Parallel Computing*, 24(3):421–444, 1998.
6. A. Cohen, S. Girbal, D. Parello, M. Sigler, O. Temam, and N. Vasilache. Facilitating the search for compositions of program transformations. In *ACM ICS'05 International Conference on Supercomputing*, pages 151–160, Cambridge, june 2005.
7. G. Dantzig. Maximization of a linear function of variables subject to linear inequalities. In T. Koopmans, editor, *Activity Analysis of Production and Allocation, Cowles Commission Monograph No. 13*, pages 339–347, New York, 1951. John Wiley & Sons, Inc.
8. A. Darte and Y. Robert. Mapping uniform loop nests onto distributed memory architectures. *Parallel Computing*, 20(5):679–710, 1994.
9. P. Feautrier. Dataflow analysis of scalar and array references. *International Journal of Parallel Programming*, 20(1):23–53, february 1991.
10. P. Feautrier. Some efficient solutions to the affine scheduling problem, part II: multidimensional time. *Int. Journal of Parallel Programming*, 21(6):389–420, december 1992.
11. B. Franke and M. O'Boyle. A complete compiler approach to auto-parallelizing c programs for Multi-DSP systems. *IEEE Transactions on Parallel and Distributed Systems (TPDS)*, 16(3):234–245, march 2005.

12. M. Griebl. Automatic parallelization of loop programs for distributed memory architectures. Habilitation thesis. Facultät für Mathematik und Informatik, Universität Passau, 2004.

13. I. Hurbain, C. Ancourt, F. Irigoin, M. Barreteau, J. Mattioli, and F. Paquier. A case study of design space exploration for embedded multimedia applications in SoCs. Technical Report A-361, CRI – École des Mines de Paris, february 2005.

14. U. Kapasi, S. Rixner, W. Dally, B. Khailany, J. Ho Ahn, P. Mattson, and J. Owens. Programmable stream processors. *IEEE Computer*, 36(8):54–62, august 2003.

15. W. Kelly and W. Pugh. A framework for unifying reordering transformations. Technical Report CS-TR-3193, University of Maryland, 1993.

16. W. Kelly, W. Pugh, and E. Rosser. Code generation for multiple mappings. In *Frontiers'95 Symposium on the frontiers of massively parallel computation*, McLean, 1995.

17. D. Kuck. *The Structure of Computers and Computations*. John Wiley & Sons, Inc., 1978.

18. H. Le Verge. A note on Chernikova's algorithm. Technical Report 635, IRISA, 1992.

19. C. Lengauer. Loop parallelization in the polytope model. In *Int. Conf. on Concurrency Theory, LNCS 715*, pages 398–416, Hildesheim, August 1993.

20. W. Li and K. Pingali. A singular loop transformation framework based on non-singular matrices. *International Journal of Parallel Programming*, 22(2):183–205, April 1994.

21. A. Lim and M. Lam. Maximizing parallelism and minimizing synchronization with affine transforms. In *PoPL'24 ACM Symp. on Principles of Programming Languages*, pages 201–214, Paris, January 1997.

22. R. Müller-Pfefferkorn, W. Nagel, and B. Trenkler. Optimizing cache access: A tool for source-to-source transformations and real-life compiler tests. In *Euro-Par 2004 Parallel Processing, 10th International Euro-Par Conference*, pages 72–81, Pisa, august 2004.

23. W. Pugh. The omega test: a fast and practical integer programming algorithm for dependence analysis. In *Proceedings of the third ACM/IEEE conference on Supercomputing*, pages 4–13, Albuquerque, august 1991.

24. W. Pugh. Uniform techniques for loop optimization. In *ICS'5 ACM International Conference on Supercomputing*, pages 341–352, Cologne, june 1991.

25. F. Quilleré, S. Rajopadhye, and D. Wilde. Generation of efficient nested loops from polyhedra. *International Journal of Parallel Programming*, 28(5):469–498, october 2000.

26. J. Ramanujam. Beyond unimodular transformations. *J. of Supercomputing*, 9(4):365–389, 1995.

27. A. Schrijver. *Theory of linear and integer programming*. John Wiley & Sons, Inc., 1986.

28. M. Wolfe. *High performance compilers for parallel computing*. Addison-Wesley, 1995.

29. J. Xue. Automating non-unimodular loop transformations for massive parallelism. *Parallel Computing*, 20(5):711–728, 1994.

# Iterative Collective Loop Fusion

T.J. Ashby[1] and M.F.P. O'Boyle[1]

Institute for Computer Systems Architecture,
University of Edinburgh, Scotland, UK
T.Ashby@ed.ac.uk, mob@inf.ed.ac.uk
http://www.icsa.inf.ed.ac.uk/compilers/

**Abstract.** Naive code generation from high-level languages that encourage modularity can give rise to large numbers of simple loops for array-based programs. Collective loop fusion and array contraction can be used on such codes to improve temporal locality and performance. The problem is typically formalised using a *loop dependence graph* (LDG), with solutions denoted by *fusion partitions*. Much previous work has concentrated on approaches to the abstract formulation. We present our technique called *iterative collective loop fusion* based on empirically evaluating different transformations, and show how it can provide speedups over existing approaches of up to 1.38. We also give results showing that applying such techniques to high-level languages can provide speedups of up to 2.45 over the original code, and outperforms an equivalent code in Fortran.

## 1 Introduction

Advanced programming languages that encourage modularity can give rise to programs with many loops, poor temporal locality and many temporary array variables when used to write scientific codes. The original motivation for this work came from the desire to optimise a package of iterative linear solvers with exactly these characteristics, written in Aldor[1], a high level mixed functional/imperative programming language for numerical and symbolic computer algebra. Such codes can benefit greatly from a systematic approach to loop fusion and array contraction. However, previous approaches to collective loop fusion have chosen transformations based on models rather than real performance. Our proposed solution to the problem is *iterative collective loop fusion*, which brings the techniques of iterative compilation to collective loop fusion.

The rest of the paper is organised as follows: Section 2 introduces the basic formalism with examples, Section 3 discusses previous work and motivates the development of our technique, Section 4 describes the technique in detail, Section 5 provides experimental results and Section 6 concludes and offers some ideas for future development.

## 2 Formulation and Example

A *loop dependence graph* (LDG) describes a *program section* that consists of basic blocks and perfectly nested loops with no additional branching for which

A. Mycroft and A. Zeller (Eds.): CC 2006, LNCS 3923, pp. 202–216, 2006.
© Springer-Verlag Berlin Heidelberg 2006

data dependencies are known. Figure 1 gives an example with pseudocode for four loops and the corresponding loop dependence graph. Nodes in the graph represent the loops of the program section, and a directed edge exists between two nodes if the target is data dependent on the source. The lack of branching in the program section ensures that its LDG is acyclic.

The LDG is used to reason about loop fusion for the program section that it represents. A *dependency path* (or just path) in the LDG is a set of edges describing a path from a source node to a destination node through the graph following the directed edges. Two loops are *conformable* if their headers are the same. The nodes representing two conformable loops are possible candidates to be directly fused if they connected by paths of length one and all the distance vectors from the source to the target are non-negative, such as loops $a$ and $b$ in Figure 1, or if they are not connected by a path. In the former case such an edge is defined as *collapsible*. A dependency path is collapsible if all its edges are collapsible, and non-collapsible otherwise.

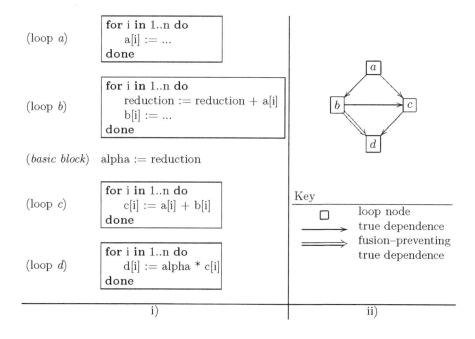

**Fig. 1.** An example LDG. i) Pseudocode for the original program section, with four loops and one basic block. Only array $d$ is live out of the program section (i.e. read at some later point), so all the other arrays can potentially be completely contracted. The loops are all conformable, and all distance vectors are 0, except for the loop-carried dependence in the second loop for a reduction variable, the dependence of the basic block on said reduction variable, and the dependence of the fourth loop on the basic block. ii) The corresponding loop dependence graph. Nodes in the graph are labelled with the name of the array that they write to.

## 2.1  Collective Loop Fusion and Fusion Partitions

A fusion partition is a partitioning of the nodes of an LDG into disjoint sets (*partitions* or *clusters*) where the nodes in each set will be fused together to produce the final transformed code. A fusion partition itself can be represented by a graph where nodes are clusters, and there is an edge between cluster nodes for every edge that exists between the loop nodes that belong to the respective partitions in the LDG. See Figure 2 for two fusion partitions of the LDG in Figure 1. The *size* of a fusion partition is the number of non-empty partitions it has (empty partitions are not allowed). For a fusion partition to be legal, it must be possible to fuse together all the nodes within a given partition, and the graph of the fusion partition must be acyclic. The first condition is satisfied by the absence of non-collapsible edges within the cluster. A given LDG has a lower bound on the size of its legal fusion partitions determined by the dependency path with the most fusion–preventing edges in it – for example, the minimum size fusion partition for the LDG in Figure 1 is two.

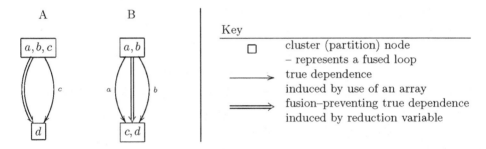

**Fig. 2.** The graphs of two possible fusion partitions of the LDG from Figure 1. Nodes in the graph (clusters) are labelled with the letters representing the loop nodes within that cluster. Both fusion partitions are the same size (2), but permit different amounts of array contraction – partition A allows two arrays to be contracted ($a$ and $b$), whereas B allows only one ($c$). This corresponds (inversely) to the inter-cluster array dependency edges in the graphs of the fusion partitions, which are labelled with the non-contracted array they correspond to – one for partition A and two for B.

## 2.2  Array Contraction

For a given array, (complete) contraction will be legal after partitioning if all the dependencies associated with it appear in the same cluster, and they all have distance zero. Applying array contraction to two fusion partitions of the same size on a given LDG can give different contraction amounts. This can be seen by the number of edges in Figure 2, and also the replacement of arrays with scalar variables in Figure 3, which represents the end product of the transformations represented in Figure 2. Conversely, different size partitions with the same amount of contraction are also possible.

A fusion partition can be labelled with a pair of numbers that denote the size of the fusion partition and the amount of array contraction that it permits. For

```
for i in 1..n do
    a := ...
    reduction := reduction + a
    b := ...
    c[i] := a + b
done
```

alpha := reduction

```
for i in 1..n do
    d[i] := alpha * c[i]
done
```

A

```
for i in 1..n do
    a[i] := ...
    reduction := reduction + a
    b[i] := ...
done
```

alpha := reduction

```
for i in 1..n do
    c := a[i] + b[i]
    d[i] := alpha * c
done
```

B

**Fig. 3.** Pseudocode representing the two fusion partitions A and B from Figure 2. Array contraction has been applied e.g. arrays $a$ and $b$ in the first loop of partition A have been reduced to scalar variables

some LDGs there will be multiple fusion partitions with the same (*contraction amount, partition size*) label.

## 3  Previous Work

### 3.1  Standard Model Based Approach

It is usual to associate a *cost function* with an LDG that ranks the possible transformations that can be applied to it. The simplest example of this is preferring more fusion over less (e.g. [2] in the context of typed loop fusion), with all fusion partitions of the same size being equal. A more sophisticated (and more common) approach is to add to the LDG a set of edges and associated weights that model the expected benefit of fusing the loops that they connect.

There have been numerous minor variations on the second approach. Some examples include transformations specifically for array contraction [3], [4], and a technique which minimises memory usage and simultaneously improves locality whilst limiting the size of any fused loop that is produced (i.e. avoiding "over fusing") [5]. One adaptation replaced edges in the cost graph with hyper edges to better capture re-use between array operands being read [6]. There have also been several composite approaches, such as a technique that prevents the creation of loops with parallelisation–preventing loop–carried dependencies [2], and a related approach that uses adjustable weights which can be altered to favour fusion for parallelism or fusion for locality [7].

The abstract formulation of various problems has been shown to be at least NP-hard [6], [8]. Consequently, most work on loop fusion is based on heuristic algorithms to find some approximation to the optimum answer for the model.

Approaches have included various greedy algorithms [4], [9], and algorithms based on max-flow min-cut heuristics [3], [6], [5].

There are two major weaknesses in previous model based fusion/contraction work. The first is the use in some approaches of overly simple search strategies to find some approximation to the solution of the idealised NP-hard problem (e.g. greedy search). As pointed out in [10], the majority of LDGs encountered in realistic programs will be small, and hence there is no real reason to emphasise the efficiency of the search so much at the cost of the quality of the approximation. The second problem is that although all the approaches discussed above target slightly different optimisations, it can be assumed that their ultimate goal is to get the best performance for a given LDG, but no authors have adequately explored the differences between their idealised problem and the implementation details of actual hardware.

For example, for a given LDG there may be many fusion partitions all ranked equal according to some abstract cost function (e.g. all with the same amount of contraction). However, for any method in the literature there is not usually any indication of how any particular one is chosen, or any indication of how the actual quality of the equally ranked LDGs varies in practice. Another illustration is the lack of any indication as to how fusion for locality and fusion for contraction may conflict, how the trade-off should be managed to get the best performance, and crucially how this may vary depending on the form of the loops and the actual processor architecture under consideration.

## 3.2   Iterative Optimisation

Current implementations of computer architectures contain a wide variety of complex structures, and consequently they are very difficult to model accurately – for one example of this see [11]. To combat this, the approach of iterative optimisation treats the goal of finding good transformations as a search problem, with the cost function as the empirical cost of executing the program that results from a candidate transformation.

Almost all previous approaches to iterative optimisation deal with trivial search spaces that are the Cartesian product of some number of options (e.g. array padding and tiling and unrolling factors for a loop [12]), where all choices are legal. A notable exception to this is [13]. Our work similarly deals with search spaces that are themselves nontrivial to generate (see Section 4.1). Also, loop fusion is rarely included in iterative optimisation work, with [13], [14] being two largely isolated examples. In the first of these papers loop fusion is implicitly included in the action of generated space-time mappings, but appears to be applied in an ad hoc fashion with no mention of choosing fusion partitions etc (in fact, fusion is almost not mentioned at all) – the primary focus of the paper is on finding parallelisation transformations with good performance. In the second, a small experiment on four loops with no fusion–preventing dependencies finds that fusing all loops together gives the best reduction in energy use, but the main emphasis is on tiling and unrolling. Again, there is no mention of fusion partitions. In both papers there is no mention at all of array contraction.

# 4   Iterative Collective Loop Fusion

The choice of fusion partition on an LDG usually involves a trade-off in locality for different pairs of references, and so the best choice depends on how the locality characteristics of the program interact with the architecture on which it is being run. These include considerations such as issue width, clock rate, cache size, miss penalty and bandwidth limits. Hence, choosing a good fusion partition with respect to temporal locality is architecture dependent and far from trivial, which is why we employ search.

To perform iterative loop fusion exhaustively we simply require a method of enumerating all the legal fusion partitions for a given LDG, and the means to empirically test their run-times. The size of the search space, that is the number of legal fusion partitions, almost always makes testing each point in it unfeasible, so there must be some method of selecting a subset of the search space to test. This is a standard problem in iterative compilation. An extra complication though is the generation of the search space of legal transformations itself, which is discussed below.

## 4.1   Generating Legal Fusion Partitions

Although clusters within a fusion partition are not distinguished, it is useful to label them with identification (ID) numbers to reason about the enumeration of the fusion partitions for an LDG. Clusters are numbered from 1 to $n$ giving a total ordering on the loops produced from a fusion partition.

The naive approach to generating fusion partitions of size $n$ is to assign each node to a partition $i$ with $1 \leq i \leq n$. The vast majority of these configurations will be illegal though, so a large number will have to be generated and tested to find each legal point. An alternative is to find some algorithmic way of enumerating only legal fusion partitions. The approach in this paper is based on node numbering, which is described below, followed by the enumeration algorithm.

**Node numbering and range finding.** Given a loop dependence graph, a target size of fusion partition, and a set of nodes with pre-assigned partition numbers, the forward node numbering procedure provides a test to determine the lower bound on the ID number of the partition to which any given (unassigned) node may belong.

Two directly connected nodes joined by at least one fusion–preventing edge must belong to different partitions. Consequently, given any path from a source to a sink, the nodes along the path can be numbered to show the earliest partition that they may belong to (as determined by this path) by grouping the nodes into sets separated by fusion–preventing edges and numbering the sets (and their elements) along the path consecutively. If a set contains a pre-assigned node with a value different from the parent set, then the set is split into two with the second set starting with the pre-assigned node and labelled with its value. Numbering along the path continues as before counting upward from the new value.

NUMBERNODESFORWARDS(*preassigned, LDG*)

**Description:** Labels each unassigned node in the LDG with the earliest partition that it may belong to.

**Input:** $\begin{cases} LDG, \text{ a loop dependence graph} \\ preassigned, \text{ a set of } (node, partitionID) \text{ pairs} \end{cases}$

**Output:** An integer label for each node as a set of (*node, partitionID*) pairs

(1)      $sources := \{(v, partitionID = 1) \mid$
                     $v \in \text{SOURCES}(LDG) \setminus \text{NODES}(preassigned)\}$
(2)      $labelled := preassigned \cup sources$
(3)      $unlabelled := \{v \mid v \in \text{NODES}(LDG) \setminus \text{NODES}(labelled)\}$
(4)      **repeat**
(5)          choose $v \in unlabelled$ s.t. $\text{PARENTS}(v) \cap unlabelled = \emptyset$
(6)          $rank_v := 0$
(7)          **foreach** $p \in \text{PARENTS}(v)$
(8)              **if** $\exists e \in \text{JOINS}(v, p)$ s.t. $\text{FUSIONPREVENTING?}(e)$
(9)                  $rank_{v,p} := 1 + \text{RANK}(p, labelled)$
(10)             **else**
(11)                 $rank_{v,p} := \text{RANK}(p, labelled)$
(12)         $rank_v := \text{MAXIMUM}(\{rank_{v,p}\})$
(13)         $labelled := labelled \cup \{(v, rank_v)\}$
(14)         $unlabelled := unlabelled \setminus \{v\}$
(15)     **until** $unlabelled = \emptyset$
(16)     **return** $labelled \setminus preassigned$

**Fig. 4.** Forward node numbering algorithm

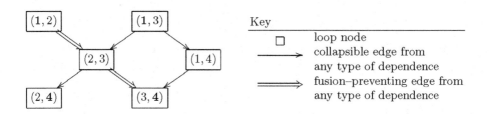

**Fig. 5.** An example showing the results produced by RANGES() when calculating possible partitionings into four clusters for a graph containing both collapsible and fusion–preventing edges. Each node is labelled with a (*minimum partition number, maximum partition number*) tuple, with numbers in bold indicating that the value results from the node being either a source or a sink in the graph.

If this procedure is repeated for all paths through the graph with each node being assigned the maximum value over all paths, then the final label $P_{min}$ will denote the earliest possible partition that the node may belong to in this LDG with these pre-assigned nodes. A pseudocode for the algorithm is provided in Figure 4. The description makes use of several simple utility functions:

- NODES(): returns the set of vertices from an aggregate data structure (either an LDG or a set of $(node, partitionID)$ pairs).
- SOURCES(): returns the set of root (source) vertices in the LDG.
- PARENTS(): returns the parents of a vertex (in the current LDG).
- JOINS(): returns the set of edges that joins two vertices (in the current LDG).
- FUSIONPREVENTING?(): returns a Boolean depending on whether the edge is collapsible or not.
- RANK(): returns from a set of $(node, partitionID)$ pairs the partition ID (integer) of a given vertex.
- MAXIMUM(): returns the maximum from a set of integers.

The algorithm does not actually enumerate all the paths through the LDG. Instead it successively selects nodes from the unassigned set only after all their parents have been processed.[1]

Given a maximum number of partitions, the same numbering can be repeated in reverse working from sinks to sources. This gives NUMBERNODES-BACKWARDS(), the result of which denotes the latest possible partition that a node may belong to, $P_{max}$. Taken together, the two procedures provide the range of partition IDs to which any unassigned node $v$ may belong $P_{v,min} \leq ID_v \leq P_{v,max}$ , and also the size of the range for that node $P_{v,max} - P_{v,min} + 1$. Any node with a range of sizes less than or equal to zero indicates that no legal fusion partitions of this size exist for this LDG. This information is provided by the RANGES() function, which essentially just calls NUMBERNODESFORWARDS() and NUMBERNODESBACKWARDS().

An example of the results produced by applying the RANGES() function to an example problem is given in Figure 5. The labelling of the graph shows for each node the earliest (minimum number) and latest (maximum number) cluster that it may belong to for the case of four partitions. Note that this is not the minimum number of partitions possible for this LDG.

**Enumeration algorithm.** The enumeration algorithm generates the fusion partitions of a given size for an LDG. It starts by finding the ranges of the nodes in the LDG, then choosing a $(node, range)$ pair. For the chosen node, the algorithm chooses a value in its range, treats the $(node, value)$ pair as a pre-assigned node, and recursively calls itself. At each step, the search is pruned if any partition will remain empty. For subsequent calls, a different value from the range of the last assigned node is chosen, until the range has been covered indicating that this recursive step is complete. Note that the ranges of unassigned nodes may change before each recursive function call, and that any unassigned node can be selected for enumeration within a call.

The enumeration algorithm is given in Figure 6. As well as the recursive call, it uses two other functions; RANGES(), explained above, and FUSIONPARTITION(),

---

[1] A similar algorithm to NUMBERNODESFORWARDS() , without the notion of accommodating preassigned nodes, can be found in an early paper on the subject [3]. However, the authors do not apply the same technique in reverse, as described here, and do not attempt to enumerate different fusion partitions.

ENUMERATEFUSIONPARTITIONS($LDG$, $size$, $fixed$)
**Description:** Enumerates the fusion partitions of an LDG

**Input:** $\begin{cases} LDG, \text{ a loop dependence graph} \\ size, \text{ the required size of fusion partition} \\ fixed, \text{ a set of } (node, partitionID) \text{ pairs} \end{cases}$

**Output:** the set of fusion partitions of size $size$ in $LDG$

(1)      **if** NODES($LDG$) \ NODES($fixed$) = $\emptyset$ **then return** FUSIONPARTITION($fixed$)

(2)      $fps := \emptyset$

(3)      $ranges :=$ RANGES($LDG$, $size$, $fixed$)

(4)      **if** $\forall p \in \{1, \ldots, size\}$ $\exists(v, p) \in fixed$ $\bigvee$ $\exists(v, r_{min}, r_{max}) \in ranges$ such that $(r_{min} \leq p \leq r_{max})$

(5)          choose $(v, rank_{v,min}, rank_{v,max})$ from $ranges$

(6)          **for** $i := rank_{v,min}$ **to** $rank_{v,max}$

(7)          $newFixed := fixed \cup \{(v, i)\}$

(8)          $fps := fps \cup$ ENUMERATEFUSIONPARTITIONS($LDG$, $size$, $newFixed$)

(9)      **return** $fps$

**Fig. 6.** Fusion partition enumeration algorithm

which makes a fusion partition data structure from a list of ($node$, $partitionID$) pairs. In the current implementation there is no special criterion for choosing nodes to fix (they are taken in whatever order they are provided in by the function that calculates the ranges) or values from their ranges (currently they are taken sequentially, from bottom to top by the loop on line 6).

### 4.2 Search Heuristics and Search Space Reduction

Although generating legal fusion partitions is relatively cheap, the total number of them means that generating and storing all of them (i.e. the search space) before choosing points to tests would take far too much time and space (see Table 1). Consequently, there needs to be some way of selecting a region of the search space to generate. The choice of this region is governed by the characteristics of the points we hope to find, and therefore determined by the search heuristics themselves:

1. More array contraction is likely to be better.
2. A smaller size fusion partition (i.e. less clusters) is likely to better.

Both heuristics stem from the goal of improving memory performance. The heuristics are not independent. Given some initial LDG, it is necessary to fuse some loops (i.e. choose a fusion partition) to uncover any more array contraction. Note that the smallest partition size may not contain the fusion partition with the most contracted arrays. However, for a non-pathological LDG derived from a typical program, more fusion and more contraction are likely to be related. This last assumption allows us to use the second heuristic to guide the generation of points in the space with the assumption that they will include (the majority of) the good points as determined by the first heuristic.

GENERATETESTCASES($LDG$, $maxCandidates$, $minPartitions$, $maxPartitions$)
**Description:** Enumerates the fusion partitions of an LDG

**Input:** $\begin{cases} LDG, \text{ a loop dependence graph} \\ maxCandidates, \text{ the maximum number of fusion partitions to generate} \\ minPartitions, \text{ the minimum size of fusion partition to generate} \\ maxPartitions, \text{ the maximum size of fusion partition to generate} \end{cases}$

**Output:** fusion partitions of $LDG$
(1)      $candidates := \emptyset$
(2)      **for** $i := minPartitions$ **to** $maxPartitions$
(3)          $fps :=$ ENUMERATEFUSIONPARTITIONS($LDG$, $i$, $\emptyset$)
(4)          $total := fps \cup candidates$
(5)          $candidates :=$ SELECTBEST($maxCandidates$, $total$)
(6)      **return** $candidates$

**Fig. 7.** Test case generation algorithm

Using the enumerating procedure, the overall algorithm for generating cases is given in Figure 7. The algorithm starts at small fusion partition sizes, and with each successive iteration the size of fusion partitions that are considered increases by one. Note that the amount of search space to generate (i.e. fusion partition size range) and the number of points to try are arguments supplied by the user. The function SELECTBEST() orders the set *total* based on the search heuristics (e.g. contraction, then partition size, then first come-first served) and then cuts it down to the first *maxCandidates* elements.

### 4.3   Code Generation

The only requirements on the code generated from the fusion partition of an LDG is that dependencies between partitions are respected in the final ordering of the loops generated from them, and similarly that the dependencies within a partition are respected in the ordering of the bodies from the original loops to form the body of the partition. The first requirement is automatically satisfied by ordering the loops according to the partition label sequence, and the second can be satisfied by a simple topological sort. Basic blocks are placed in the code between loops as early as is legal.

## 5   Experiments

### 5.1   Example LDG

The example is derived from the general step of a two-sided Krylov space algorithm, the fundamental component of several sparse linear solver and eigenvalue approximation algorithms [17], code for which is given in [15]. It is applied to a 3/4 dimensional simple stencil problem. A decorated version of the associated LDG is presented in Figure 8. All loops are conformable, and all edge weights are equal. Loop nodes are labeled with the variable they write to – scalars are denoted with greek letters ($\alpha, \beta \dots$), arrays with lower case letters or numbered

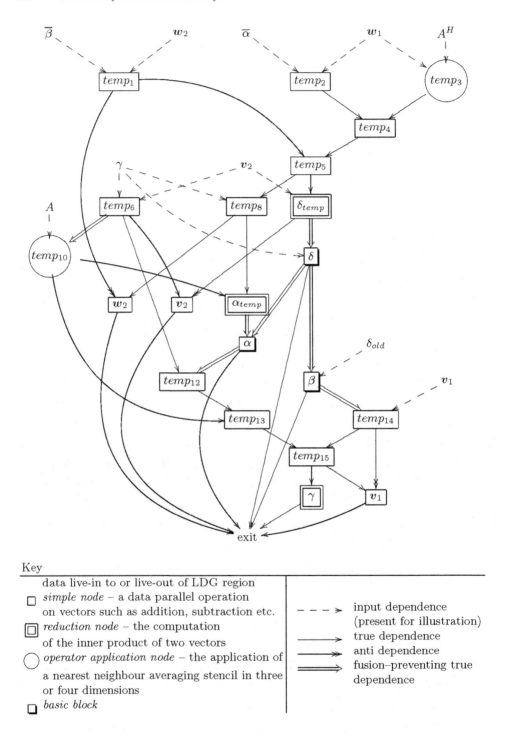

**Fig. 8.** LDG from two-sided Krylov space update

temporaries ($w_2$, $temp_9$ ...), and data for the stencil with capitals ($A$ ...). Data that is live-in and dependencies to an `exit` node for data that is live-out are added for illustration purposes.

## 5.2   Enumeration of Fusion Partitions and Compilation Times

Table 1 gives the four smallest fusion partition sizes (column 1), the number of legal fusion partitions for that size (column 2), along with the time taken to generate them (column 3). The results are further broken down to show how many partitions of that size exist with a given amount of maximum array contraction (columns 4 – 8). For example, of the 80 fusion partitions of size 3, 24 have a maximum of 9 array contractions. Our heuristics prioritise partitions with the most contraction – i.e. the column marked 10, which has a total of eight partitions from different sizes. In fact, the best result was always produced by one of these fusion partitions (although not necessarily the smallest). The table shows that there are relatively few fusion partitions with the best characteristics according to our heuristics, and so restricting empirical testing to these preferred candidates would be cheap.

The time to find a solution depends on the time spent generating the search space and testing points, both of which are under user control. Consequently compile times are determined by how much search a user is willing to do to characterise the space. The optimum points can be found for our example by testing only eight points each time, (i.e. column four from Table 5.2) but this may not be enough in all cases. A characterisation of the search spaces for multiple benchmarks on different architectures is currently in progress. Compilation times are, however, expected to be relatively long – the approach is targeted at long-running scientific/embedded applications where the investment will pay off.

**Table 1.** Number of legal fusion partitions (FPs) of certain sizes, the time taken to generate them and how many partitions with a given amount of array contraction exist for that size

| FP size | no. legal FPs | time to enumerate (in minutes) | no. FPs with $n$ contracted arrays | | | | |
|---|---|---|---|---|---|---|---|
| | | | 10 | 9 | 8 | 7 | 6 |
| 3 | 80 | 1 | 2 | 24 | 39 | 13 | 2 |
| 4 | 3557 | 1 | 4 | 174 | 960 | 1395 | 792 |
| 5 | 63801 | 4 | 2 | 366 | 4974 | 17066 | 22362 |
| 6 | 633799 | 57 | 0 | 307 | 10350 | 71951 | 178862 |

## 5.3   Comparison Against Existing Fusion Techniques

**Method.** The first set of iterative search experiments compare our search technique against two algorithms representative of those in the literature that target array contraction, a greedy [9] and a max-flow min-cut [3] algorithm, as well as the original untransformed code (i.e. without any fusion/contraction). In all cases simple Aldor code is generated from the fusion partitions by our prototype tool, followed by compilation to C code using the Aldor compiler version

**Table 2.** Times in seconds for best search, control methods and untransformed code

| stencil | machine | size | best search | greedy | max-flow min-cut | original |
|---------|---------|------|-------------|--------|------------------|----------|
| 3D | Pentium III | 50 | 136.8 | 186.3 | 163.6 | 329.6 |
|    | Pentium 4 | 70 | 55.3 | 64.2 | 76.6 | 122.3 |
| 4D | Pentium III | 18 | 118.6 | 141.3 | 148.5 | 291.1 |
|    | Pentium 4 | 24 | 59.7 | 69.7 | 79.2 | 126.9 |

**Table 3.** Times for linear solve on 3D stencil (search vs. Fortran)

| machine | size | best search | Fortran |
|---------|------|-------------|---------|
| Pentium III | 30 | 43.4 | 64.1 |
|             | 50 | 209.1 | 303.7 |
| Pentium4 | 30 | 5.26 | 7.20 |
|          | 50 | 24.5 | 33.6 |
|          | 70 | 71.6 | 95.6 |

1.01 with aggressive inlining settings. This C code is compiled using the Intel C compiler (icc) version 8.0 to run on either a 1 GHz Pentium III (Coppermine) or a 2.6 GHz Pentium 4 (Northwood). Flags for icc were set to target the specific processor (-xK/N), perform all but the most aggressive optimisations (-O2) and instrument the code for profiling. Timings were generated by executing a program that calls the main function 1000 times, to give stable results.

**Results.** A comparison of the results produced for the first set of experiments by our search method, the control techniques and the original code is given in Table 2.[2] Our technique provides speedups of up to 2.45 over the original code, and up to 1.36 and 1.38 over a greedy and a max-flow min-cut algorithms respectively. The speedup over the original code shows that there are important gains to be had from this kind of technique, and the speedup over the other methods shows that search is necessary to get the full potential benefit of the transformations.

### 5.4   Comparison Against Fortran

**Method.** The second set of experiments provide some broad comparison of the performance of Aldor code transformed with our technique against a standard Fortran 77 package containing an equivalent algorithm, QMRpack [16]. This was compiled using the Intel Fortran compiler version 8.0 (ifc) with the same flags as for icc, but also with cross-file inlining and the highest level of optimisation (-O3) to enable high-level transformations such as loop fusion. QMRpack had to be modified slightly to make the two codes more similar, by adding a stencil

---

[2] For further results, a more in-depth analysis and a discussion of how the best solution changes with respect to the problem and the architecture in question, please see [15].

and removing some conditionals that skip steps based on floating point error tolerances and may have prevented transformations such as loop fusion. Additionally, the Aldor code had to be augmented with some extra code to make it into a full QMR solver.

**Results.** Results for the second set of experiments are presented in Table 3. The transformed version outperforms the Fortran version with the relative performance gain being $\approx 1.46$ on the Pentium III and $\approx 1.35$ on the Pentium 4. These results show that using an advanced language does not necessarily mean sacrificing performance compared to lower-level languages.

# 6    Conclusion and Future Work

Iterative collective loop fusion applies heuristically guided search to select the best candidate from several fusion partition sizes and contraction amounts, and provides important performance benefits over the alternative techniques with speedups of up to 1.38. The overall approach of applying such a technique to a high-level language that is inherently very modular is promising, with performance improvements over navely generated code of up to 2.45, combining elegance of expression with performance more usually associated with traditional imperative languages.

The two most important extensions to this work will be to gather further results using more machines and LDGs derived from other codes, and to investigate how loop fusion and array contraction interact with subsequent single loop optimisations such as loop unrolling or software pipelining. In addition, investigating how to formulate the loop fusion/array contraction problem for other abstract frameworks such as the polytope model would be interesting.

# References

1. Watt, S.M. Aldor Users Guide. http://www.aldor.org
2. Kennedy, K., McKinley, K.S. Typed Fusion with Applications to Parallel and Sequential Code Generation. Techreport TR93-208. Rice University Dept. of Computer Science (1993)
3. Gao, G.R., Olsen, R., Sarkar, V., Thekkath, R. Collective Loop Fusion for Array Contraction. Proceedings of the 5th International Workshop on Languages and Compilers for Parallel Computing. Springer-Verlag (1992) 281–295
4. Lewis, E.C., Lin, C., Snyder, L. The implementation and evaluation of fusion and contraction in array languages. In: PLDI '98. Proceedings of the ACM SIGPLAN 1998 conference on Programming language design and implementation. ACM Press (1998) 50–59
5. Song, Y., Xu, R., Wang, C., Li, Z. Data locality enhancement by memory reduction. In: ICS '01. Proceedings of the 15th international conference on Supercomputing. ACM Press (2001) 50–64
6. Ding, C., Kennedy, K. The Memory Bandwidth Bottleneck and its Amelioration by a Compiler. In: IPDPS '00: Proceedings of the 14th International Symposium on Parallel and Distributed Processing. IEEE Computer Society (2000) 181–

7. Singhai, S., McKinley, K.S. A Parameterized Loop Fusion Algorithm for Improving Parallelism and Cache Locality. In: The Computer Journal **40, 6** (340–355) 1997
8. Darte, A. On the Complexity of Loop Fusion. In: PACT '99. Proceedings of the 1999 International Conference on Parallel Architectures and Compilation Techniques. IEEE Computer Society (1999) 149–
9. Kennedy, K. Fast greedy weighted fusion. In: ICS '00. ACM Press (2000) 131–140
10. Megiddo, N., Sarkar, V. Optimal weighted loop fusion for parallel programs. In: SPAA '97: Proceedings of the ninth annual ACM symposium on Parallel algorithms and architectures. ACM Press (1997) 282–291
11. Parello, D., Temam, O., Verdun, J-M. On increasing architecture awareness in program optimizations to bridge the gap between peak and sustained processor performance: matrix-multiply revisited. In: Supercomputing '02. IEEE Computer Society Press (2002) 1–11
12. Kisuki, T., Knijnenburg, P.M.W., O'Boyle, M.F.P. Combined Selection of Tile Sizes and Unroll Factors Using Iterative Compilation. In: PACT '00. IEEE Computer Society (2000) 237–
13. Nisbet, A.P. GAPS: Iterative Feedback Directed Parallelisation Using Genetic Algorithms. In: Proceedings of Workshop on Profile and Feedback-Directed Compilation at PACT98, Paris, France
14. Gheorghita, S.V., Corporaal, H., Basten, T. Iterative Compilation for Energy Reduction. Journal of Embedded Computing (To appear in 2005)
15. Ashby, T.J. Design and Optimisation of Scientific Programs in a Categorical Language. PhD Thesis, University of Edinburgh (2005)
16. Freund, R., Nachtigal, N. QMRpack. http://www.netlib.org/linalg/qmr/
17. Greenbaum, A. Iterative methods for solving linear systems. Society for Industrial and Applied Mathematics (1997)

# Converting Intermediate Code to Assembly Code Using Declarative Machine Descriptions

João Dias and Norman Ramsey

Division of Engineering and Applied Sciences, Harvard University

**Abstract.** Writing an optimizing back end is expensive, in part because it requires mastery of both a target machine and a compiler's internals. We separate these concerns by isolating target-machine knowledge in *declarative machine descriptions*. We then analyze these descriptions to automatically generate machine-specific components of the back end. In this work, we generate a *recognizer*; this component, which identifies register transfers that correspond to target-machine instructions, plays a key role in instruction selection in such compilers as vpo, gcc and Quick C--. We present analyses and transformations that address the major challenge in generating a recognizer: accounting for compile-time abstractions not present in a machine description, including variables, pseudo-registers, stack slots, and labels.

## 1  Introduction

Because of the substantial effort required to build a compiler, and because of the increasing diversity of target machines, including PCs, graphics cards, wireless sensors, and other embedded devices, a compiler is most valuable if it is easily retargeted. But in current practice, retargeting requires new machine-dependent components for each new back end: instruction selection, register allocation, calling conventions, and possibly machine-specific optimizations. Writing these components by hand requires too much effort, and it requires an expert who knows both the internals of the compiler and the details of the target machine. Our long-term goal is to minimize this effort by dividing and encapsulating expertise: compiler expertise will be encapsulated in compiler-specific optimizations and code-generator generators, and machine expertise will be encapsulated in *declarative machine descriptions*.

A declarative machine description clearly and precisely describes a property of a machine, in a way that is independent of any compiler. For example, the SLED machine-description language (Ramsey and Fernández 1997) describes the binary and assembly encodings of machine instructions, and the λ-RTL machine-description language (Ramsey and Davidson 1998) describes the semantics of machine instructions. A declarative machine description is well suited to formal analysis, and because it is independent of any compiler, it can be reused by multiple compilers and other tools. Furthermore, a declarative machine description may be checked independently for correctness or consistency (Fernández and Ramsey 1997).

Our ultimate goal is to use declarative machine descriptions to generate *all* the machine-dependent components of a compiler's back end. In this work, we generate a *recognizer*, which supports machine-independent instruction selection and optimization (Davidson and Fraser 1984). A recognizer is an integral part of Davidson and

A. Mycroft and A. Zeller (Eds.): CC 2006, LNCS 3923, pp. 217–231, 2006.

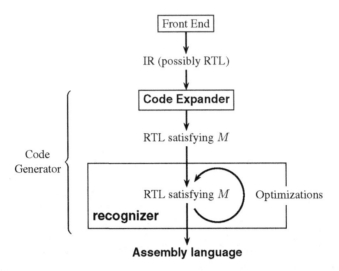

**Fig. 1.** Davidson/Fraser compiler: $M$ represents the machine invariant. Machine-dependent components and representations are in **bold**.

Fraser's compilation strategy: intermediate code is represented by machine-independent *register-transfer lists* (RTLs), but each RTL is required to be implementable by a single instruction on the target machine (Figure 1). This requirement, called the *machine invariant*, is established by a compiler phase called the *code expander*, which runs at the start of code generation. In later phases, the requirement is enforced by the recognizer: each phase is built around a machine-independent, semantics-preserving transformation, and the phase maintains the machine invariant by asking the recognizer if each new RTL can be implemented by an instruction on the target machine; if not, transformations are rolled back. For example, instead of building a peephole optimizer for each target, we build a single peephole optimizer which combines related instructions and, if the recognizer accepts the combination, replaces the original instructions with the combination. The recognizer can not only identify which RTLs correspond to machine instructions but can also emit assembly code for such instructions.

In generating a recognizer from machine descriptions, the major challenge is to account for compile-time abstractions such as variables, pseudo-registers, stack slots, and labels. Such abstractions, while essential to compilation, have no place in a machine description. The contribution of this paper is a set of analyses and transformations that enable us to bridge this "semantic gap" between instructions as viewed by a machine and instructions as viewed by a compiler. We have built these analyses and transformations into a "$\lambda$-RTL toolkit," which generates recognizers for our Quick C-- compiler.

## 2   The Semantic Gap

The $\lambda$-RTL machine-description language takes the perspective of the bare machine. Each instruction is specified as a transformation on the machine's state. This state is modeled as a collection of *storage spaces*, each of which is an array of *cells*. For example, on the x86, the storage spaces include the 'r' space for the 32-bit integer registers, the 'm' space for 8-bit addressable memory, and the 'f' space for the floating-point register stack. We refer to storage using array-index notation; for example, $r[0] refers to the first cell in the 'r' space.

Transformations on storage are specified using a formal notation for register transfers (Ramsey and Davidson 1998). For example, `$r[0] := 16 + $r[0]` adds 16 to the value in register 0, then places the sum in register 0. The register transfers needed to describe a machine are so simple that this example shows essentially all their elements: storage, assignment, literal bit vectors such as 16, and RTL operators such as +.

A compiler has a much richer model of computation. During compilation, computations may refer to source-language variables, pseudo-registers, stack slots whose locations have not yet been determined, and names defined in separately compiled modules. A compiler also distinguishes among storage spaces in ways that are not necessary in a machine description; for example, hardware registers are typically managed entirely by the compiler, whereas memory locations are managed partly by the compiler (e.g., stack slots) and partly by user code (e.g., heap). A compiler therefore needs a much richer model of register transfers than a machine-description language:

- Hardware locations are not undifferentiated storage cells; a compiler represents registers differently from memory. Moreover, compile-time locations include not only hardware locations but also variables and pseudo-registers.
- Constants include not only literal bit vectors but also late compile-time constants (e.g., the offset of a stack slot) and labels.

The differences in the representations of locations and constants constitute the semantic gap between λ-RTL's model of the machine and a compiler's model of the machine.

### 2.1   Mapping High-Level RTLs to Low-Level RTLs

To be usable at any time during compilation, a recognizer must accept RTLs containing high-level abstractions such as variables, labels,[1] stack slots, and late compile-time constants. To accept such a high-level RTL, the recognizer must know how the compiler will map that RTL down to a machine-level RTL. That way, it can accept an RTL if and only if the RTL's image (under the mapping) will be implementable by a single instruction on the target machine.

The mapping is distributed over several compiler phases, each of which eliminates one abstraction. Variables and labels are familiar, simple abstractions, but stack slots and late compile-time constants may need some explanation.

We represent a stack slot as a memory location addressed using an offset from a frame pointer. Until stack-frame layout is complete, we represent the offset as a symbolic constant (Lindig and Ramsey 2004); such a constant is called a *late compile-time constant* and is notated $k$. Furthermore, in order to save a register, our compiler uses a

---

[1] Our compiler actually works with "link-time constant expressions," which include not only labels but also such expressions as the sum of a label and a constant or the difference of two labels. But for simplicity, in this paper we refer to all of these expressions as "labels."

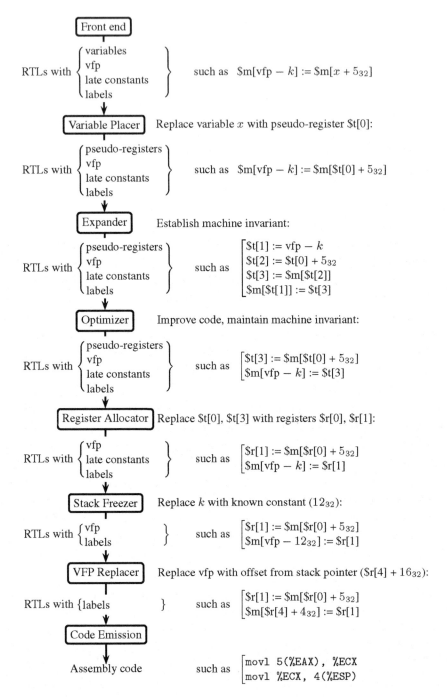

**Fig. 2.** Translation by phases. Each phase is shown in a box; each arrow between phases describes the representation passed between those phases. The examples on the right show the evolution of a memory-to-memory move instruction.

*virtual* frame pointer (vfp), which is read-only. At each program point, the virtual frame pointer is at a known offset from the stack pointer, but because the stack pointer may move, offsets may differ at different program points. After stack layout is complete, these offsets are computed by a separate dataflow pass, which also replaces each use of the virtual frame pointer with an expression of the form stack-pointer-plus-constant.

Figure 2 shows all phases of our back end; code flows from top to bottom. Phases that map high-level RTLs to low-level RTLs are interleaved with other phases, such as the code expander and the optimizer. The first phase, the variable placer, puts each variable in a pseudo-register or a stack slot. Then the code expander establishes the machine invariant: provided that suitable substitutions are made for pseudo-registers, the virtual frame pointer, late compile-time constants, and labels, each RTL can be represented by a single instruction on the target machine. The optimizer then improves the code, maintaining this form of the machine invariant. After optimization, the register allocator replaces pseudo-registers with hardware registers; the stack freezer lays out the stack frame and replaces late compile-time constants with constant bit vectors; and a final pass replaces each use of the virtual frame pointer with the correct stack-pointer-plus-offset expression. The only remaining high-level abstractions are labels, which are dealt with by the assembler.

The phases of our compiler behave as in typical compilers, with two exceptions: the expander generates very naïve code, and the optimizer works at the machine level. Generating naïve code makes it easier for the optimizer to find redundancies. And exposing the machine-level semantics of the target instructions makes it possible for the optimizer to produce better code (Benitez and Davidson 1994).

To generate a recognizer for the high-level RTLs manipulated by the compiler, we use our $\lambda$-RTL toolkit to analyze the low-level RTLs in a machine description and find the corresponding set of high-level RTLs. Specifically, our analyses recover high-level abstractions of locations and constants from the low-level RTLs in the $\lambda$-RTL machine description. The basic idea behind the analyses is to invert the compiler's mapping from high-level RTLs to low-level RTLs. Some analyses are very nearly the inverse of compiler stages; others are not. Before presenting these analyses in Section 3, we explain how the semantics and encoding of instructions are expressed in the $\lambda$-RTL and SLED machine-description languages.

## 2.2   Describing Instructions Using $\lambda$-RTL and SLED

$\lambda$-RTL and SLED share the same model of an instruction set: a simple grammar gives the abstract syntax of instructions and addressing modes. For example, the x86 8-bit add-immediate instruction is associated with the abstract syntax ADDidb (reg, i8), where ADDidb is a *constructor* and reg and i8 are integer *operands* (a register number and an 8-bit immediate operand, respectively). A constructor acts much like an opcode, but although opcodes may be overloaded in the surface syntax of an assembly language, constructor names are not overloaded; the idb suffix serves to distinguish this instruction from other add instructions.

Using this model, a $\lambda$-RTL description associates each abstract-syntax tree with a semantics (Ramsey and Davidson 1998). More precisely, each constructor is associated with a function that maps the semantics of the operands to the semantics of the instruction, which is described using a low-level RTL. For example, neglecting effects on condition codes (Section 4), the semantics of `ADDidb` is

```
ADDidb (reg, i8) is $r[reg] := $r[reg] + sx i8
```

The `ADDidb` instruction stores the sum of register `$r[reg]` and the sign-extended 8-bit immediate `i8` back into register `$r[reg]`.

In similar fashion, a SLED description associates each instruction with an assembly-language and binary representation (Ramsey and Fernández 1997). The details are beyond the scope of this paper.

Given λ-RTL and SLED machine descriptions, we generate a recognizer that matches a high-level, compile-time RTL with an instruction represented using the common abstract syntax. From this representation, we produce assembly or binary code.

## 3    Transforming λ-RTL into a Recognizer

We generate a recognizer by transforming a λ-RTL description into an automaton that can accept high-level RTLs. Broadly speaking, this transformation involves two tasks: bridging the semantic gap and working within the limitations of efficient automata.

To bridge the semantic gap, we transform the low-level RTLs in the machine description into patterns that match the high-level RTLs used in our compiler. In particular, we arrange to accept registers and memory (in place of undifferentiated storage spaces), pseudo-registers (in addition to hardware registers), stack slots, late compile-time constants, and labels. Accepting each of these high-level abstractions requires some analysis or transformation of the original λ-RTL.

The primary limitation of efficient automata is that it is not known how to accept or reject an RTL efficiently based on its semantics; we can do so only based on its syntax. This limitation affects the compiler: a transformation maintains the machine invariant only if the recognizer accepts the transformed RTLs. To manage this limitation requires both an additional compile-time invariant and additional analysis and transformation of the original λ-RTL.

We achieve these two tasks through a combination of different techniques, as detailed below. The whole is a bit of a bag of tricks, but there is one pleasantly recurring theme: binding time.

### 3.1    Bridging the Semantic Gap

We cover the high-level abstractions from the simplest to the most complex: labels, registers and memory, pseudo-registers, and stack slots.

**Labels.** Labels are easy because they are supported by the assembler and linker, which deal with the semantic gap. Coding of labels within machine instructions is the province of SLED, which handles not only labels coded as absolute addresses but also labels coded using PC-relative arithmetic. By hiding this coding, SLED simplifies the λ-RTL description and thereby our recognizer. For example, λ-RTL describes an x86 PC-relative jump instruction as follows:

```
JMP.Jb (addr) is EIP := addr
```

The jump instruction takes an address, which could be a label, and sets the program counter EIP to the value of the label. Because the SLED description identifies which operands can be labels, our toolkit need only identify addr as a possible label and generate code to match it.

**Registers and memory.** The first part of the semantic gap that requires work on our part is the classification of each storage space as registers or memory. We use a *binding-time analysis* developed by Feigenbaum (2001). Depending on when the value of an expression becomes known, Feigenbaum identifies three binding times:

- *Specification time:* The value of the expression depends only on literal constants, so it may be determined from the λ-RTL specification alone.
- *Instruction-creation time:* The value of the expression depends only on the values of an instruction's operands, so it may be determined when the instruction is created.
- *Run time:* The value of the expression depends on machine state, so it is not determined until run time.

A simple analysis determines the binding time of each expression in a machine description. To distinguish registers from memory, Feigenbaum applies this analysis to the addressing expressions used to compute cell numbers in each storage space. The resulting binding times classify the spaces:

- *Fixed space:* The value of each addressing expression is determined by the constructor used to build the instruction, so these values are known at specification time. An example on the x86 is the control-register space, which contains the program counter and the condition codes.
- *Register-like space:* The value of each addressing expression is determined by constructors and operands, so these values are known at instruction-creation time. An example on the x86 is the integer-register space.
- *Memory-like space:* The values of some addressing expressions may not be known until run time. An example on the x86 is the memory space. A more subtle example is the x86 floating-point register stack: it may be indexed using the run-time value of the floating-point stack-top pointer.

The λ-RTL toolkit classifies fixed and register-like spaces as registers; it classifies memory-like spaces as memory. It then transforms the RTLs in the machine description to distinguish between registers and memory, just like the RTLs manipulated by the compiler.

By choosing the operands used in addressing expressions in a register-like space, a compiler can control which cells are used. The compiler can therefore manage these cells using standard register-allocation techniques, justifying the name "register-like." The next step in our transformation is therefore to arrange for the recognizer to accept pseudo-registers, which will be mapped to hardware registers by the register allocator.

**Pseudo-registers.** Each pseudo-register lives in an imaginary, infinite storage space that is different from any hardware space. Pseudo-register spaces are not one-to-one with hardware register spaces; instead, each pseudo-register space corresponds to an *interchangeable set* of hardware registers. Such a set is not necessarily identified with a hardware register space; for example, on the SPARC, integer registers $r[1] to $r[31] are interchangeable in most instructions, but integer register $r[0] is not, because it is hardwired to zero. As another example, a single hardware space may include multiple, distinct register sets; on the x86, for example, the 32-bit, 16-bit, and 8-bit integer registers each form distinct sets, despite the fact that the 16-bit registers are contained entirely within the 32-bit registers, and the 8-bit registers are contained entirely within the 16-bit registers. Our $\lambda$-RTL toolkit identifies these register sets, associates each set with a pseudo-register space, and arranges for the recognizer to accept a pseudo-register if and only if it would accept *any* register from the corresponding set.

To identify sets, we use a *location-set analysis* developed by Feigenbaum (2001):

- *Fixed location set:* A fixed location set contains only a single location. A fixed location set arises if an instruction refers specifically to a location. For example, the 32-bit multiply instruction on the x86 refers to the EAX register; no other location could replace EAX in this instruction. The compiler simply uses the location; no pseudo-registers are needed.
- *Register-like location set:* A register-like location set contains a set of locations from a register-like space. For each register-like location set, the toolkit introduces a new pseudo-register space.
- *Memory-like location set:* A memory-like location set contains a set of locations from a memory-like space. For example, a load from memory on the x86 may load from any memory location.

The analysis works by examining the addressing expression in each RTL location in each instruction. If the addressing expression is always bound at specification time, the location forms a fixed location set. If the addressing expression is bound at instruction-creation time or at run time, the analysis assumes it may evaluate to any bit vector of the appropriate width, except that the value may be constrained by guards on the RTL containing the location. The location set consists of those cells whose numbers satisfy the constraints. For example, on the SPARC, most instructions are guarded by a condition specifying that the addressing expression for an integer register is nonzero, and the relevant location set contains only integer registers $r[1] to $r[31].

After the location-set analysis, the $\lambda$-RTL toolkit replaces each location in an RTL with a pattern that matches either a hardware location or an appropriate pseudo-register. The compiler and the $\lambda$-RTL toolkit must agree on the names used to represent pseudo-register spaces.

**Stack slots and late compile-time constants.** For most of compilation, a stack slot is a memory reference of the form $m[vfp + k]$, where $k$ is a (symbolic) late compile-time constant. Because the address in this form must be accepted wherever the hardware would expect a reference of the form stack-pointer-plus-constant, we must extend the recognizer to deal with both the virtual frame pointer and late compile-time constants.

The virtual frame pointer is eventually replaced with an expression of the form $sp+n$, where sp is the stack pointer and $n$ is a literal bit vector. We therefore arrange to accept the virtual frame pointer wherever $sp+n$ would be accepted. The only potentially tricky part is identifying the stack pointer. If there is only one indistinguishable set of registers used in addressing expressions, we can simply assume the stack pointer is in that set.

Otherwise, because the identity of the stack pointer is a matter of software convention, the λ-RTL toolkit must be told which register is the stack pointer.

The more difficult problem is when to accept a late compile-time constant $k$. The problem is that an instruction set may limit the number of bits of precision available for an immediate constant. For example, while the x86 supports 32-bit immediate constants, the MIPS supports only 16-bit constants, and the SPARC only 13-bit constants. The recognizer can easily determine if the value of a literal bit vector fits in 16 or 13 bits, but what should it do with a 32-bit late compile-time constant, which is symbolic?

One solution is to be pessimistic: to reject any late compile-time constant that might be too wide. This solution requires that the code expander be pessimistic as well. For example, to address a memory cell using the expression $sp + k$, the code expander might load the high bits of $k$ into a pseudo-register, add sp to that pseudo-register, and then address the cell by using the low bits of $k$ as an offset from the pseudo-register. After the stack-freezing phase determines the values of late compile-time constants, some of these extra instructions might be eliminated by the peephole optimizer, but in the meantime the compiler must deal with more instructions in the intermediate representation, as well as increased register pressure.

A better solution is to assume optimistically that a late compile-time constant fits in the width required by the instruction. This solution results in a simpler code expander, a simpler recognizer, and fewer instructions in the intermediate representation. It works well because most late compile-time constants represent offsets of stack slots, which are usually small. But when the optimistic assumption proves incorrect, the compiler must fix any incorrect code. On some machines, the compiler must reserve a register for such fixup code. Sometimes the assembler will reserve a register and do the fixup, allowing compiler writers to assume that machine instructions can handle any 32-bit constant (Kane and Heinrich 1992).

### 3.2    Limitations of Efficient Automata

A recognizer should accept any compile-time RTL that is equivalent to some RTL in the machine description. But when are two RTLs equivalent? Ideally, two RTLs would be deemed equivalent if, when executed, they had the same effect on a machine's state. But such equivalence is extremely expensive to compute—and because the recognizer is consulted in the optimizer's inner loop, it has to decide the question efficiently. The need for efficiency rules out reasoning about the effects of RTLs; instead, we decide equivalence based on syntax. It would be pleasant to be flexible and to accept multiple ways of writing such associative-commutative operations as two's-complement addition or simultaneous composition of effects, but even the equivalence relation induced by associativity and commutativity is too expensive to be decided in the inner loop. Accordingly, like vpo and `gcc`, we deem two RTLs to be equivalent only if they are syntactically identical. This impoverished equivalence relation can be decided easily and relatively cheaply at compile time, but to make it useful, we have to work harder at recognizer-generation time.

To illustrate the most frequent way in which a compiler may generate semantically equivalent but syntactically different RTLs, we return to the `ADDidb` instruction. The machine description says

```
ADDidb (reg, i8) is $r[reg] := $r[reg] + sx i8
```

The RTL $r[0] := $r[0] + 12_{32}$ is not a syntactic match for any RTL generated by the right-hand side, but we would like to accept it as a proxy for the semantically equivalent $r[0] := $r[0] + sx 12_8$, which *is* a syntactic match. We can frame the requirement in terms of binding time: the recognizer should accept a constant in place of an expression that can be evaluated at instruction-creation time. We call such an expression a *compile-time constant expression*.

It is not safe to accept *any* literal constant in place of a compile-time constant expression. For example, the literal constant $65535_{32}$ could not be obtained by sign-extending an 8-bit immediate constant. In the general case, a literal constant is acceptable only if it satisfies a *constraint*, which ensures that the constant could have been computed by the original expression. For example, for ADDidb, the $\lambda$-RTL toolkit identifies the compile-time constant expression sx i8, and it transforms sx i8 into a constrained pattern variable const:

```
ADDidb (reg, i8) is $r[reg] := $r[reg] + (const : #32 bits)
   where fits_signed(const, 8)
```

By itself, const would match any 32-bit constant; the where constraint ensures that const can be obtained by sign-extending an 8-bit quantity. Using the optimistic strategy described above, the recognizer also allows const to match expressions involving only literal bit vectors and late compile-time constants.

The transformation of sx i8 to const has one more subtle consequence. Because SLED uses the original operands of an instruction to construct the assembly or binary encoding of that instruction, the $\lambda$-RTL toolkit must generate code to reconstruct the values of those operands. In the ADDidb instruction, for example, the value of the operand i8 can be extracted directly from the value of const. The final result is an instruction with constants in place of compile-time constant expressions, with constraints to maintain the original semantics of the instruction, and with a map that can compute the values of the operands of the original instruction:

```
ADDidb (reg, i8) is $r[reg] := $r[reg] + (const : #32 bits)
   where fits_signed(const, 8)
   and   i8 = lobits(const, 8)
```

Finally, once the recognizer is geared to accept constants, the compiler must arrange that *every* compile-time constant expression is represented by a literal constant. In other words, the compiler must fold constants. Constant folding is done by the *simplifier*, which is applied to each RTL before the RTL is passed to the recognizer.

## 4    Pragmatics

In generating a recognizer, we must deal with two sets of pragmatic concerns: how to manage multiple forms of the machine invariant, and how to manage complexity in the semantics of the target machine.

As they pass through the compiler, RTLs satisfy successively stronger forms of the machine invariant, containing successively fewer high-level abstractions (Figure 2). Because the recognizer is used both in the optimizer and in the code emitter, it must accept RTLs satisfying different forms of the invariant. We could generate multiple recognizers, but it is simpler to generate a single recognizer that accepts the weakest form of the invariant. When used for code emission, this recognizer may mistakenly accept RTLs that contain pseudo-registers or late compile-time constants, but such RTLs can exist only if the register allocator or the stack freezer is broken. If necessary, we could add a function to reject any RTL containing a pseudo-register or late compile-time constant.

Another pragmatic concern is that real machines are often complicated in detail but simple in the abstract. To eliminate unwanted detail, a compiler writer can ignore unused instructions and machine state (e.g., obscure parts of the processor status word).

What about state that is used, but the details of which we wish to ignore? For example, most compiler writers don't care about the x86's six different condition-code bits; they just want to know how conditional-branch instructions interact with instructions that set condition codes. A common trick is to aggregate and abstract over such state. For example, a description of the x86 might treat the condition-code register as an aggregate instead of as six individual bits. Each effect on the aggregate could then be described as the result of some machine-specific comparison operator. For example, to describe the addition instructions, we might introduce the machine-specific operator x86_addflags, which takes two n-bit arguments and returns a new value for the entire 32-bit condition-code aggregate:

```
rtlop x86_addflags : #n bits * #n bits -> #32 bits
```

Using this kind of abstraction, the full semantics of ADDidb can be described by simultaneous composition of just two effects:

```
ADDidb (reg, i8) is $r[reg] := $r[reg] + sx i8
               | EFLAGS := x86_addflags($r[reg], sx i8)
```

Judicious use of such abstractions can simplify both a machine description and a compiler, but to ensure that such abstract RTLs are recognized, the machine description and compiler must use exactly the same abstraction to specify the semantics of each instruction.

Using these kinds of abstractions has a number of advantages:

– It is easier to write and understand code that manipulates simpler RTLs.
– The compile-time representation of a simple RTL requires less memory.
– A recognizer that only needs to match simple RTLs may be smaller and faster.

But simplifying abstractions must be used with care; they may change the semantics of instructions in subtle ways. For example, aggregation of mutable state may indicate that an instruction uses or modifies more state than it actually does. It is safe to aggregate mutable state only if no source program can tell the difference between instructions with and without this simplification. Because most source languages do not expose condition codes or status bits, it is usually safe to abstract over mutation of the entire condition-code register.

Even when it is safe, a simplifying abstraction may inhibit optimization. If the optimizer does not know the semantics of each machine-specific operator, it cannot tell when two such operators affect relevant state in the same ways, and it may miss opportunities to remove redundant code.

## 5    Generating a Recognizer

To generate a recognizer, we first use analyses from Section 3 to transform the λ-RTL description into a suitable pattern match over compiler RTLs. This match is expressed in terms of a one-off, domain-specific language. This language defines a set of nonterminals, each of which may be matched by BURG-style, linear tree patterns which are extended with constraints. After the transformations described in Section 3, we linearize the patterns: if a pattern variable occurs multiple times in one pattern, we rewrite the pattern to use distinct variables, and we add an equality constraint. At this point, we can compile the pattern match into an efficient, bottom-up tree matcher in the style of BURG (Fraser, Henry, and Proebsting 1992).

We use a few tricks to improve the quality of the compiled matcher. A bottom-up tree matcher works by associating each subtree with a *state*. Such a matcher can be table-driven; the table is indexed by a tree constructor and by the states of the subtrees. One can compress tables by identifying sub-states that are equivalent, then merging table entries for such sub-states (Chase 1987; Proebsting 1992). Table-compression heuristics work best on matches in which common patterns have been factored out. To improve factoring in the matches we generate, we use the structure of operands in the λ-RTL description. For example, if an instruction takes as operand an addressing mode with eight alternatives, we do not expand the instruction into a list of eight patterns. Instead, we introduce a pattern-match nonterminal to stand for the addressing mode. We also keep code size down by introducing a single named function to stand for any fragment of code that is common to two or more actions.

## 6    Results

We have used the λ-RTL toolkit and our match compiler to generate a recognizer for the x86 target in our Quick C-- compiler, which is implemented in Objective Caml. We used a machine description that describes 630 instructions; it is 1,160 non-blank, non-comment lines of λ-RTL code. The generated recognizer replaces a hand-written recognizer which describes only the 233 instructions used in the compiler; it is 754 non-blank, non-comment lines of Objective Caml and BURG code.

The major effort of integrating the generated recognizer with the compiler involved correcting bugs in the hand-written code expander, which often produced incorrect RTLs. For example, the RTL that represented the x86's block copy instruction was incorrect, but because the hand-written recognizer accepted the incorrect RTL, the bug went undetected. Other bugs in the hand-written expander included missing effects on floating-point condition codes. These types of bugs may be less likely to appear in a machine description: the author of a machine description is free to focus on describing the machine accurately, instead of worrying about how to convert the compiler's intermediate representation to machine code.

**Table 1.** Time and space measurements for hand-written and machine-generated recognizers

| Recognizer | Compilation Time | Recognizer Fraction | Size |
| --- | --- | --- | --- |
| Hand-written | 69.29 s | 3.99% | 189,504 B |
| Machine-generated, factored | 64.23 s | 0.69% | 555,804 B |
| Machine-generated, expanded | 65.73 s | 0.56% | 1,330,036 B |

To evaluate the quality of the generated recognizers, we compare three different recognizers: a hand-written recognizer, a machine-generated recognizer with the operands factored out, and a machine-generated recognizer with the operands expanded. Like the hand-written recognizer, the generated recognizers include only the instructions used in the compiler, and when we run the compiler on our test suite, all three recognizers match the same RTLs. For each recognizer, we measured the time spent compiling our test suite, the percentage of compilation spent in the recognizer as indicated by gprof, and the size of the stripped object file (Table 1).

Although all three recognizers are generated from variants of a BURG specification language, the machine-generated recognizers use a different match compiler, which generates faster recognizers. This match compiler, like BURG, precomputes state tables at compile-compile time; the hand-written recognizer uses a match compiler that, like iBurg (Fraser, Hanson, and Proebsting 1992), computes the state tables at run time. The use of different match compilers also helps to explain why the machine-generated recognizer with factored operands is almost three times the size of the hand-written recognizer. The size of each machine-generated recognizer includes the precomputed state tables, which are known to dominate the size of a bottom-up match compiler.

The size of the recognizer is further affected by the factoring of the BURG specification. A well-factored BURG specification can produce a smaller, more efficient recognizer, as demonstrated by the machine-generated recognizers: the factored recognizer is less than half the size of the unfactored recognizer. The hand-written recognizer benefits further because the original programmer carefully factored the BURG specification by hand, whereas the specification of the machine-generated recognizer is factored only over the operands.

## 7   Related Work

The technique of compiling RTLs using machine-independent optimizations with a machine-dependent code expander and a recognizer was developed by Davidson and Fraser (1984) and refined by Benitez and Davidson (1994). This technique is also used in gcc. It provides effective scalar, loop, and machine-level optimizations without requiring many machine-specific compiler passes.

Compiler writers have used "machine descriptions" for years, but the term is normally used loosely to mean "whatever information is needed to retarget my compiler." Recently, some other researchers have begun to use machine descriptions that have a declarative flavor. For example, Ceng et al. (2005) present a machine-description language that is similar in spirit, if not in syntax, to $\lambda$-RTL. They use a machine description to generate a BURG specification for instruction selection. After instruction selection, the code proceeds to a register allocator and a code emitter; the optimizer does not have the opportunity to exploit information about the semantics of machine instructions.

Tröger (2004) uses declarative machine descriptions to implement a dynamic binary translator. The translator uses two machine descriptions; for each effect of a guest-machine instruction, it finds host-machine instructions which execute that effect. Provided the semantics of parallel execution are preserved, the effects can be executed in sequence.

From the vast literature on bottom-up tree matching, we mention only papers that we have found directly relevant. Early work by Hoffmann and O'Donnell (1982) provides a useful overview of what are now common top-down and bottom-up tree-matching algorithms. Table-compression techniques for compile-compile-time state tables in a bottom-up tree matcher were developed by Chase (1987) and refined by Proebsting (1992). An alternative approach to bottom-up parsing is to perform shift-reduce parsing on the intermediate representation (Glanville and Graham 1978).

Pattern matching is built into many functional languages, which are typically implemented using top-down matching. Top-down matching works well on hand-written patterns with few alternatives and shallow nesting (Scott and Ramsey 2000), but a machine's instruction set has hundreds of deeply nested alternatives. For machine instructions, top-down matchers are prohibitively large, even when clever compression techniques are used (Eddy 2002).

## 8    Conclusion and Future Work

We have shown how to analyze a declarative, low-level machine description to recover the high-level abstractions used in a compiler. Leveraging these analyses, we generated a recognizer for the x86 in the Quick C-- compiler. The benefits of generating the recognizer are modest as long as the rest of the back end continues to be written by hand. Ultimately, we would like to generate *all* the machine-specific components of the back end, most notably, the code expander. Other plans include automatically checking the correctness of a $\lambda$-RTL machine description and incorporating elements of semantic matching to improve the flexibility of the recognizer.

## Acknowledgements

Thanks to Paul Govereau, Glenn Holloway, and Kevin Redwine for helpful comments on early versions of this paper. This work has been supported by NSF grant CCR-0311482 and by an Alfred P. Sloan Research Fellowship.

## Bibliography

Manuel E. Benitez and Jack W. Davidson. 1994 (March). The advantages of machine-dependent global optimization. In *Programming Languages and System Architectures*, *LNCS* volume 782, pages 105–124. Springer Verlag.

Jianjiang Ceng, Manuel Hohenauer, Rainer Leupers, Gerd Ascheid, Heinrich Meyr, and Gunnar Braun. 2005 (March). C Compiler Retargeting Based on Instruction Semantics Models. In *DATE '05*, pages 1150–1155.

David R. Chase. 1987. An improvement to bottom-up tree pattern matching. In *POPL '87*, pages 168–177.

Jack W. Davidson and Christopher W. Fraser. 1984 (October). Code selection through object code optimization. *ACM TOPLAS*, 6(4):505–526.

Jonathan Eddy. 2002 (April). A continuation-passing operator tree for pattern matching. Senior Thesis, Division of Engineering and Applied Sciences, Harvard University.

Lee D. Feigenbaum. 2001 (April). Automated translation: generating a code generator. Senior Thesis, Division of Engineering and Applied Sciences, Harvard University.

Mary F. Fernández and Norman Ramsey. 1997 (May). Automatic checking of instruction specifications. In *ICSE '97*, pages 326–336.

Christopher W. Fraser, David R. Hanson, and Todd A. Proebsting. 1992 (September). Engineering a simple, efficient code-generator generator. *ACM LOPLAS*, 1(3): 213–226.

Christopher W. Fraser, Robert R. Henry, and Todd A. Proebsting. 1992 (April). BURG—fast optimal instruction selection and tree parsing. *SIGPLAN Notices*, 27(4):68–76.

R. Steven Glanville and Susan L. Graham. 1978 (January). A new method for compiler code generation. In *POPL '78*, pages 231–240.

Christoph M. Hoffmann and Michael J. O'Donnell. 1982. Pattern matching in trees. *JACM*, 29 (1).

Gerry Kane and Joe Heinrich. 1992. *MIPS RISC Architectures*. Prentice-Hall.

Christian Lindig and Norman Ramsey. 2004 (April). Declarative composition of stack frames. In *CC '04*, *LNCS* volume 2985, pages 298–312.

Todd A. Proebsting. 1992 (June). Simple and efficient BURS table generation. *PLDI '92*, in *SIGPLAN Notices*, 27(7):331–340.

Norman Ramsey and Jack W. Davidson. 1998 (June). Machine descriptions to build tools for embedded systems. In *LCTES '98*, *LNCS* volume 1474, pages 172–188. Springer Verlag.

Norman Ramsey and Mary F. Fernández. 1997 (May). Specifying representations of machine instructions. *ACM TOPLAS*, 19(3):492–524.

Kevin Scott and Norman Ramsey. 2000 (May). When do match-compilation heuristics matter? Technical Report CS-2000-13, Department of Computer Science, University of Virginia.

Jens Tröger. 2004. *Specification-Driven Dynamic Binary Translation*. PhD thesis, Queensland University of Technology, Brisbane, Australia.

# SARA: Combining Stack Allocation and Register Allocation

V. Krishna Nandivada and Jens Palsberg

UCLA
University of California, Los Angeles

**Abstract.** Commonly-used memory units enable a processor to load
and store multiple registers in one instruction. We showed in 2003 how
to extend gcc with a stack-location-allocation (SLA) phase that reduces
memory traffic by rearranging the stack and replacing some load/store
instructions with load/store-multiple instructions. While speeding up the
target code, our technique leaves room for improvement because of the
phase ordering of register allocation before SLA. In this paper we present
SARA which combines SLA and register allocation into a single phase.
SARA creates a synergy among register assignment, spill-code generation, and SLA that makes the combined phase generate faster code than
a sequence of the individual phases. We specify SARA by an integer
linear program generated from the program text. We have implemented
SARA in gcc, replacing gcc's own implementation of register allocation.
For our benchmarks, our results show that the target code is up to 16%
faster than gcc with a separate SLA phase.

## 1 Introduction

**Background.** Processors such as Intel StrongARM together with memory such
as SDRAM enable efficient execution of multiple loads and stores in a single
instruction. We can find such a combination of processor and memory in Intel's IXP-2400 [1], Stargate (http://www.xbow.com/Products/XScale.htm), Sun
MAJC 5200 [24], etc. Multiple loads and stores are particularly useful in connection with register allocation where spill code may need to save and restore
multiple registers.

For example, on the StrongARM, the register size is 32 bits and each basic
load/store operation (called LDR/STR) operates on one register at a time. However, the SDRAM has a 64 bit bus so if we are using an LDR instruction to load
a 32 bit register, we are wasting half of the bandwidth of the bus. Fortunately,
we can use a load/store-multiple operation (we refer to them as LDM/STM) to
operate on two registers at a time, thereby taking full advantage of the bus and
saving one full LDR/STR instruction (40/50 cycles) [23].

To replace two LDR instructions with one LDM instruction we need the addresses to be contiguous and the destination registers to be different. To replace

$$\begin{array}{ll} \text{LDR } addr_1\ r_i & \text{MOV } r\ addr_1 \\ \text{LDR } addr_2\ r_j & \text{LDM } [r]\ \{r_i,r_j\} \end{array} \quad \text{by}$$

A. Mycroft and A. Zeller (Eds.): CC 2006, LNCS 3923, pp. 232–246, 2006.

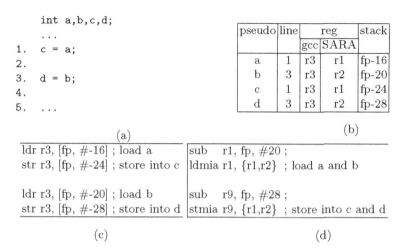

(a)

(b)

| pseudo | line | reg | | stack |
|---|---|---|---|---|
| | | gcc | SARA | |
| a | 1 | r3 | r1 | fp-16 |
| b | 3 | r3 | r2 | fp-20 |
| c | 1 | r3 | r1 | fp-24 |
| d | 3 | r3 | r2 | fp-28 |

```
ldr r3, [fp, #-16] ; load a
str r3, [fp, #-24] ; store into c

ldr r3, [fp, #-20] ; load b
str r3, [fp, #-28] ; store into d
```

(c)

```
sub    r1, fp, #20 ;
ldmia r1, {r1,r2}  ; load a and b

sub    r9, fp, #28 ;
stmia r9, {r1,r2}  ; store into c and d
```

(d)

**Fig. 1.** (a) Fragment of C code, (b) Mappings of pseudos to registers and stack locations, (c) code generated by gcc, (d) code generated by SARA

we would need $i \neq j$ and the two base addresses $addr_1$ and $addr_2$ must be contiguous at 4 byte boundaries: $addr_2 - addr_1 = 4$.

We showed in 2003 [20] how to extend gcc with a stack-location-allocation (SLA) phase that reduces memory traffic by

- moving some load and store instructions such that they occur in pairs,
- rearranging the stack such that the temporaries used in a pair of load/store instructions have neighboring stack locations, and
- replacing some loads and stores with load/store-multiple instructions.

While speeding up the target code, our technique leaves room for improvement because of the phase ordering of register allocation before SLA.

For an example of the shortcomings of gcc extended with SLA, consider the code snippet in Figure 1(a). The code snippet is part of a synthetic benchmark program in which c and d are needed somewhere after line 3. For the benchmark program, gcc spills the four pseudos a, b, c, and d to the memory locations shown in Figure 1(b) and generates the code shown in Figure 1(c); gcc extended with SLA generates exactly the same code. To see why SLA fails to merge the two loads and the two stores, notice first that the register allocator has done a good job using register r3 both when loading a and when loading b. However, the use of r3 in both load instructions and both store instructions prevents SLA from moving the instruction for loading b to the program point just before the instruction for storing into c; the code motion would change the behavior of the program. Thus, the good register allocation is *counterproductive* to merging loads and stores. The compiler can generate better code for the benchmark program by first doing a worse register allocation which uses different registers when loading a and when loading b. The reason is that now the SLA phase can safely move the two load instructions together and also move the two store instructions together, then replace those instructions with a double-load (ldmia) and a double-store (stmia), and ultimately generate the code shown in Figure 1(d).

Another weakness of gcc extended with SLA is that first the register allocator will assign stack locations to all spilled pseudos and then SLA will try to reorganize the stack as best as it can to enable double-loads and double-stores. If SLA does not manage to find the best permutation of the stack locations, then the target code may not contain the highest possible number of double-loads and double-stores. A better approach may be to let the register allocator know about double-loads and double-stores and do the spilling of pseudos accordingly.

Our observations about gcc extended with SLA suggest that a compiler can do better if register allocation and SLA are more tightly integrated.

**Question:** Can a combined phase be better than a two-phase sequence of register allocation and SLA?

**Our Results.** In this paper we present SARA which combines SLA and register allocation into a single phase. Our technique creates a synergy among register assignment, spill-code generation, and SLA that makes the combined phase generate faster code than a sequence of the individual phases. We specify SARA by an integer linear program (ILP) generated from the program text. Our ILP formulation uses an objective function which estimates the execution time of the memory instructions. We have implemented SARA in gcc, replacing gcc's own implementation of register allocation. For our benchmarks, our results show that the target code is up to 16% faster than gcc with a separate SLA phase.

We specify SARA by an ILP because (1) register allocation can be specified by an ILP [13, 14, 16, 3, 11, 19], (2) SLA can be specified by an ILP [20], and (3) ILPs are often easy to combine. We speculate that it would be much more difficult to build a one-phase combination of register allocation and SLA based on one of the classical non-ILP-based register allocators [8, 7, 6].

While solving ILPs can be slow, we note that all of the following three problems are NP-complete: (a) register assignment [22], (b) spill code generation [12], and (c) SLA [20]. The combination of (a)+(b)+(c) is also NP-complete. We view our ILP formulation of (a)+(b)+(c) as a high-level specification which, as we demonstrate, leads to good target code. We present a technique that enables us to contain the state space explosion and allow the solver to terminate in reasonable time limits. Our proposal uses the variable liveness information that is available to the register allocator in most optimizing compilers. In future work one might investigate how to implement fast approximation algorithms for our ILP formulation.

To show that the combined phase SARA works better than the individual phases performed sequentially, we specify an ILP-based register allocation phase (RA) without SLA. Our results show that RA leads to faster code than the code generated by gcc at O2 level of optimization. Next we reconfirm our results in [20] by showing that RA followed by SLA is better than RA alone. And finally we show that the combined phase SARA is better than the sequential composition of ILP-based register allocation and SLA. In slogan form, if $P$ is one of our benchmark programs, and ET denotes an execution time monitor, we have

$$\mathrm{ET}(SARA(P)) \leq \mathrm{ET}(SLA(RA(P))).$$

In related work, Bradlee et al. [5] and Motwani et al. [18] demonstrated how to combine register allocation and code scheduling to obtain faster code. Lerner et al. [15] presented a framework for composing dataflow analyses and thereby overcoming the phase ordering problem. Our approach differs from theirs in that we use and combine ILPs.

In the following section we specify an ILP-based register allocator. In Section 3 we extend the ILP-based register allocator with facilities for SLA; the result is SARA. In Section 4 we discuss how we control the state-explosion problem, and in Section 5 we present our experimental results.

## 2   ILP-Based Register Allocation

Our ILP-based register allocator does register assignment and spill code generation. We defined our register allocator with inspiration from the ILP-based register allocators of Goodwin and Wilken [13] and of Appel and George [3]. The key property of our register-allocator specification is that we can easily add SLA, as shown in the following section. We will now present the three main phases of the register allocator: model extraction, constraint generation, and constraint solving.

**Model extraction.** From the input program we extract a model consisting of sets and parameters.

| | | | | | |
|---|---|---|---|---|---|
| Insts | $\subseteq \{1..\mathrm{nInsts}\}$ | Req | : Insts × Pseudos | $\rightarrow \{0,1\}$ |
| Pseudos | $\subseteq \{1..\mathrm{nPseudos}\}$ | Def | : Insts × Pseudos | $\rightarrow \{0,1\}$ |
| Regs | $\subseteq \{1..\mathrm{nRegs}\}$ | prevInst | : Insts | $\rightarrow$ Insts $\cup \{null\}$ |
| Loc | $\subseteq \{1..\mathrm{nPseudos}\}$ | joinInst | : Insts × Insts | $\rightarrow$ Insts $\cup \{null\}$ |
| | | callInst | : Insts | $\rightarrow \{0,1\}$ |

The set of instructions, pseudos, registers, and stack locations for the pseudos is given by Insts, Pseudos, Regs, Loc, respectively. For the example shown in Figure 1, Insts = {1,2,3,4}, Pseudos = {a,b,c,d}, Regs = {1,2,3,4,5,6,7,8,9,10}. The parameter Req$(i, p)$ is set to 1 if instruction $i$ requires pseudo $p$ and hence needs $p$ to be present in a register. The parameter Def$(i, p)$ is set to 1 if instruction $i$ sets pseudo $p$. The control flow of the program is given by three parameter maps. The parameter prevInst$(i)$ is a singleton set containing the previous instruction of $i$ if it has only one previous instruction, and null otherwise. The parameter joinInst$(i)$ is the set of previous instructions of $i$ if instruction $i$ is a join point with multiple previous instructions, and null otherwise. The parameter callInst$(i)$ has value 1 if the instruction $i$ is a call instruction, and 0 otherwise.

For each instruction $i$, the parameter freq$(i)$ returns the frequency of execution of that instruction. In this paper, we use static estimates of freq$(i)$; alternatively one might use a profiling-based approach. The parameters loadCost and storeCost give the cost of one single load and one single store respectively. Also a subset of Regs is designated as caller save registers and are represented by callerSaveRegs For the target environment we have the set of caller save registers is {0,1,2,3,9,12}.

Each function must save and restore any register that is a callee save register, that is, not a caller save register.

**Constraint Generation.** From the input program we generate an ILP whose main purpose is to ensure the following properties: (1) at any instruction, each pseudo is assigned at most one register, (2) at any instruction, each register is assigned at most one pseudo, (3) at any instruction, the number of used registers is bounded by the available number of registers, (4) for every definition and use of a pseudo, the pseudo has a register assigned to it, and (5) a pseudo keeps its mapping to a register, unless the pseudo is no longer live or the pseudo is defined, loaded, or stored.

We will use the following maps. Intuitively, the map PsR maps pseudos to registers for each instruction, the map xDef gives the register map for a pseudo $p$ at a given instruction defining $p$, the maps spLoad and spStore represent the load and store instructions that need to be inserted into the program, and the map inUse tracks whether a register is used.

$$\begin{aligned}
\text{PsR} &: \text{Insts} \times \text{Pseudos} \times \text{Regs} \to \{0,1\} \\
\text{xDef} &: \text{Insts} \times \text{Pseudos} \times \text{Regs} \to \{0,1\} \\
\text{spStore} &: \text{Insts} \times \text{Pseudos} \times \text{Regs} \to \{0,1\} \\
\text{spLoad} &: \text{Insts} \times \text{Pseudos} \times \text{Regs} \to \{0,1\} \\
\text{inUse} &: \text{Regs} \qquad\qquad\qquad\quad \to \{0,1\}
\end{aligned}$$

$\text{PsR}(i,p,r)$ returns 1 if pseudo $p$ is present in register $r$ at instruction $i$. $\text{xDef}(i,p,r)$ returns 1 if pseudo $p$ is defined in instruction $i$, in register $r$. Pseudo $p$ will be present in register $r$ in the next instruction. $\text{spStore}(i,p,r)$ returns 1 if pseudo $p$ is spilled *after* instruction $i$ and is currently mapped to register $r$. $\text{spLoad}(i,p,r)$ returns 1 if pseudo $p$ is (re)loaded *before* instruction $i$ into register $r$. We generate the following constraints.

Each pseudo is assigned to at most one register and each register is assigned to at most one pseudo:

$$\forall i \in \text{Insts}, \ \forall p \in \text{Pseudos} : \sum_{r \in \text{Regs}} \text{PsR}(i,p,r) \leq 1$$

$$\forall i \in \text{Insts}, \ \forall r \in \text{Regs} : \sum_{p \in \text{Pseudos}} \text{PsR}(i,p,r) \leq 1$$

The second of the two constraints above implies that at any program point the number of pseudos that are available in registers is bounded by the number of registers available.

A pseudo that is used in an instruction has to be present in a register at that point:

$$\forall i \in \text{Insts}, \ \forall p \in \text{Pseudos} : \sum_{r \in \text{Regs}} \text{PsR}(i,p,r) \geq \text{Req}(i,p)$$

A pseudo being defined needs a register:

$$\forall i \in \text{Insts}, \ p \in \text{Pseudos} : \sum_{r \in \text{Regs}} \text{xDef}(i,p,r) = \text{Def}(i,p)$$

A pseudo $p$ retains its mapping to a register unless it is spilled or another pseudo is mapped to that register. If the instruction has only one previous instruction:

$\forall i \in$ Insts, $p \in$ Pseudos, $r \in$ Regs, $pr \in$ prevInst$(i)$ :
$$\mathrm{PsR}(i, p, r) = (\mathrm{spLoad}(i, p, r) \vee \mathrm{PsR}(pr, p, r) \vee \mathrm{xDef}(pr, p, r)) \wedge \neg\mathrm{spStore}(pr, p, r)$$

If the instruction is next to a join point and hence have multiple predecessors:

$\forall i \in$ Insts, $p \in$ Pseudos, $r \in$ Regs :
$$\mathrm{PsR}(i, p, r) = ( \bigwedge_{pr \in \mathrm{joinInst}(i)} \mathrm{PsR}(pr, p, r) \wedge \neg\mathrm{spStore}(pr, p, r)) \vee \mathrm{spLoad}(i, p, r)$$

A pseudo mapped to a caller save register loses its mapping after a call:

$$\forall i \in \text{Insts}, \ \forall p \in \text{Pseudos} \ \forall r \in \text{callerSaveRegs} : \mathrm{callInst}(i) \Rightarrow \mathrm{PsR}(i, p, r) = 0$$

A register is used if it is mapped to a pseudo:

$$\forall i \in \text{Insts}, \ \forall p \in \text{Pseudos} \ \forall r \in \text{Regs} : \mathrm{inUse}(r) \geq \mathrm{PsR}(i, p, r)$$

**Objective function.** Our objective function estimates the execution time of the inserted loads and stores for spilling and for storing and restoring the callee save registers at the beginning and end of a function. The objective of our ILP solver is to minimize SpillCost + CalleeSaveCost where

$$\mathrm{SpillCost} = \sum_{i \in \mathrm{Insts}} \mathrm{freq}(i) \times \sum_{p \in \mathrm{Pseudos}, \ r \in \mathrm{Regs}} \left( \begin{array}{c} \mathrm{spLoad}(i, p, r) \times \mathrm{loadCost} \\ + \\ \mathrm{spStore}(i, p, r) \times \mathrm{storeCost} \end{array} \right)$$

$$\mathrm{CalleeSaveCost} = \frac{1}{2} \times \sum_{r \in \mathrm{Regs-callerSaveRegs}} \mathrm{inUse}(r) \times (\mathrm{loadCost} + \mathrm{storeCost})$$

The callee save registers are loaded and stored using load/store-multiple instructions, hence the cost is reduced by a factor of two.

**Constraint Solving.** We use AMPL [9] to generate the ILP, and CPLEX (www.cplex.com) to solve it. The gcc compiler invokes the constraint generator by providing the data in a file. Once constraints are generated the constraint generator calls the solver, which returns the resulting solution to gcc in a file.

The result of solving the constraints for the running example in Figure 1 is shown in the following table. (Only tuples with non-zero values are shown.)

| PsR | $= \{(1,a,r3),(2,c,r3),(3,b,r3),(4,d,r3)\}$ |
|---|---|
| spLoad | $= \{(1,a,r3),(3,b,r3)\}$ |
| spStore | $= \{(2,c,r3),(4,d,r3)\}$ |
| xDef | $= \{(1,c,r3),(3,d,r3)\}$ |
| inUse | $= \{r3\}$ |
| SpillCost | $= 2 \times \mathrm{loadCost} + 2 \times \mathrm{storeCost} = 184$ |
| CalleeSaveCost | $= 0$ |

## 3  SARA

The advantage of using an ILP-based framework for combining multiple phases is that each phase can be added as a module on top of an already existing ILP. SARA, the combined phase of SLA and RA, is built upon the set of parameters and constraints given for the ILP-based RA in section 2. We now present the additional parameters, variables and constraints required for SARA over RA. The new phase SARA requires three additional variables:

$$
\begin{aligned}
\text{loadPair} \ &: \text{Insts} \times \text{Pseudos} \times \text{Pseudos} \rightarrow \{0, 1\} \\
\text{storePair} \ &: \text{Insts} \times \text{Pseudos} \times \text{Pseudos} \rightarrow \{0, 1\} \\
f \qquad\ &: \text{Pseudos} \times \text{Loc} \qquad\qquad \rightarrow \{0, 1\}
\end{aligned}
$$

For a given instruction $i$, and two pseudos $p_1$ and $p_2$ $(p_1 \neq p_2)$, the map loadPair$(i, p_1, p_2)$ returns 1 if we can replace the two spill loads by a pair, and 0 otherwise. The map $f$ maps a pseudo to its location: $f(p, l)$ returns 1 if pseudo $p$ is placed in location $l$. Note that not all pseudos would need a location.

A pseudo can have at most one location and a location can have at most one pseudo mapped to it.

$$
\forall p \in \text{Pseudos} : \sum_{l \in \text{Loc}} f(p, l) \leq 1 \qquad \forall p \in \text{Loc} : \sum_{l \in \text{Pseudos}} f(p, l) \leq 1
$$

A pseudo needs a location if it is spilled and/or reloaded.
$\forall i \in \text{Insts}, \ p \in \text{Pseudos} :$

$$
2 \times \sum_{l \in \text{Loc}} f(p, l) \geq \sum_{r \in \text{Regs}} (\text{spLoad}(i, p, r) + \text{spStore}(i, p, r))
$$

Two consecutive loads or stores can be replaced by an LDM or STM instruction.
$\forall i \in \text{Insts}, \ \forall p_1, p_2 \in \text{Pseudos} :$

$$
2 \times \text{loadPair}(i, p_1, p_2) \leq \sum_{r \in \text{Regs}} (\text{spLoad}(i, p_1, r) + \text{spLoad}(i, p_2, r))
$$

$$
2 \times \text{storePair}(i, p_1, p_2) \leq \sum_{r \in \text{Regs}} (\text{spStore}(i, p_1, r) + \text{spStore}(i, p_2, r))
$$

LDM and STM require that the memory locations are consecutive.
$\forall i \in \text{Insts}, \ \forall p_1, p_2 \in \text{localPseudos} :$

$$
\begin{aligned}
\text{diff}(p_1, p_2) \neq 1 &\Rightarrow \text{loadPair}(i, p_1, p_2) = 0 \\
\text{diff}(p_1, p_2) \neq 1 &\Rightarrow \text{storePair}(i, p_1, p_2) = 0 \\
\text{diff}(p_1, p_2) = ((\textstyle\sum_{l \in \text{Loc}} l \times f(p_1, l)) &- (\textstyle\sum_{l \in \text{Loc}} l \times f(p_2, l)))
\end{aligned}
$$

It may be noted that we do not need to check for the absolute value of diff. This is because the optimizing solver will consider both the options $(p_1, p_2)$ and $(p_2, p_1)$ and can pick the best one.

**Objective function.** The objective function used in SARA is similar to the one used by our ILP-based RA given in section 2. The new twist is that SpillCost takes pairs into account.

SpillCost =

$$
\sum_{i \in insts} freq(i) \times \left( \begin{array}{l} \sum_{p \in Pseudos, r \in Regs} spLoad(i,p,r) \times loadCost \quad - \\ \sum_{p_1,p_2 \in Pseudos}(loadPair(i,p_1,p_2) \times loadPairSave) \\ \\ \sum_{p \in Pseudos, r \in Regs} spStore(i,p,r) \times storeCost \quad - \\ \sum_{p_1,p_2 \in Pseudos}(storePair(i,p_1,p_2) \times storePairSave) \end{array} \right)
$$

Here loadPairSave is the savings that one gets because of replacing two loads by a load-pair and storePairSave is the savings that one gets by replacing two stores by a store-pair. If loadPairCost is the cost of executing one load-pair instruction (this will include the cost of setting the base register) then loadPairSave is given by $(2 \times loadCost - loadPairCost)$. Similarly storePairSave is calculated as $(2 \times storeCost - storePairCost)$. In the model generated by the compiler loadPairCost and storePairCost are given as parameters.

The result of solving the above constraints for the running example shown in Figure 1 is shown below. As can be seen the cost has gone down by nearly 50% as compared to the ILP-based RA in section 2. This is because of the introduction of the load-pair and store-pair instructions in the code.

| | |
|---|---|
| PsR | $= \{(1,a,r1),(2,c,r1),(3,b,r2),(4,d,r2)\}$ |
| spLoad | $= \{(1,a,r1),(3,b,r2)\}$ |
| loadPair | $= \{(1,a,b)\}$ |
| storePair | $= \{(4,c,d)\}$ |
| xDef | $= \{(1,c,r1),(3,d,r2)\}$ |
| inUse | $= \{r1,r2\}$ |
| SpillCost | $= loadPairCost + storePairCost = 94$ |
| CalleeSaveCost | $= 0$ |

Our implementation of SARA uses a superset of the constraints presented in this paper. The additional constraints take care of (1) pre-colored pseudos (pseudos that require a certain register, as required, for example, in connection with parameter passing), (2) non-spill memory instructions (generated in the presence of pointer based accesses in the code), and (3) inversions [20]. A practical register allocator has to take care of these issues to be able to generate executable code. The reader can obtain the full set of constraints from our webpage, http://compilers.cs.ucla.edu/nvk/sara.mod.

## 4   SARA Improvements

In this section we will explain three techniques that are used in SARA, namely two techniques for reducing the size of the ILP state space and one technique for improving the quality of the generated code.

**Reducing the size of the ILP state space.** Our first technique uses liveness information. Notice first that the domain of the pseudo-to-register map PsR is Insts × Pseudos × Regs. However, for a pseudo to be assigned a register, the pseudo has to be live, that is, the map PsR is valid only at those instructions where the pseudo is live. For our benchmarks, most of the pseudos are live in only small parts of the program. So we define PsR only for live pseudos. Similarly, we define spLoad, spStore, loadPair, and storePair only for live pseudos. By the same token, we define constraints only for defined ILP variables. Our focus on live pseudos let us reduce the number of variables and constraints by a big factor. We have tried a version of SARA without this optimization on our benchmark programs, and in many case the preprocessor that translates the constraints specified in high level language (AMPL) to a format that is understood by the solver (CPLEX) runs out of memory and fails. With the liveness-based optimization in place, SARA does not run out of space when handling our benchmark programs.

Our second technique manages the number of ILP variables needed to represent the generated load and store instructions. Our technique inserts a dummy instruction after each instruction, generates load instructions only before real instructions, and generates store instructions only after dummy instructions. A dummy instruction does not use any pseudos nor define any; we use dummy instructions as place holders for spill instructions. Let us now explain the details and merits of dummy instructions in more detail. We are trying to track the mapping of pseudos to registers at each instruction. However, sometimes it is not sufficient to know the mapping of a pseudo just at each instruction! For example, in the code fragment without dummy instructions:

$$i_1 : x = y + p \; ; \; // \; p \; dies \; after \; i_1$$
$$i_2 : y = y + z \; ;$$

let us assume pseudo $x$ has to be spilled (because of register pressure) to memory after the instruction labeled $i_1$ but before $i_2$, and let us assume pseudo $z$ has to be loaded before $i_2$. In the case where we do not have any more free registers, we could use the same register (say $r1$) for $p$, $x$ and $z$. Notice that because $x$ is being set, $x$ needs a register. But since $x$ will be spilled that register will be free immediately afterwards and can be used for loading $z$. So we have a mapping of $x$ to $r1$ between $i_1$ and $i_2$. But at $i_1$, $p$ is mapped to $r1$, and at $i_2$, $z$ is mapped to $r1$. This leads to the situation that $x$ does not have a mapping to $r1$ in PsR. To avoid such situations, we inserted a dummy instruction after each instruction before generating the ILP:

$$i_1 : x = y + p \; ; \; // \; p \; dies \; after \; i_1$$
$$d_1 :$$
$$i_2 : y = y + z \; ;$$
$$d_2 :$$

The register allocator can assign register $r1$ to pseudo $x$ at the dummy instruction $d_1$. Additionally, the register allocator can emit an instruction to spill $x$

after $d_1$, and an instruction to load $z$ before $i_2$, thereby establishing the desired pseudo-to-register mapping. The introduction of dummy instructions also overcomes the need to introduce dummy basic blocks as additional place holders for spill code. Our notion of dummy instructions is related to the notion of points between instructions that was used by Appel and George [3]. Instead of using dummy instructions or points between instructions, one might find a way to allow the generation of loads and stores before and after every instruction, although we believe such an approach is more awkward.

**Improving the quality of the generated code.** SARA can benefit from having freedom to move the spill and reload instructions around. Perhaps surprisingly, the use of strict (exact) liveness information can lead to the generation of inefficient code. For example, in code for copying structures, we come across patterns like:

$$
\begin{aligned}
&\quad\quad // \ x_1, \ x_2, \ y_1, \ y_2 \ are \ dead \\
i_1\colon & y_1 = x_1; \ // \ live \ x_1 \\
i_2\colon & \quad\quad // \ x_1 \ and \ y_1 \ are \ dead \\
i_3\colon & y_2 = x_2; \ // \ live \ x_2 \\
i_4\colon & \quad\quad // \ x_2 \ and \ y_2 \ are \ dead
\end{aligned}
$$

Here $x_1$, $x_2$, $y_1$, $y_2$ could be globals or be accessed by globals. We must load $x_1$ before instruction $i_1$ and $x_2$ before $i_3$. Recall that a load/store requires that the pseudo is live. Forcing such liveness constraints would constrain SARA so much that it cannot move these two loads together. The same logic holds for the spill of pseudo $y_1$ and $y_2$ after instructions $i_1$ and $i_3$. Assuming that we have an additional register for the duration of these instructions, and the liveness constraints were a bit relaxed, we would give SARA a bit more breathing room to pair up more loads and stores. For example, if we deliberately make the liveness information a bit more conservative and convey to SARA that $x_2$ is live at $i_1$ as well, then SARA could generate a load-pair for $x_1$ and $x_2$. A similar argument can be given for $y_1$ and $y_2$ as well. This leads to an interesting trade off: strict liveness reduces the search space and state space but might result in inefficient code.

We have experimented with relaxing the liveness information by different amounts: (a) strict liveness, (b) liveness extended to basic blocks—each pseudo is live from the beginning of the basic block until the end; unless it dies in between, (c) liveness relaxed by three instructions. Let us consider (c) in more detail. If a pseudo is live starting at instruction $i_1$, then the pseudo is assumed to be live starting at $i_1 - 2 \times 3$ (multiplied by 2, to take care of the dummy instructions) unless $i_1$ is one of the first three instructions in the basic block. And if it is, then the pseudo is assumed to be live starting from the beginning of the basic block until its death or end of basic block. We arrived at the magic number three from our experience with the benchmarks code. Our experience confirmed our belief that most of the need for code motion arises in code that does copying of structures, etc. In such cases, relaxing the liveness by three instructions is effective.

From our experience, we found that case (b) above, even though it gives more flexibility to the solver to move the spill code, often resulted in large data sets that causes the ILP solver to return no feasible solution even after a lengthy execution. We present in this paper our experience with cases (a) and (c). We refer to the case (c) as SARA and case (a) as $SARA_s$ (the subscript denoting *strict* liveness).

## 5    Experimental Results

We have implemented SARA in gcc-2.95.2, replacing gcc's own implementation of register allocation, and we have tested the target code from the new compiler on a Stargate platform. Stargate has a StrongArm/XScale processor and 64MB SDRAM and no cache. The impact of SARA may be different for systems with cache. We have drawn our benchmark programs from a variety of sources:

- Stanford Benchmark suite: The first four benchmarks are small and simple, but typical of the subroutines of many other benchmarks.
- NetBench: Route and url are network related benchmarks from the NetBench [17] suite. Route is an implementation of IPv4 routing according to RFC 1812, and url is a switching protocol that implements url based switching.
- Pointer-intensive benchmark: This benchmark suite is a collection of pointer-intensive benchmarks [4]. Yacr2 is an implementation of a channel router and Ft is an implementation of a minimum spanning tree algorithm [10].
- The last two benchmarks are taken from the comp.benchmarks FAQ at http://www.cs.wisc.edu/~thomas/comp.benchmarks.FAQ.html.    The    c4 benchmark is an implementation of the connect-4 [2] game and mm is an implementation of nine different matrix multiplication algorithms.

The static characteristics and compile time statistics of these benchmarks are presented in Figure 2. The static characteristics we present here include the number of lines of C code, the number of instructions seen by the ILP solver

| Benchmark | LoC | #RTLs | #Funcs | gcc+SLA | | | RA+SLA | | | SARA | | |
|-----------|-----|-------|--------|-----|------|-----|-----|------|-----|-----|------|-----|
| | | | | Mem | Pair | CSR | Mem | Pair | CSR | Mem | Pair | CSR |
| sieve | 39 | 134 | 3 | 0 | 0 | 9 | 0 | 0 | 9 | 0 | 0 | 9 |
| matmul | 56 | 254 | 6 | 9 | 2 | 22 | 9 | 0 | 20 | 7 | 6 | 19 |
| perm | 34 | 112 | 3 | 5 | 0 | 14 | 5 | 0 | 12 | 4 | 2 | 12 |
| queen | 58 | 144 | 4 | 11 | 0 | 14 | 12 | 1 | 11 | 8 | 5 | 11 |
| route | 2246 | 4672 | 23 | 519 | 4 | 110 | 506 | 6 | 116 | 546 | 19 | 107 |
| url | 790 | 1264 | 12 | 115 | 8 | 62 | 120 | 5 | 56 | 120 | 8 | 58 |
| yacr2 | 3979 | 10838 | 58 | 1060 | 8 | 123 | 1003 | 6 | 123 | 1109 | 24 | 142 |
| ft | 2155 | 3218 | 35 | 219 | 5 | 92 | 225 | 9 | 87 | 230 | 14 | 106 |
| c4 | 885 | 3388 | 21 | 189 | 3 | 289 | 190 | 7 | 305 | 184 | 18 | 320 |
| mm | 647 | 2884 | 14 | 386 | 9 | 130 | 375 | 4 | 116 | 380 | 23 | 92 |

**Fig. 2.** Benchmark characteristics and compile time statistics

(which depends on the number of RTL instructions in the intermediate representation of the program), and the number of functions. Due to space constraints, we limit ourselves to presenting compile time statistics for three different register allocators: gcc's default register allocator followed by SLA, our ILP-based RA followed by SLA, and SARA (with the liveness information extended to three instructions, see section 4). For each of these combinations we present an estimate of the number of memory accesses; the number of loads and stores (Mem), the number of load-pair/store-pair instructions (Pair) inserted, and the number of callee save registers (CSR) used.

All these benchmarks have the common characteristic that they are non-floating point benchmarks. (We had to edit a few of them to remove some code that uses floating point operations; we did so only after ensuring that the code with floating point operations is not critical to the behavior of the program.)

Studying the compile time characteristics gives a good insight into the way SARA works. We can see that in the compile time statistics, SARA outperforms both gcc+SLA and RA+SLA by a big margin in terms of the number of pairs generated. Notice, though, that SARA sometimes uses more callee save registers, because of the added register pressure that comes from pairing up loads and stores. Another point that can be easily noticed is that in some cases, such as c4, SARA and RA+SLA are generating more memory instructions than gcc. This is because the constraints use the frequency of the instruction as a parameter to compute the cost of the objective function. And in such cases, generating loads/stores outside the loop is a better option. One final point to note here is that, for benchmarks route, yacr2, ft and mm, SARA generates more loads/stores than our ILP-based register allocator. The reason is that by generating more loads and stores in non-loop code and generating load-pairs in the loops SARA is able to reduce the overall cost.

We do not give detailed compilation times; our solver sometimes took more than 30 minutes and we had to terminate CPLEX and work with a perhaps nonoptimal solution. The total compilation time for all the benchmarks is in the order of hours.

We now present the execution time numbers for the benchmarks. In Figure 3 we present the time each benchmark took to run when compiled with different compilers. Each of these is compiled at the -O2 level of optimization.

To get an overall comparison of the different register allocators, we present the normalized execution time numbers in Figure 4. Our experience can be represented in a lattice as shown in Figure 5. We use the notation $A \leq B$ to denote that time taken to execute code when compiled with $A$ less than or equal to the time taken to execute the same when compiled with $B$.

Let us now analyze the results in more detail. Sieve is one benchmark where no spill code was needed and gcc's register allocator and our register allocator both perform in the same way. For benchmarks matmul and route, gcc+SLA performs better than RA, indicating that SLA in itself is fairly powerful. For other benchmarks RA is doing better than gcc+SLA, showing that our ILP-based register allocation is giving better results than gcc's default module run

| Benchmark | Exec Time(seconds) | | | | | |
|---|---|---|---|---|---|---|
| | gcc-O2 | RA | gcc+SLA | RA+SLA | SARA$_s$ | SARA |
| sieve | 9.26 | 9.26 | 9.26 | 9.26 | 9.26 | 9.26 |
| matmul | 71.59 | 68.19 | 67.49 | 67.02 | 66.45 | 66.28 |
| perm | 154.45 | 151.26 | 146.90 | 143.24 | 140.10 | 140.10 |
| queen | 27.33 | 24.39 | 26.80 | 23.39 | 22.90 | 22.24 |
| route | 20.9 | 18.91 | 18.82 | 18.10 | 17.8 | 17.18 |
| url | 10.85 | 10.36 | 10.55 | 10.36 | 9.86 | 9.86 |
| yacr2 | 4.40 | 4.21 | 4.30 | 4.11 | 3.99 | 3.95 |
| ft | 46.25 | 45.26 | 46.15 | 45.26 | 45.26 | 43.21 |
| c4 | 42.3 | 41.1 | 42.19 | 40.53 | 40.23 | 39.65 |
| mm | 330.02 | 326.2 | 326.5 | 324.21 | 322.60 | 311.32 |

**Fig. 3.** Execution time numbers

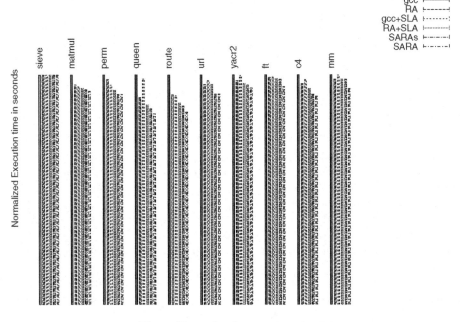

**Fig. 4.** Normalized execution times

followed by SLA. For ft, RA + SLA does not give any improvement over RA. That is because SLA could not introduce many pairs in the frequently executed code. Also SARA$_s$ is not giving much improvement either. That's because the ILP solver could not generate many pairs with the strict liveness constraints. However SARA does show an improvement which is due to the relaxed bounds. Theoretically one can imagine cases where RA+SLA could be doing better than SARA$_s$ or even SARA, but we did not find any such cases in our benchmarks. Further experimentation may reveal such cases.

A general point to note about the numbers is that there is a appreciable amount of tension between the number of callee save registers used, the number

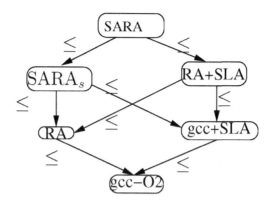

**Fig. 5.** A comparison of different register allocator schemes

of normal loads and stores, and the pairs inserted. As a result, SARA shows a significant but not earthshaking improvement over the other register allocators. Overall, we see that SARA yields improvements up to 16% compared to the gcc compiler's own register allocator extended with SLA, and up to 8% compared to our own ILP-based register allocator followed by SLA. On average (excluding the numbers for sieve), the improvements are 7.4% and 4.1% respectively.

## 6   Conclusion and Future Work

We have presented an ILP-based approach to combining register allocation and stack location allocation. We have shown that doing these optimizations together gives better results than doing them separately in sequence.

In future work, one might implement SARA using fast heuristics and compare the results to the results of solving the ILPs using CPLEX. One might also add register coalescing, register rematerialization, etc. to SARA and study the effect on code quality and compilation time.

**Acknowledgments.** We thank the anonymous reviewers for helpful comments on draft of the paper. We were supported by Intel and by a National Science Foundation ITR Award number 0401691.

## References

1. Intel(r) IXP2400 network processor.
   http://www.intel.com/design/network/products/npfamily/ixp2400.htm.
2. Victor Allis. A knowledge-based approach of connect-four–the game is solved: White wins. Technical Report IR–163, Vrije Universiteit Amsterdam, 1988.
3. Andrew W. Appel and Lal George. Optimal spilling for CISC machines with few registers. In PLDI 2001, pages 243–253.
4. Todd M. Austin, Scott E. Breach, and Gurindar S. Sohi. Efficient detection of all pointer and array access errors. In PLDI 1994, pages 290–301.

5. D. Bradlee, S. Eggers, and R. Henry. Integrating register allocation and instruction scheduling for riscs. In ASPLOS 1991, pages 122–131.
6. Preston Briggs, Keith D. Cooper, and Linda Torczon. Improvements to graph coloring register allocation. ACM TOPLAS 16(3):428–455, May 1994.
7. D. Callahan and B. Koblenz. Register allocation via hierarchical graph coloring. In PLDI 1991, pages 192–203.
8. G. J. Chaitin. Register allocation and spilling via graph coloring. *SIGPLAN Notices*, 17(6):98–105, June 1982.
9. Robert Fourer, David M. Gay, and Brian W. Kernighan. *AMPL A modeling language for mathematical programming*. Scientific Press, 1993.
10. Michael L. Fredman and Robert Endre Tarjan. Fibonacci heaps and their uses in improved network optimization algorithms. *J. ACM*, 34(3):596–615, 1987.
11. Changqing Fu and Kent Wilken. A faster optimal register allocator. In Proceedings of ACM/IEEE MICRO 2002, pages 245–256.
12. M. R. Garey and D. S. Johnson. *Computers and Intractability: A Guide to the Theory of NPCompleteness*. Freeman, 1979.
13. David W. Goodwin and Kent D. Wilken. Optimal and near-optimal global register allocations using 0-1 integer programming. *Software–Practice & Experience*, 26(8):929–968, August 1996.
14. Timothy Kong and Kent D. Wilken. Precise register allocation for irregular architectures. In Proceedings of ACM/IEEE MICRO 1998, pages 297–307.
15. Sorin Lerner, David Grove, and Craig Chambers. Composing dataflow analyses and transformations. In POPL 2002, pages 270–282.
16. Vincenzo Liberatore, Martin Farach-Colton, and Ulrich Kremer. Evaluation of algorithms for local register allocation. In CC 1999, pages 137–152, LNCS 1575.
17. G. Memik, B.Mangione-Smith, and W.Hu. Netbench: A benchmarking suite for network processors. In IEEE ICCAD 2001.
18. Rajeev Motwani, Krishna V. Palem, Vivek Sarkar, and Salem Reyen. Combining register allocation and instruction scheduling. Tech. Report CS-TN-95-22, 1995.
19. Mayur Naik and Jens Palsberg. Compiling with code-size constraints. *ACM Transactions on Embedded Computing Systems*, 3(1):163–181, 2004.
20. V. Krishna Nandivada and Jens Palsberg. Efficient spill code for SDRAM. In CASES 2003, pages 24–31.
21. R. Rivest. The md5 message-digest algorithm. *Request for Comment: 1321*, 1992.
22. Ravi Sethi. Complete register allocation problems. In ACM STOC 1973, pages 182–195.
23. Tammo Spalink, Scott Karlin, and Larry Peterson. Evaluating network processors in ip forwarding. Technical Report TR–626–00, Princeton University, 2000.
24. Marc Tremblay, Jeffrey Chan, Shailender Chaudhry, Andrew W. Conigliaro, and Shing Sheung Tse. The majc architecture: A synthesis of parallelism and scalability. *IEEE Micro*, 20(6):12–25, 2000.

# Register Allocation for Programs in SSA-Form

Sebastian Hack, Daniel Grund, and Gerhard Goos

Fakultät für Informatik,
Universität Karlsruhe
(hack, daniel, ggoos)@ipd.info.uni-karlsruhe.de

**Abstract.** As register allocation is one of the most important phases in optimizing compilers, much work has been done to improve its quality and speed. We present a novel register allocation architecture for programs in SSA-form which simplifies register allocation significantly. We investigate certain properties of SSA-programs and their interference graphs, showing that they belong to the class of chordal graphs. This leads to a quadratic-time optimal coloring algorithm and allows for decoupling the tasks of coloring, spilling and coalescing completely. After presenting heuristic methods for spilling and coalescing, we compare our coalescing heuristic to an optimal method based on integer linear programming.

## 1 Introduction

Graph coloring register allocation has been a successful approach for register allocation, mostly due to its very simple abstraction: Each variable in the program is mapped to a node in an undirected, so called *interference graph*. Whenever the compiler finds out that two variables cannot be held in the same register (they are *simultaneously live*), an edge is drawn between the two nodes in the interference graph representing the two variables. A $k$-coloring of the interference graph thus leads to a valid register allocation using at most $k$ registers.

Chaitin [1] showed that for each undirected graph $G$, there is a program which has $G$ as its interference graph. Since graph coloring is $\mathcal{NP}$-complete, so is register allocation. This leads to the well known iterative approach of graph coloring register allocators (here, we illustrate a simplified version of the allocator proposed by Briggs [2]):

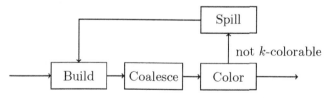

Since determining the graph's chromatic number (the minimal number of colors needed for a valid coloring) is also $\mathcal{NP}$-complete, the impact of a modification of the graph (spilling and coalescing) on its colorability cannot be determined efficiently in general. This has two unappealing consequences:

A. Mycroft and A. Zeller (Eds.): CC 2006, LNCS 3923, pp. 247–262, 2006.

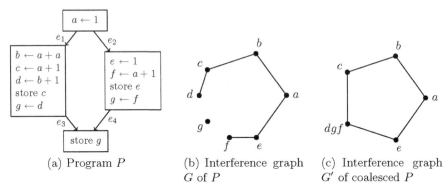

(a) Program $P$        (b) Interference graph        (c) Interference graph
                           $G$ of $P$                   $G'$ of coalesced $P$

**Fig. 1.** Program $P$ and its interference graph

1. Coalescing (the task of eliminating useless copies) may do more harm than good by increasing the chromatic number of the graph. Consider the example program $P$ in figure 1(a) and its interference graph $G$ in figure 1(b). $G$'s chromatic number $\chi(G)$ equals 2. Aggressive coalescing would merge the nodes $d, g, f$ into one producing the graph $G'$ (shown in figure 1(c)) which is not 2-colorable anymore. Thus, the register demand of $P$ is raised by merely removing some copies and thus possibly introducing spill code.

2. Since it is not clear if the spilling of a node improved the colorability of the graph, the modifications of the program caused by spilling have to be materialized, the interference graph has to be rebuilt and coloring has to be attempted again. Thus, coloring is repeated until $k$ colors suffice. Especially for a small number of available registers many iterations have to be expected, since the number of spills will be high. This is costly, since the interference graph is a large data structure which then has to be rebuilt over and over.

The situation drastically changes if we require the processed program to be in SSA-form. As we show in section 2, interference graphs of SSA-form programs are *chordal*. The two major properties of chordal graphs which make them so appealing for register allocation are:

1. Their chromatic number is equal to the size of the largest clique in the graph.
2. They can be optimally[1] colored in quadratic time (concerning the number of nodes, cf. Golumbic [3]).

Furthermore, there are several relations between SSA-form programs and their interference graphs which allow us to circumvent the deficiencies of conventional graph coloring register allocators as mentioned above:

– Cliques in the interference graph correspond to live sets in the program. This means after liveness analysis we know how many registers will be needed for the program in question. If we reduce the amount of variables live at each point in the program to at most $k$, the graph will be $k$-colorable, which

---

[1] Using as few colors as possible.

eliminates the iteration. In section 4.1, we present a simple algorithm which splits the live ranges of the variables so that the register pressure is at most $k$ at each point in the program.

- Dominance, a fundamental notion for SSA-form programs, induces an order of the interference graph's nodes which allows the interference graph $G = (V, E)$ of a SSA-form program to be colored optimally in $O(\chi(G) \cdot |V|)$ as shown in section 2.
- Finally, as shown in section 4.3, we coalesce useless copies in the shape of $\phi$-operations not by modifying the graph but by finding a $k$-coloring which assigns as many sources and targets of copies the same register. This preserves the chordality of the interference graph and thus does not change its $k$-colorability. So coalescing a copy will never cause any additional spill.

This leads to a single pass register allocator architecture looking like

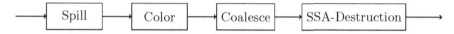

avoiding any iteration.

## 2    SSA-form Programs and their Interference Graphs

Before going into algorithmic details, let us discuss basic properties of SSA-form programs and their connection to relevant terms of register allocation like liveness and interference.

We consider a program as a standard CFG being a triple $(Labels, CF, \textbf{start})$. Each label $\ell \in Labels$ contains a single instruction

$$\ell : \underbrace{(y_1, \ldots, y_m)}_{D_\tau} \leftarrow \tau \underbrace{(x_1, \ldots, x_n)}_{U_\tau}$$

a set of control flow edges $CF$ between the labels and one designated label $\textbf{start}$ which has no control flow predecessors. As we only consider SSA-form programs from now on, each variable $v$ has a unique label where it is defined. We will denote this label by $\mathcal{D}_v$.

A fundamental notion for SSA-form programs is the one of dominance:

**Definition 1 (Dominance).** *A label $\ell$ dominates a label $\ell'$ if all paths from* **start** *to $\ell'$ contain $\ell$. We then write $\ell \preceq \ell'$.*

Essential for all later work is the notion of a strict program which was coined by Budimlić [4].

**Definition 2 (Strict program).** *A program is strict, if each usage of a variable $v$ is dominated by $\mathcal{D}_v$.*

The interference graph $G = (V, E)$ of a program $P$ contains all variables occurring in $P$ as nodes. Two variables $v$ and $w$ are connected by an edge (we then write $vw \in E$) in $G$, iff they interfere:

**Definition 3 (Interference).** *We say, two variables* interfere *if there exists a label in the program where they are both live.*

In the same paper, Budimlić gave two lemmas which establish a fundamental relationship between dominance and interference:

**Lemma 1.** *If two variables $v, w$ interfere either $\mathcal{D}_v \preceq \mathcal{D}_w$ or $\mathcal{D}_w \preceq \mathcal{D}_v$.*

**Lemma 2.** *If $v, w$ interfere and $\mathcal{D}_v \preceq \mathcal{D}_w$, then $v$ is live at $\mathcal{D}_w$.*

Based on Budimlić's lemmas we can prove our first claim of the introduction:[2]

**Theorem 1.** *For each clique $C = \{c_1, \ldots, c_n\} \subseteq V$ in the interference graph $G = (V, E)$ of a SSA-form program $P$, there exists a label $\ell \in \text{Labels}_P$ where all $c_1, \ldots, c_n$ are live.*

*Proof.* Since $C$ is a clique, $(c_i, c_j) \in E$ for each $1 \leq i < j \leq n$. By lemma 1, the labels $\{\mathcal{D}_{c_1}, \ldots, \mathcal{D}_{cn}\}$ form a totally ordered set. Thus there exists a permutation $\sigma : C \longrightarrow C$ for which $\mathcal{D}_{\sigma(c_1)} \preceq \cdots \preceq \mathcal{D}_{\sigma(c_n)}$. By lemma 2, $\sigma(c_1), \ldots, \sigma(c_n)$ are live at $\mathcal{D}_{\sigma(c_n)}$.

# 3    Coloring SSA Interference Graphs

Consider the following method to color a graph: Given an order $v_1, \ldots, v_n$ of the graph's nodes. Eliminate the $v_i$ one by one from the graph. Then, re-insert the nodes in reverse order and give each $v_i$ the first free color not used by its already re-inserted neighbors.

A well-known result from graph theory states that for each graph $G = (V, E)$ there is an ordering of all nodes in $V$ for which this procedure leads to an optimal coloring of $G$ (cf. the textbook of Diestel [6] for example). In general, as graph coloring is $\mathcal{NP}$-complete, determining such a sequence is also $\mathcal{NP}$-complete.

For the moment, let us consider the following approach to generate such an ordering: In each elimination step, search a node $v$ whose neighbors form a clique in the current graph (such a node is also called *simplicial*). The idea is, that when the node is re-inserted, all neighbors which are already colored form a clique, and thus the number of colors used for the coloring is bound by the size of the largest clique in the graph. Such an elimination order is called a *perfect elimination order (PEO)*. Consider the following example:

PEO: $a, d, b, e, c$
No PEO: $b, a, c, d, e$

Of course, not every graph allows to find such a node whose neighbors form a clique at each step in the elimination process. For instance, the diamond graph

---

[2] Bouchez [5] gave this theorem, independently from us, too.

used as an example by Briggs in [2] does not allow for perfect elimination order. It is a well-known theorem of the theory of perfect graphs, that if a graph possesses a perfect elimination order, the coloring procedure described above will generate an optimal coloring of the graph (cf. the textbook of Golumbic [3] for example).

Based on Budimlić's lemmas, we prove that the dominance relation of a program in SSA-form induces a perfect elimination order of its interference graph $G = (V, E)$.

**Lemma 3.** *Let* $ab, bc \in E$ *and* $ac \notin E$. *If* $\mathcal{D}_a \preceq \mathcal{D}_b$, *then* $\mathcal{D}_b \preceq \mathcal{D}_c$.

*Proof.* By contradiction: due to lemma 1, either $\mathcal{D}_b \preceq \mathcal{D}_c$ or $\mathcal{D}_c \preceq \mathcal{D}_b$. Assume $\mathcal{D}_c \preceq \mathcal{D}_b$. Then (by lemma 2), $c$ is live at $\mathcal{D}_b$. Since $a$ and $b$ also interfere and $\mathcal{D}_a \preceq \mathcal{D}_b$, $a$ is also live at $\mathcal{D}_b$. So, $a$ and $c$ are live at $\mathcal{D}_b$ which cannot be by precondition.

**Theorem 2.** *A variable* $v$ *can be added to a PEO of* $G$ *if all variables whose definitions are dominated by the definition of* $v$ *have already been added to the PEO.*

*Proof.* To be added to a PEO, $v$ must be simplicial. Let us assume, $v$ is *not* simplicial. Then, by definition, there exist two neighbors $a, b$ of $v$ which are not connected ($va, vb \in E$ and $ab \notin E$). By the proposition, all variables whose definitions are dominated by $\mathcal{D}_v$ have been added to the PEO and removed from $G$. Thus, $\mathcal{D}_a \preceq \mathcal{D}_v$. Then, by lemma 3, $\mathcal{D}_v \preceq \mathcal{D}_b$ which contradicts the proposition. Thus, $v$ is simplicial.

Thus, a PEO of a SSA interference graph's nodes can be easily obtained by a post order walk over the program's dominance tree. Thus, we can optimally color the interference graphs of SSA-form programs in quadratic time.

The graphs, for which perfect elimination orders exist are called *chordal* graphs or sometimes triangulated or rigid-circuit graphs. Since chordal graphs are *perfect* (cf. to [3]) the characteristic property of perfect graphs also applies to chordal graphs:

**Definition 4.** *A graph* $H$ *is perfect, iff for each induced subgraph* $H$ *of* $G$ *the chromatic number* $\chi(H)$ *is equal to the size of the largest clique* $\omega(H)$.

## 4    A Register Allocator for SSA-form Programs

Before giving a detailed description of spilling and coalescing techniques in the next subsections let us briefly outline how the theoretical results of the last section can be exploited to derive a new architecture for register allocators in general.

Theorem 2 together with definition 4 state that the chromatic number of a SSA interference graph is determined by the largest clique in the graph. By theorem 1, for each clique in the interference graph, there is a label in the program, where all variables in the clique are live. Thus, spilling can make the interference graph $k$-colorable by reducing the number of live variables at each label to $k$. This enables us to consider the spilling problem separately from the other tasks of a register allocator since checking how many variables are live at all labels in the program is easy in contrast to determining the chromatic number of an arbitrary graph. In section 4.1 we demonstrate how a well known basic block oriented spilling technique can be extended to serve as a spilling method for the whole program.

By section 3, obtaining an optimal $k$-coloring is trivial. All one has to do is to obey the coloring sequence induced by the dominance relation. Section 4.2 shows how the $\phi$-operations can be removed to obtain a non-SSA program having a valid register allocation with $k$ registers.

We consider coalescing as the task of obtaining a *good* coloring with respect to $\phi$-operations. Consider a $\phi$-operation $y \leftarrow \phi(x_1, \ldots, x_n)$. If we can assign as many of the $x_i$ the color of $y$, we save move operations on the respective edges to the $\phi$'s block. The advantage over merging the node of $y$ with the nodes of the $x_i$ in the interference graph is, that we do not modify the graph's structure (i.e. possibly rendering it non-chordal) which lets us still determine its chromatic number easily.

## 4.1 Spilling

In conventional global register allocation (like the register allocator by Briggs [2]), spilling is not activated until coloring fails. Thus, the spilling decision is tightly coupled to the way the graph is colored: If a node is popped from the coloring stack and there is no color left to assign since its neighbors use up all available colors, one of its neighbors is marked to be spilled, i.e. each use is preceded by a reload and each definition is succeeded by a store of its value. This breaks the live range apart making the variable only interfere with the variables live at the usages and definitions. So the node is spilled only because another one cannot be colored.

Since the interference graph represents the live ranges of variables, it hides relevant information concerning spilling:

- How often is a variable used?
- Where is a variable used?
- How far is the next use away from a given point?

Thus spilling in conventional global register allocation is *only* concerned with modifying the graph's structure in order to make it $k$-colorable. A lot of work has been done to make these register allocators more sensitive to the program structure (see e.g. the work by Bergner et al. [7] or by Chow and Hennessy [8]).

However, theorems 1 and 2 and definition 4 allow for using more program-sensitive, basic block oriented spilling approaches like Hsu et al. [9] and combine their results to a solution for the whole procedure. Guo et al. [10] describe the power of Belady's MIN algorithm [11] for spilling in a basic block. Belady's algorithm does *not* minimize the number of loads or stores in a basic block. Though, as the measurements of Guo show, it is still a good heuristic. In the following, we present a method how Belady's algorithm can be extended to work on a whole procedure by using the results of section 2.

**Belady's MIN Algorithm.** The main principle of Belady's MIN algorithm is to displace the variables from registers whose next use is farthest in the future (regarding the number of instructions). The algorithm starts at the entry of a basic block $B$ and visits each label $\ell$ in the block once. Assume, that all operands of the instruction of $\ell$ are read/written from/to registers. If all registers are occupied, one variable has to be displaced from the registers to make room for the result of the instruction. If a label is reached whose instruction uses a value which has been displaced, a reload must be inserted for this variable and, since the reload loads the value in a register, another variable may have to be displaced from the register set.

For example, you have 4 registers which are currently occupied by the variables $a, b, c, d$. Reaching a label

$$\ell : f \leftarrow \tau(a, e)$$

one register has to be freed to reload the variable $e$. The algorithm of Belady selects the one of $b, c, d$ whose next use is farthest away from $\ell$. Two questions arise immediately:

1. How far away is the next use of a variable $v$ which is live out at the block $B$ of consideration but not used in that block anymore?
   Since $v$ can be used on several different control flow paths from the block, it is not clear when $v$ will be used next since this depends on the taken control flow successor of $B$. Therefore we use an estimation by taking the minimum of all next use distances.
2. What is the initial occupation of the registers?
   Let us consider the set $I_B$ containing all values live in at $B$ and the results of all $\phi$-functions in $B$. All these values are passed to this block "from outside".[3]
   If $|I| > k$, we select $k$ elements from $I_B$ with the nearest next uses.
   Furthermore, if we find out that a variable $v$ in $I_B$ is displaced before it is used, it is not sensible to hold $v$ in a register at the entry of the block, thus $v$ is removed from $I_B$.

We record the occupation of the registers after the last instruction in the block $B$ in the set $O_B$.

The final step is to combine the results of the algorithm applied to all basic blocks in the program into a solution for the whole procedure. Since the register pressure is nowhere larger than $k$, we only have to assure that all variables in $I_B$

---

[3] Note that a $\phi$ is just a representative for a control flow dependent live in.

for some block $B$ are in registers on each control flow edge leading to $B$. Thus we examine each predecessor block $P$ of $B$: If $M := I_B \setminus O_P$ is not empty, we have to insert reloads for all variables in $M$ on the control flow edge from $P$ to $B$.[4]

Note that spilling a (SSA-)variable $v$ and reloading it several times actually destroys the SSA-form of the program, since $v$ has then multiple definitions, i.e. the reloads $v$. The SSA-form can be reconstructed by applying a SSA construction algorithm, e.g. the one by Cytron et al. [12].

## 4.2    SSA-Destruction

A $\phi$-operation $y \leftarrow \phi(x_1, \ldots, x_n)$ works like a control flow dependent copy operation assigning $x_i$ to $y$ if the $\phi$'s label is reached via the $i$-th control flow predecessor. Furthermore, SSA semantics state that all $\phi$-operations in a basic block have to be executed simultaneously before all other instructions in that basic block. Thus, all $\phi$-operations

$$y_1 \leftarrow \phi(x_{11}, \ldots, x_{1n})$$
$$\ldots$$
$$y_m \leftarrow \phi(x_{m1}, \ldots, x_{mn})$$

in a block work as a "bulk copy" copying the $x_{ij}$ to the $y_i$ *at once* if the block was entered via the $j$-th edge.

Conventionally, while translating out of the SSA-form, $\phi$-operations are replaced by copy instructions. Despite some other problems like the swap-problem (see Briggs et al. [13]), this kind of $\phi$ removal may raise the register demand unnecessarily as demonstrated by the example program $Q$ in figure 2(a): Replacing the $\phi$-operations by inserting the copies

$$i_3 \leftarrow i_2$$
$$j_3 \leftarrow j_2$$

on the edge $e_4$ introduces an interference between $i_3$ and $j_2$ which was not present in the SSA interference graph shown in figure 2(c). This edge creates the clique $i_3, j_2, j_3$ which raises the graph's chromatic number to 3.

So let us reconsider the bulk copy property of the $\phi$-operations in a basic block. Consider the register allocation of $Q$ shown in figure 2(d). If the block $B$ is entered via $e_1$, $R_1$ is assigned $R_1$ and $R_2$ is assigned $R_2$, so the $\phi$s do nothing on this edge. However, if $B$ is reached via $e_4$, $R_1$ is assigned $R_2$ and vice versa, *at once:* The registers $R_1$ and $R_2$ are swapped.

So generally $\phi$-operations work like permutations on registers and not like a set of copies. It depends on the registers allocated for the results of the $\phi$ and its operands how the permutation will look like. Thus, in this setting, coalescing is

---

[4] Instructions can be placed on a control flow edge by eliminating critical edges and putting the instruction in the respective block.

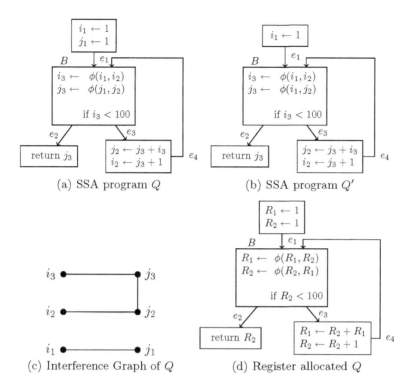

**Fig. 2.** Example programs $Q$ and $Q'$

the task of finding a register allocation in which the permutations will have as many *fixed points* (registers that are mapped to themselves) as possible.

As known from basic linear algebra, each permutation of size $n$ can be written as a sequence of *transpositions* (swaps) and thus is implementable using $n$ registers, using *no* extra register. For example, the $\phi$-operations at some label $\ell$

$$R_2 \leftarrow \phi(\ldots, R_1, \ldots)$$
$$R_3 \leftarrow \phi(\ldots, R_2, \ldots)$$
$$R_1 \leftarrow \phi(\ldots, R_3, \ldots)$$
$$R_4 \leftarrow \phi(\ldots, R_4, \ldots)$$

can be implemented by inserting the sequence

```
swap R2, R3
swap R1, R2
```

on the corresponding control flow edge entering $\ell$.

If the processor provides a swap instruction (like **xchg** on the x86), $\phi$-operations can be directly be implemented by a sequence of these. If not, one can use three exclusive ors. However, if one register is spare at the $\phi$s, we can use it to implement the permutation with moves. Note that due to theorem 1 and definition 4 we exactly know how many registers are in use at $\ell$.

Finally, there is one subtle point: The $\phi$-operations of a basic block can use a variable multiply concerning the same control flow edge like the $\phi$-operations in figure 2(b) both use $i_1$ concerning edge $e_1$. So, arriving at $B$ from $e_1$, $i_1$ must be written to $i_3$ and $j_3$. Thus, a copy from $i_1$ to either $i_3$ or $j_3$ must be inserted on edge $e_1$. This copy is inevitable since the value of $i_1$ must be present in *two* registers upon entering $B$. The decision which destination the copy has (in this example either $i_3$ or $j_3$) is deferred to coalescing since at this point in time it is not clear whether $i_1$ and $i_3$ or $i_1$ and $j_3$ can be assigned the same color.

Note that the same situation also occurs if an operand $x$ of a $\phi$ is live-in at the $\phi$'s block. Then $x$ and the $\phi$'s result interfere and cannot be given the same color. Thus a copy has to be inserted also.

### 4.3   Coalescing

As we have seen, we can eliminate $\phi$-operations in a way that no additional register demand arises. Thus, a coloring of the interference graph of the SSA-form program is a valid register allocation for the program with $\phi$-operations removed. In order to lower the number of transpositions needed for a $\phi$-operation we investigate the problem of maximizing the number of fixed points of a $\phi$.[5]

Concerning a coloring $f$, variable $x$ is a fixed point of a $\phi$-operation $y \leftarrow \phi(\ldots, x, \ldots)$ if $x$ and $y$ have been assigned the same register, i.e. $f(y) = f(x)$. Clearly, for fixed points no code has to be generated. Even more, if all $\phi$-operands are fixed points, no code has to be generated for the $\phi$ at all.

Given a SSA-form program $P$, its interference graph $G = (V, E)$ and the set $\Phi$ of all $\phi$-operations in $P$. For a valid $k$-coloring $f : V \longrightarrow \{1, \ldots, k\}$ of $G$, we define the costs of a $\phi$-operation $p : y \leftarrow \phi(x_1, \ldots, x_n)$ as follows:

$$c_f(p) = \sum_{i=1}^{n} \text{cost}_f(y, x_i) \qquad \text{with } \text{cost}_f(a, b) = \begin{cases} w_{ab} & \text{if } f(a) \neq f(b) \\ 0 & \text{else} \end{cases} \qquad (1)$$

where the $w_{ab} \geq 0$ are costs for copying $b$ to $a$. The overall costs of the program under the coloring $f$ are then

$$c_f(P) = \sum_{p \in \Phi} c_f(p)$$

**Definition 5 (SSA-Maximize-Fixed-Points).** *Given a SSA-form program $P$ and its interference graph $G$. Find a coloring $f$ of $G$ for which $c_f(P)$ is minimal.*

**Theorem 3.** SSA-MAXIMIZE-FIXED-POINTS *is $\mathcal{NP}$-complete depending on the number of $\Phi$-operations. For a proof see [14].*

---

[5] Note that optimizing fixed points is only an approximation corresponding to the traditional coalescing paradigm but does not generally minimize the number of transpositions.

**A Heuristic Approach for SSA-Maximize-Fixed-Points.** In contrast to existing approaches we do *not* merge nodes in the interference graph but try to alter the coloring (as obtained with theorem 2) in order to assign operands of $\phi$-operations and their results the same color. So, instead of changing the graph's structure, we search for a "better" $k$-coloring wrt. the cost function defined in equation 1. Thus, it will never happen that additional spill code is caused by assigning two nodes the same color, in contrast to the example in figure 1. Unlike other techniques, our method is not limited to the immediate neighborhood of the node pair to base its decision whether to coalesce or not.

The algorithm considers each $\phi$-operation separately. The aim is to color as many operands of the $\phi$ equally to the $\phi$'s result. Therefore we consider an excerpt (later called conflict graph) from the interference graph containing the $\phi$'s result and its operands. Then we try to assign these nodes the same color. As this may lead to conflicts (as this color may already be in use by neighbors), we try to resolve these conflicts by recursively adjusting the conflicting nodes' colors. If we cannot resolve the conflicts for a node, we mark this node as incompatible.

For each $\phi$-operation, we build an *optimization unit (OU)* $\omega = (y, x_1, \ldots, x_m)$ consisting of the $\phi$'s result $y$ and the arguments $x_1, \ldots, x_m$ of the $\phi$ which do not interfere with $y$. An argument interfering with $y$ can trivially never be assigned $y$'s color. For each OU a minimization of the costs is then tried separately. The minimization of an OU is not allowed to touch the results of all already processed OU. The processing of every $\omega = (y, x_1, \ldots, x_m)$ consists of three phases:

**Init.** For each allowed color **c** for $y$, we insert an entry $E_{\mathbf{c}} = (\mathbf{c}, C_{\mathbf{c}}, S_{\mathbf{c}})$ into a priority queue. An entry consists of:

- a color **c**.
- a conflict graph $C_{\mathbf{c}}$. Initially, $C_{\mathbf{c}}$ equals to the subgraph of the interference graph induced by $y, x_1, \ldots, x_m$.
- a maximum weighted stable set $S_{\mathbf{c}}$ of $C_{\mathbf{c}}$.[6] $S_{\mathbf{c}}$ represents all nodes in the conflict graph which shall be assigned the color **c**. Each $x_i$ in the OU is assigned the weight $w_{yx_i}$ as defined in the cost function in equation 1. The weight of $y$ is arbitrary, because $y$ is contained in every maximum stable set by construction. This property is preserved throughout the optimization process.

The gain of $E_{\mathbf{c}}$ is the sum of the weights of the nodes contained in $S_{\mathbf{c}}$. The priority queue is ordered decreasingly by the gain of the entries. Thus, the first entry in the queue represents a coloring which provides the largest gain (or causes the fewest costs).

**Test.** The first entry $E_{\mathbf{c}}$ is removed from the priority queue. We then attempt to adjust the coloring of the interference graph in a way, that the nodes in $S_{\mathbf{c}}$ are assigned the color **c**. Note, that until the testing phase is not completed for an OU, color changes are only virtual and rolled back if the optimization fails for the OU.

---

[6] A weighted stable set is a set of nodes equipped with weights for which no node is connected to the other.

We try to change the color for each $u \in \{y, x_1, \dots, x_m\}$ to **c**. If a neighbor $n$ of $u$ is also colored with **c**, we annotate $n$ with the former color of $u$. This may provoke further conflicts which are then resolved recursively. Swapping the color of a node $v$ originally initiated by changing the color of $u$ to **c** ends in one of the three cases:

1. Changing $v$'s color does not generate new conflicts.
2. $v$'s color has already been pinned (see phase **Apply**) by the processing of another optimization unit. Then, changing $v$'s color would increase the costs incurred by this other OU. $uu$ is added to $C_{\mathbf{c}}$. Thus, $u$ is excluded from every possible stable set of $C_{\mathbf{c}}$. Then, $S_{\mathbf{c}}$ is recomputed and the entry is reinserted into the queue.
3. If $v$ is a pinning candidate for the current OU, $u$ and $v$ are somehow interdependent. The algorithm cannot assign **c** to $u$ and $v$ at the same time. As we require $y$ to be always contained in each $S_{\mathbf{c}}$, if $v = y$, we add the edge $uu$, otherwise the edge $uv$ to $C_{\mathbf{c}}$. Afterwards, $S_{\mathbf{c}}$ is recomputed and the entry is reinserted into the queue.

If all conflicts caused by changing $u$'s color to **c** have been resolved (all ended in case 1), then $u$ is marked as a *pinning candidate*, else all color annotations caused by re-coloring $u$ are discarded.

If all $y, x_1, \dots, x_m$ are marked as pinning candidates, testing ends for this OU.

**Apply.** If the testing phase produced at least two pinning candidates (some $x_i$ and $y$ could be colored with the same color), the pinning candidates become *pinned* and all color changes annotated by the testing phase are applied to $G$.

Note, that the **Test**-Phase always terminates, since in each step an edge is added to the conflict graph, if testing was not successful. Thus, in the worst case, the stable set will finally consist of the $\phi$-result only and is *not* re-inserted into the priority queue. Thus, the whole algorithm terminates.

## 5   Measurements

We implemented our coalescing heuristic into our research compiler system Firm [15] and ran the complete C/C++-subset of the SPEC2000 benchmark suite through it. The architecture compiled for is a virtual RISC machine, to determine the effect of our approach on different register file sizes. Therefore, we did not measure the execution times of the compiled programs but investigated the quality of the heuristic's solutions in terms of costs of the target function as defined in equation 1 in section 4.3. The weights $w_{ij}$ are determined by the loop nesting depth to the power of two.

To assess the quality of the heuristic, we implemented an ILP formulation of SSA-MAXIMIZE-FIXED-POINTS (for details on the implementation, see [14]). Since ILP solving occasionally takes very long, the ILP solver was stopped after one minute of computation and thus did sometimes *not* produce an optimal solution.[7] As this happened in only 7% of all cases, we consider the solutions of the ILP solver as the best ones we could get and call the remaining costs after applying the ILP solver *unoptimizable*.

The measurements were conducted as follows: We compiled all C/C++- functions in the SPEC2000 benchmark suite for 8, 16 and 32 registers. We measured the costs incurred by the $\phi$-functions at three stages in the compiler: After coloring with no coalescing done, after performing the heuristic and after applying the ILP solver. The solution of the heuristic was fed into the ILP solver as a start solution.[8] The row Non-Opt gives the percentage of functions for which the ILP solutions were not proven optimal. The results of the three measurements are reflected by the rows Initial, Heuristic and ILP in the table below. The Elim row shows the quotient (Initial − Heuristic)/(Initial − ILP) representing the fraction of optimizable costs the heuristic has eliminated. One can see that the heuristic eliminates always more than 95.0% of all optimizable costs.

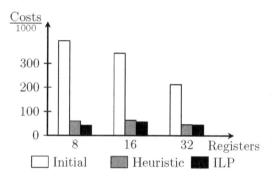

| Registers | 8 | 16 | 32 |
|---|---|---|---|
| Non-Opt | 6.7% | 3.7% | 1.3% |
| Initial | 394592 | 342842 | 213544 |
| Heuristic | 60114 | 63506 | 46060 |
| ILP | 42738 | 57010 | 43479 |
| Elim | 95.0% | 97.7% | 98.4% |

# 6    Conclusions and Further Work

SSA-form programs allow for a new architecture of register allocators. Due to the chordality of their interference graphs, spilling and coalescing can be completely decoupled, thus avoiding the iterative approach in common graph coloring register allocators.

Based on the direct correspondence between the variables live at a label in the program and the cliques in its interference graph, we showed how an already existing, heuristic method for spilling in basic blocks can be extended to work on a whole procedure. Furthermore, we showed that an optimal coloring of the interference graph $G = (V, E)$ can be obtained in $O(\chi(G) \cdot |V|)$.

We investigated the $\mathcal{NP}$-complete problem of copy coalescing, presented a heuristic method for its solution and compared its quality to (near-) optimal solutions computed by an integer linear program. As our measurements show,

---

[7] To be precise, the solver could not prove the optimality of its best known feasible solution within time.

[8] Thus the solution of the ILP solver is always feasible and as good as or better than the heuristic's one.

the proposed coalescing heuristic eliminated more than 95% of all optimizable costs for 8, 16 and 32 registers.

Finally, we showed how a $k$-register allocation of a SSA program can be immediately turned into a $k$-register allocation of a non-SSA program. Thus, *optimizing* SSA-destruction is no longer necessary since it is handled by the coalescing phase.

As using SSA-form for register allocation demands a complete new backend architecture, we only had a prototype implementation running at the point in time this paper was written. The implementation of conventional register allocators is also work in progress and has not been completed.

As anticipated in section 4.3 optimal copy minimization is *not* achieved by maximizing the fixed points of a $\phi$-operation but by minimizing the number of transpositions of the register permutation the $\phi$ stands for. Future work could investigate this problem.

# 7    Related Work

The first coalescing technique concerning graph coloring register allocation, called *aggressive coalescing,* was given by Chaitin et al. [1]. It recklessly coalesced all copies if the source and target did not interfere. It thus often introduced additional spill code by degrading the graph's colorability. Since then, a lot of work has been done on developing coalescing techniques which do not degrade the colorability of the graph, basically by stating criteria under which coalescing two nodes never will introduce a spill. Briggs et al. [2] introduced *conservative coalescing* which refuses to merge two nodes if the merged node will have more or equal than $k$ neighbors. George and Appel [16] developed *iterated coalescing* which is able to remove more copies than conservative coalescing by interleaving it with the simplification phase of the register allocator. Park and Moon [17] present *optimistic coalescing* which adapts aggressive coalescing and integrate it into the Briggs allocator, allowing to undo coalescing if the coalesced node is selected to be spilled.

In his inspiring paper [18] Andersson tested a huge amount of interference graphs from the SML/NJ compiler published by Appel and George for the so called 1-perfectness property and found for all graphs he investigated, $\omega(G)$ was equal to $\chi(G)$. Following Andersson's work, Pereira and Palsberg [19] tested the interference graphs of the Java standard library compiled with the JoeQ compiler for chordality and found that 95% of them were chordal. They propose a register allocator without iteration for non-SSA programs and give heuristics both for spilling and coalescing. Since their approach works with non-SSA programs and even non-chordal interference graphs, they cannot utilize the theoretic properties presented in section 2.

A more technical proof (without using perfect elimination orders) of the chordality of SSA interference graphs by one of the authors can be found in [20]. Brisk [21] gives a proof for the perfectness of the interference graphs of SSA-form programs. Bouchez [5] extensively studies the complexity of the spilling problem for SSA-form programs. He proves the problem of reducing the number of live variables for each label to $k$ while minimizing the number of reloads to be $\mathcal{NP}$-complete wrt. to the chromatic number of the interference graph of the SSA program.

## Acknowledgements

We want to thank our colleagues Michael Beck, Rubino Geiß, Götz Lindenmaier for many fruitful discussions. Fernando Pereira, Jens Palsberg, Philip Brisk and Daniel Berlin provided many helpful insights. Also, this paper greatly benefitted from discussions arising from a seminar at the Computer Laboratory of Cambridge University.

## References

1. Chaitin, G.J., Auslander, M.A., Chandra, A.K., Cocke, J., Hopkins, M.E., Markstein, P.W.: Register allocation via graph coloring. Journal of Computer Languages **6** (1981) 45–57
2. Briggs, P., Cooper, K.D., Torczon, L.: Improvements to graph coloring register allocation. ACM Trans. Program. Lang. Syst. **16** (1994) 428–455
3. Golumbic, M.C.: Algorithmic Graph Theory And Perfect Graphs. Academic Press (1980)
4. Budimlić, Z., Cooper, K.D., Harvey, T.J., Kennedy, K., Oberg, T.S., Reeves, S.W.: Fast copy coalescing and live-range identification. In: Proceedings of the ACM SIGPLAN 2002 Conference on Programming language design and implementation, ACM Press (2002) 25–32
5. Bouchez, F.: Allocation de registres et vidage en mémoire. Master's thesis, ÉNS Lyon (2005)
6. Diestel, R.: Graph Theory. 3 edn. Volume 173 of Graduate Texts in Mathematics. Springer (2005)
7. Bergner, P., Dahl, P., Engebretsen, D., O'Keefe, M.: Spill code minimization via interference region spilling. In: PLDI '97: Proceedings of the ACM SIGPLAN 1997 conference on Programming language design and implementation, New York, NY, USA, ACM Press (1997) 287–295
8. Chow, F.C., Hennessy, J.L.: The priority-based coloring approach to register allocation. ACM Trans. Program. Lang. Syst. **12** (1990) 501–536
9. Hsu, W.C., Fisher, C.N., Goodman, J.R.: On the Minimization of Loads/Stores in Local Register Allocation. IEEE Trans. Softw. Eng. **15** (1989) 1252–1260
10. Guo, J., Garzaran, M.J., Padua, D.: The Power of Belady's Algorithm in Register Allocation for Long Basic Blocks. The 16th International Workshop on Languages and Compilers for Parallel Computing (2003)
11. Belady, L.: A Study of Replacement of Algorithms for a Virtual Storage Computer. IBM Systems Journal **5** (1966) 78–101
12. Cytron, R., Ferrante, J., Rosen, B.K., Wegman, M.N., Zadek, F.K.: Efficiently computing static single assignment form and the control dependence graph. ACM Transactions on Programming Languages and Systems **13** (1991) 451–490
13. Briggs, P., D.Cooper, K., Harvey, T.J., Simpson, L.T.: Practical Improvements to the Construction and Destruction of Static Single Assignment Form. Software: Practice and Experience **28** (1998) 859–881

14. Hack, S., Grund, D., Goos, G.: Towards Register Allocation for Programs in SSA-form. Technical Report 2005-27, Universität Karlsruhe (2005)
15. Lindenmaier, G., Beck, M., Boesler, B., Geiß, R.: Firm, an intermediate language for compiler research. Technical Report 2005-8, University of Karlsruhe (2005)
16. George, L., Appel, A.W.: Iterated register coalescing. ACM Trans. Program. Lang. Syst. **18** (1996) 300–324
17. Park, J., Moon, S.M.: Optimistic register coalescing. ACM Trans. Program. Lang. Syst. **26** (2004) 735–765
18. Andersson, C.: Register Allocation By Optimal Graph Coloring. In Hedin, G., ed.: CC 2003. Volume 2622 of LNCS., Heidelberg, Springer-Verlag (2003) 33–45
19. Pereira, F.M.Q., Palsberg, J.: Register allocation via coloring of chordal graphs. In: Proceedings of APLAS'05. (2005)
20. Hack, S.: Interference Graphs of Programs in SSA-form. Technical Report 2005-15, Universität Karlsruhe (2005)
21. Brisk, P., Dabiri, F., Macbeth, J., Sarrafzadeh, M.: Polynomial time graph coloring register allocation. In: 14th International Workshop on Logic and Synthesis, ACM Press (2005)

# Enhanced Bitwidth-Aware Register Allocation

Rajkishore Barik and Vivek Sarkar

IBM T.J. Watson Research Center

**Abstract.** Embedded processors depend on register files for performance, just like general-purpose processors in desktop and server systems. However, unlike general-purpose processors, the power consumption of register files poses a significant challenge for embedded processors, making it desirable for embedded processors to use as few registers as possible. Past research has indicated the potential for leveraging *bitwidth analysis* and *bitwidth-aware register allocation* to reduce register usage in embedded applications.

This paper makes the following contributions in evaluating and enhancing bitwidth-aware register allocation for embedded applications. First, we compare the Tallam-Gupta bitwidth analysis with an idealized *limit study*, and show significant opportunities for enhancements. Second, we show how bitwidth-aware register allocation can be enhanced by *enhanced bitwidth analysis* for scalar and array variables, and also by *enhanced coalescing* of variables. Third, we use our prototype implementation of bitwidth-aware register allocation in *gcc* to compare the number of dynamic spill load/store instructions resulting from a) *bitwidth-unaware* allocation, b) *bitwidth-aware* allocation, c) *enhanced bitwidth-aware* allocation, and d) *ideal profile-driven bitwidth-aware* allocation. Our results show that our enhancements can reduce the number of dynamic spill load/store instructions to between 3% and 27% of the number obtained from the Tallam-Gupta algorithm.

## 1 Introduction

Embedded applications operate extensively on *subword* data values *i.e.,* data values with narrower width than the standard data width (word size) supported by the underlying embedded processor *e.g.,* 32 bits or 64 bits. As indicated by Tallam and Gupta [20], the register usage of embedded applications can be reduced by employing *bitwidth-aware register allocation.* A reduction in register usage can then be leveraged to reduce the power requirements of the embedded application on an embedded system [11]. Similarly, *bitwidth analysis* has been used to reduce the number of registers needed in the context of silicon compilation [19] and reconfigurable architectures. The opportunities for reducing register usage are even more promising when moving to embedded processors with a 64-bit word size (compared to a 32-bit word size).

One cornerstone of bitwidth-aware register allocation lies in its underlying *bitwidth analysis.* Stephenson et al. introduced a bitwidth analysis for silicon compilation [19] and showed how it can be used to reduce the total number of

A. Mycroft and A. Zeller (Eds.): CC 2006, LNCS 3923, pp. 263–276, 2006.

*register bits* in the generated RTL. However, the silicon compilation problem differs from register allocation, because there is no notion of *register spills* in silicon compilation. The Tallam-Gupta algorithm addresses this problem more directly by providing a register allocation algorithm that is capable of packing multiple subwords into a single register. There is an underlying trade-off when performing bitwidth-aware register allocation viz., reducing the number of registers used can save power, but may introduce additional overhead for subword access. This trade-off is well suited to new embedded processors in which the overhead of subword access is reduced by direct hardware support, and where the benefits of using fewer registers is clearly visible in reduced power.

Another cornerstone lies in the *coalescing heuristics* employed by bitwidth-aware register allocation. Unlike coalescing in conventional register allocation, it is permissible to coalesce two interfering variables in bitwidth-aware register allocation (provided that the sum of their bitwidths does not exceed the register word size). As shown in Figure 5, the estimates for coalescing provided in [20] can be improved significantly to perform a better coalescing of live ranges.

This paper makes the following contributions in evaluating and enhancing bitwidth-aware register allocation for embedded applications:

1. A *limit study* (Section 2) that compares compare the Tallam-Gupta bitwidth analysis algorithm [20] with dynamic profile-driven bitwidth information, and show significant opportunities for enhancements.
2. An *enhanced bitwidth analysis* algorithm (Section 3) that performs more detailed scalar analysis and array analysis for improved bitwidth information than in [20].
3. An *enhanced coalescing* algorithm (Section 4) that performs less conservative (more aggressive) coalescing than in [20].
4. Experimental results from a prototype implementation of bitwidth-aware register allocation in *gcc* to compare the effect of the two main enhancements listed above.

Our results show that our enhancements can reduce the dynamic number of load/store instructions significantly, compared to the Tallam-Gupta bitwidth-aware allocation algorithm. In the best case, our enhancements resulted in a reduction of the load/store instructions to 3% of the bitwidth-unaware case (for 6 registers). As can be seen in Table 4, the reductions delivered by our enhancements can also be smaller — the "worst" case is a reduction to 27% of the orginal dynamic number of load/store instructions. To the best of our knowledge this is the first study that reports on the dynamic number of load/store instructions (spill instructions) resulting from bitwidth-aware register allocation. (The results reported in [20] were for static register requirements and static numbers of live ranges and interference graph nodes.)

Davidson and Jinturkar [8] proposed a compiler optimization that exploits narrow width data. They used memory coalescing to improve cache performance of a program. It will be interesting to see how the approach advocated in this paper for register allocation could be extended in the future to improve cache performance.

The rest of this paper is organized as follows. Section 2 introduces metrics such as the *Active Compression Factor* (ACF) to compare the Tallam-Gupta bitwidth analysis with an idealized *limit study*, and thereby show significant opportunities for enhancements. Section 3 shows how bitwidth-aware register allocation can be improved by enhanced analysis of scalar and array variables. Section 4 shows how additional improvements can be obtained by enhancements to the coalescing algorithm and its underlying framework. Section 5 reports on our experimental results obtained from our prototype implementation of bitwidth-aware register allocation. Finally, Section 6 contains our conclusions.

## 2   Limit Study of Bitwidth Usage

Our first step in studying bitwidth-aware register allocation was to perform a *limit study* that compares the bitwidth usage computed by the *static* compile-time bitwidth analysis algorithm in [20] with *dynamic* bitwidth information obtained from an execution profile. The infrastructure used for this study was based on the GCC compiler, as depicted in Figure 1. The register allocation phase in gcc was modified to accept input from the box labeled "Bitwidth analysis", which can either generate compile-time or profile-driven bitwidth information. In general, the width of a variable at a program point can be represented by three parts: a leading part of unused bits, a middle part of active bits, and a trailing part of unused bits. We implemented the Tallam-Gupta algorithm in the GCC compiler to obtain this information for the compile-time case. For the profile-driven case, we instrumented the code generated by GCC so as to perform a "logical or" of the values dynamically assigned to a each variable. The major motivation for performing the limit study is that the prior work by Gupta and Tallam reported static benefits of bitwidth-aware register allocation (fewer registers used, smaller cliques in the interference graph), but did not provide any indication of what additional opportunities remain for improved bitwidth analysis.

The benchmarks used in this paper were all taken from the Bitwise benchmark set [1], so as to be representative of embedded applications. Our evaluation was performed on 9 out of the 15 programs in the full benchmark set. The following five programs were not used because they did not contain a return value, thereby making it possible for gcc to optimize away the entire program as dead code — *bilint, levdurb, motiontest, sha, softfloat*. In addition, the *life* program was not used, because the Bitwise benchmark set already contains a *newlife* program which is very similar to *life*. All experiments were performed using the *-O3* option and the *–param max-unroll-times=0* option[1] with version 4.1 of gcc targeted to the x86 platform.

Table 1 lists the total number of variables (pseudoregisters) available for register allocation in each benchmark, followed by the number of variables that were

---

[1] This option disables loop unrolling. Loop unrolling can create more candidates for register allocation, but the relative impact of unrolling depends on the benchmark so it was disabled.

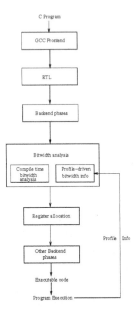

**Fig. 1.** GCC modification for limit study

identified to have varying bitwidth by static analysis, and next by the number of variables that were identified to have variable bitwidth by profile information. The results in the table indicate that there is opportunity for significant improvement in compile-time bitwidth analysis, compared to the static analysis obtained from the Tallam-Gupta algorithm.

We now introduce another metric called the *active compression factor* (ACF) to measure the effectiveness of the bit sensitive analysis. Let $AB_{ij}$ denote the number of *active bits* in register operand $j$ at statement $i$ (obtained either from static analysis or from profile information), and $TB_j$ denote the number of *total bits* in register operand $j$ (in other words, the statically defined size of $j$). Let

**Table 1.** Comparison of compile-time and profile-driven bitwidth analysis: Number of and percentage of variables with bitwidth $< 32$ bits

| Benchmark | Total # variables | Total # and % of variables with variable bitwidth (Compiler analysis) | (Profile-driven) |
|---|---|---|---|
| adpcm | 26 | 20 (76.92%) | 25 (96.15%) |
| bubblesort | 20 | 11 (55.00%) | 20 (100.00%) |
| convolve | 8 | 6 (75.00%) | 7 (87.50%) |
| edge_detect | 107 | 20 (18.69%) | 76 (71.02%) |
| histogram | 29 | 16 (55.17%) | 23 (79.31%) |
| jacobi | 36 | 13 (36.11%) | 23 (63.88%) |
| median | 33 | 9 (27.27%) | 26 (78.78%) |
| mpegcorr | 30 | 13 (43.33%) | 21 (70.00%) |
| newlife | 62 | 19 (30.64%) | 48 (77.41%) |

$FREQ_i$ denote the dynamic frequency of statement $i$. We define the active compression factor as follows:

$$ACF = \frac{\sum_{i \in INSN} \sum_{j \in REGOPERAND} FREQ_i * TB_j}{\sum_{i \in INSN} \sum_{j \in REGOPERAND} FREQ_i * AB_{ij}}$$

Note that $ACF$ must be $\geq 1$ since $TB_j \geq AB_{ij}$.

Table 2 shows $ACF$ values for the compile-time and profile-driven cases. The same execution profile information is used for the $FREQ_i$ values in both cases – the difference lies in the computation of the $AB_{ij}$ values. A larger $ACF$ value indicates a greater opportunity for bitwidth-aware register allocation. The results in Table 2 show ACF values in the range of 1.0 to 1.37 for the compile-time case, and in the range of 1.45 to 3.90 for the profile-driven case. Once again, this shows opportunity for improved bitwidth analysis, compared to the results obtained from the Tallam-Gupta algorithm.

**Table 2.** Active Compression Factor (ACF) comparison across static and profile-driven bitwidth analysis without loop unrolling

| Benchmark | Compile-time compression | Profile-driven compression |
|---|---|---|
| adpcm | 1.37 | 3.39 |
| bubblesort | 1.21 | 3.90 |
| convolve | 1.00 | 3.05 |
| edge_detect | 1.04 | 2.26 |
| histogram | 1.10 | 2.09 |
| jacobi | 1.00 | 1.67 |
| median | 1.01 | 2.14 |
| mpegcorr | 1.03 | 1.94 |
| newlife | 1.05 | 2.67 |

## 3   Enhanced Bitwidth Analysis

In this section, we outline two key enhancements that we made to the bitwidth analysis in the Tallam-Gupta algorithm, both of which were motivated by the opportunities identified by the limit study in the previous section.

1. *Enhanced Scalar Analysis.* The Tallam-Gupta algorithm performs a data flow analysis that includes a forward *zero bit section* analysis and a backward *dead bit section* analysis. We added a *recurrence analysis* (using the algorithm in [3]) that can identify general induction variables and other patterns with closed form solutions. This is more general than the scalar range analysis presented by Stephenson et al [19].

2. *Enhanced Array Analysis.* A key limitation of the Tallam-Gupta algorithm is that it performs no analysis of array variables. We added an *array range analysis* that tracks the values being assigned to arrays, and integrates the array analysis with the enhanced scalar analysis. This enhancement performs

a flow-insensitive analysis of all accesses to an array variable. In the future, we plan to implement a flow-sensitive version, based on the Array SSA form algorithm for element-level constant propagation [13].

```
#define NSAMPLES 2407
. . .
int sbuf[NSAMPLES];
. . .
  for(i=0;i<NSAMPLES;i++) {
    sbuf[i]=i & 0xFFFF;
  }
. . .
    for ( i = 0; i < NSAMPLES; i++ ) {
      val = sbuf[i];
. . .
```

**Fig. 2.** Code fragment from BITWISE adpcm benchmark

```
. . .
  for (i=0; i<SIZE/2; i++) {
    sortlist_even[i] = (SIZE-(i << 1)        ) | (1 << (WIDTH-1));
    sortlist_odd[i]  = (SIZE-((i << 1) | 1) ) | (1 << (WIDTH-1));
  }

  for(top=SIZE-1;top>0;top--) {
    for(i=0;i<top;i++) {
      io = i >> 1;
      ie = io + (i & 1);
      s1=sortlist_even[ie];
      s2=sortlist_odd[io];
      if(s1 > s2 ^ (i & 1)) {
        sortlist_even[ie] = s2;
        sortlist_odd[io]  = s1;
      }
    }
  }
. . .
```

**Fig. 3.** Code fragment from BITWISE bubblesort benchmark

We use two code examples to illustrate the benefits of these two enhancements, and how they are used in conjunction with each other. Figure 2 contains a code fragment from the Bitwise *adpcm* benchmark. While it may not be standard practice in general, it is common practice in embedded applications for loop iterations to be bounded by constants defined in the program. When analyzing the expression, i & 0xFFFF, our enhanced analysis determines that variable i must be in the range, 0 . . . 2406. Further, the constant 0xFFFF value has a bitwidth of 16 bits. Hence, each element assigned to the **sbuf** array has a lower bound of 0, and an upper bound of $\min(2406, 65535) = 2406$, or a maximum bitwidth of 12 bits (The min function is applied when a bitwise-and operator is being analyzed.). Scalar variable *val* is then bounded by a maximum bitwidth of 12 bits.

Figure 3 contains a code fragment from the Bitwise *bubblesort* benchmark. There are two static definitions each for arrays `sortlist_even` and `sortlist_odd`. However, the values of `s2` and `s1` that appear in the right-handside of the second pair of definitions originate from the same arrays. Therefore, our data flow analysis determines that the bitwidth of the array elements must be bounded by their initial definition i.e., 17 bits.

## 4    Enhanced Coalescing for Bitwidth-Aware Register Allocation

In this section, we outline improvements in the *coalescing* heuristics used in bitwidth-aware register allocation. Figure 4 contains a summary of the Tallam-Gupta bitwidth-aware register allocation algorithm, as presented in Figure 13 in [20]. The key step that implements the coalescing heuristic is Step 7. As shown later in our experimental results, enhancements to the coalescing heuristic can have a significant impact on the effectiveness of bitwidth-aware register allocation. Note that the coalescing step in bitwidth-aware register allocation is different from coalescing in classical register allocation. In classical register allocation, two *non-interfering* variables can be coalesced so as to use the same register. Bitwidth-aware register allocation allows two *interfering* variables to be coalesced provided the sum of their bitwidths does not exceed the register word size.

We now discuss three key characteristics of the Tallam-Gupta algorithm, and outline how they were extended/replaced in our algorithm:

1. Coalescing is performed *conservatively* in the Tallam-Gupta algorithm *i.e.,* coalescing is restricted to cases when the node created by coalescing two nodes has fewer than $k$ neighbors with degree of $k$ or more (where $k$ is the number of registers available for allocation). However, our experimental results show that this restriction is too conservative in many cases, so we use *aggressive* coalescing algorithm originally proposed by Chaitin [7].
2. If nodes $A$ and $B$ are coalesced, and both have an edge to another node, $C$, it is necessary to compute a new label for the edge from the new coalesced node, $AB$ to $C$. As discussed in Section 4.1 below, the heuristic used in the Tallam-Gupta algorithm can result in edge labels that are unnecessarily large, thereby precluding some possible coalescing heuristics. Our algorithm performs a more precise update of the edge label.
3. The priority function for live ranges used in the Tallam-Gupta algorithm for selecting nodes in Step 3 is defined as follows:

$$Priority(lr) = \frac{\text{Estimated Load/Store Savings}}{\text{Live Range Area}}$$

$$= \frac{\text{Estimated Load/Store Savings}}{\sum_{\text{Program point } p} width(lr, p)}$$

However, our experience has shown that this priority function often favors short-lived live ranges which have a small area, even though they may not offer a large savings in load/store instructions. Our enhancement was to remove the denominator term in the priority function, so that all live ranges are prioritized (largest-first) according to the estimated absolute load/store savings.

These three enhancements together result in the "Enhanced Coalescing" experimental results presented in Section 5.

1. Construct *interference graph.*
2. Label edges with *interference widths.*
3. Construct *prioritized node list.*
4. **while** node list $\neq \phi$ **do**
5.      Get a node, say $n$, from prioritized node list.
6.      **for** each node $a$ in $n$'s *adjacency list* **do**
7.          *Attempt coalescing* $a$ with $n$. // **Coalescing heuristic**
8.          If successful, update interference graph and prioritized node list.
9.      **end for**
10. **end while**
11. Replace each coalesced variable set with a new name.
12. Introduce *intravariable moves.*
13. Perform graph *coloring* register allocation

**Fig. 4.** Tallam-Gupta Bitwidth-aware Register Allocation

### 4.1 Updating Edge Labels After Coalescing

As mentioned earlier, the update of edge labels after coalescing can be unnecessarily large in the Tallam-Gupta algorithm. Each edge $(X, Y)$ is labeled with an ordered pair, $(X_y, Y_x)$, such that $X_y$ and $Y_x$ estimate the maximum widths of $X$ and $Y$ at a program point corresponding to the maximum interference width of $X$ and $Y$. A key constraint is that nodes $X$ and $Y$ cannot be coalesced if $X_y + Y_x$ is larger than the register word size.

Let us consider the interference graph shown in Figure 5 as an example in which we attempt to coalesce nodes $A$ and $B$. The upper right section of Figure 5 shows the actual number of bits required by variables $A$, $B$ and $C$ in the instruction stream. The Tallam-Gupta algorithm uses an Estimated Maximum Interference Width (EMIW) computation that results in the edge label $(28, 8)$ as shown on the lower left of Figure 5 (Refer to $E_{int}$ in [20]). In this case, node $AB$ cannot be coalesced later with $C$, since $28 + 8 = 36$ is larger than the 32-bit word size assumed in this example. However, if we use our enhanced estimates as illustrated in the lower right of Figure 5, the resulting edge label is $(21, 8)$, which would permit nodes $AB$ and $C$ to be coalesced next. The key point is that the Tallam-Gupta algorithm conservatively estimates the bitwidth of $AB$ after coalescing to be 28, though it should actually be 21.

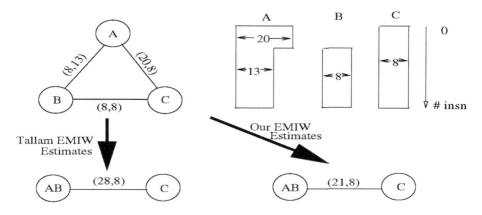

**Fig. 5.** Example Interference Graph

The details of our more precise estimate of edge labels can be obtained from the equations listed below, which we used to add to the equations for Case II in Figure 7 of [20]. $NODEMAX$ denotes the *maximal width* of a node across all program points. We have also proved that this more precise estimation satisfies the *intermediate value theorem* in [20]. The proofs are included in Appendix A.

$$E_1 = A_b + B_a + NODEMAX(C)$$
$$E_2 = A_c + C_a + NODEMAX(B)$$
$$E_3 = C_b + B_c + NODEMAX(A)$$
$$E_4 = B_a + C_a + MAX(A_b, A_c) \text{ if } E_{min} = E_a \text{ and } E_4 \geq E_{min}$$
$$E_5 = A_b + C_b + MAX(B_a, B_c) \text{ if } E_{min} = E_b \text{ and } E_5 \geq E_{min}$$
$$E_6 = A_c + B_c + MAX(C_a, C_b) \text{ if } E_{min} = E_c \text{ and } E_6 \geq E_{min}$$

$$EMIW(A, B, C) = MIN(E_{int}, E_1, E_2, E_3, E_4, E_5, E_6)$$

$$(AB_c, C_{ab}) = (A_b + B_a, NODEMAX(C)) \text{ if } EMIW(A, B, C) = E_1$$
$$(AB_c, C_{ab}) = (A_c + NODEMAX(B), C_a) \text{ if } EMIW(A, B, C) = E_2$$
$$(AB_c, C_{ab}) = (B_c + NODEMAX(A), C_b) \text{ if } EMIW(A, B, C) = E_3$$
$$(AB_c, C_{ab}) = (B_a + MAX(A_b, A_c), C_a) \text{ if } EMIW(A, B, C) = E_4$$
$$(AB_c, C_{ab}) = (A_b + MAX(B_a, B_c), C_b) \text{ if } EMIW(A, B, C) = E_5$$
$$(AB_c, C_{ab}) = (A_c + B_c, MAX(C_a, C_b)) \text{ if } EMIW(A, B, C) = E_6$$

## 5    Experimental Results

In this section, we report on experimental results obtained from our prototype implementation of bitwidth-aware register allocation based on gcc. Figure 6

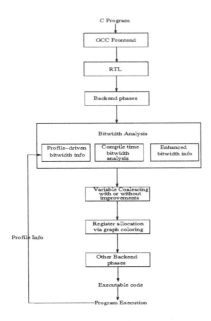

**Fig. 6.** GCC modification for register allocation

depicts how the bitwidth-aware register allocator is inserted into the phases of the gcc compiler. A standard graph coloring register allocator [7] was used instead of GCC's local and global register allocator. Note that we now have three options for Bitwidth Analysis — the Tallam-Gupta algorithm, *enhanced bitwidth* analysis, and *profile-driven* information. The enhanced analysis results were obtained by our implementation of the enhanced scalar and array analysis outlined in Section 3. Also, there are two options for Variable Coalescing — the Tallam-Gupta algorithm or the *enhanced coalescing* algorithm outlined in Section 4.

The experimental results reported in this section will be used to compare five different cases:

1. Bitwidth-Unaware — a standard graph coloring algorithm is used with no support for bitwidth-aware register allocation.
2. + Bitwidth-Aware — enhancement of the previous case by using the Tallam-Gupta bitwidth-aware register allocation.
3. + Enhanced Coalescing — addition of the enhanced coalescing techniques introduced in Section 4 of this paper.
4. + Enhanced Bitwidth — addition of the enhanced scalar and array bitwidth analysis techniques introduced in Section 3 of this paper.
5. + Profiled Bitwidth — like the previous case, but with profiled bitwidth information from the limit study used instead of statically analyzed bitwidth information.

The benchmark programs being used in this section are the same as those that were used for the limit study described in Section 2.

**Table 3.** Comparison of number of coalesce node-pairs with different levels of bit-sensitive register allocation for the number of available registers = 8

| Benchmarks | Bitwidth-Aware (Tallam-Gupta) | + Enhanced Coalescing | + Enhanced Bitwidth | + Profiled Bitwidth |
|---|---|---|---|---|
| adpcm | 0 | 7 | 15 | 18 |
| bubblesort | 1 | 1 | 12 | 12 |
| convolve | 0 | 0 | 2 | 2 |
| edge_detect | 0 | 0 | 25 | 64 |
| histogram | 1 | 1 | 15 | 15 |
| jacobi | 0 | 0 | 15 | 16 |
| median | 0 | 0 | 16 | 17 |
| mpegcorr | 0 | 0 | 10 | 13 |
| newlife | 0 | 2 | 40 | 41 |

As can be seen in Figure 6, the same register allocator based on graph coloring is used in all cases. Therefore, the only way for the bitwidth-aware heuristics to demonstrate an improvement compared to bitwidth-unaware allocation, is for the heuristics to perform some coalescing of nodes.

Table 3 reports the number of node-pairs coalesced when processing all nine benchmark programs for number of available registers 8. Note that the coalescing pre-pass for Tallam-Gupta depends on the number of available registers (conservative coalescing) whereas our modified approach does not (aggressive coalescing). The results show that our combined heuristic (Case 4 above) performs significantly more coalescing than the Tallam-Gupta algorithm.

Next, Table 4 compares the number of dynamic load/store instructions arising from register spills for the five different cases. Each row represents the case for a certain number of available registers, and each entry represents the sum of the dynamic load/store spill instructions for the nine benchmarks.

As seen in Table 4, the Tallam-Gupta algorithm had zero impact on reducing the number of dynamic load/store spill instructions, for the cases studied, and essentially yielded the same dynamic spill load/store instruction count as the bitwidth-unaware. However, the techniques introduced in our paper (cases 3

**Table 4.** Comparison of dynamic spill load/store instructions with different levels of bit-sensitive register allocation for the number of available registers = 8

| Number of registers | Bitwidth-Unaware (Standard Coloring) | + Bitwidth-Aware (Tallam-Gupta) | + Enhanced Coalescing | + Enhanced Bitwidth | + Profiled Bitwidth |
|---|---|---|---|---|---|
| 4 | 2427150 | 2427150 | 1973769(81.00) | 669469(27.00) | 622421(25.00) |
| 6 | 836687 | 836687 | 267324(31.00) | 26443(3.00) | 18953(2.00) |
| 8 | 58633 | 58633 | 36967(63.00) | 6909(11.00) | 5370(9.00) |
| 10 | 19581 | 19581 | 19571(99.00) | 3342(17.00) | 1803(9.00) |
| 12 | 9945 | 9945 | 9945(100.00) | 1824(18.00) | 527(5.00) |
| 14 | 6378 | 6378 | 6378(100.00) | 548(8.00) | 0(0) |
| 16 | 4860 | 4860 | 4860(100.00) | 10(0) | 0(0) |
| 18 | 3342 | 3342 | 3342(100.00) | 0(0) | 0(0) |

and 4 above) reduced the dynamic spill load/store instruction count to 3% to 27% of the bitwidth-unaware case. This is a significant reduction.

# 6    Conclusions and Future Work

In this paper, we studied the problem of enhancing bitwidth-aware register allocation. Our *limit study* showed significant opportunities for improvement, compared to the algorithm pioneered by Tallam and Gupta. We used our prototype implementation of bitwidth-aware register allocation in *gcc* to compare the dynamic number of load/store instructions) resulting from a) *bitwidth-unaware* allocation, b) *bitwidth-aware* allocation, c) *enhanced bitwidth-aware* allocation with improved bitwidth analysis and improved coalescing, and d) *ideal profile-driven bitwidth-aware* allocation. Our results show that our enhancements can reduce the dynamic number of spill load/store instructions to 3% to 27% of the number obtained from the Tallam-Gupta algorithm.

In future, we would like to study the overhead of bit-aware register allocation (number of extra instructions added), effect on run-time performance and energy reduction.

# References

1. Bitwise benchmarks. http://www.cag.lcs.mit.edu/bitwise/bitwise_benchmarks.htm.
2. Gcc compiler. http://gcc.gnu.org/, 2004.
3. Daniel Berlin, David Edelsohn, and Sebastian Pop. High-level loop optimizations for gcc. In *The 2004 GCC Developers' Summit*, 2004.
4. Preston Briggs, Keith D. Cooper, and Linda Torczon. Improvements to graph coloring register allocation. *ACM Transactions on Programming Languages and Systems*, 16(3):428–455, May 1994.
5. David Brooks and Margaret Martonosi. Dynamically exploiting narrow width operands to improve processor power and performance. In *HPCA '99: Proceedings of the The Fifth International Symposium on High Performance Computer Architecture*, page 13, Washington, DC, USA, 1999. IEEE Computer Society.
6. Mihai Budiu, Majd Sakr, Kip Walker, and Seth Copen Goldstein. Bitvalue inference: Detecting and exploiting narrow bitwidth computations. In *Euro-Par '00: Proceedings from the 6th International Euro-Par Conference on Parallel Processing*, pages 969–979, London, UK, 2000. Springer-Verlag.
7. Gregory J. Chaitin. Register allocation and spilling via graph coloring. In *Proceedings of the ACM SIGPLAN '82 Symposium on Compiler Construction*, pages 98–105, Jun. 1982.
8. Jack W. Davidson and Sanjay Jinturkar. Memory access coalescing: a technique for eliminating redundant memory accesses. In *PLDI '94: Proceedings of the ACM SIGPLAN 1994 conference on Programming language design and implementation*, pages 186–195, New York, NY, USA, 1994. ACM Press.
9. Rajiv Gupta, Eduard Mehofer, and Youtao Zhang. A representation for bit section based analysis and optimization. In *CC '02: Proceedings of the 11th International Conference on Compiler Construction*, pages 62–77, London, UK, 2002. Springer-Verlag.

10. W. Harrison. Compiler analysis of the value ranges for variables. *IEEE Transactions on Software Engineering*, (3), May 1977.
11. Johnson Kin, Munish Gupta, and William H. Mangione-Smith. The filter cache: an energy efficient memory structure. In *MICRO 30: Proceedings of the 30th annual ACM/IEEE international symposium on Microarchitecture*, pages 184–193, Washington, DC, USA, 1997. IEEE Computer Society.
12. Kathleen Knobe and Vivek Sarkar. Array ssa form and its use in parallelization. In *POPL '98: Proceedings of the 25th ACM SIGPLAN-SIGACT symposium on Principles of programming languages*, pages 107–120, New York, NY, USA, 1998. ACM Press.
13. Kathleen Knobe and Vivek Sarkar. Conditional constant propagation of scalar and array references using array SSA form. In Giorgio Levi, editor, *Lecture Notes in Computer Science, 1503*, pages 33–56. Springer-Verlag, 1998. Proceedings from the *5th International Static Analysis Symposium*.
14. Samuel Larsen and Saman Amarasinghe. Exploiting superword level parallelism with multimedia instruction sets. In *PLDI '00: Proceedings of the ACM SIGPLAN 2000 conference on Programming language design and implementation*, pages 145–156, New York, NY, USA, 2000. ACM Press.
15. Bengu Li and Rajiv Gupta. Bit section instruction set extension of arm for embedded applications. In *Proceedings of the international conference on Compilers, architecture, and synthesis for embedded systems*, pages 69–78. ACM Press, 2002.
16. Bengu Li, Youtao Zhang, and Rajiv Gupta. Speculative subword register allocation in embedded processors. In *Proceedings of the LCPC 2004 Workshop*, 2004.
17. Unsal O.S., Wang Z., Koren I., Krishna C.M., and Moritz C.A. On memory behavior of scalars in embedded multimedia systems. In *MPI Workshop, ISCA01*, 2001.
18. Massimiliano Poletto and Vivek Sarkar. Linear scan register allocation. *ACM Transactions on Programming Languages and Systems*, 21(5):895–913, 1999.
19. Mark Stephenson, Johnathan Babb, and Saman Amarasinghe. Bitwidth analysis with application to silicon compilation. In *ACM SIGPLAN Conference on Programming Language Design and Implementation*, Vancouver, British Columbia, June 2000.
20. Sriraman Tallam and Rajiv Gupta. Bitwidth aware global register allocation. In *POPL '03: Proceedings of the 30th ACM SIGPLAN-SIGACT symposium on Principles of programming languages*, pages 85–96, New York, NY, USA, 2003. ACM Press.
21. Omri Traub, Glenn H. Holloway, and Michael D. Smith. Quality and speed in linear-scan register allocation. In *SIGPLAN Conference on Programming Language Design and Implementation*, pages 142–151, 1998.

# A    Appendix

**Theorem 1.** *The estimates $E_1$, $E_2$ and $E_3$ are safe i.e., each of $E_1$, $E_2$ and $E_3$ is greater than or equal to $MIW(A,B,C)$.*

*Proof.* Let $MIW(A,B,C) = W_A + W_B + W_C$, where $W_A$, $W_B$, and $W_C$ are contributions of $A$, $B$, and $C$ to $MIW(A,B,C)$. By definition of $MIW$ it is true that:

$$W_A + W_B \leq A_b + B_a$$

Similarly, by definition of $NODEMAX$ it must be the case that:

$$W_C \leq NODEMAX(C)$$

Combining the above two equations:

$$W_A + W_B + W_C \leq A_b + B_a + NODEMAX(C)$$

$\Rightarrow$

$$E_1 \geq W_A + W_B + W_C$$

$E_1$ is safe. In a similar fashion we can prove that $E_2$ and $E_3$ are safe.

**Theorem 2.** *The estimates $E_4$, $E_5$ and $E_6$ are safe i.e., each of $E_4$, $E_5$ and $E_6$ is greater than or equal to $MIW(A,B,C)$.*

*Proof.* By definition of $MIW$,

$$A_b + B_a \geq W_A + W_B$$

$$A_c + C_a \geq W_A + W_C$$

$\Rightarrow$

$$B_a + C_a + A_b + A_c \geq W_B + W_C + 2W_A$$

$\Rightarrow$

$$B_a + C_a + MAX(A_b, A_c) \geq W_B + W_C + W_A + W_A - MIN(A_b, A_c)$$

$\Rightarrow$ If $W_A \geq MIN(A_b, A_c)$, then

$$B_a + C_a + MAX(A_b, A_c) \geq W_A + W_B + W_C$$

$\Rightarrow$ If $W_A \geq MIN(A_b, A_c)$, then

$$E_4 \geq W_A + W_B + W_C$$

Whether $W_A \geq MIN(A_b, A_c)$ is obtained the following way.
If $E_{min} = E_a$ ($E_{min}$ and $E_a$ are estimates in Figure 7 of [20]), and $E_4 \geq E_{min}$ then estimate $E_4$ can be used, because the following two things can happen:

- if $E_{min} \geq MIW(A, B, C)$ then $E_4 \geq E_{min} \geq MIW(A, B, C)$. $E_4$ is safe.
- if $E_{min} < MIW(A, B, C)$ then $B_c + C_b + max(A_b, A_c) < W_A + W_B + W_C$. By definition of $MIW$, $B_c + C_b < W_B + W_C$. This implies $W_A > MAX(A_b, A_c) \geq MIN(A_b, A_c)$. $E_4$ is safe.

Similarly, $E_5$ and $E_6$ can be proven to be safe.

# Author Index

# Lecture Notes in Computer Science

For information about Vols. 1–3806

please contact your bookseller or Springer

Vol. 3851: P.J. Narayanan, S.K. Nayar, H.-Y. Shum (Eds.), Computer Vision – ACCV 2006, Part I. XXXI, 973 pages. 2006.

Vol. 3850: R. Freund, G. Păun, G. Rozenberg, A. Salomaa (Eds.), Membrane Computing. IX, 371 pages. 2006.

Vol. 3849: I. Bloch, A. Petrosino, A.G.B. Tettamanzi (Eds.), Fuzzy Logic and Applications. XIV, 438 pages. 2006. (Sublibrary LNAI).

Vol. 3848: J.-F. Boulicaut, L. De Raedt, H. Mannila (Eds.), Constraint-Based Mining and Inductive Databases. X, 401 pages. 2006. (Sublibrary LNAI).

Vol. 3847: K.P. Jantke, A. Lunzer, N. Spyratos, Y. Tanaka (Eds.), Federation over the Web. X, 215 pages. 2006. (Sublibrary LNAI).

Vol. 3846: H. J. van den Herik, Y. Björnsson, N.S. Netanyahu (Eds.), Computers and Games. XIV, 333 pages. 2006.

Vol. 3845: J. Farré, I. Litovsky, S. Schmitz (Eds.), Implementation and Application of Automata. XIII, 360 pages. 2006.

Vol. 3844: J.-M. Bruel (Ed.), Satellite Events at the MoD-ELS 2005 Conference. XIII, 360 pages. 2006.

Vol. 3843: P. Healy, N.S. Nikolov (Eds.), Graph Drawing. XVII, 536 pages. 2006.

Vol. 3842: H.T. Shen, J. Li, M. Li, J. Ni, W. Wang (Eds.), Advanced Web and Network Technologies, and Applications. XXVII, 1057 pages. 2006.

Vol. 3841: X. Zhou, J. Li, H.T. Shen, M. Kitsuregawa, Y. Zhang (Eds.), Frontiers of WWW Research and Development - APWeb 2006. XXIV, 1223 pages. 2006.

Vol. 3840: M. Li, B. Boehm, L.J. Osterweil (Eds.), Unifying the Software Process Spectrum. XVI, 522 pages. 2006.

Vol. 3839: J.-C. Filliâtre, C. Paulin-Mohring, B. Werner (Eds.), Types for Proofs and Programs. VIII, 275 pages. 2006.

Vol. 3838: A. Middeldorp, V. van Oostrom, F. van Raamsdonk, R. de Vrijer (Eds.), Processes, Terms and Cycles: Steps on the Road to Infinity. XVIII, 639 pages. 2005.

Vol. 3837: K. Cho, P. Jacquet (Eds.), Technologies for Advanced Heterogeneous Networks. IX, 307 pages. 2005.

Vol. 3836: J.-M. Pierson (Ed.), Data Management in Grids. X, 143 pages. 2006.

Vol. 3835: G. Sutcliffe, A. Voronkov (Eds.), Logic for Programming, Artificial Intelligence, and Reasoning. XIV, 744 pages. 2005. (Sublibrary LNAI).

Vol. 3834: D.G. Feitelson, E. Frachtenberg, L. Rudolph, U. Schwiegelshohn (Eds.), Job Scheduling Strategies for Parallel Processing. VIII, 283 pages. 2005.

Vol. 3833: K.-J. Li, C. Vangenot (Eds.), Web and Wireless Geographical Information Systems. XI, 309 pages. 2005.

Vol. 3832: D. Zhang, A.K. Jain (Eds.), Advances in Biometrics. XX, 796 pages. 2005.

Vol. 3831: J. Wiedermann, G. Tel, J. Pokorný, M. Bieliková, J. Štuller (Eds.), SOFSEM 2006: Theory and Practice of Computer Science. XV, 576 pages. 2006.

Vol. 3830: D. Weyns, H. V.D. Parunak, F. Michel (Eds.), Environments for Multi-Agent Systems II. VIII, 291 pages. 2006. (Sublibrary LNAI).

Vol. 3829: P. Pettersson, W. Yi (Eds.), Formal Modeling and Analysis of Timed Systems. IX, 305 pages. 2005.

Vol. 3828: X. Deng, Y. Ye (Eds.), Internet and Network Economics. XVII, 1106 pages. 2005.

Vol. 3827: X. Deng, D.-Z. Du (Eds.), Algorithms and Computation. XX, 1190 pages. 2005.

Vol. 3826: B. Benatallah, F. Casati, P. Traverso (Eds.), Service-Oriented Computing - ICSOC 2005. XVIII, 597 pages. 2005.

Vol. 3824: L.T. Yang, M. Amamiya, Z. Liu, M. Guo, F.J. Rammig (Eds.), Embedded and Ubiquitous Computing – EUC 2005. XXIII, 1204 pages. 2005.

Vol. 3823: T. Enokido, L. Yan, B. Xiao, D. Kim, Y. Dai, L.T. Yang (Eds.), Embedded and Ubiquitous Computing – EUC 2005 Workshops. XXXII, 1317 pages. 2005.

Vol. 3822: D. Feng, D. Lin, M. Yung (Eds.), Information Security and Cryptology. XII, 420 pages. 2005.

Vol. 3821: R. Ramanujam, S. Sen (Eds.), FSTTCS 2005: Foundations of Software Technology and Theoretical Computer Science. XIV, 566 pages. 2005.

Vol. 3820: L.T. Yang, X.-s. Zhou, W. Zhao, Z. Wu, Y. Zhu, M. Lin (Eds.), Embedded Software and Systems. XXVIII, 779 pages. 2005.

Vol. 3819: P. Van Hentenryck (Ed.), Practical Aspects of Declarative Languages. X, 231 pages. 2005.

Vol. 3818: S. Grumbach, L. Sui, V. Vianu (Eds.), Advances in Computer Science – ASIAN 2005. XIII, 294 pages. 2005.

Vol. 3817: M. Faundez-Zanuy, L. Janer, A. Esposito, A. Satue-Villar, J. Roure, V. Espinosa-Duro (Eds.), Nonlinear Analyses and Algorithms for Speech Processing. XII, 380 pages. 2006. (Sublibrary LNAI).

Vol. 3816: G. Chakraborty (Ed.), Distributed Computing and Internet Technology. XXI, 606 pages. 2005.

Vol. 3815: E.A. Fox, E.J. Neuhold, P. Premsmit, V. Wuwongse (Eds.), Digital Libraries: Implementing Strategies and Sharing Experiences. XVII, 529 pages. 2005.

Vol. 3814: M. Maybury, O. Stock, W. Wahlster (Eds.), Intelligent Technologies for Interactive Entertainment. XV, 342 pages. 2005. (Sublibrary LNAI).

Vol. 3813: R. Molva, G. Tsudik, D. Westhoff (Eds.), Security and Privacy in Ad-hoc and Sensor Networks. VIII, 219 pages. 2005.

Vol. 3812: C. Bussler, A. Haller (Eds.), Business Process Management Workshops. XIII, 520 pages. 2006.

Vol. 3811: C. Bussler, M.-C. Shan (Eds.), Technologies for E-Services. VIII, 127 pages. 2006.

Vol. 3810: Y.G. Desmedt, H. Wang, Y. Mu, Y. Li (Eds.), Cryptology and Network Security. XI, 349 pages. 2005.

Vol. 3809: S. Zhang, R. Jarvis (Eds.), AI 2005: Advances in Artificial Intelligence. XXVII, 1344 pages. 2005. (Sublibrary LNAI).

Vol. 3808: C. Bento, A. Cardoso, G. Dias (Eds.), Progress in Artificial Intelligence. XVIII, 704 pages. 2005. (Sublibrary LNAI).

Vol. 3807: M. Dean, Y. Guo, W. Jun, R. Kaschek, S. Krishnaswamy, Z. Pan, Q.Z. Sheng (Eds.), Web Information Systems Engineering – WISE 2005 Workshops. XV, 275 pages. 2005.